AF814413

All in One

Recommended by **Teachers**
Trusted by **Toppers**

# PHYSICAL EDUCATION
## Class 11

**EVERYTHING YOU NEED TO SCORE**

- Simplified Theory
- All Types of Questions; VSA, SA & LA
- CBQs; MCQs, A-R, Picture Based
- Sample Question Papers

**CBSE Exams 2026**

All in One®

Recommended by **Teachers**
Trusted by **Toppers**

# PHYSICAL EDUCATION
## Class 11

**EVERYTHING YOU NEED TO SCORE**

- Simplified Theory
- All Types of Questions; VSA, SA & LA
- CBQs; MCQs, A-R, Picture Based
- Sample Question Papers

**CBSE Exams 2026**

*Author*
Saumya Aggarwal

arihant
SUCCESS AND NOTHING LESS

arihant
SUCCESS AND NOTHING LESS

**ARIHANT PRAKASHAN**
(School Division Series)
All Rights Reserved

卐 © PUBLISHER
No part of this publication may be re-produced, stored in a retrieval system or by any means, electronic, mechanical, photocopying, recording, scanning, web or otherwise without the written permission of the publisher. Arihant has obtained all the information in this book from the sources believed to be reliable and true. However, Arihant or its editors or authors or illustrators don't take any responsibility for the absolute accuracy of any information published and the damage or loss suffered thereupon.

All disputes subject to Meerut (UP) jurisdiction only.
卐 ADMINISTRATIVE & PRODUCTION OFFICES

*Regd. Office*
'Ramchhaya' 4577/15, Agarwal Road, Darya Ganj, New Delhi -110002
Tele: 011- 47630600, 43518550; Fax: 011- 23280316

卐 *Head Office*
Kalindi, TP Nagar, Meerut (UP) - 250002, Tel: 0121-7156203, 7156204

卐 SALES & SUPPORT OFFICES
Agra, Ahmedabad, Bengaluru, Bareilly, Chennai, Delhi, Guwahati, Hyderabad, Jaipur, Jhansi, Kolkata, Lucknow, Nagpur & Pune.

*PO No : TXT-XX-XXXXXXX-X-XX*

Published By Arihant Publications (India) Ltd.

For further information about the books published by Arihant, log on to www.arihantbooks.com or e-mail at info@arihantbooks.com

Follow us on

卐 PRICE ₹300.00

**PRODUCTION TEAM**

*Publishing Managers*
Mahendra Singh Rawat & Keshav Mohan

*Cover Designer*
Salman Shaikh

*Inner Designer*
Ankit Tyagi

*Project Head*
Shivam Gupta

*Page Layouting*
Jashoda

*Proof Reader*
Priya

# Index *cum* Study Planner

## PART A Theory

# One Book- Endless Features

*to Help you Succeed*

## Complete Theory in Each Chapter

Each chapter has Complete, Easy to Understand and Simplified theory covering latest syllabus. Theory is developed in such a way that it is suitable for all types of learners.

## Concept of Physical Education

The concept of 'physical education' is in use from ancient times as fitness is essential for survival. The foundation of physical educatio in ancient Greece when philosophers like Socrates, Aristotle and P strongly advocated physical training and knowledge for the youth.

Physical education is derived from the phrase 'physical fitness', wh to the capacity of a person to meet the physical demands of daily l carry out regular activities without undue fatigue. It is the integral the general education which promotes harmonious growth and de of an individual.

## Sample Question Papers

To make students practice of examination in real sense, there are 3 Sample Question Papers at the end. All these Sample Questions Paper are exactly prepared on the latest syllabus & pattern of examination.

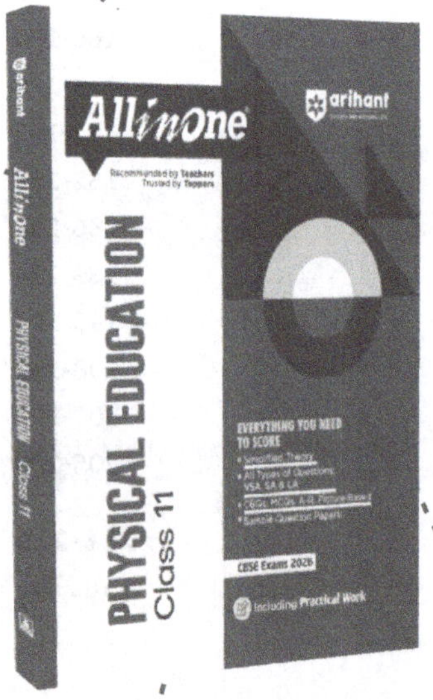


## CHAPTER PRACTICE

**OBJECTIVE TYPE QUESTIONS**

Multiple Choice Questions (MCQs)

1 The foundation of physical education was laid in
(a) England (b) Greece
(c) USA (d) Italy
Ans (b) Greece

2 Which of the following is not the objective of physical education?
(a) Physical development
(b) Social development
(c) Emotional development
(d) Technical development
Ans (d) Technical development

3 According to JB Nash, the objectives of physical education are
(a) Neuromuscular development
(b) Organic development
(c) Interpretative development
(d) All of the above
Ans (d) All of the above

8 What are the objectives of Fit India Movement?
(a) To promote fitness as easy, fun and free
(b) To encourage indigenous Sports
(c) To make fitness reach every school, college and university
(d) All of the above
Ans (d) All of the above

9 A Committee has been formed to advice government on Fit India Movement, consisting of
(a) Various government officials
(b) Members of Indian Olympics Association
(c) National Sports Federations
(d) All of the above
Ans (b) All of the above

Fill in the Blanks

10 Physical education is derived from the ___ phrase which refers to the capacity of person to meet physical demands of daily life.
Ans physical fitness

11 ___ objective of physical education is related to the mental development of an individual

## Chapter Practice

Chapter Practice have all types of questions; MCQs, VSA, SA & LA Type Questions.

## SAMPLE QUESTION PAPER 1

A Highly Simulated Sample Question Paper for CBSE Class XI Examination

**PHYSICAL EDUCATION**

**General Instructions**

- The question paper consists of 5 sections and 34 Questions.
- Section A consists of question 1-18 carrying 1 mark each and is multiple choice questions. All questions are compulsory.
- Sections B consist of questions 19-23 carrying 2 marks each and are very short answer types and should not exceed 60-90 words. There is internal choice available

*Time : 3 hours* *Max. Marks : 70*

**SECTION A**

1 Identify the given asana. (1)

4 Career options through physical education are (1)
(a) Sports Departments
(b) Sports Facilities Management
(c) Sports Journalism
(d) All of the above

5 Which of the following is not the component of wellness? (1)
(a) Physical

## Self Assessment

Complete Test of chapter in Exam format.

## SELF ASSESSMENT

**OBJECTIVE ANSWER TYPE QUESTIONS**

1 Which of the following philosophers strongly advocated physical training for the youth?
(a) Socrates (b) Aristotle
(c) Plato (d) All of these

2 The first 'Khelo India School Games' which are part of Khelo India Programme were held in
(a) Mumbai (b) Kolkata
(c) New Delhi (d) Chennai

3 Which of the following is the career options in communication media?
(a) Writing (b) Sports facilities management
(c) Teaching (d) Coaching

# Latest Course *Structure*

## THEORY

**Max. Marks 70**

### UNIT I Changing Trends & Career in Physical Education

- Concept, Aims & Objectives of Physical Education
- Development of Physical Education in India-Post Independence
- Changing Trends in Sports- playing surface, wearable gears and sports equipment, technological advancements
- Career Options in Physical Education
- Khelo-India and Fit-India Program

### UNIT II Olympism Value Education

- Olympism – Concept and Olympics Values (Excellence, Friendship & Respect)
- Olympic Value Education- Joy of Effort, Fair Play Respect for Others, Pursuit of Excellence, Balance Among Body, Will & Mind
- Ancient and Modern Olympics
- Olympics - Symbols, Motto, Flag, Oath, and Anthem
- Olympic Movement Structure - IOC, NOC, IFS, Other members

### UNIT III Yoga

- Meaning & Importance of Yoga
- Introduction to Ashtanga Yoga
- Yogic Kriyas (Shat Karma)
- Pranayama and its types
- Active Lifestyle and Stress Management through Yoga

### UNIT IV Physical Education & Sports for CWSN (Children with Special Needs - Divyang)

- Concept of Disability and Disorder
- Types of Disability, its causes & nature (Intellectual disability, Physical disability)
- Disability Etiquette
- Aim & Objective of Adaptive Physical Education
- Role of various professionals for children with special needs (Counsellor, Occupational Therapist, Physiotherapist, Physical Education Teacher, Speech Therapist & Special Educator)

### UNIT V Physical Fitness, Health and Wellness

- Meaning and Importance of Wellness, Health and Physical Fitness
- Components/Dimensions of Wellness, Health and Physical Fitness
- Traditional Sports & Regional Games for promoting wellness

- Leadership through Physical Activity and Sports
- Introduction to First Aid-PRICE

## UNIT VI Test, Measurement & Evaluation

- Define Test, Measurement & Evaluation
- Importance of Test, Measurement and Evaluation in Sports
- Calculation of BMI, Waist-Hip Ratio, Skin Fold Measurement (3-site)
- Somato Types (Endomorphy, Mesomorphy & Ectomorphy)
- Measurement of Health-related fitness

## UNIT VII Fundamentals of Anatomy, Physiology in Sports

- Definition and Importance of Anatomy and Physiology in Exercise and Sports
- Functions of Skeletal system, Classification of bone and types of joints
- Properties and Functions of Muscles
- Structure and Function of Circulatory System and Heart
- Structure and Function of Respiratory System

## UNIT VIII Fundamentals of Kinesiology and Biomechanics in Sports

- Definition and Importance of Kinesiology and Biomechanics in sports
- Principles of Biomechanics
- Kinetics and Kinematics in Sports
- Types of Body Movements - Flexion, Extension, Abduction, Adduction, Rotation, Circumduction, Supination & Pronation
- Axis and Planes – Concept and its application in body movements

## UNIT IX Psychology & Sports

- Definition & Importance of Psychology in Physical Education & Sports
- Developmental Characteristics at Different Stages of Development
- Adolescent Problems & Their Management
- Team Cohesion and Sports
- Introduction to Psychological Attributes: Attention, Resilience, Mental Toughness

## UNIT X Training and Doping in Sports

- Concept and Principles of Sports Training
- Training Load: Over Load, Adaptation and Recovery
- Warming-up & Limbering Down-Types, Method & Importance
- Concept of Skill, Technique, Tactics & Strategies
- Concept of Doping and its Disadvantages

# Practicals

**Practicals should be conducted alongside the concepts taught in theory classes**

***Max. Marks 30***

| | | |
|---|---|---|
| 01. | Physical Fitness Test: SAI Khelo India test, Brockport Physical Fitness Test (BPFT) * | 6 Marks |
| 02. | Proficiency in Games & Sports (Skill of any one IOA recognised Sport/Game of choice) ** | 7 Marks |
| 03. | Yogic Practices | 7 Marks |
| 04. | Record File** | 5 Marks |
| 05. | Viva Voce (Health/Games & Sports/Yoga) | 5 Marks |

* Test for CWSN (any 4 items out of 27items but 1 item from each component: Aerobic function, Body Composition, Muscular strength & endurance, range of motion or flexibility)

**CWSN (Children With Special Needs – Divyang): Bocce/Boccia , Sitting Volleyball, Wheel Chair Basketball, Unified Badminton, Unified Basketball, Unified Football, Blind Cricket, Goalball, Floorball, Wheel chair races and throws, or any other sport/games of choice.

**Children With Special Needs can also opt any one sport/game from the list as alternative for Yogic Practices. However, the sport/game must be different from Test-'Proficiency in Games & Sports'.

### **Record File shall include:

Practical-1: Fitness Tests Administration (SAI Khelo India Test)

Practical-2: Procedure for Asanas, Benefits & Contraindication for any two Asanas for each lifestyle disease.

Practical-3: Any one IOA recognised Sport/Game of choice. Labelled diagram of field & equipment. Also mention its Rules, Terminologies & Skills.

# Part A
# Theory

CHAPTER

01

# Changing Trends and Career in Physical Education

## Concept of Physical Education

The concept of 'physical education' is in use from ancient times as physical fitness is essential for survival. The foundation of physical education was laid in ancient Greece when philosophers like Socrates, Aristotle and Plato strongly advocated physical training and knowledge for the youth.

Physical education is derived from the phrase 'physical fitness', which refers to the capacity of a person to meet the physical demands of daily life and to carry out regular activities without undue fatigue. It is the integral part of the general education which promotes harmonious growth and development of an individual.

Physical education is an integral part of general education. This branch of education promotes harmonious growth and development along with behavioural modifications, so that an individual is able to bring efficiency in his/her ability to work.

Physical education develops a child physically, mentally, socially and emotionally and prepares him/her to face various challenges in life.

### Aims of Physical Education

Different people have expressed their opinion in their own ways about the aims of physical education.

Some of them are given below

According to **JF Williams,** "Physical education should aim to provide skilled leadership, adequate facilities and ample time for the individual and groups to participate in activities that are physically wholesome, mentally stimulating and satisfying, and socially sound."

CHAPTER CHECKLIST

- Concept of Physical Education
- Development of Physical Education in India Post-Independence
- Career Options in Physical Education
- Changing Trends in Sports
- Khelo India Programme

According to **Central Advisory Board of Physical Education,** "the aim of physical education is to make every child physically, mentally and constitutionally fit. To develop in him/her such personal and social qualities that will help him/her to live happily with others and build him up as a good citizen."

Thus, the aims of physical education is to enable the students to

- Understand the value of physical education.
- Develop a high level of physical fitness to undertake a variety of physical activities.
- Perform physical exercises to their optimum level.
- Develop personal and social qualities to experience enjoyment and satisfaction in life.
- Demonstrate the knowledge, skills and techniques learned with enthusiasm, commitment and initiative.
- Develop social skills which demonstrate the importance of teamwork and cooperation in group activities.

## Objectives of Physical Education

The objectives of physical education have been expressed by various educationists such as

- **Hetherington** have classified five objectives of physical education *viz.* immediate objectives, remote objectives, developmental objectives, social standard objectives and objectives in control of health conditions.
- According to **JB Nash**, the objectives of physical education are, neuromuscular development, organic development, interpretative development and emotional development.
- **Leslie** has categorised objectives of physical education as organic aspect of development, emotional aspect of development, neuromuscular aspect of development, intellectual aspect of development, and social aspect of development.

On the basis of above mentioned objectives, the main objectives of the physical education can be elaborated as follows

### Physical Development

It is the first and foremost objective of physical education. This refers to the proper growth of the body.

It ensures smooth working of the internal organs and the systems such as digestive system, circulatory system, respiratory system, nervous system and muscular system. By performing physical activities, these systems work smoothly, bring efficiency in activities and help in developing proper neuromuscular coordination, so as to develop a good personality.

Therefore, doing physical activities regularly and taking active part in them with full enthusiasm develops the ability and capacity of an individual which ultimately results into a healthy body.

### Psychological Development

This objective is related to the mental development of an individual by developing positive thoughts, behaviour, attitude, alertness of mind, concentration, confidence and calculated movements.

Participation in physical activities helps in mental development as an individual learns to concentrate, draw conclusions, face challenges, understand new situations and take decisions independently.

This directs the person's growth in a sequential manner, makes the person active and develops a sound mind, which are all essential to lead a well-balanced life.

### Social Development

This objective is related to the development of social skills that are needed to live in society. Social qualities like cooperation, courtesy, sportsmanship, tolerance, friendship, sincerity and adjustment are essential to live in society.

Physical education provides good opportunities to come closer, form friendships and adjust according to different situations.

It creates a healthy social environment within the society and helps to develop the socialisation process among children. This objective also helps to overcome social evils and brings prosperity alongwith communal harmony.

### Emotional Development

This objective relates to bringing about emotional development so that an individual is able to deal appropriately with various emotions.

Every individual has various types of emotions like jealousy, hate, fear, anger, love, pleasure, distress, hope etc. It is essential that an individual is able to express, manage and control emotions depending upon the situation.

Physical education provides opportunities through various games, physical exercises, programmes and activities to bring about proper emotional development.

By participating in programmes of physical education regularly, one can have a good control over his emotions.

Thus, it can be concluded that aim is the highest possible achievement or goal, while on the other hand, objectives are many and may change from time to time.

## Development of Physical Education in India Post - Independence

The Government of India took many steps for development of physical education after Independence. Many organisations were set up and various other steps were taken to improve the condition of physical education. These are as follows

- **National Credit Corps** (NCC) and **Auxiliary Credit Corps** (ACC) were introduced at school and college level in 1948 to popularise importance of physical education in youth.
- In 1950, the Government of India established the **Central Advisory Board of Physical Education and Recreation (CABPER)**. It advised the government on various steps for the development of physical education.

  Important recommendations given by board are
  - Development training of leaders in physical education
  - Scholarship for research in physical education
  - Financial assistance to the collages of physical education
  - Giving direction to the state government regarding the development of physical education in respective states
- In 1953, the Government of India started **Rajkumari coaching scheme** with the aim of training good athletes. Major figures like Major Dhyan Chand and Dr Ram Singh also worked under this scheme.
- In the same year 1953, the Ministry of Education established All India Council with the purpose to establish link between Central government and various sports associations and federations. The role of this council is to facilitate the financial assistance to these federations and check proper utilisation of funds.
- A National syllabus of physical activities was formed in the year 1956.
- Lakshmi Bai College of Physical Education established in 1957, it was given status of National importance in 1973.
- **National Institute of Sports** was established in **Patiala** in 1961. In 1973, it was renamed as Netaji Subhash National Institute of Sports.
- Sports Authority of India was formed on 25th March, 1984. It was formed to raise the standards of sports in India.
- Health and physical education was included in core curriculum for school education by NCERT in the year 1988, which was revised in the year 1992 and 2000.
- **Ministry of Youth Affairs and Sports**, an independent ministry for development of sports and physical education was established in the year 2000. The role its departments is to create the infrastructure and promote capacity building for broad-based sports as well as for achieving excellence in various competitive events at national and international levels.

## Career Options in Physical Education

The career options in physical education were very limited earlier and mostly related to teaching in schools and colleges or coaching players. These are called **traditional careers** in physical education.

The situation changed after 1950 as a number of institutions providing education and training in physical education came into existence.

New options for careers opened up in the field of physical education that are related to health, sports performance, sports management, administration, media, communication etc. These are called as **emerging careers.**

The career options are discussed below

### Career in Teaching

Physical education has traditionally been considered as a professional field.

This profession offers many rewards to the teachers whether they are engaged in elementary schools, middle schools, high schools, senior secondary schools, colleges or universities.

This career is generally considered to have many benefits and provides internal satisfaction. This career provides job security, flexible timings, and commands deep respect.

Teaching opportunities in the field of physical education at different levels are described below

### Primary Schools

Physical education is important for young children, as it focuses on their all round development.

Teaching physical education at primary level includes various activities like running, throwing, catching, jumping, climbing, kicking etc.

In India, there is no specialised subject of physical education at the primary level, so other subject teachers teach physical activities. This is the major drawback in India.

Implementation of physical education as a subject in primary schools will open more job opportunities in physical education and will help to make good and fit persons.

### Middle Schools

Teaching physical education in middle schools *i.e.* for classes VI, VII and VIII, is very limited. This is because a separate syllabus for physical education is prescribed by only a few boards like Central Board of Secondary Education (CBSE).

This is available only in big cities. In towns and villages, physical education is not considered a separate subject. So, mostly other subject teachers teach this subject and hence job opportunities are limited in middle schools also.

### Secondary/ High Schools

The requirement of physical education teachers for higher classes is more as compared to junior classes. Specialised teachers for physical education are appointed in both government and private schools to teach physical education subjects theoretically and practically.

They also prepare students for various inter-school sports competitions and zonal level tournaments.

### Senior Secondary Schools

In senior secondary classes *i.e.* class XI and XII, physical education is an optional subject. There is a prescribed course which needs to be covered.

Specialised teachers are appointed for physical education; they are qualified and proficient in teaching the theory and practical aspects.

The teachers are also required to maintain school discipline and prepare students for inter-school competitions.

### College and University

Colleges and universities provide ample employment options in the field of physical education.

They offer many different degree, diploma and certificate courses in physical education, such as Certificate Course in Physical Education (CPEd), Diploma Course in Physical Education (DPEd), Bachelor Degree in Physical Education (BPEd), Certificate Course in Yoga, B.Sc in Physical Education, Masters Degree in Physical Education, etc.

At the post-graduate level, there are many short and long-term courses in Test and Measurement in Sports, Sports Psychology, Sports Sociology, Sports Medicine, Sports Biomechanics, Exercise Physiology, Sports Management, Sports Administration, Sports Nutrition etc.

In countries, like USA, UK, Germany, France and Russia, teaching of physical education is also carried out in sports clubs, community organisations, teaching centres for elders, in resorts etc.

## Career in Coaching

Field of physical education also provides coaching as a career option. Coaching can be done in combination with teaching of physical education or can be taken up separately.

Coaches are required to coach a team for inter-school, inter-collegiate and inter-university competitions.

Coaching opportunities are available in private schools, state sports departments, Sports Authority of India, professional teams, commercial sports clubs, hotels and private enterprises, etc.

To become a professional coach, NIS training course, Certificate or Diploma Course in Coaching or Master of Sports Degree (MS) can be undertaken.

Coaches should be efficient enough to give interviews. They must be able to speak in front of groups and keep themself updated with latest rules and current trends of the sport in which they are coaching.

This career provides many advantages like good salary, respect, excitement of winning, extra income of coaching during vacations etc.

However, the disadvantage is that coaches undergo tremendous pressure if their teams are not performing well.

Coaching includes tasks like conducting practice sessions, reviewing results, planning and counselling of the players, etc besides coaching individual sportspersons. Also, there are no fixed salary norms for coaches.

## Health Related Career

The health related career opportunities in the field of physical education have expanded during recent years. It is because people have become more health conscious and they want to be healthy and fit. Everyone wants to lead a healthy lifestyle.

Moreover, people want themselves to keep away from various types of diseases like hypertension, heart diseases and disorders such as obesity, diabetes, mellitus, etc.

So, it can be said that the people have realised the value of health, due to which, health related career have emerged.

Health and weight control clubs are one of the significant areas under health related career.

These clubs are based on individual's desire to be physically fit, to have slim and trim figure and to look smart. These health clubs are managed by the owners or are in the form of franchise, thus, it has become an industry.

Physical educators may find a number of opportunities in such health and weight control clubs. The activities and services provided by these clubs vary but fitness activities remain the same.

The facilities provided by these clubs include various games such as squash, tennis, swimming, etc.

**Athletic Training** is another field of career under health related career, which is available at the national level in India.

Athletic trainers work with national teams of games and sports, while there is little scope of job opportunities in schools and colleges as compared to Western countries.

An athletic trainer's responsibilities are many but their main responsibility is related to prevention of sports injuries and rehabilitation of injured athletes. They also work with coaches in making and supervising conditioning programmes.

## Career in Sports Management

It is related to administration and management of tournaments and sports institutions. This career provides job security, as most of the jobs are available in the public sector. The careers related to sports administration are given below

### Sports Departments

There are ample job opportunities related to administration in sports departments. The post of Director and Assistant Director in the Sports Departments of States and District Sports Officer in every District are available in the public sector.

The Director of Sports is responsible for the administration of men's and women's sports and games. He supervises coaches and assistant coaches.

Director of sports must have adequate knowledge regarding the rules and regulations of sports competition.

He is also responsible for fixing dates of competitions, arranging officials, lodging and boarding, preparing sports budget, etc.

Jobs related to sports administration are also available in State's Sports Department, such as District Sports Officers at District level.

These officers administer the work of coaches of various games and sports and other officials.

There are intramural or campus recreation programmes in Western countries whose administrative work is performed by the Director of Intramurals or the Director of Campus Recreation.

The director is mainly responsible to promote participation and has other responsibilities which are same as in other sports departments.

### Department of Physical Education

There are administrative posts in the departments of colleges and universities that have physical education courses.

The Head or Chairman of the department is responsible for all the teachers and clerical staff working under him. These jobs are available in both private and public sector.

There is no requirement for separate management qualifications for this post in India, as it is generally based on seniority.

### Private Sector Jobs in Administration

Apart from the government sector, there are many administrative jobs in private companies that undertake sports related programmes such as recreational competitions, sports meets and such other events.

The responsibilities include establishing programme venue, listing of activities, scheduling of activities, setting up teams and formation of various committees like transportation committee, refreshment committee, health and safety committee etc.

### Sports Facilities Management

This relates to the management of the facilities that are required in various sports such as managing the facility of gymnasium, health clubs, fitness centres, stadiums, sports complexes, swimming pools etc.

The sports facilities manager has to be sure that the facilities and equipments are well-maintained as well as to ensure safety according to the accepted standards.

For instance, a manager of a swimming pool has to see that, apart from maintenance and cleanliness of the pool, there are adequate safety measures taken.

Since, the number of sports clubs is increasing, the need to maintain the facilities is also rising and hence the job opportunities are also growing in this field.

## Career in Communication Media

Sports related communication through television, radio, newspapers and magazines has opened up career opportunities in the communication media.

Also, cable television channels like Ten Sports, Star Sports, ESPN etc provide 24 hours coverage of sports events. Therefore, this career has many different opportunities.

The careers related to communication media are given below

### Sports Journalism

This career option is available for physical educators who are good at writing and can communicate well. Sports journalists are required to write about sporting events or any aspect of sports, create stories related to sports, compile statistics, do research and then publish the articles in newspapers and magazines.

They also conduct interviews of players, sportspersons, coaches etc, and provide their views on a particular topic.

Therefore, sports journalists should have in-depth knowledge about current sports and should be aware of the latest trends as well as the rules and regulations of the sport they are writing about. The advantages of this career option are good media exposure, popularity and good scope of earning.

### Sports Broadcasting

A career in sports broadcasting is related to doing commentary or reporting a sports event over radio and television. Sports broadcasting requires not only the knowledge of the game but also the ability to communicate clearly.

Since the broadcast relays at the local, national and international levels, the commentators or reporters should have very good communication skills and language proficiency.

They should be able to report the sports performances in an easy way and report every action, each moment of the game with adequate technical information for the sports enthusiast.

In the case of radio commentary, reporting has to be more detailed and interesting. The commentator should be knowledgeable about the skills, techniques, tactics, rules and terms of the game.

### Writing

Another career opportunity in sports communication is writing books in the field of physical education. This is a very broad field and has a lot of scope, as very few books have been written.

The books can be written on general topics or on a sub-discipline of physical education such as sports psychology, sports sociology, exercise physiology, sports medicine, sports biomechanics etc.

This career option does not provide regular employment opportunities, so it can be taken up on a part-time basis.

Keen interest in the subject, in-depth knowledge, ability to do some research and writing talent are the requirements to take up book writing as a career.

### Sports Photography

It is another career which can be taken up by physical educators. The sports photography career is for those who have a keen interest in photography and a desire to communicate the real meaning of sports to public through photographs.

Photographs of the players, sportspersons, coaches as well as photographs and videos of actions in the field during a match or tournament are published in newspapers and magazines as well as are being shown on television channels.

This is the reason why this field offers lucrative career opportunities. One should have keen interest and knowledge about photography and videography.

Sports Photography

In this career, knowledge about other sub-disciplines of physical education can be very helpful.

For instance, knowing about biomechanics is helpful in taking the photograph of a player in action from the best angle.

The essential requirements for a career in this field are a degree in physical education and a course in photography and videography.

### Career in Sports Equipments Sales and Marketing

With more number of children learning various games and sports from a very young age and increase in the interest in sports, the sale and marketing of sports equipments and sports goods has increased.

Companies require people who have knowledge about various sports equipments and can demonstrate their proper usage to customers.

Therefore, physical educators are needed for sales and marketing also.

Jobs available under sales and marketing are marketing managers, sales representatives, salespersons etc. Courses in business management and accounting along with courses in physical education can provide very good career opportunities.

### Career in Sports Industry

Setting-up small scale units for manufacturing sports equipments or sports goods can also be a career option. For this, knowledge of physical education is essential, as research has to be undertaken to design the goods according to the changing needs and requirements of the sports concerned.

Small scale units can undertake the manufacturing of different types of sports goods such as swim suits or track suits, hockey sticks or a host of different items needed in sports.

Adidas and Reebok are some of the popular companies selling quality sports shoes and form an important part of the sports industry.

## Changing trends in Sports

### Playing surface

Playing surface means any outdoor area used or capable of being used for any organised sport or recreation. Playing surface is an important factor which affects the performance of an individual, in modern times when the course of the sports has been totally changed due technical advancements, the changes in the playing surfaces also become very important, specially in athletics.

Construction of Artificial Turf (AT) playing fields has increased, therefore the number of athletes playing on AT has increased. Performance variables, such as speed, appear to improve on AT, however injury rate has increased. To date, few publications have studied the effect of playing surfaces on markers of athletic performance.

### Wearable Gears and Sports Equipment

Sports equipment is constantly advancing thanks to the evolution of technology, and coaches are taking notice. There are several smart sports gear products able to track an athlete's performance and allow coaches to help enhance their abilities. InfoMotion Sports created a basketball which measures the player's ball-handling skills. This product includes nine accelerometers that detect movement and track the ball's speed and rotation when shot through the air.

For tennis players, Babolat created a useful tool, called the **Play Pure Drive tennis racquet**. This product is similar to the 94Fifty basketball because of its ability to monitor tennis movements including serves, forehands, and backhands. This analysed data is available through a smartphone app, in which users can deliver information to their app and observe their performance.

As a result of recent advances in technology, smart sports gear now provides better safety and wellness to athletes and their coaches. Professionals within the healthcare field expressed positive thoughts toward mobile apps and wearable trackers, according to an infographic created by Arizona State University. Eighty-six percent of those interviewed said these tools have the ability to increase their knowledge of patient conditions.

### Technological Advancements in Sports

Within the last five years, the athletic world has been entirely transformed by emerging sports technology. These technologies make it easier than ever for fans to get into the game, and for athletes to optimise their performance.

### Sensors

Arguably, the greatest of all sport technology advancements has been the development of devices that can measure different metrics during a game or race. Today, there are sport-specific sensor devices for virtually every athletic activity under the Sun.

Sensors have also taken the pro sports world by storm, as the information gleaned from these devices offers access to tons of advanced statistical detail we've never had access to before. These advanced stats are then used by teams to inform scouting, personnel decisions, and much more within the front office. For fans, these new stats allow them to dive even deeper into the numbers to measure player performance.

### Protective Gears

From helmets to cleats, new technology in sports equipment has revolutionised the way that manufacturers keep athletes safe from injury. Helmet manufacturers are leveraging years of impact data and combining them with technologically advanced materials to produce safer and more comfortable helmets. The same holds for companies that make pads, gloves, and other gear.

These advancements provide players with the gear they need to stay safe, without compromising their ability to play at their peak.

## Khelo India Programme

Sports and fitness are integral part of humans' life. Sports help to inculcate team spirits, develops strategic and analytical thinking, leadership skills, goal setting and risk taking. It is believed that a healthy and fit person can make equally healthy society and strong nation.

For harmonious development of our nation, sports plays an extremely important role.

But in the last few years in the field of sports and games, India has made a steady progress.

Thus, it's time to inculcate sports spirit in young talented minds and provide top level facilities and world class training to them.

There is a much required need to inspire young people to take participation in various sports and games which would enable them to show their actual potential.

The aim of 'Khelo India Programme' is to revive the sports culture in India at the grassroots level by building a strong framework for all sports played in our country and thereby establish India as a great sporting nation. It was launched in the year 2017-18 by the Ministry of Sports and Youth Affairs.

The first Khelo India School Games, which are a part of Khelo India Programme were held in New Delhi from 31st January to 8th February, 2018.

KHELO INDIA
Ministry of Youth Affairs and Sports

### Objectives of Khelo India Programme

The objectives of the Khelo India Programme are discussed as follows

- **Playfield Development** The aim of the programme is to develop many playfields at various state and district level, so that basic facilities may be provided to sportsperson.
- **Community Coaching Development** Skill development and certification system for sports coaching is another important goal of this programme. Its aim is to evolve and identify physical education teachers and to train them as master trainers.
- **State Level Khelo India Centre** Supporting better utilisation of sports infrastructure in relation to States/UTs is another goal of this programme.
- **Annual Sports Competition** This programme provides a good platform to talented children in order to exhibit their talent in sports. To identify such talents, various games are organised like athletics, basketball, volleyball, boxing, handball, etc except cricket.
- **Talent Search and Development** This programme aims to search new young and upcoming talent in sports with the help of best scientific methods. The identification of talent to be done by the committee.

- **Utilisation, Creation and Upgradation of Sports Infrastructure** The programme aims at developing sports infrastructure at schools and universities which have high sports potential.
- **Support to National/Regional/State Sports Academics** Another important aim of this programme is to provide financial, technical and developmental support for expediting long-term athlete development programmes.
- **Physical Fitness of School-going Children** Development of physical fitness of school-going children is one of the important objectives of this programme. Under this scheme, tool kit is provided to schools to measure the physical fitness of school-going children.
- **Sports for Women** The programme encourages and promotes women's participation in different sports activity. It organises competitions in those sports/games where women participation is less.
- **Promotion of Sports among Specially Abled Persons** The programme focuses on promoting sports among disabled (divyang) persons. Financial assistance will be given to States/UTs and Sports Authority of India for creation of sports infrastructure for such people. Coaching facilities will also be arranged for them.
- **Promotion of Rural and Indigenous/Tribal Games** The programme seeks to organise Annual Sports Competitions in rural and indigenous/tribal games on alternate basis. It's aim is to enhance sports participation in such games.

# Fit India Movement

Fit India Movement was launched on 29th August, 2019 by Honourable Prime Minister with a view to make fitness an integral part of our daily lives. The mission of the Movement is to bring about behavioural changes and move towards a more physically active lifestyle. Towards achieving this mission, Fit India proposes to undertake various initiatives and conduct events to achieve the following objectives

- To promote fitness as easy, fun and free.
- To spread awareness on fitness and various physical activities that promote fitness through focused campaigns.
- To encourage indigenous sports.
- To make fitness reach every school, college/university, panchayat/village, etc.
- To create a platform for citizens of India to share information, drive awareness and encourage sharing of personal fitness stories .
- A committee has been formed to advice government on this campaign. It is composed of various government officials, members of Indian Olympic Association, national sports federations, private bodies and fitness promoters.

# CHAPTER PRACTICE

## OBJECTIVE TYPE QUESTIONS

### Multiple Choice Questions (MCQs)

**1** The foundation of physical education was laid in

(a) England (b) Greece
(c) USA (d) Italy

*Ans* (b) Greece

**2** Which of the following is not the objective of physical education?

(a) Physical development
(b) Social development
(c) Emotional development
(d) Technical development

*Ans* (d) Technical development

**3** According to JB Nash, the objectives of physical education are

(a) Neuromuscular development
(b) Organic development
(c) Interpretative development
(d) All of the above

*Ans* (d) All of the above

**4** Career options through physical education are

(a) Sports Departments
(b) Sports Facilities Management
(c) Sports Journalism
(d) All of the above

*Ans* (d) All of the above

**5** Inter-State Athletic Championship is organised by

(a) Athletic Federation of India
(b) The State Athletic Association
(c) Association of Indian Universities
(d) All England Championship

*Ans* (a) Athletic Federation of India

**6** When did the revival of Olympic games took place?

(a) 1895 (b) 1896 (c) 1899 (d) 1892

*Ans* (b) 1896

**7** Fit India Movement was launched on ......... .

(a) August, 2020 (b) February, 2019
(c) August, 2019 (d) February, 2018

*Ans* (c) August, 2019

**8** What are the objectives of Fit India Movement?

(a) To promote fitness as easy, fun and free
(b) To encourage indigenous Sports
(c) To make fitness reach every school, college and university
(d) All of the above

*Ans* (d) All of the above

**9** A Committee has been formed to advice government on Fit India Movement, consisting of

(a) Various government officials
(b) Members of Indian Olympics Association
(c) National Sports Federations
(d) All of the above

*Ans* (b) All of the above

### Fill in the Blanks

**10** Physical education is derived from the ......... phrase which refers to the capacity of person to meet physical demands of daily life.

*Ans* physical fitness

**11** ......... objective of physical education is related to the mental development of an individual.

*Ans* Psychological development

**12** In Senior Secondary Classes (XI-XII), physical education is an ......... subject.

*Ans* optional

**13** ......... career option is available for physical educators who are good at writing and can communicate well.

*Ans* Sports Journalism

### State True or False

**14** In coaching job, a coach should be efficient enough to give interviews.

*Ans* True

**15** Khelo India Programme has been introduced to revive the sports culture in India at the grassroots level.

*Ans* True

## Assertion-Reason

**16** **Assertion** (A) Physical education is integral part of the education system.
**Reason** (R) The aim of physical education is to make every child physically, mentally and constitutionally fit.
In the context of above two statements, which one of the following is correct?

**Codes**
(a) Both A and R are true and R is the correct explanation of A
(b) Both A and R are true, but R is not the correct explanation of A
(c) A is true, but R is false
(d) A is false, but R is true

*Ans.* (a) Both A and R are true and R is the correct explanation of A

**17** **Assertion** (A) Field of physical education also provides coaching as a career option.
**Reason** (R) The health related career opportunities in the field of physical education have expanded during recent years.

**Codes**
(a) Both A and R are true and R is the correct explanation of A
(b) Both A and R are true, but R is not the correct explanation of A
(c) A is true, but R is false
(d) A is false, but R is true

*Ans.* (b) Both A and R are true, but R is not the correct explanation of A

**18** **Assertion (A)** Asian Games are organised by International Association of Athletics Federation.
**Reason** (R) Olympic Games began in ancient Greece.

**Codes**
(a) Both A and R are true and R is the correct explanation of A
(b) Both A and R are true, but R is not the correct explanation of A
(c) A is true, but R is false
(d) A is false, but R is true

*Ans.* (d) A is false, but R is true

## VERY SHORT ANSWER TYPE QUESTIONS

**19** Explain the meaning of physical education with the help of a definition.

*Ans* According to R Cassidy, "Physical education is the sum of the changes in the individual caused by experiences involving motor activities."
It means physical education involves movements that help in keeping us fit and healthy.

**20** What is psychological development?

*Ans* Psychological development is an objective of physical education that is related to the mental development of an individual by developing positive thoughts, behaviour, attitude, alertness of mind, concentration, confidence and calculated movements.

**21** How does physical education develop neuromuscular coordination?

*Ans* By performing physical activities regularly, the internal organs and systems in the body such as digestive system, circulatory system, respiratory system, nervous system and muscular system work smoothly. This develops neuromuscular coordination.

**22** Define physical education as given by the Central Advisory Board of Physical Education and Recreation, Government of India.

*Ans* According to the Central Advisory Board of Physical Education and Recreation, "Physical education is an education through physical activities for the development of the total personality of the child to its fullness and perfection in body, mind and spirit."

**23** How does physical education promote harmonious growth and development?

*Ans* Physical education promotes harmonious growth and development, as it aims for all round development of a person that relates to physical, psychological, social and emotional development, all at the same time.

**24** Which qualifications are required by physical instructors to teach in schools?

*Ans* Physical instructors should have a Bachelor Degree of Education in Physical Education to teach the subject in schools.

**25** What is the changing trend that can be seen in careers related to physical education?

*Ans* The changing trend is that earlier only traditional careers were available in physical education i.e. teaching and coaching, but now emerging careers in health, sports management and sports broadcasting as well as others are also available.

**26** What avenues are open for health related careers in physical education?

*Ans* The avenues open in health related careers are fitness trainer, aerobics trainer, yoga instructor, weight training expert, physical training instructor etc.

**27** Are there any jobs related to physical education in private sector?

*Ans* Yes, private sector also provides many job opportunities, as private companies undertake sports related programmes such as recreational competitions, sports meet etc where physical educators are needed.

**28** What is a sports facility?

*Ans* Sports facilities are the facilities required in various sports, games and other activities such as the facility of gymnasium, equipment in health clubs and fitness centres, swimming pools, stadium, sports complexes etc.

**29** Define sports journalism.

*Ans* Sports journalism is a career option in which the journalist is required to write about a sporting event or any aspect of sports or compile statistics or do some research on sports and then publish the information as articles in newspapers and magazines.

**30** Why was Khelo India Programme introduced in India?

*Ans* Khelo India Programme was introduced in India to revive the sports culture at the grassroots level by building a strong framework for all sports played in our country.

## SHORT ANSWER TYPE QUESTIONS

**31** How does physical education develop the ability and capacity of an individual?

*Ans* Physical education tells us about the benefits of physical activities. Regular physical activities ensure smooth working of the internal organs of the body like heart, lungs, liver and kidney.

Physical activity also ensures smooth functioning of all the different systems working in our body such as digestive system, circulatory system, respiratory system, nervous system and muscular system.

When these systems work smoothly, our body works in a better way and develops our ability and capacity to work.

**32** Participation in physical activities helps in proper mental development. Justify.

*Ans* By participating in physical activities like games and sports, an individual learns to concentrate and face challenges, as there are many competitors.

The players learn to take quick decisions by understanding existing situations and guessing the moves of the opponents.

This helps in developing positive thoughts and also develops positive behaviour and attitude.

At the same time, physical activities improve alertness of the mind, increase concentration, build confidence and help to calculate movements.

This directs growth in a sequential manner and thus helps in proper mental development.

**33** Discuss the short and long-term courses available in the field of physical education in India by giving examples.

*Ans* Short-term courses are for a duration of a few months to 1-2 years. Diploma and certificate courses are short-term courses.

There are many such courses like Diploma in Physical Education, Diploma in Adaptive Physical Education etc.

Certificate courses are available in Aerobics, Yoga Science, Coaching, Sports Administration etc.

Long-term courses available in physical education are degree courses like Bachelor of Arts in Physical Education, Master of Arts in Physical Education, M. Phil. in Physical Education etc.

**34** Discuss the career opportunities available in coaching.

*Ans* There are many career opportunities available in coaching, which can be taken in combination with teaching or separately. Coaching is required by a team preparing for inter-school and inter-collegiate competitions.

Therefore, job options in coaching are available in private schools, government schools, colleges, State Sports Departments and Sports Authority of India.

In the private sector, coaching jobs are available in commercial sports clubs, hotels, private enterprises etc. Professional teams taking part in national and international sports events also hire coaches.

**35** What are the pros and cons of taking up sports performance related careers?

*Ans* Sports performance related careers give very good scope of earning through participation in sports tournaments, sponsorships and commercial advertisements.

Government also provides jobs to sportspersons. Such persons have the chance to get absorbed in defence services, railways, banks and private companies.

The disadvantage of taking a sports performance related career is that it is very short-lived, as it requires consistent performance that can be achieved till a certain age only.

**36** What do you mean by sports industry? How can physical educators make a career in sports industry?

*Ans* Sports industry refers to setting up small scale manufacturing units for the production of sports equipments or sports goods like sports shoes, cricket kits etc.

Physical educators have a knowledge of the various sub-disciplines of physical education like sports physiology, bio-mechanics, sports psychology etc.

This helps them in designing sports goods and equipments according to the changing needs and requirements of the players.

So, physical educators can understand how to manufacture suitable sports goods and sell them in the market.

**37** Write a short note on playing surface.

*Ans* Playing surface means any outdoor area used or capable of being used for any organised sport or recreation Playing surface is an important factor which affects the performance of an individual, in modem times when the course of the sp.orts has been totally changed due technical advancements, the changes in the playing surfaces also become very important, specially in athletics.

Construction of artificial turf (AT) playing fields has increased, therefore the number of athletes playing on AT has increased. Performance variables, such as speed, appear to improve on AT, however injury rate has increased. To date, few publications have studied the effect of playing surfaces on markers of athletic performance.

**38** Write about athletic training as career under health related career.

*Ans* The athletic training is another field of career under health related career which is available at the national level in India.

Athletic trainers work with national teams of games and sports, while, there is little scope of job opportunities in schools and colleges as compared to Western countries.

The responsibility of athletic trainers are many but their main responsibility is related to prevention of sports injuries and rehabilitation of injured athletes.

They also work with coaches in making and supervising programmes.

They also work at hospitals and fitness centres. Professional sports team employ some athletic trainers. This is a physically demanding job.

**39** Discuss about wearable gears and sports equipments in brief.

*Ans* Sports equipment is constantly advancing thanks to the evolution of technology, and coaches are taking notice. There are several smart sports gear products able to track an athlete's performance and allow coaches to help enhance their abilities .. InfoMotion Sports created a basketball which measures the player's ball-handling skills. This product includes nine accelerometers that detect movement and track the ball's speed and rotation when shot through the air.

For tennis players, Babolat created a useful tool, called the Play Pure Drive tennis racquet. This product is similar to the 94Fifty basketball because of its ability to monitor tennis movements including serves, forehands, and backhands. This analysed data is available through a smartphone app, in which users can deliver information to their app and observe their performance.

Thanks to recent advances in technology, smart sports gear now provides better safety and wellness to athletes and their coaches. Professionals within the healthcare field expressed positive thoughts toward mobile apps and wearable trackers, according to an infographic created by Arizona State University. Eighty-six percent of those interviewed said these tools have the ability to increase their knowledge of patient conditions.

**40** Explain the meaning of physical education with the help of definition.

*Ans* Physical education is the accumulation of wholesome experiences through participation in large mascular activities that promote optimum growth and development.

It is an integral part of the total education process which has its aim at the development of physically, mentally, emotionally and socially fit citizens through the medium of physical activities which have been selected with a view to realising these outcomes.

Government of India, defines Physical Education as "an education through physical activities for the development of total personality of the child to its fullness and perfection in body, mind and spirit."

**41** What are the main aims of teaching physical education in school?

*Ans* The main aims of teaching physical education in school are as follows:

- Understand the value of physical education.
- Develop a high level of physical fitness to undertake a variety of physical activities.
- Perform physical exercises to their optimum level.
- Develop personal and social qualities to experience enjoyment and satisfaction in life.
- Demonstrate the knowledge, skills and techniques learned with enthusiasm, commitment and initiative.
- Develop social skills which demonstrate the importance of teamwork and cooperation in group activities.

**42** Write a short note on the social development.

*Ans.* Social development is related to the development of social skills that are needed to live in society. Social qualities like cooperation, courtesy, sportsmanship, tolerance, friendship, sincerity and adjustment are essential to live in society.

Physical education provides good opportunities to come closer, form friendships and adjust according to different situations. It creates a healthy social environment within the society and helps to develop the socialisation process among children. This objective also helps to overcome social evils and brings prosperity alongwith communal harmony.

**43** What is scope of career in the sports broadcasting?

*Ans* A career in sports broadcasting is related to doing commentary or reporting a sports event over radio and television.

Sports broadcasting requires not only the knowledge of the game but also the ability to communicate clearly. Since the broadcast relays at the local, national and international levels, the commentators or reporters should have very good communication skills and language proficiency.

**44** Explain the major objective of the Khelo India Programme.

*Ans.* Khelo India Programme was launched in the year 2018. Its main objective are as follows

- **Talent Search and Development** This programme aims to search new young and upcoming talent in sports with the help of best scientific methods. The identification of talent to be done by the committee.
- **Utilisation, Creation and Upgradation of Sports Infrastructure** The programme aims at developing sports infrastructure at schools and universities levels, which have high sports potential.
- **Support to National/Regional/State Sports Academics** Another important aim of this programme is to provide financial, technical and developmental support for expediting long-term athlete development programmes.

**45** John is a student of class 12th in XYZ school. He wants to build his career in physical education but he is not clear about career options in the physical education. So he take information about building his career from his physical education teacher.

(i) Which of the following career options John can choose to build his career in physical education?

(a) Teaching
(b) Sales and Marketing
(c) Communication Media
(d) All of the above

(ii) Which of the following is the reason for limited scope of teaching physical education in middle schools?

(a) The syllabus for physical education is prescribed by only a few boards.
(b) This subject is taught by teachers of physical education only.

CHAPTER PRACTICE

(c) Physical education is considered as a separate subject in towns and villages.
(d) None of the above

(iii) Which of the following institution provide job opportunities if a person chose career in coaching?
(a) Private enterprises
(b) Sports Authority of India
(c) Sports Departments
(d) All of the above

*Ans* (i) (d) All of the above
(ii) (a) The syllabus for physical education is prescribed by only a few boards.
(iii) (d) All of the above

## LONG ANSWER TYPE QUESTIONS

**46** Define physical education. Explain the aims of physical education.

*Ans* According to Brownell and Hagman, "Physical education is the accumulation of wholesome experiences through participation in large muscular activities that promote optimum growth and development."

Thus, physical education stresses on balanced development of body and mind equally. The aim of physical education, as given by JF Williams, is to develop skilled leadership, adequate facilities and ample time for the individual and groups to participate in activities that are physically wholesome, mentally stimulating and satisfying and socially sound.

The aim of physical education is to enable the students to

- Understand the value of physical education.
- Develop a high level of physical fitness to undertake a variety of physical activities.
- Perform physical exercises to their optimum level.
- Develop personal and social qualities to experience enjoyment and satisfaction in life.
- Demonstrate the knowledge, skills and techniques learned with enthusiasm commitment and initiative.
- Develop social skills which demonstrate the importance of teamwork and cooperation in group activities.

It can be summarised that the main aim of physical education is to promote good health.

**47** Explain briefly the objectives of physical education.

*Ans* For answer, refer to page no. 2 and 3 under Objectives of Physical Education heading.

**48** Discuss the teaching careers available in physical education.

*Ans* Teaching as a career in physical education provides job security, flexible timings, deep respect and satisfaction. The career options in teaching are

(i) **Teaching in Primary Schools** This is related to teaching physical education in primary classes. Here the teacher teaches basic motor skills like running, throwing, climbing, kicking etc.

In India, there is less scope because the schools do not have a separate subject of physical education.

(ii) **Teaching in Middle Schools** It is related to teaching in classes VI, VII and VIII. This is also limited because there is no separate syllabus, so other subject teachers take up teaching of physical education in these classes.

(iii) **Secondary Schools** In these classes, the requirement of physical education teachers is more. Specialised teachers are appointed, so there is a good scope of teaching in these classes.

(iv) **Senior Secondary Schools** In classes XI and XII, Physical Education is an optional subject for which there is a prescribed syllabus. Therefore, there is need for teachers and hence the demand for teachers is high. So, this is a good career option.

(v) **College and Universities** There are ample job opportunities in colleges and universities as a teacher of physical education. The teachers also prepare students for competitions.

Therefore, teaching provides good job opportunities for physical educators.

**49** Discuss the career options available in administration of physical education.

*Ans* The career options available in administration of physical education are

(i) **Sports Department** The job opportunities available within the sports departments in government are Director and Assistant Director of Sports, District Sports Officer at the district level and other officials working in the department.

(ii) **Department of Physical Education** There are opportunities available for administrative posts in physical education departments of colleges and universities.

(iii) **Private Sector** Private colleges also have administrative posts in their physical education departments. Private companies also hire physical educators who can undertake the administration of various sports events run by the companies.

So, there are a number of jobs in the private sector related to sports administration.

(iv) **Sports Facilities Management** This relates to the various facilities provided by the different health clubs, fitness centres, gyms, sports complexes etc.

The administrative duties relate to the overall supervision of the work at these facilities. Since the number of sports clubs are rising in the urban areas, the job opportunities are also growing in this field.

**50** Explain the technological advancement in Sports.

*Ans* Within the last five years, the athletic world has been entirely transformed by emerging sports technology. These technologies make it easier than ever for. fans to get into the game, and for athletes to optimize their performance Sensors Arguably the greatest of all sport technology advancements has been the development of devices that can measure different metrics during a game or race. Today, there are sport-specific sensor devices for virtually every athletic activity under the sun.

Sensors have also taken the pro sports world by storm, as the information gleaned from these devices offers access to tons of advanced statistical detail we've never had access to before. These advanced stats are then used by teams to inform scouting, personnel decisions, and much more within the front office. For fans, these new stats allow them to dive even deeper into the numbers to measure player performance.

Protective Gears From helmets to cleats, new technology in sports equipment has revolutionized the way that manufacturers keep athletes safe from injury. Helmet manufacturers are leveraging years of impact data and combining them with technologically advanced materials to produce safer and more comfortable helmets. The same holds for companies that make pads, gloves, and other gear.

These advancements provide players with the gear they need to stay safe, without compromising their ability to play at their peak.

**51** Describe about the objectives of Khelo India Programme.

*Ans* The objectives of the Khelo India Programme are discussed as follows

(i) **Playfield Development** The aim of the programme is to develop many playfields at various state and district level, so that basic facilities may be provided to sportsperson.

(ii) **Community Coaching Development** Skill development and certification system for sports coaching is another important goal of this programme.

Its aim is to evolve and identify physical education teachers and to train them as master trainers.

(iii) **State Level Khelo India Centre** Supporting better utilisation of sports infrastructure in relation to States/UTs is another goal of this programme.

(iv) **Annual Sports Competition** This programme provides a good platform to talented children in order to exhibit their talent in sports. To identify such talents, various games are organised like athletics, basketball, volleyball, boxing, handball etc. except cricket.

(v) **Talent Search and Development** This programme aims to search new young and upcoming talent in sports with the help of best scientific methods. The identification of talent to be done by the committee.

(vi) **Utilisation, Creation and Upgradation of Sports Infrastructure** The programme aims at developing sports infrastructure at schools and universities which have high sports potential.

(vii) **Support to National/Regional/State Sports Academics** Another important aim of this programme is to provide financial, technical and developmental support for expediting long-term athlete development programmes.

(viii) **Physical Fitness of School-going Children** Development of physical fitness of school-going children is one of the important objectives of this programme. Under this scheme, tool kit is provided to schools to measure the physical fitness of school-going children.

(ix) **Sports for Women** The programme encourages and promotes women's participation in different sports activity. It organises competitions in those sports/ games where women participation is less.

(x) **Promotion of Sports among Specially Abled Persons** The programme focuses on promoting sports among disabled (divyang) persons. Financial assistance will be given to States/UTs and Sports Authority of India for creation of sports infrastructure for such people. Coaching facilities will also be arranged for them.

(xi) **Promotion of Rural and Indigenous/Tribal Games** The programme seeks to organise Annual Sports Competitions in rural and indigenous/ tribal games on alternate basis. It's aim is to enhance sports participation in such games.

**52** Describe about FIT India Campaign.

*Ans* FIT India Movement was launched on 29th August, 2019 by Honourable Prime Minister with a view to make fitness an integral part of our daily lives. The mission of the Movement is to bring about behavioural changes and move towards a more physically active lifestyle. Towards achieving this mission, Fit India proposes to undertake various initiatives and conduct events to achieve the following objectives:

- To promote fitness as easy, fun and free.
- To spread awareness on fitness and various physical activities that promote fitness through focused campaigns.
- To encourage indigenous sports.
- To make fitness reach every school, college/university, panchayat/village, etc.
- To create a platform for citizens of India to share information, drive awareness and encourage sharing of personal fitness stories.

A committee has been formed to advice government on this campaign. It is composed of various government officials, members of Indian Olympic Association, national sports federations, private bodies and fitness promoters.

# SELF ASSESSMENT

## OBJECTIVE ANSWER TYPE QUESTIONS

1 Which of the following philosophers strongly advocated physical training for the youth?

(a) Socrates
(b) Aristotle
(c) Plato
(d) All of these

2 The first 'Khelo India School Games' which are part of Khelo India Programme were held in

(a) Mumbai
(b) Kolkata
(c) New Delhi
(d) Chennai

3 Which of the following is the career options in communication media?

(a) Writing
(b) Sports facilities management
(c) Teaching
(d) Coaching

4 FIT India Movement was launded on ......... .

(a) August, 2020
(b) February, 2019
(c) August, 2019
(d) February, 2018

5 What are the objectives of Fit India Movement?

(a) To Promote fitness as easy, fun and free
(b) To encourage indigenous sports
(c) To make fitness reach every school, college and university
(d) All of the above

6 A Committee has been formed to advice government on Fit India Movement consisting of

(a) Various government officials
(b) Members of Indian olympics association
(c) National Sports federations
(d) All of these

## VERY SHORT ANSWER TYPE QUESTIONS

7 Physical education is a sum total of other parts of education. How?

8 Which psychological qualities are developed through physical education?

9 The Bachelors and Masters degrees in Physical Education are recognised by which government institutions?

10 In which classes is physical education an optional subject?

## SHORT ANSWER TYPE QUESTIONS

11 How does physical education develop the overall health of a person?

12 According to the aims of physical education, what will students be enabled to achieve through it?

13 Enumerate the pros and cons of taking up coaching as a career.

## LONG ANSWER TYPE QUESTIONS

14 Explain how the definition of physical education given by the Central Advisory Board of Physical Education and Recreation matches the objectives of physical education.

15 Explain how social and emotional development can be brought about in people through physical education.

16 Write about the significance of Khelo India Programme. Also, enumerate its four objectives.

CHAPTER

# 02

# Olympism

CHAPTER CHECKLIST

- Olympics
- Olympic Symbols
- Olympism
- Olympic Movement Structure

## Olympics

The Olympic genesis and its importance can better be understood under the two major heads *i.e.* ancient olympics and modern olympics.

### Ancient Olympics

The Ancient Olympic Games came into existence in 776 BC in the city of Olympia in Greece. These games were held in honour of the Greek God 'Zeus'. The people of Olympia constructed a magnificent temple and started the tradition of offering sacrifices. Later on, Hercules, the son of Zeus, started these games and sports competitions in honour of his father.

The ancient Olympic Games consisted of races of 100, 200 and 400 yards, wrestling, chariot racing, boxing, javelin throwing etc. The winners were crowned with an olive wreath made of wild olive leaves from a sacred tree near the temple of Zeus at Olympia. These games were held at Olympia every four years thereafter.

However, the tradition of Olympic Games was broken when the Roman Emperor Theodosius banned them in 394 AD. The statue of Zeus was also broken and the stadium was destroyed. But even after that, the memory of these games remained in the hearts of the people like a burning fire. They could not forget these games even after many centuries.

#### Rules for Competitions

When the Olympic Games were organised in 776 BC, certain rules were framed for competitors of various sports competitions which were engraved on a bronze plate. These rules are given below

- The competitor must only be a Greek, completely from a Hellenic race and must be physically fit. Slaves and criminals were not allowed to participate in these games.

- The competitors had to stay in Olympia for one month before the beginning of the games and engage themselves in practise during this time.

  They had to take an oath that they had already taken training lasting for 10 months in their State.
- Women were not allowed to participate in competitions or witness these games.
- Only amateur sportsmen could participate in these games, professionals were not allowed.

**Arena : Ancient Olympic Games**

## Opening Ceremony

The opening ceremony of Ancient Olympic Games had a spectacular ceremony. In the opening ceremony, all the players, their brothers, fathers and trainers used to gather in the stadium.

The experts in sports and games made them take the oath that they would participate in the games as per the rules and that they had trained for ten months.

After that, a pig was killed and offered to the God Zeus. After the completion of the ritual, one by one, all the players used to come out of the sports arena.

Exactly at that time, the players were introduced to the spectators. If any of the spectators had any objection against any player, the player was not allowed to participate in the competitions.

The rest of the players were allowed to participate. After that, the declaration was made to start the games.

With the passage of time, the number of sports kept on changing like, 400 yards walking was included in 724 BC. Three miles race was included in 720 BC, pentathlon in 708 BC, boxing in 688 BC and horse race in 648 BC. The games used to be organised for five days.

The events of Olympics continued for five days in following way

- On the first day, only religious functions were performed.
- The second day was reserved for march past and introduction and after that chariot race, horse race and Pentathlon were held.
- On the morning of the third day, the ritual of sacrifice of an animal was performed. After that, competitions of races, wrestling and boxing were held.
- The fourth day was fixed for athletic events, wrestling and boxing.
- On the final day, recreational programmes were organised.

## Awards

In the Ancient Olympic Games, less attention was paid to awards. Only foodgrains and animals were given as a reward. After that, a crown made of olive leaves was given to the winners.

More emphasis was laid on respect and honour, instead of awards, to the players. In ancient Olympic games, Statues were also made of the winners.

Poems were also composed in praise of the winners and their names were recorded in the annals of history. Sportsmen participated in these games for respect and honour and not for the sake of awards.

# Modern Olympics

The credit of reviving the lost tradition of Olympic Games and give it a modern look goes to Baron Pierre de Coubertin. He was born in 1862 in an Italian family that was settled in France.

He believed that various national and international problems could be solved through holding the Olympic Games, as it would give a common platform for the countries to meet.

For this purpose, he called a meeting of various countries in 1893. Some countries *viz.* Italy, Greece, Spain and Sweden were in favour of commencing these games, whereas other countries opposed the holding of these games.

In another conference held on 16th June, 1894, the motion, that sports events should be held every fourth year and every nation should be invited to participate, was passed.

With his efforts and support from other leaders of that time, the first modern Olympics were held in 1896 in Athens, Greece. Only 9 countries participated in it. However, this number gradually increased over the years and in the 2016 Rio de Janeiro (Brazil) Olympic Games, 206 countries participated.

Women participated for the first time at the 1900 Paris games with the inclusion of women's events in Lawn Tennis. Athletics and gymnastics events for women were held for the first time in 1928.

The games scheduled to be held in 1916, 1940 and 1944 were cancelled due to two World Wars. Apart from that, Olympic Games have been held regularly every 4 years. These are now also known as **Summer Olympics**.

## Rules for Competitions

Originally, the rule was that all males and females can participate in Olympic Games if they are amateur. But, nowadays, professionals are also allowed to participate in some sports.

The participants are sent by their National Olympic Committee. No sportsperson can participate in these games without the approval as well as recommendation of their National Olympic Committee.

## Opening Ceremony

Much before the games actually start, the Olympic torch is lit through the rays of the sun in the Olympia a village in Greece and brought *via* a relay of athletes to the city where the Olympic games are going to be held. The President or Prime Minister of the host country declares the games open in the stadium.

Before this process, all the sportspersons take part in a march past and they take a Olympic oath. Later on, recreational and cultural programmes are organised.

The Olympic flag is hoisted and the Olympic flame of the stadium is kindled by the torch. This flame remains lit throughout the games till the closing ceremony.

## Closing Ceremony

Sportspersons from all the countries assemble in the stadium for the closing ceremony on the last day of the games.

The Mayor of the host city and the President of the managing committee escort the President of the International Olympic Committee to the stadium. He declares the games closed.

After that, the Olympic flag is lowered and it is given to the Mayor of the city where the next Olympic Games will be held. Various cultural programmes are organised. The Olympic flame is extinguished. At last, the games come to an end with the Olympic song.

**Year and Venue of Olympic Games**

| S. No. | Year | City | Country |
|---|---|---|---|
| I | 1896 | Athens | Greece |
| II | 1900 | Paris | France |
| III | 1904 | St. Louis | USA |
| IV | 1908 | London | England |
| V | 1912 | Stockholm | Sweden |
| VI | 1916 | (Not held due to World War I) | |
| VII | 1920 | Antwerp | Belgium |
| VIII | 1924 | Paris | France |
| IX | 1928 | Amsterdam | Holland |
| X | 1932 | Los Angeles | USA |
| XI | 1936 | Berlin | Germany |
| XII | 1940 | (Not held due to World War II) | |
| XIII | 1944 | (Not held due to World War II) | |
| XIV | 1948 | London | England |
| XV | 1952 | Helsinki | Finland |
| XVI | 1956 | Melbourne | Australia |
| XVII | 1960 | Rome | Italy |
| XVIII | 1964 | Tokyo | Japan |
| XIX | 1968 | Mexico City | Mexico |
| XX | 1972 | Munich | Western Germany |
| XXI | 1976 | Montreal | Canada |
| XXII | 1980 | Moscow | Russia |
| XXIII | 1984 | Los Angeles | USA |
| XXIV | 1988 | Seoul | South Korea |
| XXV | 1992 | Barcelona | Spain |
| XXVI | 1996 | Atlanta | USA |
| XXVII | 2000 | Sydney | Australia |
| XXVIII | 2004 | Athens | Greece |
| XXIX | 2008 | Beijing | China |
| XXX | 2012 | London | England |
| XXXI | 2016 | Rio de Janeiro | Brazil |
| XXXII | 2020 | Tokyo | Japan (Held in 2021 due to the COVID-19 Pandemic) |

# Olympic Symbols

Various symbols and ideals associated with the mega sporting event, the Olympic Games, are representative of the olympic values educations. These are as follows

## Olympic Flag

It was designed by **Baron Pierre de Coubertin** in 1913. The Olympic flag is made of white silk without any border and displays five interlocking rings in the center.

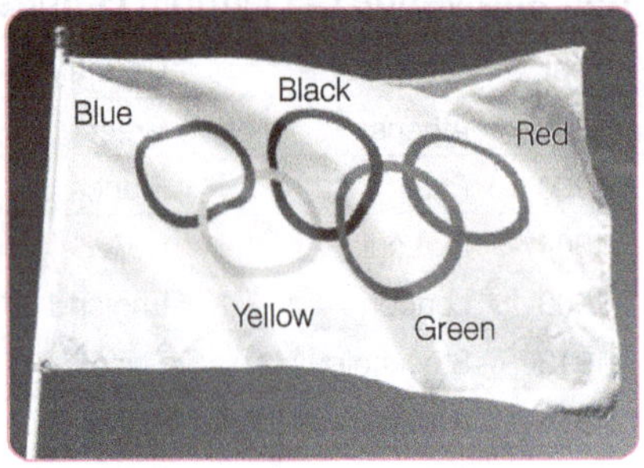


**Olympic Flag**

Each ring has a specific colour *i.e.* Blue, Black, Red, Yellow and Green and represents a particular continent *i.e.* America, Africa, Asia, Australia and Europe. At least one of these five colours is also present on the flags of all the nations.

The rings are interlocked which represents friendship, brotherhood and unity among all the people. The flag was used for the first time in the Olympic Games of 1920 in Antwerp, Belgium.

## Olympic Flame

The concept of the lighting of the Olympic flame came from Ancient Greece. The Olympic flame is a symbol used in the Olympic movement. It is also a symbol of continuity between ancient and modern games.

The Olympic flame was first introduced into Modern Olympics in 1928, Games held in Amsterdam, Netherlands. Since then, the flame symbolises the light of spirit, knowledge and life.

The Olympic flame or torch is lighted in Olympic Village of Greece and is carried by the runners to the place where the Olympic Games are going to be organised. During this process, it keeps on burning.

At the end of the closing ceremony of the games, this flame is extinguished.

**Olympic Flame**

## Olympic Mascot

Olympic mascots are fictional characters in animal or human form that are native to the country which hosts the Olympic event.

The mascots have also become symbols of the Olympics. The first mascot was 'Schuss', a stylised skier in the Winter Olympics of 1968 held in Chamonix, France.

**Rio Olympic 2016 Mascot—Vinicius**

## Olympic Medals

Sportspersons winning the first, second and third positions in the Olympic events are awarded with Gold, Silver and Bronze medals respectively.

A certificate is also given to them. The next five position holders are also given certificates.

## Olympic Motto

The Olympic motto represents the Olympic ideal which is taken from the sermons of a Dominician priest, Father Didon.

The Olympic motto is 'Citius, Altius, Fortius' which are Latin words means 'Faster, Higher and Stronger'. The motto was proposed by **Baron Pierre de Coubertin.**

### Olympic Oath

The Olympic oath is one of the rituals of every Olympic Games. It is taken by an athlete of the host country on behalf of all the athletes. At present, the oath is "In the name of all competitors, I promise that we shall take part in these Olympic Games, respecting and abiding by the rules that govern them, committing ourselves to a sport without doping and without drugs, in the true spirit of sportsmanship, for the glory of sport and the honour of our teams."

Similar oaths are also taken by the officials (judges, referees etc.) as well as the coaches of the athletes.

## Olympic Anthem

Olympic Anthem is a choral cantata by opera composer Spyridon Samaras (1861–1917), with lyrics by Greek poet Kostis Palamas. The anthem was performed for the first time for the ceremony of opening of the first edition at the 1896 Summer Olympics in Athens, Greece.

The anthem by Samaras and Palamas was declared the official Olympic Anthem by the International Olympic Committee in 1958 at the 54th Session of the IOC in Tokyo, Japan. The anthem was performed in English at the 1960 Winter Olympics in Squaw Valley and since then it has been played at each Olympic Games, during the opening ceremony when the Olympic flag is hoisted, and during the closing ceremony when the Olympic flag is lowered.

# Olympism

Olympism refers to the philosophy of the Olympic games. The fundamental principles of Olympism are outlined in the Olympic Charter. Olympism seeks to create a way of life by blending sport with culture, education and international cooperation. It is based on the joy of effort, the educational value of a good example, social responsibility and respect for universal fundamental ethical principles.

According to the principles of Olympism, the practice of sport is a human right. Every individual must have the possibility of practicing sport, without discrimination of any kind and in the Olympic spirit, which requires mutual understanding with a spirit of friendship, solidarity and fair play.

## Objectives and Values of Olympism

### Olympic Objectives

The objectives of the Olympics are as follows

- To develop physical education and healthy sports competition among people.
- To develop moral values, strong personality, etc.
- To promote sports ethics and fair play in competitions.
- To promote physical activities and sports among youth.
- To promote cooperation, brotherhood and friendship between countries.
- To promote international peace and understanding.
- To end discrimination on the basis of race, religion or caste.
- To bring the rich and poor nations on one platform and thereby promote cooperation.

### Olympic Values

The Olympic values are given below

- **Friendship** The Olympic movement provides good opportunities to develop friendship among players, coaches and officials of different countries, which brings nations closer to each other.
- **Solidarity** The Olympic movement develops unity and mutual agreement which gives a feeling of brotherhood among different countries. It creates cohesion among the participants and nations.
- **Fair Play** Fair play is based on the value of justice. The value of fair play i.e. no cheating, no kind of partiality and not using unfair means, helps in bringing out the best in the athletes.
- **Freedom from Discrimination** The Olympic movement lays stress on ending discrimination on the basis of caste, race and religion. Thus, it inculcates the value of equality.
- **Joy of Effort** Participants challenge themselves and each other in games, sports and physical activities in order to develop and practice their intellectual, behavioural and physical skills. Children many times show signs that they are not interested towards acertain sport due to the reason of them being forced to engage in a certain sport. Children who are younger in age are naturally active but, they tend to be less active as they grow older. Thus, inspirational methods and activities should be used to encourage young people to engage in sports.

- **Respect for Others** The sports itself develops this and it is promoted at international level by Olympic movement. This value motivates the players to show sportsman spirit. Every player respects the opponents, rules of game and environment.
- **Pursuit of Excellency** This value motivates a person to give the best performance onfield and outside the field is excellency and comes with hard work.
- **Balance among Body, Mind and Will** The process of learning includes the whole body, learning of morals and intellect can be developed with the help of learning through movement. This concept became the cornerstone of Pierre de Coubertin's interest in reviving Olympic Games. Coubertin has illustrated on the extreme compartmentalisation of modern education where each strength acts in isolation deprived of any link or contact with its neighbours. For example, if one discusses the topic of muscles, only the subject matter of function will be discussed. The human brain is furnished in a manner similar to tiny, air tight compartments. To open it, one must learn through movement which built a balance of body,will and mind.

## Olympic Movement Structure

The three main constituents of the Olympic Movement are the International Olympic Committee (IOC), the National Olympic Committees (NOCs) and the International Sports Federations (IFS).

### International Olympic Committee

The Modern Olympic Games are organised by the International Olympic Committee (IOC) that has its headquarters in Lausanne, Switzerland.

It is committed to support and promote participation in sports throughout the world.

The IOC was established by Baron Pierre de Coubertin on 23rd June, 1894. Demetrios Vikelas was its first President. Its membership consists of 105 active members and 32 honorary members.

It organises both Summer and Winter Olympics. The IOC selects the dates, sites and venues of the Olympic Games. The IOC consists of members from different countries.

The President of IOC is elected for a term of eight years. The four Vice-Presidents are elected for four years. The President, four Vice-Presidents and members of the Executive Board are elected by all the members of the IOC.

### Functions of IOC

The IOC performs various functions which are summarised below

- The IOC organises the Olympics, decides about the host country and the city where Olympic Games will be held.
- It ensures the smooth flow of all the events held in the Olympics.
- IOC sets the general guidelines, rules and regulations of the different sporting events.
- It encourages fair play without any discrimination.
- It fights against doping practices in sports.
- It encourages youth to participate in games and sports.
- It opposes any kind of political or commercial movement associated with international sports.
- It promotes regular celebration of the Olympic Games after every four years.
- It encourages and supports the promotion of women in sports at all levels.

### International Sports Federation

The International Sports Federations are international non-governmental organisations recognised by the International Olympic Committee (IOC) as administering one or more sports at world level. The national federations administering those sports are affiliated to them. While conserving their independence and autonomy in the administration of their sports, International Sports Federations seeking IOC recognition must ensure that their statutes, practice and activities conform with the Olympic Charter.

The IFS have the responsibility and duty to manage and to monitor the everyday running of the world's various sports disciplines, including for those on the programme, the practical organisation of events during the Games. The IFS must also supervise the development of athletes practising these sports at every level. Each IFS governs its sport at world level and ensures its promotion and development. They monitor the everyday administration of their sports and guarantee the regular organisation of competitions as well as respect for the rules of fair play.

The IFs may formulate proposals addressed to the IOC concerning the Olympic Charter and the Olympic Movement in general, including the organising and holding of the Olympic Games; give their opinions concerning the candidatures for organising the Olympic Games, particularly concerning the technical capabilities of the candidate cities; collaborate in the preparation of the Olympic Congresses; and participate in the activities of the IOC commissions.

The International Sports Federations (IFS) establish the rules that govern their sport and ensure that they are applied. They are responsible for the technical aspects of their sport at the Olympic Games. The IFs ensure that their sport is developed worldwide and disseminate the values of Olympism through their activities.

## National Olympic Committee (NOC)

A National Olympic Committee (NOC) is a national constituent of the worldwide Olympic movement. Subject to the controls of the International Olympic Committee, NOCs are responsible for organising their people's participation in the Olympic Games. They may nominate cities within their respective areas as candidates for future Olympic Games. NOCs also promote the development of athletes and training of coaches and officials at a national level within their geographies.

## International Sports Federations (IFS)

The International Sports Federations are international non-governmental organisations recognised by the International Olympic Committee (IOC) as administering one or more sports at world level. The national federations administering those sports are affiliated to them. While conserving their independence and autonomy in the administration of their sports, International Sports Federations seeking IOC recognition must ensure that their statutes, practice and activities conform with the Olympic Charter.

## Functions of IFS

The major functions of IFS are

The IFS have the responsibility and duty to manage and to monitor the everyday running of the world's various sports disciplines, including for those on the programme, the practical organisation of events during the Games.

The IFS must also supervise the development of athletes practising these sports at every level.

Each IFS governs its sport at world level and ensures its promotion and development. They monitor the everyday administration of their sports and guarantee the regular organisation of competitions as well as respect for the rules of fair play.

The IFS may formulate proposals addressed to the IOC concerning the Olympic Charter and the Olympic Movement in general.

## Other Members

In addition to its three main constituents, the Olympic Movement also encompasses the Organising Committees of the Olympic Games (OCOGs), the national associations, clubs and persons belonging to the IFS and NOCs, particularly the athletes, whose interests constitute a fundamental element of the Olympic Movement's action, as well as the judges, referees, coaches and the other sports officials and technicians. It also includes other organisations and institutions as recognised by the IOC.

# CHAPTER PRACTICE

## OBJECTIVE TYPE QUESTIONS

### Multiple Choice Questions (MCQs)

**1** In which BC, the Ancient Olympic Games were started?
(a) 778 BC (b) 776 BC
(c) 772 BC (d) 775 BC

*Ans* (b) 776 BC

**2** The first Modern Olympic Games were held in Athens, Greece in which year?
(a) 1893 (b) 1894 (c) 1896 (d) 1861

*Ans* (c) 1896

**3** The Olympic flag displays how many interlocking rings in the centre?
(a) Three (b) Five (c) Two (d) Six

*Ans* (b) Five

**4** The International Olympic Committee was established by whom?
(a) Baron Pierre de Coubertin
(b) Carl Lewis
(c) Jesse Owens
(d) Jim Thorpe

*Ans* (a) Baron Pierre de Coubertin

**5** Which of these is/are the functions of International Olympic Committee?
(a) It sets the general guidelines, rules and regulations of the different sporting events.
(b) It fights against doping practices in sports.
(c) It decides the host country where Olympic Games will he held.
(d) All of the above

*Ans* (d) All of the above

**6** What does the term 'citius' mean?
(a) Stronger (b) Faster
(c) Higher (d) Slower

*Ans* (b) Faster

### Fill in the Blanks

**7** The tradition of Olympic Games was broken when the Roman Emperor ......... banned them in 394 AD.

*Ans* Theodosius

**8** The colours of interlinked Olympic flags are Blue, Black, Red, Green and ......... .

*Ans* Yellow

**9** The Olympic flame was first introduced into Modern Olympics games in 1928 held in ......... .

*Ans* Amesterdam, Netherlands

**10** The headquarters of Modern Olympic Games is in ......... .

*Ans* Lausanne, Switzerland

### State True or False

**11** In the Olympic Games, which were organised in 776 BC, slaves and criminals were not allowed to participate.

*Ans* True

**12** Indian Hockey team (men), who was sent first time to Olympics in 1928, won a gold medal.

*Ans* True

**13** The Olympic Motto is 'Citius, Altius, Fortius' which means 'Slower, Higher and Stronger'.

*Ans* False. The Olympic Motto is 'Citius, Altius, Fortius' which means 'Faster, Higher and Stronger'.

**14** In Antwerp, Belgium the flag was used for the first time in the Olympic games of 1920.

*Ans* True

### Assertion-Reason

**15** **Assertion** (A) The Ancient Olympic Games came into existence in 770 BC.
**Reason** (R) Hercules, the son of Zeus, started these games and sports in honour of his father.
In the context of above two statements, which one of the following is correct?
**Codes**
(a) Both A and R are true and R is the correct explanation of A
(b) Both A and R are true, but R is not the correct explanation of A
(c) A is true, but R is false
(d) A is false, but R is true

*Ans* (d) A is false, but R is true

**16** **Assertion** (A) In the Ancient Olympic Games, less attention was paid to awards.
**Reason** (R) More emphasis was laid on respect and honour.
In the context of above two statements, which one of the following is correct?
**Codes**
(a) Both A and R are true and R is the correct explanation of A
(b) Both A and R are true, but R is not the correct explanation of A
(c) A is true, but R is false
(d) A is false, but R is true

*Ans* (a) Both A and R are true and R is the correct explanation of A

**17** **Assertion** (A) International Olympic Committee only organises Summer Olympics.
**Reason** (R) Olympics promotes cooperation, brotherhood and friendship between countries.
In the context of above two statements, which one of the following is correct?
**Codes**
(a) Both A and R are true and R is the correct explanation of A
(b) Both A and R are true, but R is not the correct explanation of A
(c) A is true, but R is false
(d) A is false, but R is true

*Ans* (d) A is false, but R is true

## VERY SHORT ANSWER TYPE QUESTIONS

**18** What were the winners awarded with in the ancient Olympic Games?

*Ans* In the ancient Olympic Games, till the sixth games, the winners were awarded cattle and corn. Afterwards, the winners were awarded a wreath made of wild olive leaves from a sacred tree near the temple of Zeus.

**19** Who started the modern Olympic Games?

*Ans* The modern Olympic Games were started by Baron Pierre de Coubertin.

**20** Why were the Olympics scheduled in 1916, 1940 and 1944 not held?

*Ans* The Olympic Games of these three years were not held because of the two World Wars.

**21** What does the Olympic flame signify?

*Ans* The Olympic flame signifies knowledge, light, happiness and peace.

**22** How do the Olympic Games develop the value of friendship?

*Ans* The Olympic Games provide good opportunities to develop the value of friendship as they bring players, coaches and officials of different countries closer to each other.

**23** Who selects the sites and dates of the Olympic Games?

*Ans* It is the role of the International Olympic Committee to select the sites and dates of the Olympic Games.

**24** Mention the year and place where the first Winter Olympics were held.

*Ans* The first Winter Olympics were held in 1924 at Chamonix in France.

## SHORT ANSWER TYPE QUESTIONS

**25** What is the role of International Sports Federation in olympics?

*Ans* The International Sports Federations are international non-governmental organisations recognised by the International Olympic Committee (IOC) as administering one or more sports at world level. The national federations administering those sports are affiliated to them. While conserving their independence and autonomy in the administration of their sports, International Sports Federations seeking IOC recognition must ensure that their statutes, practice and activities conform with the Olympic Charter.

**26** Why does the Olympic flag have five rings?

*Ans* The five rings in the Olympic flag are of different colours (blue, black, red, yellow and red) and represent five different continents *i.e.* Europe, Africa, America, Asia and Oceania.

The rings are interlocked, which means that players of all the countries participate in this sporting event. It poses that there will not be any discrimination on the basis of race, caste, religion, economic condition or political boundaries. These rings signify friendship, universal brotherhood and unity.

**27** Write a short note on the Ancient Olympics Games.

*Ans* The 'Ancient Olympic Games' came into existence in 776 BC in the town of Olympia in Greece. At that time, the events consisted of sports like races of 100, 200 and 400 yards, wrestling, chariot races, boxing, javelin throw etc. These events were held in the honour of Greek God Zeus.

The winners of these sporting events were respected in society and awarded with an olive wreath and other gifts.

However, this sporting event came to an abrupt end in 394 AD with the orders of the Roman Emperor Theodosius I banning these sports.

**28** Describe the ceremonies associated with the Olympic flame.

*Ans* The Olympic flame is an important symbol of the Olympics. The flame is lighted at the opening ceremony of the Olympic Games.

Participants, coaches, referees, judges and other officials of all the countries taking part in the Olympics also take part in the opening ceremony. The Olympic flame burns throughout the sporting event.

In the closing ceremony, which is held on the final day of the Olympic event, this flame is extinguished. In this way, the Olympic flame marks the opening and closing of the world's biggest sporting event.

**29** Who started the modern Olympics? What was his aim behind it?

*Ans* The modern Olympics was started by Baron Pierre de Coubertin in the late nineteenth century. The main aim behind starting this grand sporting event was to develop peace, understanding and cooperation between countries.

He believed that a common platform where people of different countries can meet will help to solve various national and international problems.

Therefore, he proposed the idea of organising a grand sporting event where sports representatives of all countries will meet and compete.

**30** Write a brief note on the Ancient Olympics.

*Ans* The Ancient Olympic Games came into existence in 776 BC in the city of Olympia in Greece. These games were held in honour of the Greek God 'Zeus'. The people of Olympia constructed a magnificent temple and started the tradition of offering sacrifices. Later on, Hercules, the son of Zeus, started these games and sports competitions in honour of his father.

The ancient Olympic Games consisted of races of 100, 200 and 400 yards, wrestling, chariot racing, boxing, javelin throwing etc. The winners were crowned with an olive wreath made of wild olive leaves from a sacred tree near the temple of Zeus at Olympia. These games were held at Olympia every four years thereafter.

**31** In Ancient Olympics less attention was given on awards. Examine.

*Ans* In Ancient Olympics less attention was given on awards. During these Olympics only food grain and animals were given as a reward. Players as well as organiser paid more exphasis on respect and honour instead of awards. Participant at this period had a broad mind, they understood the real spirit behind the organisation of the Olympics.

Award is just a piece of tangible product which can be created or achieved through different means. But, Olympics Games are much above than that of Awards. The spirit of participation is most important in the whole scenario. The participant who take part in it with the objective only winning the award, they defeat the noble cause behind the Games.

**32** What are main features of the Olympic flag?

*Ans* The main features of the Olympic flag are as follows
- It was designed by **Baron Pierre de Coubertin** in 1913.
- The Olympic flag is made of white silk without any border and displays five interlocking rings in the center.
- Each ring has a specific colour *i.e.* Blue, Black, Red, Yellow and Green and represents a particular continent *i.e.* America, Africa, Asia, Australia and Europe.
- The rings are interlocked which represents friendship, brotherhood and unity among all the people.

**33** Identify the main objectives of the Olympics.

*Ans* The main objectives of the Olympics are as follows
- To develop physical education and healthy sports competition among people.
- To develop moral values, strong personality, etc.
- To promote sports ethics and fair play in competitions.
- To promote physical activities and sports among youth.
- To promote cooperation, brotherhood and friendship between countries.

- To promote international peace and understanding.
- To end discrimination on the basis of race, religion or caste.
- To bring the rich and poor nations on one platform and thereby promote cooperation.

## LONG ANSWER TYPE QUESTIONS

**34** Discuss in detail about International Sports Federation.

*Ans* The International Sports Federations are international non-governmental organisations recognised by the International Olympic Committee (IOC) as administering one or more sports at world level. The national federations administering those sports are affiliated to them. While conserving their independence and autonomy in the administration of their sports, International Sports Federations seeking IOC recognition must ensure that their statutes, practice and activities conform with the Olympic Charter.

The IFS have the responsibility and duty to manage and to monitor the everyday running of the world's various sports disciplines, including for those on the programme, the practical organisation of events during the Games. The IFS must also supervise the development of athletes practising these sports at every level. Each IFS governs its sport at world level and ensures its promotion and development. They monitor the everyday administration of their sports and guarantee the regular organisation of competitions as well as respect for the rules of fair play.

The IFS may formulate proposals addressed to the IOC concerning the Olympic Charter and the Olympic Movement in general, including the organising and holding of the Olympic Games; give their opinions concerning the candidatures for organising the Olympic Games, particularly concerning the technical capabilities of the candidate cities; collaborate in the preparation of the Olympic Congresses; and participate in the activities of the IOC commissions.

The International Sports Federations (IFS) establish the rules that govern their sport and ensure that they are applied. They are responsible for the technical aspects of their sport at the Olympic Games. The IFs ensure that their sport is developed worldwide and disseminate the values of Olympism through their activities.

**35** Write the Olympic objectives in brief.

*Ans* The objectives of Olympics are

- To develop physical education and healthy sports competition among people.
- To develop moral values, strong personality and character.
- To promote sports ethics and fair play in competitions.
- To promote physical activities and sports among the youth.
- To promote cooperation, brotherhood and friendship between countries.
- To promote international peace and understanding.
- To end discrimination on the basis of race, religion or caste.
- To bring the rich and poor nations on one platform and thereby promote cooperation.

**36** What is the Olympic oath? Explain it's meaning.

*Ans* The Olympic oath represents the Olympic ideal of holding a sporting event which is based on fair competition which is free from any discrimination.

The Olympic oath, which is taken by all participants at the Olympic Games, says,

*"In the name of all competitors, I promise that we shall take part in these Olympic Games, respecting and abiding by the rules that govern them, committing ourselves to a sport without doping and without drugs, in the true spirit of sportsmanship, for the glory of sport and the honour of our teams."*

Thus, the oath means that the participating players, officials and all the people associated with the sporting event will take the competitions in their true spirit so that their glory is maintained.

**37** What values are promoted by organising the Olympic event?

*Ans* The Olympics event promotes certain values which are explained as follows

(i) **Friendship** The Olympic movement provides good opportunities to develop friendship among players, coaches and officials of different countries, which brings nations closer to each other.

(ii) **Solidarity** The Olympic movement develops unity and mutual agreement which gives a feeling of brotherhood among different countries. It creates cohesion among the participants and nations.

(iii) **Fair Play** Fair play is based on the value of justice. The value of fair play, i.e. no cheating, no kind of partiality and not using unfair means, helps in bringing out the best in the athletes.

(iv) **Freedom from Discrimination** The Olympic movement lays stress on ending discrimination on the basis of caste, race and religion. Thus, it inculcates the value of equality.

**38** What is IOC? When was it formed? Explain three roles of the IOC.

*Ans* IOC is International Olympic Committee. It was formed on 23rd June, 1894 with the purpose of organising international sporting events like Summer and Winter Olympics, selecting the site, venue and date of those events etc.

Three roles of IOC are

(i) The IOC organises the Olympic events, decides about the host country and the city where the Olympics will be held.

(ii) IOC sets the general guidelines, rules and regulations of the different sporting events.

(iii) It opposes any kind of political or commercial movement associated with international sports.

**39.**

(i) What do the five rings on the Olympic symbol represent?

(ii) The Olympic flag was used for the first time in the Olympic Games of ................. .

(iii) The concept of the lightening of the Olympic flame came from ................. .

(iv) The headquarters of Modern Olympic Games is in .................. .

*Ans.* (i) Five continents

(ii) 1920 in Belgium

(iii) Ancient Greece

(iv) Lausanne, Switzerland

# SELF ASSESSMENT

## OBJECTIVE ANSWER TYPE QUESTIONS

1 The Ancient Olympic Games consisted of how many races?
(a) 100 yards (b) 200 yards
(c) 400 yards (d) All of these

2 Where were the Winter Olympic of 1968 held?
(a) Chamonix France (b) Munich
(c) Rio de Janeiro (d) Seoul

3 The President of IOC is elected for how many years?
(a) Five years (b) Four years
(c) Six years (d) Three years

## VERY SHORT ANSWER TYPE QUESTIONS

4 The Modern Olympic Games started from which country?

5 When was athletics for women introduced in the Olympics?

6 When is the Olympic flame lighted?

## SHORT ANSWER TYPE QUESTIONS

7 Highlight the features of the Olympic flag.

8 How are the values of Olympics achieved through the Olympic motto?

## LONG ANSWER TYPE QUESTIONS

9 What do you understand by objectives of the Olympics?

10 Discuss about role of IFS in Olympics.

CHAPTER

# 03

# *Yoga*

The practice of Yoga is believed to have started with the very start of the Indian Civilisation. Many ancient sculptors, scriptures, seals and fossil remains of the Indus Valley Civilisation suggest that yoga was a part of the ancient Indian culture. Yoga has also been mentioned in *Mahabharata*, *Ramayana* and the *Upanishads* along with many other Indian scriptures.

Though Yoga was practiced in the ancient period, it was the great Sage Patanjali, who compiled *Yoga Sutras* in 147 BC, which presented its existing knowledge in a very systematic manner. Yoga has played a significant role in maintaining the mental and physical well-being of people all across the world.

### CHAPTER CHECKLIST

- Meaning of Yoga
- Ashtanga Yoga
- Yogic Kriyas
- Pranayama

## Meaning of Yoga

The word 'Yoga' is derived from the Sanskrit word '*yuj*', which means 'to join' or 'to unite'. This means that Yoga unites the individual's soul with the divine soul (*i.e.* God), a unification of *Atma* with *Parmatma*.

It implies the unification of the physical, mental, intellectual and spiritual aspects of a human being. It is also considered as a science which develops a person's consciousness.

The following definitions can be helpful to understand the meaning of Yoga

- According to **Maharishi Ved Vyas**, "Yoga is attaining the pose."
- According to **Patanjali**, "Suppression of modifications of the mind is Yoga."
- According to **Agam**, "The knowledge of Shiva and Shakti is Yoga."
- According to **Bhagwad Gita**, "Yoga is skill in action."

## Importance of Yoga

The modern age is the age of stress, tension and anxiety. The improper lifestyle and the lack of proper relaxation make people physically tired and mentally tense.

Their lives are full of problems. They are always in a hurry and have no time for leisure. As a result, most of them be it rich or poor, do not live a peaceful, healthy or a happy life.

* *The Yogic Practices or Asanas discussed in this chapter are also to be included in Practical.*

At such a juncture, yoga becomes very significant. The practice of yoga is not merely an exercise for the body. In fact, it is the knowledge that our ancestors developed to live a healthier, happier, peaceful and meaningful life. Thus, yoga is important in many ways, which are described as follows

1. **Brings about Physical Purity**
   Internal organs of our body can be cleansed by various yogic exercises.
   According to Ayurveda, our body is made of *Vaat* (airy elements), *Pitt* (fiery elements) and *Kaph* (watery elements). These elements must remain balanced for us to remain healthy.
   Yogic exercises which keep our bodies healthy and clean include *Basti, Dhoti, Kapalbhati, Nauli, Tratak* etc. For proper cleanliness and purity of our internal organs, we should perform these yogic exercises regularly.
2. **Prevents and Cures Diseases**
   There are various diseases which usually hamper the smooth functioning of our body. Yoga protects us from these diseases and also cures them. Various yogic exercises increase the body's immunity.
   Diseases which can be cured by some *asanas*, if performed regularly, are given in the table below

| Disease which can be Cured | Asanas to be Performed Regularly |
|---|---|
| Poor functioning of thyroid gland | *Halasana* / Plough pose and *Matsyasana* / Fish pose |
| PCOS in women (excess male hormone production) | *Dhanurasana* / Bow pose and *Bhujangasana* / Cobra pose |
| Arthritis | *Shishuasana / Child pose* and *Adho Mukha Svanasana* / Downward facing dog pose |
| Lower back pain | *Supta Matsyendrasana* / Supine Spinal Twist and *Marjaryasana*/Cat or Cow pose |
| Diabetes | *Ardha Matsyendrasana* / Half Spinal Twist and *Chakrasana* / Wheel pose |
| Indigestion / stomach disorder | *Apanasana* / Knees to chest pose and *Paschimottanasana* / Seated forward bend pose |
| Migraine (recurrent headache) | *Padmasana* / Lotus pose and *Padangusthasana*/Big Toe Pose |
| Liver problems | *Ardha Bhekasana* / Half Frog pose and *Parighasana* / Gate Pose |
| Depression | *Baddha Konasana* / Bound Angle pose and *Sukhasana* / Easy pose |
| Kidney disorders | *Salamba Bhujangasana* / Sphinx pose and *Naukasana* / Boat pose |

3. **Improves Health in General**
   Yoga maintains and improves our health by making our respiratory, circulatory, nervous, digestive and excretory systems more efficient as well as strengthening our muscles.
4. **Reduces Mental Tension**
   In the modern world, most people are under constant stress and tension. Without peace of mind, people feel upset and disturbed. Yoga helps to reduce any stress and tension.
   The *Pratyahara, Dharana* and *Dhyana* elements of Yoga help in bringing peace of mind. Some *asanas* like *Makarasana, Shavasana, Shalabhasana* and *Bhujangasana* benefit us by reducing stress and tension.
5. **Reduces Obesity and Beautifies the Body**
   Everyone wants to have a beautiful body. Obesity is a universal problem today and makes people prone to many diseases like high blood pressure, diabetes, heart diseases, stroke, gall bladder stones, cancer, gout, breathing problems etc.
   *Pranayam* and yogic *asanas* like *Mayurasana* reduce obesity and make the body more beautiful.
6. **Gives Relaxation**
   When we indulge in any work, after some time we feel tired. At such times, we are unable to work further as we need relaxation.
   *Asanas* like *Padmasana, Shavasana* and *Makarasana* as well as *Pranayama* helps in relaxing the body and mind, thus removing fatigue.
7. **Helps Maintain the Correct Posture**
   Due to the modern lifestyle of city dwellers, where most jobs are performed while being seated, deformities in posture are becoming common. Practising *asanas* like *Sarvangasana, Mayurasana, Chakrasana, Bhujangasana, Vajrasana* and *Dhanurasana* helps to cure postural deformities and makes the practitioners of these *asanas* maintain correct posture.
8. **Increases Flexibility**
   Flexibility helps in moving the body efficiently. *Chakrasana, Dhanurasana, Shalabhasana, Halasana* and *Bhujangasana* helps in improving flexibility and prevents sports related injuries.

9. **Develops People Spiritually**
   *Padmasana* and *Siddhasana* improve the power of meditation and give better control over the mind to develop people spiritually. *Pranayama* also helps in spiritual development that brings peace in life.
10. **Improves Moral and Ethical Values**
   Nowadays, there is a declining trend in moral and ethical values. Following the first two elements of Yoga, *i.e. Yama* (meaning universal moral guidelines) and *Niyama* (meaning self-purification by discipline) helps in the development of moral and ethical values.

## Ashtanga Yoga

In his description of the ancient Indian classical Yoga, Patanjali had classified Yoga into eight elements or *Ashtanga* (eight limbs).

These elements are also called the eight-fold paths or steps. These steps form a sequence from outer to inner self. Through this sequence, the ultimate goal of yoga, *i.e.* union of our soul with the divine can be achieved.

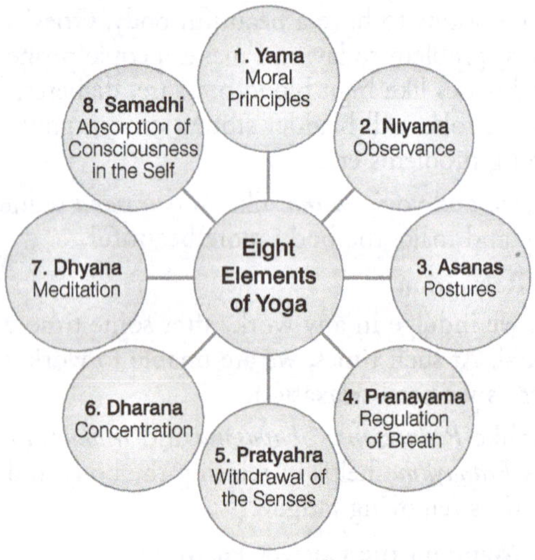

**Elements of Yoga**

These elements are as follows

1. **Yama**
   Yama contains the ethical rules of Hinduism. With the practice of Yama, one learns to self-restraint from struggle for survival. Yama contains 5 moral vows or codes of conduct, which are as follows
   - **Ahimsa** (Non-violence) It means that we must stay away from negative emotions like jealousy, hate anger, etc. and not harm any other living being.
   - **Satya** (Truthfulness) It means that we must be truthful in our thoughts, words and deeds at any cost.
   - **Asteya** (Non-stealing) It means that we must not use or even think of using others' objects, money or thoughts for our own benefit. We must be satisfied with what we have.
   - **Brahmacharya** (Celibacy) It means that we must stay away from anything that stimulates sexual desires. We must also not indulge in any sexual relations.
   - **Aparigraha** (Non-possessiveness) It means that we must live our life with minimum requirements. We must not desire to own any material possessions.
2. **Niyama**
   *Niyamas* are ethical practices that are related to the individual's body and senses. It contains essential teachings for self-maintenance including *Saucha, Santosh, Tapa, Swadhyaya* and *Isvara Pranidhana,* which are as follows
   - **Saucha** (Maintaining Cleanliness/Purity) It means that we must keep our mind, body and speech clean and pure.
     In yoga, special emphasis is given to cleanliness of internal organs using six *Shudhikriyas* or *Shatkarmas* such as *Neti kriya, Dhauti kriya* etc.
   - **Santosh** (Contentment) It means that we must develop a feeling of satisfaction in all situations of life.
   - **Tapa** (Discipline) It means that we must bear the difficulties, obstacles and complex situations in our life, in order to achieve the goal. We should also have the same spirit for all conflicts in our life like pleasure and pain, loss and gain.
   - **Swadhyaya** (Introspection or Study of the Self) It means the study of the various scriptures such as Vedas, Granths, Upanishads, etc. with devotion as well as the study of self.
   - **Ishvara Pranidhana** (Prayer or Surrendering to God) It means that as a devotee, a person must dedicate all the deeds to God. He/she must think that all the facilities and prosperity such as body, mind, intelligence, etc. available to him are due to God. There must not exist any pride, ego and other impurities within him/her.
3. **Asanas**
   *Asanas* are a set of physical postures that improve strength and balance. These *asanas* are beneficial for the inner organs.
   *Asanas* also enhance the beauty of the body by reducing inappropriate accumulation of fat in the body. They help to regulate blood and oxygen flow. They bring flexibility and agility by stretching of muscles. They have no age restrictions and even old people can perform *asanas.*

There are various types of *asanas* such as corrective *asanas*, relaxative *asanas* and meditative *asanas*. These types of *asanas* have different types of effects on our body.

4. **Pranayama**
   It involves controlled breathing and is also practised with some *asanas*. It consists of three simple exercises, *i.e. Puraka* (Inhale), *Kumbhaka* (Retain the breath) and *Rechaka* (Exhale).
   It is considered beneficial for lungs and helps in boosting the count of red blood corpuscles. It improves heart and lung functioning and increases longevity.
   *Ujjayi, Digra, Bahya, Aulom-Vilom Sheetali, Bhastrika, Nadi Sodhana, Kapalabhati* etc are various types of *Pranayama*.
5. **Pratyahara**
   Pratyahara means to control our mind and senses. It is a self-control process where people become able to control their various senses.
   In other words, an individual stops responding to the external sensory world such as touch, taste, smell, etc. that hinders mental concentration and self-welfare. As a result, one starts meditating into the inner self.
6. **Dharana**
   It is the concentration of the mind and the first stage of meditation. You focus all your energy at one point without letting your mind get distracted, and discard all your random thoughts. The mind is fixed on one subject, topic or place.
7. **Dhyana**
   It is a process of complete constancy of mind. *Dharana* sets the stage for *dhyana*. When one starts focussing on a topic, the mind starts actively engaging with its focus.
   Thus, *dhyana* is the active modification of knowledge in complete stability and calmness.
8. **Samadhi**
   It is the ultimate union of an individual's soul with God. It is the stage where a person lose himself to God. The concepts of 'I', 'me' and 'mine' hold no significance for that person and he forgets himself completely.

## Benefits of Ashtanga Yoga

The benefits of Ashtanga yoga are

- It is known to be strenuous, so it is great for athletes and people that are looking for a good workout. Like most styles of hatha yoga, Ashtanga focuses on breath, poses, and meditation.
- A regular yoga practice can improve your flexibility, breathing, and balance. It can increase stamina, bone density and muscle strength, control your bodyweight, lowers blood pressure and relieve stress.
- The benefits of the Ashtanga yoga are not only limited to physical factors. It also helps mentally and spiritually by boosting mental clarity, creating mental calmness and developing better concentration in daily life.

# Yogic Kriyas

The human body requires both internal and external cleanliness for proper functioning. Generally, we carry out outer cleanliness, which is very easy, but inner cleanliness is slightly difficult.

Inner cleanliness of our body can be accomplished by practising six yogic *Kriyas*, also called *Shatkarmas* or *Shudhhi Kriyas*. These are as follows

1. **Neti** Nasal cleansing.
2. **Dhauti** Cleaning of digestive tract, especially oesophagus and stomach.
3. **Nauli** Abdominal massage.
4. **Kapalabhati** Purification of lungs and frontal lobe of brain.
5. **Basti** Colon cleaning.
6. **Trataka** Purification of the eye to overcome eye problems.

### Benefits of Yogic Kriyas

The general benefits of performing these *kriyas* are as follows

- They help in overcoming many diseases completely, so they are effective in Yoga therapy.
- The practice of the *shatkarmas* creates harmony between body and mind.

- The different systems of the body are purified by the practice of the *shatkarmas*, so energy can flow through the body freely.
- Practising the *shatkarmas* increases the capacity to work, think, digest, taste, feel, experience etc.

## Pranayama

The word '*Paranayama*' is composed of two words, *prana* (meaning 'life') and *ayam* (meaning 'control'). Thus, it means 'control and regulation of the vital life force *i.e.* 'breathing.'

*Pranayama* strengthens the respiratory system, purifies the blood, soothes the nervous system, improves digestion, develops endurance and tones up the whole body.

It consists of three parts

1. **Puraka** (Inhale)
   When we breathe in, the chest expands, the diaphragm contracts and the ribs move outwards and up.
2. **Kumbhaka** (Retain)
   It consists of two parts, retaining the breath after complete inhalation (called 'internal *Kumbhaka*') and retaining the breath after complete exhalation (called 'external *Kumbhaka*').
3. **Rechaka** (Exhale)
   When we breathe out, the chest contracts, the diaphragm relaxes and the ribs move inwards and down.

### Types of Pranayama

There are essentially various types or methods of *pranayama*. Some of them are

- *Suryabhedi pranayama* or right nostril breathing,
- *Ujjayi pranayama* or victorious breath,
- *Sheetkari pranayama* or the hissing breath,
- *Sheetali pranayama* or cooling breath,
- *Bhastrika pranayama* or bellows breath,
- *Bhramari pranayama* or bee breathing technique,
- *Plavini pranayama* or the floating breath,
- *Morcha pranayama* or swooning breath, etc.

## Active Lifestyle and Stress Management through Yoga

Mental and physical relaxation is enhanced by yoga, which helps reduce stress and anxiety. The physical postures of yoga improve flexibility, relieve tension, and reduce pain.

Yoga poses may help to release physical blockages like muscle knots, helping release emotions and tension. They also promote the release of mood-boosting endorphins, which are the feel-good hormones that can positively affect how you handle stress.

Focusing on the present moment during your yoga practice enhances your awareness, boosts your concentration, and centers your mind.

One become aware of the transitory nature of your bodily sensations, thoughts, and feelings, you may find it easier to let go of attachments to positive, negative, and neutral experiences. It also cultivates feelings such as love, joy, and serenity.

According to a 2018 study, yoga had a positive result on women who practiced Hatha yoga 3 times a week for 4 weeks. After 12 sessions, they experienced significant reductions in stress, depression, and anxiety.

The results suggest that yoga can act as medicine and may decrease the need for other medicines.

A small 2020 study in adult men suggested that yoga stretches reduce cortisol levels and have a positive effect on parasympathetic nerve activity, which encourages relaxation.

Researchers in an another 2020 study found that people who did an 11-minute yoga nidra meditation for 30 days reduced their stress levels, enhanced their overall well-being, and improved their sleep quality.

Practicing yoga nidra also boosted mindfulness and reduced negative emotions. These benefits stayed the same at a follow-up 6 weeks later.

# CHAPTER PRACTICE

## OBJECTIVE TYPE QUESTIONS

### Multiple Choice Questions (MCQs)

**1** From where do we derive the elements of yoga?

(a) Bhagwad Gita (b) Yoga-sutra
(c) Upanishads (d) Ramayana

*Ans* (b) Yoga-sutra

**2** Yoga has been mentioned in

(a) Mahabharata (b) Ramayana
(c) Upanishads (d) All of these

*Ans* (d) All of these

**3** Who compiled Yoga Sutras in 147 BC?

(a) Kabir Das (b) Surdas
(c) Patanjali (d) None of these

*Ans* (c) Patanjali

**4** According to whom "Yoga is attaining the pose"?

(a) Patanjali (b) Maharishi Ved Vyas
(c) Agam (d) None of these

*Ans* (b) Maharishi Ved Vyas

**5** The yogic elements that includes the study of self is

(a) Pratyahara (b) Dhyana
(c) Swadhayana (d) Rechaka

*Ans* (c) Swadhayana

**6** When an individual starts to think, imagine, contemplate and recollect, the state is called

(a) Dharana
(b) Isvara Pranidhana
(c) Samadhi
(d) Dhyanavastha

*Ans* (d) Dhyanavastha

### Fill in the Blanks

**7** Asetya means ............ .

*Ans* non-stealing

**8** Cleaning of digestive tract is a part of ......... .

*Ans* dhauti kriya

**9** The first stage of meditation is ............ .

*Ans* dharana

### State True or False

**10** The practice of yama and niyama does not help in making an individual strong morally and ethically.

*Ans* False. The practice of yama and niyama help in making an individual strong morally and ethically.

**11** Yoga essentially means the unification of the self with nature.

*Ans* False. Yoga essentially means unification of Atma with Parmatma.

**12** Samadhi is the ultimate goal of yoga.

*Ans* True

### Match the Following

**13**

| List I | List II |
|---|---|
| A. Santosh | (i) Non-possessiveness |
| B. Brahmacharya | (ii) Purity |
| C. Saucha | (iii) Contentment |
| D. Aparigraha | (iv) Celibacy |

**Codes**

| | A | B | C | D | | A | B | C | D |
|---|---|---|---|---|---|---|---|---|---|
| (a) | (iii) | (iv) | (ii) | (i) | (b) | (i) | (ii) | (iii) | (iv) |
| (c) | (ii) | (iii) | (i) | (iv) | (d) | (iv) | (i) | (iii) | (ii) |

*Ans* (a)

### Assertion-Reason

**14** **Assertion** (A) Yoga unites the individual's soul with the divine soul.

**Reason** (R) The word 'Yoga' is derived from the Sanskrit word 'Yuj' which means 'to unite'.

In the context of above two statements, which one of the following is correct?

**Codes**

(a) Both A and R are true and R is the correct explanation of A
(b) Both A and R are true, but R is not the correct explanation of A
(c) A is true, but R is false
(d) A is false, but R is true

*Ans* (b) Both A and R are true, but R is not the correct explanation of A

**15** **Assertion** (A) Yoga is not effective for depression.
**Reason** (R) Yoga helps in maintaining correct posture.
In the context of above two statements, which one of the following is correct?
**Codes**
(a) Both A and R are true and R is the correct explanation of A
(b) Both A and R are true, but R is not the correct explanation of A
(c) A is true, but R is false
(d) A is false, but R is true

*Ans* (c) A is true, but R is false

**16** **Assertion** (A) Pratyahara is the ultimate union of an individual's soul with God.
**Reason** (R) Pranayama involves controlled breathing.
In the context of above two statements, which one of the following is correct?
**Codes**
(a) Both A and R are true and R is the correct explanation of A
(b) Both A and R are true, but R is not the correct explanation of A
(c) A is true, but R is false
(d) A is false, but R is true

*Ans* (d) A is false, but R is true

## VERY SHORT ANSWER TYPE QUESTIONS

**17** In which epics and ancient Sanskrit texts has Yoga been mentioned?

*Ans* Yoga has been mentioned in the *Ramayana*, *Mahabharata* and the *Upanishads*.

**18** What does the word 'Yoga' imply?

*Ans* The word 'Yoga' implies the unification of the physical, mental, intellectual and spiritual aspects of a human being.

**19** What are the constituents of pranayama?

*Ans* *Pranayama* consists of three simple exercises - *Puraka* (Inhale), *Kumbhaka* (Retain) and *Rechaka* (Exhale).

**20** What do you mean by shatkarmas or yogic kriyas?

*Ans* *Shatkarmas* or yogic *kriyas* are six practices which help in externally and internally cleaning the human body to make it function properly.

## SHORT ANSWER TYPE QUESTIONS

**21** Enlist nine reasons, why the practice of Yoga is important for us.

*Ans* Nine reasons why the practice of Yoga is important for us are
- It brings about physical purity.
- It prevents and cures diseases by providing immunity to the body.
- It reduces mental tension.
- It reduces obesity and beautifies the body.
- It relaxes the body and mind.
- It corrects and maintains posture.
- It increases flexibility.
- It develops people spiritually.
- It improves moral and ethical values.

**22** What do you mean by Yama? What are the five basic virtues mentioned in it?

*Ans* *Yama* is the first element of Yoga, which teaches that we should not corrupt our souls by indulging in wrongful activities. It contains five basic virtues which everyone should have. These are as follows
- *Ahimsa* (non-violence)
- *Satya* (truthfulness)
- *Asteya* (non-stealing)
- *Brahmacharya* (celibacy)
- *Aparigraha* (non-possessiveness)

**23** What is the meaning of the second element of Yoga? What are its five parts?

*Ans* The second element of Yoga is called *Niyama*, which contains five essential teachings for self-maintenance. These teachings are
- *Shaucha* (maintaining cleanliness of the body, both internal and external)
- *Santosh* (contentment)
- *Tapas* (discipline)
- *Svadhyaya* (introspection or studying the self
- *Isvarapranidhana* (prayer or surrendering to God)

**24** What do you understand by pranayama? Describe its three parts in detail.

*Ans* The word *pranayama* is composed of two words, *prana* (meaning 'life') and *ayam* (meaning 'control'). Thus it means 'control and regulation of the vital life force or energy'.

It consists of three parts

(i) **Puraka** (Inhale) When we breathe in, the chest expands, the diaphragm contracts and the ribs move outwards and up.

(ii) **Kumbhaka** (Retain) It consists of two parts, retaining the breath after complete inhalation (called 'internal *Kumbhaka*') and retaining the breath after complete exhalation (called 'external *Kumbhaka*').

(iii) **Rechaka** (Exhale) When we breathe out, the chest contracts, the diaphragm relaxes and the ribs move inwards and down.

**25** What are the six yogic kriyas and what are the functions of these kriyas?

*Ans* The six yogic *kriyas* and the function of each of them are given in the table below

| Name of Kriya | Function |
|---|---|
| *Neti* | Nasal cleansing |
| *Dhauti* | Cleaning of oesophagus and stomach |
| *Nauli* | Abdominal massage to improve functioning of the whole digestive system |
| *Kapalabhati* | Purification of lungs and frontal lobe of brain |
| *Basti* | Colon cleaning |
| *Trataka* | Purification of the eye to overcome eye problems |

**26** Create a flow chart of elements of Yoga and explain any two of them.

*Ans* Flow chart of elements of Yoga are

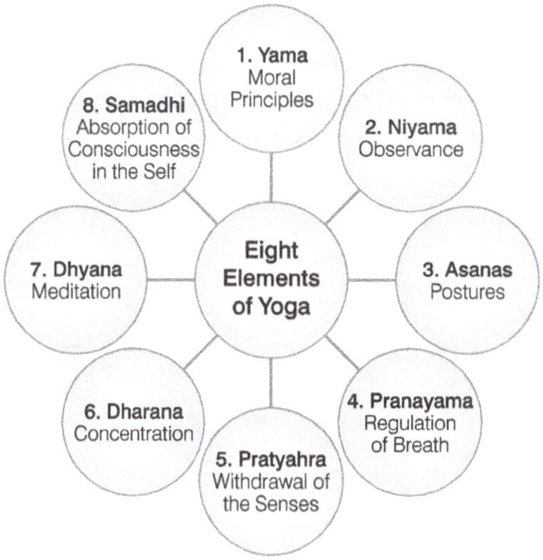


**Elements of Yoga**

- **Dharana** It is the concentration of the mind and the first stage of meditation. You focus all your energy at one point without letting your mind get distracted and discard all your random thoughts. The mind is fixed on one subject, topic or palce.
- **Pranayama** It involves controlled breathing and is also practised with some asanas. It consists of three simple exercises, i.e., Puraka (Inhale), Kumbhaka (Retain the breath) and Rechaka (Exhale).

## LONG ANSWER TYPE QUESTIONS

**27** Yoga is known to prevent and cure various diseases. List in tabular form, five lifestyle diseases which can be cured by performing yogic asanas and two asanas which help in curing / preventing each of these diseases.

*Ans* Five lifestyle diseases and the yogic *asanas* which cure and prevent these diseases are given below

| Lifestyle Disease | Yogic Asanas which Cure and Prevent the Disease |
|---|---|
| Lower back pain | *Supta Matsyendrasana* / Supine Spinal Twist and *Marjaryasana* / Cat or Cow pose |
| Diabetes | *Ardha Matsyendrasana* / Half Spinal Twist and *Chakrasana* / Wheel pose |
| Stomach disorder | *Apanasana* / Knees to chest pose and *Paschimottanasana* / Seated Forward Bend Pose |
| Liver problems | *Ardha Bhekasana* / Half Frog pose and *Parighasana* / Gate pose |
| Depression | *Baddha Konasana* / Bound Angle pose and *Sukhasana* / Easy pose |

**28** What is Yoga? Discuss the Ashtanga Yoga in brief.

*Ans* The word 'Yoga' is derived from the Sanskrit word *yuj*, which means 'to join' or 'to unite'. Thus, Yoga unites the individual's soul with the divine soul (i.e. God).

It also implies the unification of the physical, mental, intellectual and spiritual aspects of a human being.

According to Patanjali, Yoga has eight elements known as Ashtanga. These eight elements are as follows

(i) **Yama** This contains five basic ethical rules that every person should possess. These five moral codes of conduct are *Ahimsa* (Non-violence), *Satya* (Truthfulness), *Asteya* (Non-stealing), *Brahmacharya* (Celibacy) and *Aparigraha* (Non-possessiveness).

(ii) **Niyama** It contains essential teachings for self-maintenance including *Saucha* (Maintaining cleanliness of the body/purity), *Santosh* (Contentment), *Tapa* (Discipline), *Swadhyaya* (Introspection or studying the self) and *Isvara Pranidhana* (Prayer or surrendering to God).

(iii) **Asanas** These are a set of physical postures that improve strength and balance. These *asanas* are beneficial for the inner organs, help to regulate blood and oxygen flow, bring flexibility and agility by stretching of muscles and help to maintain posture.

(iv) **Pranayama** It consists of three simple exercises *Puraka* (Inhale), *Kumbhaka* (Retain) and *Rechaka* (Exhale). It involves controlled breathing, improves heart and lung functioning, and increases longevity.

(v) **Pratyahara** It means to control our mind and senses. In other words, an individual stops responding to the external sensory world such as touch, taste, smell, etc. that hinders mental concentration and self-welfare.

(vi) **Dharana** It is the first stage of meditation. You focus all your energy at one point without letting your mind get distracted. The mind, then, get focused on one topic object or thing.

(vii) **Dhyana** *Dharana* sets the stage for *dhyana*. It is a process of complete constancy of mind. When one starts focusing on a topic, the mind starts actively engaging with its focus. Thus, *dhyana* is the active modification of knowledge in complete stability and calmness.

(viii) **Samadhi** It is the ultimate union of ones soul with God. It is the stage where one loses oneself to God. The concepts of 'I', 'me' and 'mine' hold no significance for that person.

**29** Write the procedure for performing Naukasana and also write its benefits.

*Ans* The procedure for performing Naukasana is as follows

- Lie on your back with your feet together and arms beside your body.
- Take a deep breath in and as you exhale, lift your chest and feet off the ground, stretching your arms towards your feet.
- Your eyes, fingers and toes should be in a line.
- Feel the tension in your navel area as the abdominal muscles contract.
- Keep breathing deeply and easily while maintaining the pose.
- As you exhale, come back to the ground slowly and relax.

Naukasana has various benefits, which are as follows

- It strengthens the back and abdominal muscles.
- It tones the leg and arm muscles.
- It is useful for people with hernia.
- It helps to remove belly fat.
- It improves digestion.
- It improves the circulation of blood.
- It gives strength to thigh, hips, shoulder and neck.
- It helps in regulating the sugar level in the blood.

# SELF ASSESSMENT

## OBJECTIVE ANSWER TYPE QUESTIONS

**1** According to whom, "The knowledge of Shiva and Shakti is Yoga"?
(a) Bhagwad Gita
(b) Maharishi Ved Vyas
(c) Patanjali
(d) Agam

**2** Which of the following is/are Ashtanga?
(a) Yama
(b) Niyama
(c) Asanas
(d) All of these

**3** Which one of the following is not an example of yama?
(a) Truthfullness
(b) Non-stealing
(c) Self-introspection
(d) Celibacy

**4** **Assertion** (A) Yoga increases the body's immunity.
**Reason** (R) Yoga also help in reducing stress and tension.
In the context of above two statements, which one of the following is correct?

**Codes**
(a) Both A and R are true and R is the correct explanation of A
(b) Both A and R are true, but R is not the correct explanation of A
(c) A is true, but R is false
(d) A is false, but R is true

## VERY SHORT ANSWER TYPE QUESTIONS

**5** Explain the meaning of the word 'yuj'.

**6** What is the meaning of pranayama?

**7** What do you understand by dharana?

**8** Name three yogic kriyas related to the digestive tract of the body.

## SHORT ANSWER TYPE QUESTIONS

**9** What are the benefits of yogic kriyas?

**10** How yoga is important physically?

## LONG ANSWER TYPE QUESTION

**11** Explain the importance of Yoga in mentally, spiritually and morally developing a person.

CHAPTER

04

# Physical Education and Sports for CWSN
## (Children with Special Needs: Divyang)

Today, even physically challenged people (Divyang) have the opportunity to participate in all physical education events with full enthusiasm. The education programme that enables them to do so is called adaptive physical education.

Such an education includes various special education teachers who train children with disabilities to participate in various local, state, national, and even international sports events such as Special Olympics, Paralympics, Deaflympics, etc.

The phrase 'differently abled' was first proposed in 1980s as an alternative to terms like 'disabled', 'handicapped', etc. on the grounds that it gave a more positive message to the society and to avoid discrimination. Disability and disorder are two separate terms that stand for different types of physical and mental conditions. Disability, whether it is physical or mental, is permanent in nature but a disorder can be temporary or permanent.

### CHAPTER CHECKLIST

- Concept of Disability
- Disability Etiquettes
- Concept of Disorder
- Adaptive Physical Education
- Role of Professionals for Children with Special Needs

## Concept of Disability

Disability is a physical, mental, cognitive or developmental condition that impairs, interferes with or limits a person's ability to engage in certain tasks or actions or participate in typical daily activities and interactions. Disability may be present since birth or acquired during the liftime of the person. Disability reduces the functional ability of a person and limits the activities of that person.

Therefore, disability is conceptualised as multi-dimensional as it affetts a person's life in many ways. It has been defined differently in different societies of the world.

According to WHO, "Disability is a restriction or lack of ability to perform an activity in the manner or within the range considered normal for a human being."

"A disability is defined as a condition or function judged to be significantly impaired relative to the usual standard of an individual or group."

# Types of Disability

Disability is conceptualised as multi-dimensional as it may affect the organs and body parts of a person in many ways.

Disability is of many types like intellectual disability, physical disability, etc. These types of disabilities are discussed below

## Intellectual Disability

Intellectual disability is a disability characterised by significant limitations in both intellectual functioning and adaptive behaviour. This disability originates before the age of 18.

The nature of this disability is also mental since the intellectual domain is related to using the capacity of mind. It is a disability characterised by significant limitations in both personal and social behaviour.

This is characterised by low Intelligence Quotient (IQ) score (under 70) and significant problems in the ways learners adapt to new situations.

### Symptoms of Intellectual Disability

- Very little interpersonal skills.
- Not understanding or following rules and instructions.
- Lack of practical skills like activities of daily living, personal care, etc.
- Reduced capacity to learn, solve problems and reasoning.

## Physical Disability

Physical disability is the long-term loss or impairment of a body part that limits the body's physical function. A person with physical disability cannot perform many actions independently.

It may be a motor deficiency or a sensory impairment. Motor deficiency is related to spinal cord, causing paralysis to some or all parts of the body. It may also lead to brain damage, which may occur before or after birth or after a stroke.

On the other hand, sensory impairment is related to an individual's visual or hearing impairments. The nature of this disability is physical as it is related to physical functioning of the body parts including sense organs.

This refers to the limitation on a person's physical functioning, mobility, dexterity or stamina.

This includes upper or lower limb loss, poor manual dexterity, visual impairment, hearing loss or disability in coordination with different organs of the body.

Apart from these, blindness, respiratory disorders, epilepsy and sleep disorders are also considered as physical disability.

Physical Disability

### Symptoms of Physical Disability

- Body's lack of full range of mobility.
- Problems related to senses such as sight, hearing or speech impairment.
- Lack of motor skills and missing developmental milestones.
- Lack of control of the limbs or the body parts.

# Causes and Nature of Disability

There are various causes and nature of disability which are discussed below

1. **Accidents** A wide variety of disabilities, especially those associated with traumatic brain injury result from vehicular accidents, burns, etc.

   Workplace accidents, especially in less regulated sectors such as construction, agriculture, mining and smaller businesses are also a common source of disability.
2. **Poverty** Poverty is one of the biggest causes of disability. Poor people are most vulnerable to disability because they are forced to live and work in unsafe environment with poor sanitation, crowded living conditions and with little access to education, clean water or enough good food. This gives rise to various diseases such as tuberculosis, polio etc.

3. **War** Land mines, cluster bombs, bullets and chemicals used in wars cause more disabilities in the world today than anything else.

   Explosions cause people to become deaf, blind and lose their limbs, as well as causing other injuries. Their mental health is also affected by such violence.

4. **Nuclear Accidents** Many people have suffered after being exposed to massive amounts of radiation. One of the incident that we can refer is when USA dropped nuclear bombs on Japan in 1945. This incident caused widespread destruction and death from exposure to radiation.

   The people who survived these accidents and bombing attacks have suffered mainly from cancer, and tumors in various body parts of the body, especially in the thyriod gland, or leukemia, all of which causes an early death. In communities where these nuclear incidents happened, there has also been an increase in number of children born with learning difficulties, such as down syndrome.

5. **Poor Access to Healthcare** Good health care can prevent various disabilities. Trained birth attendants who can identify risks and handle emergencies, can prevent babies from being born with many disabilities. Immunisation can also prevent many disabilities. But many times, vaccines are not available, or people who are poor or live far from cities cannot afford them, or there are not enough facilities available for everyone, which leads to various disabilities.

6. **Inherited Disabilities** Disabilities also pass from one generation to another. Such disabilities are referred to as inherited disabilities. These are also known as genetic disabilities.

   Some disabilities are known to be inherited, such as spinal muscular dystrophy *i.e.* diseases of muscles and of nerve cells that carry signals from the brain to the muscle, making the muscles of the body get weaker and weaker and slowly stop working.

7. **Illness** Illness is one of the most important factors of disabilities. There are various causes of illness such as virus, bacteria, pathogens, etc.

   For instance, illness of a pregnant woman can cause birth defect to her body when born. Some illnesses that a baby or a small child may get, can also cause disability, such as meningitis, polio and measles. It is important for newborn babies to get immunisation for protection.

8. **Malnutrition** It is one of the major causes of disability, especially witnessed in our country. Malnutrition and under nutrition in older adults can also increase the likelihood of breaking bones, including hip fractures, which can lead to limited physical mobility.

   Problems with physical mobility, after illness or injury, can leave older adults physically unable to obtain or prepare food for themselves.

   Micro nutrient and macro nutrient deficiencies are risk factors for physical, sensory and cognitive impairment.

   For instance, regarding micro nutrient associated disability, each year between 2,50,000 and 5,00,000 children become blind as a result of Vitamin A deficiency.

9. **Poisons and Pesticides** Poison such as Lead found in paints or pesticides found in various products can cause disabilities in people and cause birth defects in babies growing in the womb.

   Smoking or chewing tobacco, inhaling smoke and drinking alcohol during pregnancy can also harm a child before he/she is born.

10. **Lack of Education** Due to lack of education among the people, it leads to disability as they are not aware regarding the symptoms of a certain diseases. They fall into the trap of certain diseases which can be avoided by using scientific methods or by taking precautions.

    But due to ignorance and lack of knowledge, they do not adopt such precautionary measures. Hence, this leads to disability among them.

11. **Medicines and Vaccines** Both medicines and vaccines are essential to protect health and prevent disability, but there are number of practitioners in the medical field who are not qualified or registered. They don't take proper care while dealing with patients. The use of unclean syringes may cause serious diseases like Hepatitis or HIV/AIDS. Improperly stored as well as wrong vaccines may cause allergic reactions, poisoning and deafness to the child.

12. **Dangerous Working Conditions** If individuals are working in factories, mines or agricultural fields under improper working conditions, they may be exposed to dangerous machinery, tools or chemicals and wide variety of health hazards. In such conditions, they may get disabilities in the long-run.

## Disability Etiquettes

Disability etiquette is a set of guidelines that explain how to approach or how to deal with the people facing physical or mental disabilities. The term serves to communicate people with disabilities more respectfully in all types of situations.

It refers to educate people regarding disabilities. It involves treating people with disabilities with respect and care, and try to bring them into a normal life. There is no certain time period as to when it started, but it is believed to come into existence in 1970.

The **Disability Rights Movement** that came around in the same period is said to divert the attention of the world towards disabled people. As part of Civil Rights, it was felt necessary to write about disability etiquettes in order to understand and respect the disabled people.

## Disability Etiquettes in General

The rules of etiquette for the disabled people are generally the same as the rules for good etiquette in society. The disability etiquettes are as follows

- It is always important to respect the dignity of disabled people. So, talk to them with respect so that their self-esteem and confidence is built up.
- When introduced to a person with disability, it is appropriate to offer shake hands.
- Never patronise people who use wheelchairs by patting them on the head or shoulder.
- Respect the individuality of the person. So, avoid generalising the disabled people and call them by their names.
- Talk to the person and address him/her directly instead of talking through a friend or an interpreter who may also be present.
- If you offer assistance, wait until the person responds. Then, listen carefully to his/her instructions.
- Do not speak about the disabled people as if they are invisible or cannot understand what is being said.
- Do not show extra attention or added care as it may give a feeling of sympathy. Treat them with the same attention and care as with normal people.
- Respect the privacy of the person. Do not ask unnecessary questions about the disability or how they are coping with it.
- When people with disability ask for any assistance, respond to it graciously.

## Disability Etiquette Guidelines

Apart from general guidelines, the etiquette guidelines can also be classified according to the different types of disabilities. The disability etiquette guidelines for people with speech difficulties, hearing loss, vision loss, cognitive impairments and mobility impairments are discussed below

### Persons with Speech Difficulties

- Give attention to the person who has difficulty in speaking.
- Keep manner to encourage rather than correcting.
- Give extra time for the conversation with these people and be patient.
- If you have difficulty in understanding, don't pretend that you do. Repeat as much as you do understand.
- Use short sentences with simple and concrete words.

### Persons with Hearing Loss

- Get the person's attention with a wave of the hand, or a tap on the shoulder.
- Speak clearly and slowly, but without exaggerating your lip movements or shouting.
- Many persons with hearing loss read lips. Place yourself facing the light source and keep hands, cigarettes and food away from your mouth while talking, in order to provide a clear view of your face.
- When an interpreter accompanies a person, direct your remarks to the person rather than to the interpreter.
- Look directly at the person and speak expressively.
- Use sign language if you and the person are familiar with it.

### Persons with Vision Loss

- When you enter a room, indicate who you are. Let the person know when you are leaving the room.
- Remember that you will need to communicate any written information orally.
- When talking to a person with a visual impairment, begin identifying yourself by name and that you are speaking to them.
- When offering your assistance, do not grab a person's cane or arm.
- If you are walking with a person who is blind, offer your arm for him to hold.

- Walk at the normal pace. It is helpful to speak casually and naturally about the environment, objects and buildings you are passing as you walk.
- Not all visually impaired people read Braille. Ask the person what alternative format they prefer.

### Persons with Cognitive/ Language Impairment

- Use a calm voice and be comfortable. Use simple and short sentences.
- Do not argue with the person.
- Treat each person as an individual with talents and abilities, deserving of respect and dignity.
- Give extra time for the person to process what you are saying and to respond.
- Look for signs of stress and/or confusion.
- Keep your manner encouraging rather than correcting.

### Persons with Mobility Impairment

Mobility impairment means difficulty in movement. To cope up with this difficulty, wheelchairs, walking sticks and several other things are used.

The disability etiquettes for mobility impairment are as follows

- Don't push, pull or touch the wheelchair, walking sticks or other objects that the person might be using.
- Be aware of the person's reach limits. For that, place the item where it is easily reachable.
- Be prepared to offer assistance to the disabled people with reaching, grasping or lifting objects, opening doors, operating vending machines and other equipments.
- Step down or bend to enquire about the person who is sitting on a wheelchair.

The rules of etiquettes and good manners to deal with people with disabilities, generally focus on treating the disabled people with respect and care as well as acknowledging their individuality.

These guidelines address specific issues which frequently arise for people with disabilities.

## Concept of Disorder

Disorder is an ailment that disturbs the health of a person, hinders a person's performance and diminishes his/her efficiency.

Disorder changes the behaviours, thoughts and emotions that may cause significant distress to either self or others.

A person with a disorder, is not able to meet his personal needs on his own or is at a danger to himself or to others. Disorder grows inside a person. It is small in the beginning, but may become serious and grow into a disability.

There are many kinds of disorders like mental disorder, neurological disorder, hyper activity disorder, eating disorder, addiction disorder, attention disorder, etc.

"Disorder can be defined as a blip (temporary deviation) in the usual functioning of a person."

According to **Medical Journal**, "Disorder is a significant behavioural or psychological syndrome or pattern that occurs in an individual and is associated with present distress or increased risk of suffering of self or others."

Regular exercise reduces the incidence of disorders by preventing risk factors which cause impairment. Physical education increases mental concentration and improves functional fitness.

## Adaptive Physical Education

Adaptive physical education programmes are school based programmes for children with disabilities like deafness/hearing impairment, blindness, speech impairment, any type of physical impairments, autism, mental retardation etc.

Children with disabilities have special needs because they are not able to participate in regular physical exercises and activities. So the adapted physical education programme is specially designed for individuals with disabilities.

It can be defined as, "Adapted physical education is the art and science of developing, implementing and monitoring a carefully designed physical education instructional programme for learners with disabilities."

In other words, it is a diversified programme which includes developmental activities, games, sports, etc, that suit the interests, capacities and limitation of children with disabilities.

It is a sub disciple of physical education that focuses on the creation of individualised programmes for students who may safely or successfully engage in unrestricted participation in physical education programmes.

Adaptive physical education provides safe, personally satisfying and successful experiences of physical ability to children who are differently abled.

Adaptive physical education programmes focus on the development of composition, posture, balance, coordination motor skills, etc. It teaches modified and suitable alternative activities which are more helpful in different circumstances.

## Aims of Adaptive Physical Education

The aims of an adaptive physical education programme is as follows

- Providing physical education that meets the unique needs of such children.
- Development of the student's motor skills.
- To assist differently abled students in achieving mental, emotional, physical and social growth.
- Achieving meaningful success and positive education outcomes.
- Developing self-esteem and improving socialisation skills.
- Coping with disabilities through an active and healthy lifestyle.
- Developing cognitive abilities to improve education results.

## Objectives of Adaptive Physical Education

The objectives are discussed as follows

1. **To Develop Motor Skills** According to this objective, the emphasis is onto develop motor skills of students with disabilities. Motor skills are necessary for performing not only specific skills but daily routine activities also.

   These skills enable physically disabled students to be active and smart.
2. **To Improve Physical Fitness** It is an important objective of adaptive physical education in which modified or adaptive exercises are provided in the programmes to improve physical fitness of students.
3. **To Ensure Students Participation in Physical Education Programmes** This objective focuses on ensuring that each students actively participates in physical education programmes regularly. It also ensures that the student is integrated into regular education programme whenever possible.
4. **To Promote Sportsmanship Qualities** It is another vital objective of adaptive physical education to promote sportsmanship qualities among the differently abled students. Participation in adaptive physical education programmes naturally improves sportsman qualities.
5. **To Ensure Services to Differently Abled Students** This objective ensures that the differently abled students are provided with the physical education services that meet their special needs properly.
6. **To Improve Social Adjustments** Participation in programmes of adaptive physical education helps the differently abled students to make social adjustments, as such adjustments are most important especially in present day society.
7. **To Develop Knowledge of Good Mechanism** This objective helps each individual to develop knowledge and sense of appreciation with regard to good body mechanics. Overall, the aims and objectives of adapted physical education programmes is to make the children with special needs cope with their disabilities in a better way.

# Role of Professionals for Children with Special Needs

The professionals who work with children with special needs have to focus on their overall development. They help and support such children in achieving their full potential, giving ability to communicate properly, etc.

The professionals working with these children are counsellors, occupational therapists, physiotherapists, physical education teachers, speech therapists and special educators.

The roles of these professionals are discussed below

## Counsellor

A counsellor is a trusted professional who provides a safe and supportive environment. The role of the counsellor is to discuss the concerns of the child with special needs and understand the feelings, emotions and sentiments of the child.

A counsellor also counsels the parents, guardians and teachers of the child with special needs. He provides guidance and helps the child to adapt to different situations because he understands the mental and physical needs of the child.

A counsellor helps students with special needs with their academic goals, their social, personal and career development.

He also carries out various development programmes related to stress management, anger management, conflict management, positive thinking, etc.

He provides social support to the child along with exploring ways to make the disability more manageable. A counsellor helps the child to cope better with the disability.

## Occupational Therapist

An occupational therapist is a professional who helps the children with special needs to develop fine and gross motor skills like eating, dressing, bathing, drinking etc.

An occupational therapist also helps them develop their sensory and cognitive abilities. This is done by teaching simple activities like grasping, reaching, picking, dressing, feeding etc.

The primary aim of an occupational therapist is to maximise the child's potential to participate in activities of everyday life by minimising the impact of their disability.

The role of an occupational therapist is to develop physical coordination among the children with special needs like hand-eye coordination to improve skills such as hitting a ball or copying from a blackboard, etc. This professional also arranges for any specialised equipment if required by the child.

## Physiotherapist

The role of the physiotherapist is to manage children with movement disorders. He teaches them how to balance their movements while walking, rolling, sitting and crawling. For this, various exercises are taught that also prevent the development of deformities.

Another role of the physiotherapist is to encourage a child's independence and mobility, thereby helping in building self-esteem.

He evaluates movements and functions of the body with special reference to physical mobility, balance, posture, gain, fatigue, etc.

He uses range of techniques like massage, exercise, electrotheraphy and hydrotheraphy, etc.

A physiotherapist also identifies the type of equipment that can help a child in managing movement disorders.

## Physical Education Teacher

Physical education teacher generally determines the abilities of students with special needs and also the procedures that may need to be implemented to support their participation in sports and physical fitness.

The physical education teachers help students with special needs to improve their physical fitness. They help in improving hand-eye coordination, flexibility, muscular strength, endurance and even cardiovascular efficiency of students with special needs.

The physical education teachers also teach physical activities which may help in reducing stress tension, depression and anxiety of the students with special needs.

They also help students with special needs in developing a feeling of self-esteem and social awareness as the students with special needs may often feel isolated and removed from the group.

They organise various physical activities for students with special needs to promote their mental and physical health.

## Speech Therapist

The role of a speech therapist is to build the communication of children with special needs. This is done by teaching them how to use words, sounds of speech, gestures and maintenance of eye contact.

His essential job is to help the children to express themselves using oral communication skills or sounds and gestures. This helps in emotional development as well as building confidence in children with special needs.

Speech therapist also helps such students who have fluency disorders like stoppages, repetitions or prolonging sounds in words, etc.

## Special Educator

The role of a special educator is to work for the overall development of children with special needs. This is done by developing teaching aids and instructional materials as well as through remedial teaching.

Special educators are concerned with the overall success of children with special needs. Their role is to improve a student's ability to function in social, emotional and behavioural capacities.

Another role of special educator is to encourage family involvement, working with other school staff to better understand the needs of the specific child, etc. For this purpose, collaborating with school and community professionals is also required.

# CHAPTER PRACTICE

## OBJECTIVE TYPE QUESTIONS

### Multiple Choice Questions (MCQs)

**1** The aim of adaptive physical education is to help whom?

(a) Adults
(b) Differently abled students
(c) Athelets
(d) All of the above

*Ans* (b) Differently abled students

**2** What is the role of physiotherapist?

(a) To manage special needs children with movement disorder
(b) Help special needs children to develop fine and gross motor skills
(c) To build communication of children with special needs
(d) To work for the overall development of children with special needs

*Ans* (a) To manage special needs children with movement disorder

**3** Which of the following term is defined as "a blip in the usual functioning of a person"?

(a) Disability (b) Impulsive
(c) Disorder (d) None of these

*Ans* (c) Disorder

**4** Regular physical exercise results in ......... .

(a) improved functional status
(b) quality of life
(c) improved cognitive abilities
(d) All of the above

*Ans* (d) All of the above

**5** Which type of instructional strategies must be used for performing various types of physical activities for children with special needs?

(a) Verbal
(b) Visual
(c) Peer teaching
(d) All of the above

*Ans* (d) All of the above

### Fill in the Blanks

**6** The ......... helps in improving hand-eye coordination, flexibility and muscular strength.

*Ans* physical education teacher

**7** The role of ......... is to build the communication of children with special needs.

*Ans* Speech Therapist

### State True or False

**8** Adaptive physical education is a direct service not a related service.

*Ans* True

**9** Speech therapist helps students to develop fine and gross motor skills.

*Ans* False. An occupational therapist helps in the development of fine and gross motor skills.

**10** Counsellors work extensively with families too.

*Ans* True

### Assertion-Reason

**11** **Assertion** (A) Children with disabilities have special need.
**Reason** (R) These children are not able to participate in regular physical exercises and activities.
In the context of above two statements, which one of the following is correct?

**Codes**

(a) Both A and R are true and R is the correct explanation of A
(b) Both A and R are true, but R is not the correct explanation of A
(c) A is true, but R is false
(d) A is false, but R is true

*Ans* (a) Both A and R are true and R is the correct explanation of A

**12** **Assertion** (A) Disability affects a person's life in many ways.
**Reason** (R) Disability is multi-dimensional concept.
In the context of above two statements, which one of the following is correct?

**Codes**

(a) Both A and R are true and R is the correct explanation of A
(b) Both A and R are true, but R is not the correct explanation of A
(c) A is true, but R is false
(d) A is false, but R is true

*Ans.* (a) Both A and R are true and R is the correct explanation of A

**13** **Assertion** (A) For health benefits, physical activity should be of moderate intensity.
**Reason** (R) Regular physical activity resulted in improved functional status and quality of life among children with special needs.
In the context of above two statements, which one of the following is correct?
**Codes**
(a) Both A and R are true and R is the correct explanation of A
(b) Both A and R are true, but R is not the correct explanation of A
(c) A is true, but R is false
(d) A is false, but R is true

*Ans.* (b) Both A and R are true, but R is not the correct explanation of A

## VERY SHORT ANSWER TYPE QUESTIONS

**14** How can we define adaptive physical education?

*Ans* Adaptive physical education can be defined as the art and science of developing, implementing and monitoring a carefully designed physical education instructional programme for learners with disabilities.

**15** How are adaptive sports different from normal sports?

*Ans* Adaptive sports have some modifications in the rules or use some special equipment to suit the needs of the participants compared to normal sports.

**16** Which professions are specially designated to work for children with special needs?

*Ans* Professions like counsellor, occupational therapist, physiotherapist, physical education teacher, speech therapist and special educator work for children with special needs.

**17** How does a physiotherapist help a child with disability?

*Ans* A physiotherapist helps a child with disability to manage movement disorders, thereby encouraging a child's mobility and independence.

**18** What is the role of a speech therapist for children with special needs?

*Ans* The role of a speech therapist is to build the communication of children with special needs by teaching them the use of words, sounds, gestures etc to express themselves.

## SHORT ANSWER TYPE QUESTIONS

**19** What are the types of disability? Explain briefly. **CBSE 2018**

*Ans* Disability is of two types, which are as follows

(i) **Intellectual Disability** Intellectual disability is a disability characterised by significant limitations in both intellectual functioning and adaptive behaviour. It is more severe in nature as the child is not able to perform even the daily activities along with difficulty in learning.

(ii) **Physical Disability** Physical disability is a long-term loss or impairment of a body part that limits the body's physical function. A person with physical disability cannot perform many actions independently. It may be a motor deficiency or a sensory impairment.

**20** Explain physical disability and its symptoms.

*Ans* Physical disability is the long-term loss or impairment of a body part that limits the body's physical function. A person with physical disability cannot perform many actions independently.

Symptoms of physical disability are as follows
- Body's lack of full range of mobility.
- Problems related to senses such as sight, hearing or speech impairment.
- Lack of motor skills and missing developmental milestones.
- Lack of control of the limbs or the body parts.

**21** Write any three causes of disability?

*Ans* Three causes of disability are discussed below

(i) **Accidents** A wide variety of disabilities especially those associated with traumatic brain injury result from vehicular accidents, burns, falls etc.

(ii) **Poverty** Poverty is one of the biggest cause of disability. Poor people are most vulnerable to disability because they are forced to live and work in unsafe environments with poor sanitation, crowded living conditions and with little access to education, clear water or enough good food.

(iii) **War** Land mines, cluster bombs, bullets and chemicals used in wars, cause more disabilities in the World today than anything else.

**22** Explain the adaptive physical education programme.

*Ans* The adaptive physical education programme is a school based programme for children with disabilities.

Children with special needs like deafness/hearing impairment, blindness, speech impairment, autism, mental retardation etc. are not able to participate in regular physical exercises and activities.

The adaptive physical education programme is not only for differently alled but also for the people of all ages.

The adaptive physical education programme focuses on the development of composition, posture, balance, coordination motor skills etc.

The programme teaches modified and suitable alternative activities which are more helpful in different circumstances.

**23** Explain the role of a counsellor in developing a supportive environment for children with special needs.

*Ans* The role of a counsellor is to develop a safe and supportive environment for children with special needs. He does this by understanding the feelings, emotions and sentiments of the child.

The counsellor counsels the child's parents, guardians and teachers on how to deal with different situations related to the child. The counsellor also develops social support for the child so that the child could manage his / her disability in a better way.

A counsellor also comes out with developmental programmes related to stress management.

So, a counsellor guides the child, its parents and society in developing a supportive environment.

**24** How can an occupational therapist help a child with special needs?

*Ans* An occupational therapist is a professional who can help a child with special needs by developing its fine and gross motor skills. This is done by teaching simple activities like grasping, reaching, picking, dressing etc.

These activities increase physical coordination among such children. When the child is able to do simple activities independently, it builds confidence in the child. The occupational therapist also arranges for any special equipment needed by the child.

**25** Differentiate between counsellor and physiotherapist on the basis of their work.

*Ans* The differences between counsellor and physiotherapist are as follows

| Counsellor | Physiotherapist |
|---|---|
| • The role of the counsellor is to discuss the concerns of the child with special needs and understand the feelings, emotions and sentiments of the child. | • The role of the physiotherapist is to manage children with movement disorder. He teaches them how to balance their movement while walking, sitting etc. |
| • A counsellor also counsels the parents, guardians and teachers of the child with special needs. | • Physiotherapist evaluates movements and functions of the body with special reference to physical mobility, balance, posture etc. |

## LONG ANSWER TYPE QUESTIONS

**26** Enumerate the objectives of adaptive physical education.

*Ans* The objectives of adaptive physical education are as follows

(i) **To Develop Motor Skills** This objective emphasis on developing motor skills of students with disabilities. They are necessary for performing not only specific skills but daily routine activities.

(ii) **To Improve Physical Fitness** This objective is to provide modified or adaptive exercises to students in order to improve their physical fitness.

(iii) **To Ensure Students Participation in Physical Education Programmes** This objective ensure that each student actively participate in physical education programmes regularly at his/her own level.

(iv) **To Promote Sportsmanship Qualities** This objective ensures promotion of sportsmanship qualities among differently abled students.

(v) **To Ensure Services to Differently Abled Students** This objective ensures that the differently abled student is provided with the physical education services that meet his/her needs properly.

(vi) **To Improve Social Adjustments** This objective is essential especially in present day world as the participation in programmes of adaptive physical education helps differently abled students to make social adjustments.

**27** Explain five strategies to make physical activities accessible for children with special needs.

*Ans* The five strategies to make physical activities accessible for children with special needs are as follows

(i) **Medical Check-up** If we want to make physical activities accessible for the children with special needs, we need to understand the type of disabilities of children and for this purpose complete medical check-up of the children is required.

(ii) **Assistive Technology** It refers to creating devices, tools or equipments that help children with special needs to participate in learning activities like bigger balls, balls with bells, balls attached to strings etc. This kind of new technology makes physical activities accessible for children with special needs.

(iii) **Adaptive Physical Education** Adapted physical education means developing, implementing and monitoring a carefully designed physical education instructional programme for a learner with a disability.

(iv) **Creating Specific Environment** This means making a friendly atmosphere by keeping in mind the specific needs of the children with disability. In this way, it shows that they are also wanted in society and like other children of their age, they can also play.

(v) **Activities based on Interests** Physical activities must be based on interest, aptitudes, abilities, previous experience and limitations of children with special needs, The teachers of physical education should have deep knowledge of limitations, interests and aptitudes of children.

**28.** In relation to the given picture, answer the following questions.

(i) Name the teacher who is specially trained to work with CWSN.

(ii) Give any one symptom of physical disability.

(iii) A disorder that may also be categorised as an intellectual disability is.................... .

(iv) .................... refers to the limitation on a persons' physical functioning, mobility, dexterity or stamina.

*Ans.* (i) Special educator

(ii) Lack of motor skills and missing developmental milestones.

(iii) down syndrome

(iv) Physical disability

# SELF ASSESSMENT

## OBJECTIVE ANSWER TYPE QUESTIONS

**1** Intellectual disability orginates before the age of ............... .

(a) 15 (b) 10 (c) 18 (d) 20

**2** ......... help in improving hand eye coordination, flexibility, muscular strength and endurance.

(a) Physiotherapist (b) Physical Education Teacher
(c) Occupational therapist (d) Counsellor

**3** .................. can be defined as a blip (temporary deviation) in the usual functioning of a person.

(a) Disorder (b) Intellectual disability
(c) Physical disability (d) None of these

## VERY SHORT ANSWER TYPE QUESTIONS

**4** Which physical education programme is designed specially for individuals with disabilities?

**5** Which professional aims to work on developing the communication skills of the children with special needs?

## SHORT ANSWER TYPE QUESTIONS

**6** Define adapted physical education. Write its aims.

**7** Discuss the concept of disability.

## LONG ANSWER TYPE QUESTION

**8** Discuss the role of a special educator in the overall development of children with special needs.

CHAPTER

# 05

# *Physical Fitness, Health and Wellness*

## Meaning of Physical Fitness

Physical fitness refers to the maximum functional capacity of all systems of the body. Various people have different view points with regard to physical fitness. For a common person, to have a good physique is a symbol of physical fitness, whereas for a doctor, the proper functioning of physiological system is physical fitness.

In reality, physical fitness has a wider meaning. For a common person, physical fitness means to carry out the routine work without getting fatigued or tired and after doing his/her work, he/she has the capacity to do more work with quick recovery.

Physical fitness is more than the possession of strength and endurance. It can also be termed as having the best possible health with the capacity to do one's everyday task, engage in recreational pursuits and meet emergencies when they arise.

An individual who is energetic, works happily and carry out emergency work with vigour, may be considered as physically fit. It implies a relation between the task to be performed and the individual's capability to perform it. Physical fitness differs according to the kind of work, individual's size, shape of the body, age, etc. There are number of mechanisms required to maintain physical fitness like an efficient motor mechanism, efficient organic mechanism, an efficient mental functioning, etc.

Following definitions of physical fitness will help us to understand the term in more appropriate manner

- According to **Webster's Collegiate Encyclopedia**, "It is the ability of a person to do daily routine work without fatigue; moreover, to participate in playful activities and still reserve enough capacity to meet any emergency."
- According to **David R Lamb**, "Physical fitness is the capacity to meet the present and potential physical challenges of life with success."

### CHAPTER CHECKLIST

- Meaning of Physical Fitness
- Meaning of Wellness
- Meaning of Health
- Components of Physical Fitness
- Components of Wellness
- Components of Health Related Fitness
- Leadership through Physical Activity and Sports
- Introduction to First Aid-PRICE

- According to **Hoskins**, "Physical fitness is the human body's ability to move with the desired speed, balance, agility and strength gained through proper exercise and nutrition."
- According to **Kroles**, "Physical fitness is the successful adaptation to the stresses of one's lifestyle."

Therefore, it can be concluded that, a physically fit person should have enough reserve of energy to meet the sudden demands in which a person is unexpectedly called upon to perform activities which requires unusual expenditure of strength, energy and adaptive ability under unfavourable conditions.

# Meaning of Wellness

Wellness is an active process of becoming aware of and making choices towards a healthy and fulfilling life. Wellness is more than just being free from illness; it is a dynamic process of change and growth.

The concept of wellness, *i.e.* staying healthy and achieving the highest potential for well-being, has gained popularity in the past few years.

According to **World Health Organisation** (WHO), "A state of complete physical, mental and social well-being, and not merely the absence of disease or infirmity."

According to **National Wellness Institution, USA,** "A conscious, self-directed and evolving process of achieving full potential."

Wellness covers all areas of health which includes physical, emotional, spiritual, social, environmental, financial, intellectual, nutritional and mental wellness. These are basically the components in one's life that can affect one's overall well-being.

In India, number of corporations have designed wellness programmes such as Apollo's Life Coporate Wellness Programme, TCS Corporate Wellness Programme, Wipro Wellness Programme, etc.

The number of positive outcomes of such programmes like increase in employee productivity, decrease in abseentism, better employees health, etc. has influenced these companies to invest in these programmes.

The basic objective of these wellness programmes is to impart knowledge related to proper nutrition, regularity and suitable physical exercises, to prohibit smoking, alcohol, drugs, weight control, stress management, etc.

These programmes also encourage individuals to develop the abilities to take part in various meaningful and satisfying sports activities and teach them about various techniques of stress management.

## Importance of Physical Fitness and Wellness

Physical fitness and wellness are very important to lead a healthy life. The importance can be summarised as

1. **Quality of Life**
   Physical fitness and wellness are the key components in improving the quality of anyone's life. A physically fit person can manage daily activities effectively and efficiently. He/She may also possess the qualities like good human relations, high ethical standards, etc.
2. **Proper Growth and Development**
   Proper growth and development is essential for a person to keep himself/herself physically fit. Physical education has a direct relation with growth and development.
   Physical Exercises helps to promote muscle strength and improve the efficiency of various organs. It enables the body physiological system to function more efficiently and effectively.
3. **Prevention of Diseases**
   Regular fitness exercises play a vital role in preventing many diseases, especially heart related diseases as a physically fit person has a low level of cholesterol in his body.
   A person is also able to prevent himself/herself from various other diseases as physical fitness and wellness also helps to boost the immune system of a person.
4. **Improves Abilities**
   A person who is physically fit can develop various abilities such as speed, strength, sharpness etc. These abilities help in overall development, which further brings fitness and wellness.
5. **Improves Posture**
   Physical fitness improves muscular coordination which ensures a good posture. Poor posture can cause back pain and many other problems.

Maintaining an optimal level of physical fitness and wellness is absolutely crucial to live a higher quality of life. They matter because everything we do and every emotion we feel relates to our well-being. In turn, our well-being directly affects our actions and emotions.

Thus, it is important for everyone to achieve optimal level of fitness and wellness in order to remove stress, reduce the risk of illness and ensure positive interactions.

## Traditional Sports and Regional Games for Promoting Wellness

Many people see the traditional/Indigenous games as a strong indicator that their culture can survive. In this way traditional/Indigenous games are not only helping youth to get physically fit but also inspiring older members of the Indigenous community.

Physical activity is decreasing in our society, especially in children as they mature. Clear evidence suggests that physical activity has numerous favourable beneficial physiologic effects that result in demonstrable reductions in cardiovascular and other disease endpoints.

Daily exercise substantially alters the expression of a substantial proportion of the genes that comprise the human genome. Traditional/Indigenous games are inclusive games and not competitive. For example, if a player gets 'out' in some games they can immediately rejoin the game once leaving the field.

### Benefits of Indigenous/Traditional Games

Benefits of bringing traditional Indigenous games back to life include

- Bringing-together of Indigenous and non-Indigenous people.
- Help reconnect urban Indigenous youth to their culture.
- Boost education retention in economically poor section.
- Promote reconciliation(Reunion).
- Provide essential training in social interaction.
- Enhance physical health.

### Indigenous Sports of India

Traditional sports of India can be traced back to Vedic times, when indigenous sports such as archery, chariot racing, wrestling, yoga and swimming were popular with royalty. After Independence, Team India garnered laurels at various international sports events in disciplines such as hockey, cricket, shooting, wrestling and tennis. Today, sports such as basketball, football, cricket, athletics and martial arts are gaining in popularity with the youth.

India has a strong tradition of traditional sports and games that are played all over the country. Some games like Kabaddi and Kho Kho are popular nationwide, while other indigenous sports of India are specific to a certain state or region. The National Sports Policy, 2001 aims to promote traditional sports through various schemes related to rural sports. According to this policy, high priority will be accorded to the development of sports in rural areas to harness local talent available there.

## Meaning of Health

Health, according to the World Health Organisation, is a state of complete physical, mental and social well-being and not merely the absence of disease and infirmity. A variety of definitions have been used for different purposes over time.

Health can be promoted by encouraging healthful activities, such as regular physical exercise and adequate sleep, and by reducing or avoiding unhealthful activities or situations, such as smoking or excessive stress.

Some factors affecting health are due to individual choices, such as whether to engage in a high-risk behavior, while others are due to structural causes, such as whether the society is arranged in a way that makes it easier or harder for people to get necessary healthcare services. Still other factors are beyond both individual and group choices, such as genetic disorders.

## Importance of Health

The importance of health is

- **Lead a Productive Life** A healthy person would serve his/her community and nation. Only when a person is not affected by any disease, he/she is considered healthy. This inturn would help them to serve better.
- **Prevent Diseases** The most important concept of leading a healthy life is to provide immunity strength against various diseases. The immune system is the body's natural defence mechanism to fight against foreign agents that cause harm to the body.
- **Improve Mental Health** Having a bad lifestyle would result in poor mental health. Adapting a healthy lifestyle would relax the mind and improve the mood. Only when a person is happy mentally, they would perform productively. Mental health is equally important as physical health.
- **Improve Longevity** If a person doesn't have a healthy lifestyle, it would affect the daily routine of a person. When the body gets proper nutrition, it becomes more fit and healthy, improving longevity.

# Components of Physical Fitness

There are five components of physical fitness. The development of each component is essential for physical fitness; however, each component has to be developed in different amounts to perform successfully in different sports. These are as follows

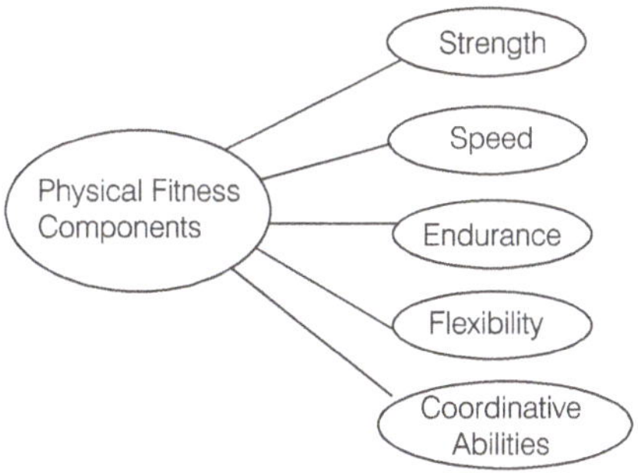


**Components of Physical Fitness**

## Strength

Strength is the ability of a muscle to exert force in a single muscle contraction. It can also be understood as the ability to overcome resistance. It is required in various games and sports like shot put, discus throw, hammer throw, javelin throw, wrestling, judo, weightlifting etc.

Though, strength is of paramount importance for a sportsperson, but it is also essential for a common man upto a certain level.

**Strength**

For a better understanding of this term, we can divide it into two parts *i.e.* dynamic and static.

These are as follows

### Dynamic Strength

It is also called isotonic strength because it is related to movement. In pull-ups and push-ups, we require dynamic strength. While doing such workouts for some time, there is a diminishing tendency in dynamic strength and as a result, after some time the muscles refuse to work. At this juncture, a person is not able to even do one extra pull-up or push-up.

Movements are clearly visible when someone uses dynamic strength. It can be divided into three types

1. **Maximum Strength** It is the greatest force that is possible in a single maximum muscle contraction. It can be defined as the ability of muscles to overcome maximum resistance.

   It is used in sports where very heavy resistance is to be tackled, like weightlifting and all throwing events. It can be measured by throw attempt and power lifting.

2. **Explosive Strength** It is the ability to overcome resistance with a fast contraction. Explosive strength is a combination of strength and speed abilities. For developing explosive strength, intensity is below-maximum and repetitions are performed as fast as possible.

   It is generally used in sprint starts, weightlifting, shot put, hammer throw, javelin throw, discuss throw, high jump, triple jump, long jump as well as some endurance events, specially in the start and spurt phases. This strength can be measured by dynamometer or by jumps chinning test.

   In simple words, explosive strength is the ability of muscle to perform forceful movement at quickest possible time. It is applied just like an explosion, so it is called as explosive strength.

3. **Strength Endurance** It is a combination of strength and endurance ability. It is the ability to overcome a resistance under conditions of fatigue. Here, it means that the player has the strength and endurance to carry on even in fatigue.

   It is used in sports like judo, swimming, long distance races, road cycling, etc. Strength endurance can be measured through chin-ups.

### Static Strength

It is also called as isometric strength. It is the ability of the muscles to act against resistance. It can be measured by a dynamometer. This type of strength is not experienced directly. It is not usually applied in sports except in weightlifting.

## Speed

It is the ability to cover a certain distance in the minimum possible time or the ability to perform movement of similar pattern as fast as possible.

In other words, it is the quickness of movement of body parts.

Speed is needed in sports where activities are needed to be covered speedily, like sprint races of 100 m, 200 m, 400 m, running between wickets in cricket, running while attacking or defending in football/ hockey etc.

**Speed**

Speed generally depends upon the two type of muscle fibres, *i.e.* **fast twitch** fibres and **slow twitch** fibres.

The fast twitch fibres are able to contract rapidly and produce maximum force, thus they fatigue quickly, while slow twitch fibres contract slowly and produce less force, thus, fatigue slowly.

In general, speed has following different forms which are seen in most sports. These are as follows

1. **Reaction Speed** It is the ability to respond to a given stimulus as quickly as possible.
2. **Movement Speed** It is the ability to do a single movement in the minimum time. Movement speed is of high relevance in cyclic sports e.g. jumping, throwing, kicking etc.
3. **Acceleration Speed** It is the ability to increase speed from minimum to maximum. This form of speed, to a great extent, depends upon explosive strength, frequency of movement and technique.

## Endurance

Endurance is the ability to carry out sports movements with the desired quality and speed under the conditions of fatigue.

According to **Harre** (1986), "Endurance is the ability to resist fatigue." It is measured by the duration of an activity or how long an exercise can be continued.

Types of endurance are

1. **Anaerobic Endurance or Short-term Endurance** It is the ability to carry on physical activities without an adequate supply of oxygen. It is required in sports where the energy requirement is heavy but for a short duration. e.g. Hockey, football.
2. **Aerobic Endurance or Long-term Endurance** It is the ability to carry on physical activities with a supply of oxygen for energy production even when the body is under condition of fatigue. This endurance is helpful when the activity is done for longer duration and the intensity or speed is slower.

## Flexibility

Flexibility is a necessary component of physical fitness. It is the ability to perform a joint action through a range of movements. An individual who has proper flexibility can perform his/her work very easily.

Flexibility is not only a significant factor in sports but also equally significant for an individual in his/her daily life.

Flexibility ensures good posture, good personality and efficiency in movement. The joints, tendons, ligaments and muscles work together to bring flexibility in movement.

Flexibility is related to genetic factors as well as physical activity programmes. Flexibility is essential in sports like gymnastics, swimming, athletics etc.

Flexibility is of two types, which are as follows

1. **Passive Flexibility** It is the ability to perform movement with greater range using external help. For example, doing a stretching movement with the help of a partner.
   This flexibility is generally dependent on the anatomy of the joint and extensibility of the muscles and ligaments.
2. **Active Flexibility** It is the ability to perform movement with greater range without using external help, *i.e.* with the help of muscular force. For example, stretching with the help of muscular force alone. Active flexibility can further be divided into two parts, which are as follows
   - **Static Flexibility** It is usually required by a sportsperson when he remains in a static position. For example, while diving, lying, sitting, etc.
   - **Dynamic Flexibility** It is needed for carrying out movements over greater distances when an individual is in motion.

## Coordinative Abilities

The ability to control the movements of different parts of our body, so that they work well together is called coordinative ability.

All sports require the coordination of eyes, hands, feet, an implement and/or a ball. Racket sports (e.g. tennis) require coordination of hand and racket to connect to the ball as well as to position our body in an appropriate position to return the ball in an efficient and effective manner.

Hockey requires the coordination of hands, eyes and hockey stick to connect with the ball, football primarily requires the coordination of feet, eyes and ball and rugby requires the coordination of hands, eyes and ball.

Coordinative ability depends upon the nervous system which is controlled by the brain. The different types of coordinative ability are rhythm ability, balance ability, adaptation ability, reaction ability, coupling ability etc.

These types of abilities can be enhanced through general or specific exercises.

Coordinative ability is required in gymnastics, badminton, lawn tennis, basketball, kho-kho, football, hockey, cricket and other games.

## Components of Wellness

Wellness is referred to as the quality or state of being healthy. The components of wellness are as follows

1. **Physical Wellness** It refers to physical appearance which can be achieved by taking nutritious food, doing regular exercises, getting in shape, having a glowing skin and a youthful appearance.

   For attaining physical wellness, an individual should do various physical activities such as jogging, swimming etc and should participate in games and sports.

   They should also breathe in fresh air in the open for some time.
2. **Emotional Wellness** It is the ability to control stress, manage anger and anxiety, and express feelings appropriately. It also lays stress on getting more out of every day with laughter and enjoyment.

   Stress management techniques, watching comedy films, recreational activities etc help in emotional wellness.
3. **Social Wellness** It refers to the ability to work with different people, to communicate well and interact with the community. Here, social values like cooperation, tolerance, sympathy and helpfulness bring social wellness.
4. **Spiritual Wellness** This refers to the wellness developed on ethical and moral grounds which helps in character building, enhances learning and helps face new challenges. Meditation, faith in religion, family values and ethics help to develop spiritual wellness.
5. **Intellectual Wellness** This refers to making sound decisions, alertness, focus and critical thinking abilities. It lays stress on creativity, openness to new ideas and motivation. This type of wellness is required for overall development of a person's personality.
6. **Nutritional Wellness** It refers to eating a balanced diet that provides all the essential nutrients to the body. Individual should avoid junk food and cold drinks as well as drinking plenty of water. This leads to better absorption of nutrients which raises the energy levels.
7. **Environmental Wellness** It refers to the physical environment that also affects the body and mind. The natural environment should be pollution free, for which suitable measures should be taken. One should lay stress on the three R's *i.e.* reduce, reuse and recycle.
8. **Financial Wellness** For improving it, an individual should set money management goals, get out of debt, set up saving plans and donate some savings to charity.

## Components of Health Related Fitness

Health related fitness refers to overall fitness which enables a person to work efficiently without undue fatigue. It is essential for all people throughout their life.

The main objective of health related physical fitness is to achieve and maintain the qualities that enhances the working efficiency of an individual and his/her standard of health.

It can be achieved by adhering to proper nutrition, effective stress management, regular exercises, control and prevention of diseases and also by avoiding harmful habits like smoking, drinking, etc.

Even the risk of various diseases like heart attack, obesity, depression, etc can be overcome through proper physical activities.

There are five main components which make up health related fitness. They are as follows

1. **Cardiovascular Endurance** It refers to the physical activity of an individual to indulge in aerobic exercise for longer period of time. It is also known as cardiorespiratory endurance.

Cardiovascular endurance can also be referred to as the ability of the heart, lungs and blood vessels to supply oxygen and nutrients to the working muscles and the ability of those muscles to allow sustained exercise.

If you have good cardiovascular endurance, then you will have healthy lungs, heart and vascular system. It implies that there will be less stress on heart and lungs, and therefore less vulnerability to cardiovascular diseases.

The endurance system can be improved by carrying out the activities like walking, swimming, cycling, etc.

2. **Muscular Strength** This refers to the ability of the muscles to exert force during an activity. Muscular strength of the different muscles can be improved by lifting weights, rapidly climbing the stairs etc.
3. **Body Composition** It refers to the relative amount of muscles, fat, bone and other vital parts of the body. It is basically the percentage of lean body mass *i.e.* bones, tendons, muscles, ligaments organs, etc in comparison to body fat.

   This percentage differs from person to person. A fit person has relatively low percentage of body fat. A healthy amount of fat for men is between 15 to 18 percent, while in women, it is 20 to 25 percent.

   Keeping the facts in view, it is essential to maintain a healthy percentage of body fat as the excess of fat can cause many health problems like heart diseases, diabetes, etc.

   The extra amount of fat may place strain on joints, muscles and bones which increases the risk of injuries. For reducing the percentage of body fat, one can do jogging, swimming, cycling, etc.
4. **Muscular Endurance** This refers to the ability of the muscles to continue to perform repetitive exercises without fatigue. Muscular endurance can be improved by doing cardio-respiratory activities like walking, cycling, jogging, dancing etc.

Muscular Endurance

5. **Flexibility** It refers to the maximum range of movements possible at a joint. It depends on the structure of joints, muscles length, tendons, ligaments and other factors.

   An individual having a good flexibility will be able to move his/her joints through a full range of motion while performing activities. He/She will also be able to perform his/her daily routine activities smoothly, efficiently and easily.

   Flexibility is helpful in number of ways like it helps to prevent injuries, improve body posture, reduce low back pain, etc. Flexibility can be improved by performing gymnastics, yoga, swimming and stretching exercises.

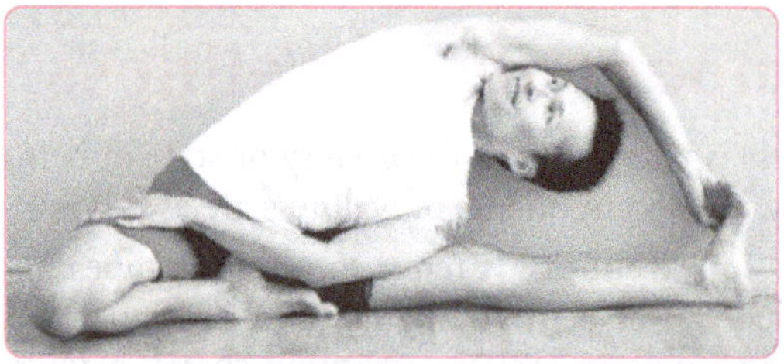

Flexibility

## Leadership through Physical Activity and Sports

Leadership can be described as the ability of an individual to influence, motivate, and enable others to contribute toward the effectiveness and success of an organization or a group of which they are members. Leader is a person who can bring about change.

The qualities of a good leader are

- A leader should be aware of different scenarios.
- The leader should be passionless enough to motivate other players.
- A leader should be full of energy and enthusiasm to do and lead for any task.
- A leader should be able to make quick decisions.
- A leader should be skilled enough to solve any technical problem occurred during any task.
- A leader should be innovative so that he can derive new and fresh concepts.

### Role of a Leader in Sports

- A good leader in sports is a good organiser in organising different sports events.

- A good leader plays the role of guardian. He understands the personalproblem of an athlete and provides solution for the problems.
- A good leader in sports performs the role of a teacher by helping participants in developing teaching techniques, educate them and improve their range of styles.
- A good leader plays the role of a psychologist. He knows the mental skills and toughness of their players.

Physical activity simply means movement of the body that uses energy. The four main types of physical activities are

1. Aerobic
2. Muscle – strengthening
3. Bone – strengthening
4. Stretching

## Creating Leaders through Physical Education

Leaders can be created through physical education in the following ways.

- One should be given responsibility to organise and coordinate various events.
- Leadership training programs should be organised in form of classrooms and seminars.
- One should be provided opportunities to give his/her views.
- Recognise achievements of one by facilitating them at different forms.
- Have faith and confidence in your student if they are defaulters.

## Introduction to First Aid-PRICE

PRICE is a five-step process for treating a muscle or joint injury such as an ankle sprain, which is short for Protection, Rest, Ice, Compression, and Elevation. It can be used even by someone without first-aid training, and should be used immediately when an injury occurs – the earlier, the better – while further medical attention is being sought. If the athlete experiences too much pain during the process, stop immediately. This process is discussed below

- **'P' for Protection** Protect the injured person and the area being treated but also protect yourself. If the injury occurs on the sports field, stop the game. Protect the area being treated with a splint if possible. If the athlete can move, carefully move them to a safer area using a stretcher or a crutch, but if there is any doubt, do not move the injured athlete.
- **'R' is for Rest** When an athlete is injured, the body responds in an effort to defend, localize, protect, and clean up the injured area, a response called inflammation. At the time of injury small blood vessels at the injury site rupture and cause tissue bleeding, which, in turn, can cause bruising and swelling. It is at that time important to bring body at rest first to treat the injury.
- **'I' is for Ice** As soon as possible after injury, begin applying ice continuously for the first 15-20 minutes to decrease swelling and pain.

  An ice bag can be applied directly to the skin (except on the outside of the knee) unless the child has a known cold allergy.

  The safest form of icing is to use a plastic bag with ice cubes or crushed ice, or instant cold packs.

  Do not use 'blue ice' or 'gel packs'.

  While icing will be uncomfortable at first, in 2 to 3 minutes, the skin will go numb and the ice bag will feel more comfortable.

  The ice bag can be secured in place using an elastic bandage, but the compression should not be too tight.

  Icing for 15-20 minutes with an ice bag is unlikely to cause nerve damage or frostbite; however, any loss of sensation and any changes in tissue coloration in areas other than the area that is being iced indicate that the application is no longer safe.
- **'C' is for Compression** After icing, to further prevent swelling, wrap the injured area with an elastic bandage or compression sleeve.

  Take the wrap and start farthest away from the injured body part to the heart.

  Continuously wrap, always making sure to cover half of the previously wrapped area. As you get closer to the end of the wrap, you don't need to wrap as tightly.

  You will know you have wrapped correctly when the hurt part ends up in the middle of the wrap. Tension should be firm but still comfortable. Tingling or pain means it's too tight. Incorrect application of an elastic wrap could cause further pain and damage and delay healing.
- **'E' is for Elevation** For both upper and lower limb injuries, it is equally important to keep the limb elevated to minimize swelling. Elevation to the level of the heart or above allows for excess fluid to be pumped back into the blood vessel system and will help prevent further swelling from occurring.

# CHAPTER PRACTICE

## OBJECTIVE TYPE QUESTIONS

### Multiple Choice Questions (MCQs)

**1** Who said that "Physical fitness is the capacity to meet the present and potential physical challenges of life with success"?
(a) Don Hoskins (b) Kroles
(c) D R Lamb (d) Harre

*Ans* (c) D R Lamb

**2** What does person require to maintain physical fitness?
(a) Efficient motar mechanism
(b) Efficient organic mechanism
(c) Efficient mental functioning
(d) All of the above

*Ans* (d) All of the above

**3** Which one of the following is not a component of physical fitness?
(a) Speed (b) Flexibility
(c) Strength (d) Cardiovascular endurance

*Ans* (d) Cardiovascular endurance

**4** Which of the following is not a characteristic of static strength?
(a) It is also called isotonic strength
(b) It can be measured by dynamometer
(c) It is not usually applied in sports
(d) This strength is not experienced directly

*Ans* (a) It is also called isotonic strength

**5** Which type of flexibility is required/needed for carrying movements over greater distances, when an individual is in motion?
(a) Passive flexibility (b) Dynamic flexibility
(c) Static flexibility (d) None of these

*Ans* (b) Dynamic flexibility

**6** Which of the following is/are health-related components?
(a) Muscular Strength (b) Body Composition
(c) Flexibility (d) All of these

*Ans* (d) All of these

**7** Which of the following is not the component of wellness?
(a) Physical (b) Emotional
(c) Muscular strength (d) Nutritional

*Ans* (c) Muscular strength

**8** Which component of Wellness refers to "As the ability to work with different people, to communicate well and interact with the community"?
(a) Emotional Wellness (b) Intellectual Wellness
(c) Social Wellness (d) Environmental Wellness

*Ans* (c) Social Wellness

**9** What should be the body fat percentage in women?
(a) 5 to 10 (b) 10 to 15 (c) 15 to 20 (d) 20 to 25

*Ans* (d) 20 to 25

**10** Which of the following is/are the indigenous Sports of India?
(a) Kho-Kho (b) Kabbadi
(c) Archery (d) All of these

*Ans* (d) All of these

**11** What are the benefits of bringing traditional games back to life?
(a) Bunging together of indigenous and non-indigenous people.
(b) Help reconnect urban indigenous youth to their culture.
(c) Enhance physical health
(d) All of the above

*Ans* (d) All of the above

**12** Identify the component of physical fitness from the activity given in the picture below.

(a) Flexibility (b) Endurance
(c) Strength (d) Speed

*Ans* (b) Endurance

### Fill in the Blanks

**13** ......... is another component of physical fitness like speed and strength.

*Ans* Endurance

**14** Explosive strength is the ability to overcome ......... with high speed.

*Ans* resistance

**15** Fast twitch fibres fatigue ........., on the other hand slow twitch fibres fatigue ......... .

*Ans* quickly, slowly

**16** Flexibility of a body can be increased by performing ............ exercises.

*Ans* stretching

**17** The body fat percentage in women is ......... percent.

*Ans* 20-25

## State True or False

**18** For a doctor to have a good physique is a symbol of physical fitness.

*Ans* False. For a doctor, the proper functioning of physiological system is a symbol of physical fitness.

**19** Reaction speed is the ability to carry out sports movement with high speed.

*Ans* False. Reaction speed is the ability to respond to a given stimulus as quickly as possible.

**20** Emotional wellness is the ability to control stress, manage anger and anxiety and express feelings.

*Ans* True

**21** Physical fitness differs according to shape of the body only.

*Ans* False. Physical fitness differs according to the kind of work, individual's size, shape of the body, age, etc.

**22** Only efficient motor mechanism is required to maintain, physical fitness.

*Ans* False. There are number of mechanisms required to maintain physical fitness like an efficient motor mechanism, efficient organic mechanism, an efficient mental functioning etc.

## Match the Following

**23**

| List I (Types of Speed) | List II (Characteristics of Speed) |
|---|---|
| A. Movement Speed | (i) It is the ability to increase speed from minimum to maximum. |
| B. Acceleration Speed | (ii) It is the ability to carry out sports movement with high speed. |
| C. Endurance Speed | (iii) It is the ability to do a single movement in the minimum time. |

**Codes**

| | A | B | C |
|---|---|---|---|
| (a) | (iii) | (i) | (ii) |
| (b) | (ii) | (i) | (iii) |
| (c) | (ii) | (iii) | (i) |
| (d) | (i) | (iii) | (ii) |

*Ans* (a)

**24**

| List I (Health Related Components) | List II (Characteristics) |
|---|---|
| A. Muscular Strength | (i) It refers to the range of motion around a movement. |
| B. Cardiovascular Endurance | (ii) It is the percentage of lean body mass in comparison to body fat. |
| C. Body Composition | (iii) It refers to the ability of muscle to exert force during an activity. |
| D. Flexibility | (iv) It refers to the physical activity of an individual to indulge in aerobic exercises. |

**Codes**

| | A | B | C | D | | A | B | C | D |
|---|---|---|---|---|---|---|---|---|---|
| (a) | (i) | (ii) | (iii) | (iv) | (b) | (iii) | (ii) | (i) | (iv) |
| (c) | (iii) | (iv) | (ii) | (i) | (d) | (ii) | (i) | (iv) | (iii) |

*Ans* (c)

## Assertion-Reason

**25** **Assertion** (A) Physical fitness refers to the maximum capacity of all systems of body.
**Reason** (R) Physical fitness is requires regular exercises and nutritional food.
In the context of above two statements, which one of the following is correct?

**Codes**

(a) Both A and R are true and R is the correct explanation of A
(b) Both A and R are true, but R is not the correct explanation of A
(c) A is true, but R is false
(d) A is false, but R is true

*Ans* (b) Both A and R are true, but R is not the correct explanation of A

**26** **Assertion** (A) Healthy life style prevents diseases.
**Reason** (R) Strength is the ability to perform a joint action through a range of movements.
In the context of above two statements, which one of the following is correct?

**Codes**
(a) Both A and R are true and R is the correct explanation of A
(b) Both A and R are true, but R is not the correct explanation of A
(c) A is true, but R is false
(d) A is false, but R is true

*Ans* (c) A is true, but R is false

**27** **Assertion** (A) Movement speed is ability to respond to a given stimulus as quick as possible.
**Reason** (R) Acceleration is the ability to increase speed from minimum to maximum.
In the context of above two statements, which one of the following is correct?

**Codes**
(a) Both A and R are true and R is the correct explanation of A
(b) Both A and R are true, but R is not the correct explanation of A
(c) A is true, but R is false
(d) A is false, but R is true

*Ans* (d) A is false, but R is true

**28** **Assertion** (A) Coordinative abilities play significant role in the sports.
**Reason** (R) All sports require the coordination of eyes, hands, feet etc.
In the context of above two statements, which one of the following is correct?

**Codes**
(a) Both A and R are true and R is the correct explanation of A
(b) Both A and R are true, but R is not the correct explanation of A
(c) A is true, but R is false
(d) A is false, but R is true

*Ans* (c) A is true, but R is false

## VERY SHORT ANSWER TYPE QUESTIONS

**29** Define physical fitness.

*Ans* According to Webster's Collegiate Encyclopedia, physical fitness is the ability of a person to do daily routine work without fatigue, participate in playful activities and still reserve enough capacity to meet any emergency.

**30** What do you understand by wellness?

*Ans* Wellness is the capacity of an individual to lead a well balanced life. It consists of multiple dimensions such as physical, mental, emotional, spiritual, occupational, social and environmental.

**31** Why is a person not able to do even small tasks due to lack of physical fitness?

*Ans* Physical fitness ensures smooth working of the organs and the body systems. Thus, in the absence of physical fitness, these organs and systems will not function properly, due to which a person feels difficulty in doing even small tasks.

**32** What do you understand by endurance?

*Ans* It is that component of physical fitness which can be defined as the ability to carry out movements with the desired quality and speed under the conditions of fatigue.

**33** What is coordinative ability?

*Ans* Coordinative ability is the ability to control the movements of different parts of our body, so that they work together in coordination.

**34** In which sports is explosive strength needed?

*Ans* Explosive strength is needed in all jumping events like high jump, long jump, triple jump and wherever jumping is needed, like basketball.

**35** What do you mean by body composition?

*Ans* Body composition refers to the relative amount of muscles, fat, bone and other vital parts of the body. Body composition determines the ability of a body to work.

## SHORT ANSWER TYPE QUESTIONS

**36** Why is a person required to be physically fit?

*Ans* A physically fit person is able to perform all routine activities properly. This is because all the organs like heart, liver, lungs, kidney and all the systems working in the body like digestive system, respiratory system, circulatory system, nervous system etc run smoothly.
This gives more energy to do work and hence the person is able to perform all the tasks efficiently. Therefore, a person is required to be physically fit.

**37** Discuss social, spiritual and intellectual wellness.

*Ans* **Social Wellness** refers to the ability to work with different people, to communicate well and interact with the community. Social values like cooperation, tolerance, sympathy, helpfulness etc. bring social wellness.

**Spiritual Wellness** refers to wellness developed on ethical and moral grounds that helps to face challenges, develop faith in religion, inculcate family values etc.

**Intellectual Wellness** refers to making sound decisions, alertness of mind, focus, critical thinking, creativity, openness to new ideas etc.

**38** What is strength? Give examples from sports where different kinds of strength are needed.

*Ans* Strength is the ability of the muscles to exert force in a single muscle contraction. It is also the ability to overcome resistance.

Maximum strength is needed to overcome maximum resistance like in weightlifting.

Explosive strength is needed in all jumping events, e.g. high jump, long jump and in basketball.

Strength endurance is needed to overcome resistance under conditions of fatigue such as in judo, swimming etc.

**39** Why is speed considered an essential component of physical fitness?

*Ans* Speed is the ability to perform movements of similar pattern as fast as possible. It is an essential component of physical fitness because speed can be achieved only when a person is physically fit.

Physical activities and exercises that keep a person physically fit also increase the ability of the person to work faster and take the shortest possible time in completing movements.

**40** Why is flexibility essential in sports, games and other physical activities?

*Ans* Flexibility is the ability to perform a joint action through a range of movements. The joint action takes place when joints, tendons, ligaments and muscles work together in perfect coordination to bring efficiency.

In sports and games, flexibility is essential because these activities involve stretching, movement, extensibility of the muscles and exercise of the ligaments. Without flexibility, these activities cannot be performed. In sports like gymnastics, swimming and athletics, etc. flexibility is essential.

**41** Explain coordinative abilities in detail.

*Ans* Coordinative abilities are the abilities that controls the movements of the different parts of our body, so that they work well together.

It is that component of physical fitness that is required in all kinds of sports. For example, Racket sports such as badminton or football where the coordination of the feet, eyes and ball is required.

These abilities depends on the nervous system which is controlled by the brain. The different types of coordinative ability are rhythmic ability, balance ability, adaptation ability, reaction ability, etc.

These types of abilities can be enhanced through general or specific exercises. Some sports wherein coordinative exercises play a main role include kho-kho, lawn tennis, hockey, cricket, etc.

**42** What do you mean by physical fitness?

*Ans* Physical fitness refers to the maximum functional capacity of all systems of the body.

Physical fitness is more than the possession of strength and endurance. It can also be termed as having the best possible health with the capacity to do one's everyday task, engage in recreational pursuits and meet emergencies when they arise.

An individual who is energetic, works happily and carry out emergency work with vigour, may be considered as physically fit. It implies a relation between the task to be performed and the individual's capability to perform it.

**43** Elaborate the concept of wellness.

*Ans* Wellness is an active process of becoming aware of and making choices towards a healthy and fulfilling life. Wellness is more than just being free from illness; it is a dynamic process of change and growth.

The concept of wellness, *i.e.* staying healthy and achieving the highest potential for well-being, has gained popularity in the past few years.

Wellness covers all areas of health which includes physical, emotional, spiritual, social, environmental, financial, intellectual, nutritional and mental wellness. These are basically the components in one's life that can affect one's overall well-being.

**44** Name the component of Physical fitness. Discuss any one of them.

*Ans* There are five components of physical fitness, which are as follows:

- Strength
- Speed
- Endurance
- Flexibility
- Coordinative ability

**Strength** It is the ability of a muscle to exert force in a single muscle contraction. It can also be understood as the ability to overcome resistance. It is required in various games and sports like shot put, discus throw, hammer throw, javelin throw, wrestling, judo, weightlifting etc.

**45** Define speed and discuss its type?

*Ans* **Speed** It is the ability to cover a certain distance in the minimum possible time or the ability to perform moment of similar pattern as fast as possible.

Types of speed

(i) **Reaction Speed** It is the ability to respond to a given stimulus as quickly as possible.

(ii) **Movement Speed** It is the ability to do a single movement in the minimum time. Movement speed is of high relevance in cyclic sports e.g. jumping, throwing, kicking etc.

(iii) **Acceleration Speed** It is the ability to increase speed from minimum to maximum. This form of speed, to a great extent, depends upon explosive strength, frequency of movement and technique.

**46** Describe any three components of the wellness.

*Ans* The three components of the wellness are as follows:

(i) **Physical Wellness** It refers to physical appearance which can be achieved by taking nutritious food, doing regular exercises, getting in shape, having a glowing skin and a youthful appearance.

(ii) **Emotional Wellness** It is the ability to control stress, manage anger and anxiety, and express feelings appropriately. It also lays stress on getting more out of every day with laughter and enjoyment.

(iii) **Social Wellness** It refers to the ability to work with different people, to communicate well and interact with the community.

## LONG ANSWER TYPE QUESTIONS

**47** Write a short note on

(i) Type of speed

(ii) Type of flexibility

*Ans* (i) In general, speed has the following different forms which are seen in most sports. These are

(a) **Reaction Speed** It is the ability to respond to a given stimulus as quickly as possible.

(b) **Movement Speed** It is the ability to do a single movement in the minimum time. Movement speed is of high relevance in cyclic sports.

For example, jumping, throwing, kicking, etc.

(c) **Acceleration Speed** It is the ability to increase speed from minimum to maximum. This form of speed, to a great extent, depends upon explosive sports, frequency of movement and technique.

(ii) Flexibility is of two types, which are as follows

(a) **Passive Flexibility** It is the ability to perform movement with greater range using external help. For example, doing a stretching movement with the help of a partner.

This flexibility is generally dependent on the anatomy of the joint and extensibility of the muscles and ligaments.

(b) **Active Flexibility** It is the ability to perform movement with greater range without using external help, *i.e.* with the help of muscular force. For example, stretching with the help of muscular force alone.

It can be further divided into two categories

- **Static Flexibility** It is usually required by a sportsperson when he remains in a static position. For example, while diving, lying, sitting etc.
- **Dynamic Flexibility** It is needed for carrying out movements over greater distances when an individual is in motion.

**48** Describe the five components of health related fitness.

*Ans* The five components of health related fitness are

(i) **Cardiovascular Endurance** It refers to the physical activity of an individual to indulge in aerobic exercises for longer period of time.

It can also be referred to as the ability of heart, lungs and blood vessels to supply oxygen and nutritients to the working muscles and the ability of those muscles to allow sustained exercise.

The endurance system can be improved through the activities like cycling, walking, etc.

(ii) **Muscular Strength** This refers to the ability of the muscles to exert force during an activity. Muscular strength of the different muscles can be improved by lifting weights, rapidly climbing the stairs, etc.

(iii) **Muscular Endurance** This refers to the ability of the muscles to continue to perform repetitive exercises without fatigue. Muscular endurance can be improved by doing cardio-respiratory activities like walking, cycling, jogging, dancing, etc.

(iv) **Body Composition** It refers to the relative amount of muscles, fat, bone and other vital parts of the body. It is basically the percentage of lean body mass i.e. bones, tendons, muscles, ligaments, etc. in comparison to body fat.

This percentage differs from person to person. A fit person has relatively low percentage of body fat one can have good body composition by having proper diet and exercise. For reducing percentage of body fat one can do jogging, climbing stairs, etc.

(v) **Flexibility** It refers to the maximum range of movements possible at a joint. It depends on the structure of joints, muscles length, tendons, ligaments and other factors.

An individual having a good flexibility will be able to move his/her joints through a full range of motion while performing activities. Flexibility can be improved through regular yoga, gymnastics and basic stretching exercises.

**49** In relation to the given picture, answer the following questions.

*Ans.*

(i) The ability to maximum turn and twist on the joints of the body is ................ .

(ii) The ability to perform maximum efforts in a short period of time is known as ..................... .

(iii) What refers to the ability of the muscles to continue to perform repetitive exercises without fatigue?

(iv) Which component of fitness can be defined as the ability of muscles to overcome maximum resistance?

*Ans.* (i) flexibility (ii) speed

(iii) Endurance (iv) Strength

# SELF ASSESSMENT

## OBJECTIVE ANSWER TYPE QUESTIONS

1 Which of the following is/are important for physical fitness and wellness?
(a) Proper growth and development (b) Quality of life
(c) Prevention of diseases (d) All of these

2 Which type of strength is required in pull and push ups?
(a) Maximum strength (b) Explosive strength (c) Static strength (d) Strength endurance

3 In which of the following games, coordinative abilities are required?
(a) Gymnastics (b) Hockey (c) Law Tennis (d) All of these

4 **Assertion** (A) Health and wellness do not include mental and social condition.
**Reason** (R) Wellness is a dynamic concept.
In the context of above two statements, which one of the following is correct?
(a) Both A and R are true and R is the correct explanation of A
(b) Both A and R are true, but R is not the correct explanation of A
(c) A is true, but R is false
(d) A is false, but R is true

## VERY SHORT ANSWER TYPE QUESTIONS

5 How does physical fitness increase longevity?

6 Give two examples to show the use of co-ordination in sports.

7 Name some sports that enhance endurance and flexibility.

8 Mention the components of wellness.

## SHORT ANSWER TYPE QUESTIONS

9 Discuss how physical fitness is closely related to wellness.

10 Differentiate between physical fitness and wellness.

11 Explain the three types of endurance along with the sports in which they are needed.

12 What is intellectual wellness ? How can it be a measure of being healthy?

## LONG ANSWER TYPE QUESTIONS

13 What is physical fitness? How do its components help in achieving physical fitness?

14 Enlist and explain the components of physical fitness in relation to the different sports in which they are needed.

CHAPTER

# 06

# Test, Measurement and Evaluation

In the field of health and physical education, we set certain objectives that we aim to reach. With the set objectives, it becomes essential for us to see or check whether such goals or objectives are met or not. For this purpose, various test, measurement and evaluation techniques are applied.

The tests, measurements and evaluation techniques in physical education are the devices through which we collect the essential data and details regarding the needs, capacities, abilities and attitude of a sportsperson.

### CHAPTER CHECKLIST

- Concept of Test
- Concept of Measurement
- Concept of Evaluation
- Calculation of BMI, WHR and Skin fold Measurement
- Somatotypes : Endomorphy, Mesomorphy and Ectomorphy
- Measurement of Health-related Fitness

## Concept of Test

A test may be called as a tool, question or examination which is used to measure a particular characteristic of an individual or a sportsperson.

In other words, it is a tool that is used to get a response to gain information on skills such as fitness, sports knowledge, values etc. It may be either subjective or objective, in order to reach the conclusion or result.

In physical education, there are many tests including Kraus Weber Test, One Mile Test, Miller Volleyball Test, National Physical Efficiency Test, etc.

## Concept of Measurement

Measurement is the process of tests and techniques that is used to collect information or data regarding the level of fitness or skill of an individual. It is the record of performance that involves the assignment of numerical values to whatever is being tested. It is quantitative in nature.

The recording of measurement includes two parts
- A number indicating the magnitude
- A unit

Measurement is a quantitative process in which level of performance, fitness, ability etc are measured through various specific tests.

There are various methods of measurement used in sports for testing and reporting physical fitness levels such as Johnson Basketball Ability Test, AAHPERD Physical Test, FITNESSGRAM Test, Miller Volleyball Test etc.

## Concept of Evaluation

Evaluation is a technique by which we can identify to what extent the objectives of a programme are being achieved.

It is a process of decision-making in which a grade and ranking has to be given based on a systematic and objective assessment of the information available.

It helps in reaching a conclusion of relevance, effectiveness, efficiency, impact and sustainability of any subject matter.

In the process of evaluation, information from previous monitoring processes is used to understand the ways in which the project or programme has developed and stimulated change.

Some of the definitions of evaluation are

- According to the **Oxford Dictionary,** evaluation is "The making of a judgment about the amount, number or value of something."
- According to the **Merriam-Webster Dictionary,** evaluation can be defined as "Determination of the significance, worth, or condition of someone or something by careful appraisal and study."
- According to **Barrow** and **Megee,** "It is the process of education that involves collection of data from the products which can be used for comparison with preconcieved criteria to make judgement."

In physical education, evaluation helps to judge or evaluate students or sportspersons through their physical strength, skill and knowledge in the field of sports.

## Importance of Test, Measurement and Evaluation in Sports

Test, measurement and evaluation are very important tools in the process of physical education and in sports. Without proper test, measurement and evaluation, the level of achievement cannot be determined. Test, measurement and evaluation in physical education and sports are important because they

1. **Give Information about Progress** These tools are very helpful to check the progress level of sportspersons. Checking the progress level has significance for both the teacher as well as the student of physical education. Without these tools, objectivity cannot be established.
2. **Allow Effective Planning** These tools help in identifying errors and help develop methods for better planning of programmes in future.
3. **Motivate Sportspersons** Motivation is progressive in nature. Test, measurement and evaluation function as a filter to know the reality of the situation. They are vital devices for a sportsperson to help in achieving better performance. Thus, they motivate sportspersons.
4. **Discover the Need of Participation** These tools help in discovering the need for participation, as they are helpful in identifying the strengths and weaknesses of the participants.
5. **Help in Determining Ability and Capacity** Test, measurement and evaluation are capable of checking the ability and capacity of sportspersons, so that they help in conceiving a remedial programme.
6. **Help in Classifying Sportspersons** Sportspersons would be given training loads according to their individual capability. Test, measurement and evaluation help in taking such decisions based on the basis of the sportsperson's physical, mental and psychological capacity.
7. **Determine Future Achievement** The performance of a sportsperson can be accurately analysed with the help of test, measurement and evaluation so that the future achievement of the sportsperson can be determined or predicted.
8. **Help Research and Development** These tools are very significant for research in the field of sports and physical education as they help in finding various shortcomings in training programmes.

They help to bridge the gap between existing knowledge and future perspectives. They help develop new styles as well as convenient tools and techniques for future development. Thus, good research depends on proper testing, measurement and evaluation.

Consequently, it can be observed that these tools i.e. test, measurement and evaluation are very much significant in the field of physical education as well as the sports world.

# Calculation of BMI, WHR and Skin Fold Measurement

## Body Mass Index (BMI)

The Body Mass Index (BMI), which is also known as Quetelet Index, was developed by Adolphe Quetelet. It is a measure of body composition. It is calculated by taking the weight of a person and dividing it by the square of the height. It provides a simple numeric measure to estimate the body bulk.

With the help of this measurement, we can easily calculate whether a person is underweight, normal, overweight or in the category of obese. The calculation of BMI requires information about the height in metres and weight in kilograms of a person.

The formula for BMI is

$$\text{Body Mass Index (BMI)} = \frac{\text{Body Weight (kg)}}{\text{Height} \times \text{Height } (\text{m}^2)}$$

BMI can also be calculated in FPS units that use pounds in place of kilograms and inches in place of metres.

$$\text{BMI} = \frac{\text{Weight in pounds}}{(\text{Height in inches})^2} \times 703$$

For instance, suppose the body weight of an individual is 70 kg and height is 1.67 m. The BMI will be

$$\text{BMI} = \left(\frac{70}{1.67 \times 1.67}\right) = \frac{70}{2.79} = 25.1 \text{ kg/m}^2$$

The World Health Organisation (WHO) developed criteria to calculate the individual's categorisation into underweight, normal, overweight or obese.

We can understand these criteria with the help of the following table

| Category | BMI |
|---|---|
| Underweight | < 18.5 |
| Normal | 18.5-24.9 |
| Overweight | 25.0-29.9 |
| Obese-I | 30.0-34.9 |
| Obese-II | 35.0-39.9 |
| Obese-III | >40.0 |

Now, take a look at the result of the individuals BMI which is 25.1 kg/m$^2$; it falls in the category of overweight, but only slightly.

### Precautions During BMI Measurement

Precautions needed during BMI measurement are

- Use a reliable and accurate weighing machine.
- While taking body weight, wear less/minimum clothes.
- While measuring height, stand on the height board in a straight position.

## Waist Hip Ratio (WHR)

Waist hip ratio is the ratio of the waist circumference to the hip circumference.

$$\text{WHR} = \left(\frac{\text{Waist Circumference}}{\text{Hip Circumference}}\right)$$

It is a tool that looks at the proportion of fat stored on the waist compared to the hips and buttocks.

Researches show that people with weight concentrated around the middle of the waist, referred to as 'apple shape', may face more health risk. Weight concentrated around the hips is referred to as pear shaped figure; they have less risk than apple shaped persons.

### Method of Measurement

To measure whether you have a healthy waist hip ratio or not, use a tape to check the waist circumference and the distance around the largest area of the hips.

$$\text{WHR} = \frac{\text{Waist Circumference (inches / cm)}}{\text{Hip Circumference (inches / cm)}}$$

The degree of health risk can be understood better by observing both BMI and WHR, as given in the table below

| BMI | Waist Hip Ratio (Males) | | | Waist Hip Ratio (Females) | | |
|---|---|---|---|---|---|---|
| | < 0.85 | 0.85 – 1.0 | > 1.0 | < 0.70 | 0.70 – 0.85 | > 0.85 |
| 20 to < 25 | Very low | Low | Moderate | Very low | Low | Moderate |
| 25 to < 30 | Low | Moderate | High | Low | Moderate | High |
| 30 to < 35 | Moderate | High | Very high | Moderate | High | Very high |
| 35 to < 40 | High | Very high | Very high | High | Very high | Very high |
| ≥ 40 | Very high | Very high | Very high | Very high | Very high | Very high |

## Skin Fold Measurement (3-Site)

Skinfold testing, also known as caliper testing is a commonly used method to determine the body fat percentage.

### Procedures for Skinfold Measurement

You need to firmly grasp a fold skin between your thumb and index finger and lift this up. The skinfold should include two thicknesses; one of skin and one of the subcutaneous fat, but no muscle or fascia.

Place the contact surface of the callipers at a 90-degree angle to the skinfold approximately 1cm below the fingers. Slightly release the pressure between the fingers, but remain holding the skinfold so that a greater pressure is applied by the callipers. Release the handle of the callipers and read the needle to the nearest 0.1mm approximately 4 seconds after the pressure is released.

**Equipment** The equipment used for measuring all skinfold widths is a standard skinfold calliper. A number of callipers are in use. But the most reliable are Harpenden, Lange and Lafayette skinfold callipers.

# Somatotypes : Endomorphy, Mesomorphy and Ectomorphy

In this world, no two persons or human beings are the same. Even twins are not the same in many ways. There are differences on the basis of their physique, strength, weight, height etc.

Undoubtedly, there are many individual differences, but there are some similarities too. On the basis of these similarities, scientists strive to classify them.

These classifications are made on the basis of physical as well as mental appearances. The classification given by WH Sheldon on the basis of appearance is generally accepted.

## Classification by WH Sheldon

Somatotype or body type is a classification of human physique. WH Sheldon categorised the human physique and named the three categories as Endomorph, Mesomorph and Ectomorph. These appearances of human physique are detailed below

1. **Endomorph** Such persons have a large amount of mass on their bodies. They have a round head, a large, round abdomen, large internal organs relative to their size, rather short arms and legs with fat upper arms and thighs, but slender wrists and ankles. They cannot lose weight easily. They can become fat or obese easily because they have high capacity to store fat.

   They have a pear shaped body and their mass makes it difficult for them to compete in most sports, because most sports require high levels of agility or speed. However, they can compete in sports requiring strength like weightlifting or power lifting.

2. **Mesomorph** This human physique is marked by greater than average muscular appearance. Mesomorphs have a square, massive head, broad, muscular chest and shoulders, a large heart, heavily muscled arms and legs, and minimal body fat. They can develop muscles easily. They have a well developed rectangular shaped body. However, they may become overweight due to leading a sedentary lifestyle and consuming a high calorie diet.

A Mesomorphic structure makes them a strong contestant in any sport. They excel in sports requiring high strength, short bursts of energy and high power.

3. **Ectomorph** People with this physique have a tendency of linearity. They are considered slim. The extreme ectomorph has a thin face with high forehead, reduced chin, narrow chest and abdomen, a narrow heart, long and thin arms and legs, little body fat and little muscle. However, they have a large skin surface and a large nervous system. An ectomorphic physique is suitable for aerobic activities like gymnastics, swimming and cycling.

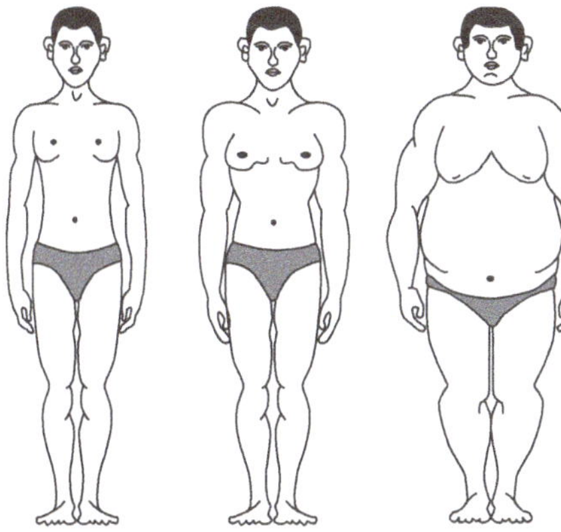


# Measurements of Health-Related Fitness

The Health Related Fitness measure the five major health-related components of physical fitness, namely cardiorespiratory fitness, muscular strength, muscular endurance, body composition and flexibility.

Measurement of Muscular Strength Muscular strength refers to the amount of force the muscle or group of muscles can exert against

resistance for short duration like in anaerobic activities. Muscular strength can be measured by Kraus Weber Test.

## Kraus Weber Test

Kraus Weber Test originated in a posture clinic and was developed as a diagnosis and treatment of low back pain. Soon, it became familiar as Kraus Weber test of minimum muscular fitness.

The test consists of six items which indicate the level of muscular strength and flexibility of key muscle groups.

### Measurement of Cardiovascular Fitness

Cardiovascular fitness is the ability of the heart and lungs to supply oxygen, rich blood to the working muscle tissues and the ability of the muscles to use oxygen to produce energy for movements. This type of fitness is required.

### Harvard Step Test

This test is also known as Aerobic Fitness test. It was developed by Brouha and others in 1943. It is used to measure the cardiovascular fitness or aerobic fitness by checking the recovery rate. Equipment

Required Bench 20 inches high, for men and 16 inches for women, stopwatch and metronome.

# CHAPTER PRACTICE

## OBJECTIVE TYPE QUESTIONS

### Multiple Choice Questions (MCQs)

**1** Test is generally used to measure
(a) a specific skill
(b) a specific body type
(c) the level of skill
(d) the abilities of a sportsperson

*Ans* (a) a specific skill

**2** Which of the following is not an example of measurement?
(a) AAHPERD (b) Miller volleyball test
(c) FITNESS GRAM (d) None of these

*Ans* (d) None of these

**3** ............ helps in understanding the ways in which a project or programme can be stimulated and developed.
(a) Evaluation (b) Test
(c) Measurement (d) None of these

*Ans* (a) Evaluation

### Assertion-Reason

**4** **Assertion** (A) Measurement is a process of administrating a test to obtain quantative data.
**Reason** (R) Measurement is a qualitative process.
In the context of above two statements, which one of the following is correct?
**Codes**
(a) Both A and R are true and R is the correct explanation of A
(b) Both A and R are true, but R is not the correct explanation of A
(c) A is true, but R is false
(d) A is false, but R is true

*Ans* (c) A is true, but R is false

**5** **Assertion** (A) Evaluation is important in sports.
**Reason** (R) Evaluation helps in improving performance.
In the context of above two statements, which one of the following is correct?
**Codes**
(a) Both A and R are true and R is the correct explanation of A
(b) Both A and R are true, but R is not the correct explanation of A
(c) A is true, but R is false
(d) A is false, but R is true

*Ans* (a) Both A and R are true and R is the correct explanation of A

## VERY SHORT ANSWER TYPE QUESTIONS

**6** What do you understand by a test?

*Ans* A test may be called a tool, question or examination which is being used to measure a particular characteristic of an individual or a sportsperson.

**7** What is measurement?

*Ans* It is the process of tests and techniques to collect information or data regarding the level of fitness or skill of sportspersons.

**8** What is evaluation?

*Ans* It is a technique by which we can know to what extent the objectives of a programme are being achieved.

**9** For what range of BMI is the health risk very high for males with a WHR > 1.0?

*Ans* For males with a waist hip ratio > 1.0, the health risk is very high if the BMI is 30 or more.

**10** What is the formula for calculating BMI in the FPS system?

*Ans* BMI= Weight in pounds/ (Height in inches)$^2$ × 703.

**11** What do you understand by waist hip ratio?

*Ans* It is the ratio of waist circumference to hip circumference.
WHR= Waist Circumference/ Hip Circumference

## SHORT ANSWER TYPE QUESTIONS

**12** Discuss the applicability of test and measurement in sports.

*Ans* Tests are processes to collect information about a specific skill, knowledge, behaviour, attitude etc. It refers to any specific instrument or technique used by administrators to obtain information from sportspersons or others.
Measurements are associated with physical measurements such as height, weight, capacity, achievement etc. It refers to the process of administrating a test to obtain quantitative data in the field of sports.

**13** What is the importance of tests in sports? Give three points.

*Ans* Tests are important in sports because

(i) **They Inform about Progress** Tests help to check the level of progress of a sportsperson. This checking of the progress level is significant for the educator/ coach as well as the student/ sportsperson concerned.

(ii) **Allow Effective Planning** Tests help in identifying errors and help develop tools for better planning of programmes in future.

(iii) **Help in Determining Ability and Capacity** Tests are capable of checking the ability and capacity of sportspersons, so that they help in conceiving a remedial programme.

**14** How do test, measurement and evaluation help in future research? Mention three reasons.

*Ans* Test, measurement and evaluation are tools which are very significant for research in the field of sports and physical education because they help to

(i) **Find Shortcomings** These tools help in finding various shortcomings in training programmes, as the results of measurement can be compared with the expected outcomes to research particular areas.

(ii) **Bridge Gaps** Evaluation of the measurements made in the tests helps to bridge the gap between existing knowledge and any viewpoint to be researched in the future.

(iii) **Develop New Techniques** Evaluation of the effectiveness of the tests helps develop new styles, convenient tools and techniques for development in the future.

Thus, good research depends on proper testing, measurement and evaluation.

**15** Determine the degree of health risk for a man by calculating the BMI and WHR based on the data given below.

| Gender | Weight (kg) | Height (cm) | Circumference of Waist (cm) | Circumference of Hips (cm) |
|---|---|---|---|---|
| Male | 57 | 174 | 180 | 190 |

*Ans* The formula for BMI is

$$\text{Body Mass Index (BMI)} = \frac{\text{Body Weight (kg)}}{\text{Height} \times \text{Height}\,(\text{m})^2}$$

Thus, in this case, BMI = 57/(1.74 × 1.74) = 24.4

The formula for WHR is

$$\text{Waist Hips Ratio (WHR)} = \left(\frac{\text{Waist Circumference}}{\text{Hip Circumference}}\right)$$

Thus, in this case, WHR = 180/190 = 0.95

According to the degree of health risk table, for a male having a BMI less than 25 and a WHR between 0.85 and 1.0, the health risk is low.

**16** What are the major physical characteristics of the three Somatotypes, as classified by Sheldon?

*Ans* The major physical characteristics of the three Somatotypes, as classified by Sheldon, are

(i) **Endomorph** Such persons have a large amount of mass on their physique. They have a pear shaped body, a round head, a large, round abdomen, large internal organs relative to their size, rather short arms and legs with fat upper arms and thighs, but slender wrists and ankles.

(ii) **Mesomorph** Such persons have an above average muscular appearance, a square, massive head; broad, muscular chest and shoulders; a large heart; heavily muscled arms and legs; and minimal body fat. They have a well-developed rectangular shaped body.

(iii) **Ectomorph** Such persons have a tendency of linearity. They are considered slim. The extreme ectomorph has a thin face with high forehead, reduced chin, narrow chest and abdomen, a narrow heart, long and thin arms and legs, little body fat and little muscle. However, they have a large skin surface and a large nervous system.

## LONG ANSWER TYPE QUESTIONS

**17** What is the purpose of evaluation in sports? Explain the planning- evaluation cycle in detail.

*Ans* The purpose of evaluation in sports is to know to what extent the objectives of a programme are being achieved. It is a process of decision-making in which a grade and ranking has to be given based on a systematic and objective assessment of the information available.

To make the evaluation more reliable and analytical, an evaluation cycle has been developed. This is referred to as the 'Planning-Evaluation Cycle'. The stages of this cycle are

(i) **Planning** In this stage, a set of potential actions, programmes or technologies is considered and the best is selected for implementation. This stage may include steps like

- Formulating the problem, issue or concern.
- Conceptualising the major alternatives.
- Detailing these alternatives and their. potential implications.

- Evaluating the alternatives.
- Selecting the best one.
- Implementing the selected alternative.

(ii) **Evaluating** In this stage, the method of evaluation is designed, formulated and operationalised, the resultant data is analysed and utilised. It includes steps like

- Formulating the major objectives, goals, and hypotheses of the program or technology.
- Conceptualising and operationalising the major components of the evaluation – the programme, participants, setting and measures.
- Designing the evaluation and detailing how these components will be coordinated.
- Analysing the information, both qualitative and quantitative.
- Utilising the evaluation results.

**18** Define evaluation. Why are test, measurement and evaluation important? Write eight reasons in brief (one sentence each).

*Ans* Evaluation is defined as "Determination of the significance, worth, or condition of someone or something by careful appraisal and study." Test, measurement and evaluation are important because they

(i) **Give Information about Progress** They help to check the progress level of sportspersons objectively.

(ii) **Allow Effective Planning** These tools help in identifying errors and help develop methods for better planning of programmes in future.

(iii) **Motivate Sportspersons** They function as a filter to know the reality of the situation, thus motivating sportspersons for better performance.

(iv) **Discover the Need of Participation** These tools help in discovering the need for participation, as they are helpful in identifying the strengths and weaknesses of the participants.

(v) **Help in Determining Ability and Capacity** They are capable of checking the ability and capacity of sportspersons, so that they help in conceiving a remedial programme.

(vi) **Help in Classifying Sportspersons** By evaluating sportspersons based on their physical, mental and psychological capacities, the sportspersons would be given training loads according to their individual capability.

(vii) **Determine Future Achievement** The performance of a sportsperson can be accurately analysed with the help of test, measurement and evaluation so that the future achievement of the sportsperson can be determined or predicted.

(viii) **Help Research and Development** These tools are very significant for research in the field of sports and physical education as they help in finding various shortcomings in training programmes and help to bridge the gap between existing knowledge and future perspectives.

**19** For what purpose was the concept of BMI developed? Explain its method of calculation. State the ranges and categories of BMI in tabular form.

*Ans* The concept of BMI was developed by the World Health Organisation (WHO) to calculate an individual's health and classify the individual into the categories of underweight, normal, overweight or obese.

Its method of calculation is

(i) The height in metres and weight in kilograms of the person are measured.

(ii) Then the following formula is used to calculate the BMI

Body Mass Index (BMI)

$$= \frac{\text{Body Weight(kg)}}{\text{Height} \times \text{Height}(\text{m}^2)}$$

The ranges and categories of BMI are given in the table below

| BMI | Category |
|---|---|
| < 18.5 | Underweight |
| 18.5 – 24.9 | Normal |
| 25.0 – 29.9 | Overweight |
| 30.0 – 34.9 | Obese - I |
| 35.0 – 39.9 | Obese - II |
| > 40.0 | Obese - III |

# SELF ASSESSMENT

## OBJECTIVE ANSWER TYPE QUESTIONS

**1** Which of the following is not a component of health related fitness?

(a) Flexibility
(b) Speed
(c) Muscular endurance
(d) Strength

**2** A person with BMI of 25 is considered in which of the following categories?

(a) Underweight
(b) Normal
(c) Overweight
(d) Obese

**3** Which among the following human physiques is marked by greater than average muscular appearances?

(a) Mesomorph
(b) Endomorph
(c) Ectomorph
(d) None of these

## VERY SHORT ANSWER TYPE QUESTIONS

**4** Distinguish between evaluation and measurement.

**5** What is a somatotype?

**6** How do we calculate waist hip ratio?

## SHORT ANSWER TYPE QUESTIONS

**7** What is the importance of measurement in sports?

**8** Explain the precautions to be taken for measurement of parameters required for calculating BMI.

**9** Briefly narrate how Waist Hip Ratio is calculated.

**10** Write the differences between mesomorphy and endomorphy.

## LONG ANSWER TYPE QUESTIONS

**11** Explain the importance of testing, measurement and evaluation in sports.

**12** Elaborate on the calculation method of BMI and WHR.

CHAPTER

# 07

# *Fundamentals of Anatomy and Physiology in Sports*

## Anatomy and Physiology

Strong and fit body is an inevitable asset in the field of sports. Study of anatomy, physiology and kinesiology helps a sportsperson to understand the structure and function of different parts of human body and to acquire a fit and healthy body.

### Meaning of Anatomy

The word 'Anatomy' is derived from a Greek word '*anatome*' which means 'to dissect' or 'to cut apart'. According to its meaning, anatomy is a branch of biology which deals with the identification and description of internal body structure of an organism or living being.

In other words, it is a dissection or a detailed analysis of the structure shape, size, weight and location of all organs of a human body.

### Meaning of Physiology

The word 'Physiology' consists of two words '*physio*' which means 'nature' and '*ology*' meaning 'study'. Thus, physiology can be defined as a branch of biology which deals with the functions and activities of all the systems of the human body and their mutual relationships.

In fact, it is the study of all mechanical, physical and biochemical processes that support the human body and its functioning.

In this field, one studies the functions of the various organ systems, organ cells and the biomolecules that allow a living organism to survive, grow, and develop.

CHAPTER CHECKLIST

- Anatomy and Physiology
- Skeletal System
- Muscular System
- Respiratory System
- Circulatory System

There are mainly 9 organ systems in a human body. They are

1. Skeletal system
2. Glandular system
3. Muscular system
4. Excretory system
5. Circulatory system
6. Reproductive system
7. Respiratory system
8. Digestive system
9. Nervous system

In the field of physical education, four of these systems play a central role in overall growth and development of an athlete.

## Importance of Anatomy and Physiology

The following points clearly depict the importance of anatomy and physiology in the field of physical education

1. **Useful in Selection of Sportspersons** Human anatomy and physiology helps in the selection of proper sportspersons for each sport because different types of sports require different anatomical and physiological structures. With the help of anatomy and physiology, we can easily identify the various requirements that an individual should possess to participate in a particular sport or game.

   For instance, a long distance runner should have less body weight, good cardiovascular endurance and a higher amount of red twitch muscular fibres. This knowledge can be gained by knowing about the sportsperson's anatomy and physiology.

2. **Help in Designing Better Training Sessions** A physical trainer can design better training sessions for sportspersons by knowing their physiological capacities and limitations. If training sessions are not designed keeping this knowledge in mind, it can even harm the sportsperson.

3. **Prevent Sports Injuries** Proper knowledge about the interrelated functioning of bones, muscles, tendons and ligaments helps in designing better protective equipment for the soft and delicate organs of the body.

   Thus, sports related injuries like fracture, dislocation, contusion, sprain etc. may be prevented by proper use of such equipment by sportspersons.

4. **Speedy Rehabilitation from Sports Injuries** Knowledge of the human anatomy helps in the speedy rehabilitation of sportspersons from injuries, if they occur.

   Initially, proper first-aid must be provided, for which knowledge of human anatomy is essential, otherwise the injury may worsen.

   Further, knowledge of the physical structure, bones, joints, ligaments etc. helps in designing of better and efficient rehabilitation programmes.

5. **Knowledge about Chemical Changes can Improve Performance** A number of chemical changes take place in our body during exercise or participating in sports. Human physiology provides detailed knowledge of these changes. On the basis of this knowledge, a proper diet can be designed for the sportsperson concerned, so that his performance can be improved.

6. **Recovery from Fatigue by Providing Massage** Providing massage to a sportsperson is a time tested technique for enabling a sportsperson to recover from fatigue either during training or after a competition.

   A proper sports massage will rectify or settle any imbalances in soft tissues which develop by doing strenuous exercise either during training or in a competition. Further, it enhance the performance of a sportsperson. A proper way of massaging can only be developed with adequate knowledge about human anatomy and physiology.

7. **Understanding Differences between Males and Females** With the knowledge of anatomy and physiology, the difference between males and females can be understood properly.

   This knowledge of anatomical and physiological differences between males and females helps in designing proper sport and training programmes for both genders. For instance, the weights of discuss, hammer, shot and javelin are different for both males and females.

8. **Understanding Environmental Effects on Sportspersons** To understand the effect of environment on sportspersons, we must have good knowledge of their anatomy and physiology. How and what type of problems sportspersons are facing can be found by knowing the physiological changes that occur in their bodies.

   For instance, when training or competing at a high altitude, where the air is rarefied, the red blood cell count goes up, unused air sacs in the lungs are activated and heart and respiratory rates go up. The effects of these changes can be studied better with proper knowledge of human physiology.

## Skeletal System

Human body is made up of a framework consisting of many large and small bones called a skeleton.

This skeleton consists of 206 bones as well as a network of tendons, ligaments and cartilages that connect them together, and this system of the body is called the skeletal system.

The skeletal system can be mainly classified into two categories which are as follows

1. **Axial Skeleton** Consists the bones such as Skull (28), Sternum (1), Ribs (24), Hyoid bone (1) and Vertebral column (26).
2. **Appendicular Skeleton** Consists bones in the upper limbs (64) and lower limbes (62).

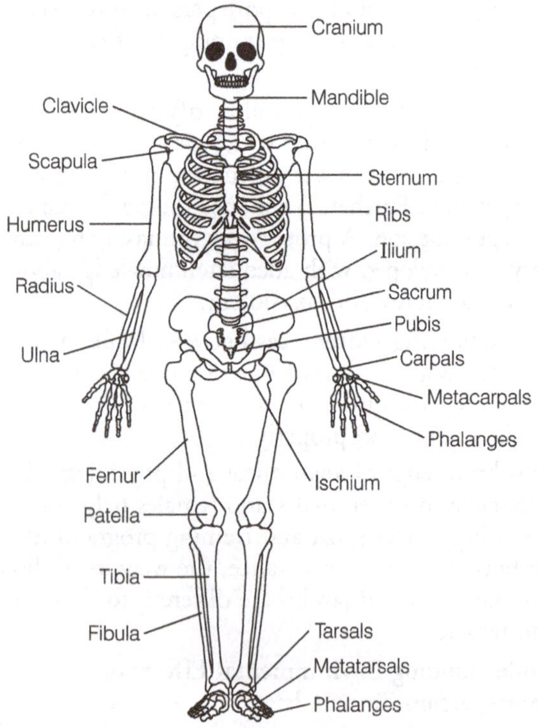


**Human Skeleton**

### Functions of the Skeletal System

The skeletal system together with the muscular system performs various vital functions as given below

1. **Support** Bones of the skeletal system provide structural support to the entire human body.
2. **Protection** The skeleton provides mechanical protection for internal organs of the body. It reduces the risk of injury to the body. Most of the soft tissues of the body are protected by bony structures.
   For instance, cranial bones of the skull protect the brain, vertebrae protect the spinal cord and the ribcage protects the heart and lungs.
3. **Movement** Body movements are possible only with the help of the skeletal system. With the interaction of muscular and skeletal system, the body is able to move voluntarily.
4. **Production of Blood Cells** It assists in production of red blood cells in the bone marrows present in the long bones.
5. **Mineral Storage** Bone tissues store several minerals including calcium and phosphorus. Bones release minerals into the blood whenever it is required to facilitate the balance of minerals in the body. These minerals are released into the bloodstream when needed by the body.
6. **Attachment of Muscles** Bones in our body provides a surface for the attachment of the skeletal muscles. This bony system affords attachment for the soft parts, maintains them in right position, covers them, and helps to control and direct varying pressures to give stability to the shape and structure of the body.
7. **Leverage** The articulation of bones creates levers that change the magnitude and direction of the forces exerted by muscles. These help in doing work easily.

### Classification of Bones

On the basis of their shapes and formation, bones are classified into the following types

1. **Long Bones** These bones are found mainly in the upper and lower limbs, and act as a lever in our body which helps in making movements possible.
   They are primarily compact and have a large amount of a spongy material at the end. Long bones such as humerus and femur consists of a shaft and two extremities each.
   Some long bones present in our body are the Femur, Tibia, Fibula, etc.
2. **Short Bones** A short bone is one that is cube-like in shape, being approximately equal in length, width and thickness. Short bones provide stability and support as well as some amount of motion.
   The only short bones in the human skeleton are in the carpals of the wrists and the tarsals of the ankles.

3. **Flat Bones** Flat bones are thin, flattened and usually curved. They provide a large surface for muscle attachments and protect internal organs. Examples includes bones of the skull, the pelvis, the sternum and the scapulae.
4. **Irregular Bones** Irregular bones have complicated shapes. They are primarily spongy bones that are covered with a thin layer of compact bone. The vertebrae and some of the bones in the skull are irregular bones.
5. **Sesamoid Bones** These are small, round bones shaped like a sesame seed. These bones are found in tendons where a great deal of pressure is generated in a joint. The sesamoid bones protect tendons by helping them overcome compressive forces.

   They vary in number and placement from person to person, but are typically found in tendons associated with the feet, hands and knees.
6. **Sutural Bones** These are very small bones located within the sutural joints between the cranial bones. These are classified by their location and not by shape.

   The number of sutural bones varies considerably because different people have different numbers of sutural bones.

## Joints

The bones present in our body are joined by a network of tendons, ligaments and cartilages. The junction at which two or more bones are joined is called a joint. It is mainly a mechanism of movements in a hard and rigid skeleton.

The joints present in the human body are formed in such a way that they maintain a balance between the movement, stability and strength of the human skeleton.

### Types of Joints

In the study of joints (also called arthrology), joints are classified into various types on the basis of structural as well as functional basis.

These types are as follows

1. **Immovable Joints or Synarthrosis Joints** In this type, the bones are held together by means of fibrous tissue or ligaments. So, these joints are also called fibrous joints. Due to the presence of fibrous tissue, these joints are immovable. These joints are found in the skull and face.

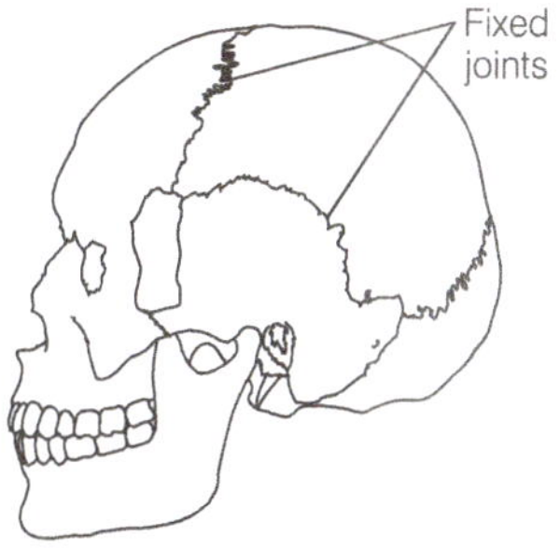


**Immovable Joints**

2. **Slightly Movable Joints or Amphiarthrosis Joints** These joints are slightly movable. A pad of cartilage lies between the bone surface and the fibrous capsule which holds the bone and cartilage in place. The cartilages of such joints also act as shock absorbers. For instance, intervertebral discs between the bodies of vertebrae strengthen the cartilage by extra collagen fibres.

   There are two types of such joints

   (i) **Synchrondrosis** It is a temporary form of joint that exist only while the skeleton is growing. These are replaced by bones once the skeleton grows completely. An example is the joint between first pair of ribs and the sternum.

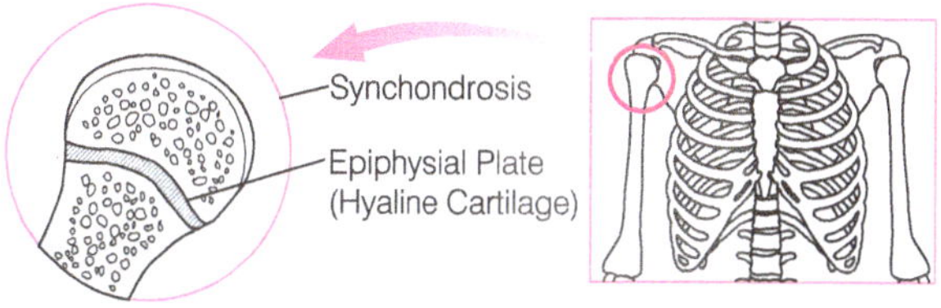


   (ii) **Symphysis** The joint consists of a compressible fibro-cartilage pad that connects two bones. This type of joint allows for some movement.

   The hip bones, connected by the pubic symphysis, and the vertebrae connected by inter-vertebral discs, are two examples of symphysis.

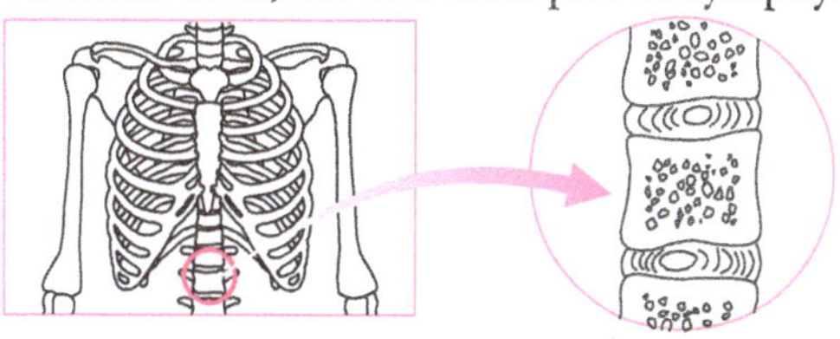


3. **Freely Movable Joints** These joints are also called as synovial joints. These joints include most of the joints present in the body. In freely movable joints, there is synovial cavity present between two ends of the bone which are covered with hyaline cartilage and are surrounded by a fibrous articular capsule.

The synovial cavity is filled with synovial fluid which helps hyaline cartilage to provide smooth surface for the opposing bones.

Further, these joints are supported by ligaments. The fluid covering the bone allow frictionless movement and protects the bones, while the ligaments gives elasticity and prevents injury.

As a result, these bones have a capacity to move freely.

The freely movable joints are further classified into six categories, which are as follows

(i) **Gliding Joint** These joints move against each other or glide on a single plane.

The ends of one of the gliding joints are slightly concave and the other is slightly convex.

These joints provide only gliding movements. Examples of such joints are bones of wrist and ankle.

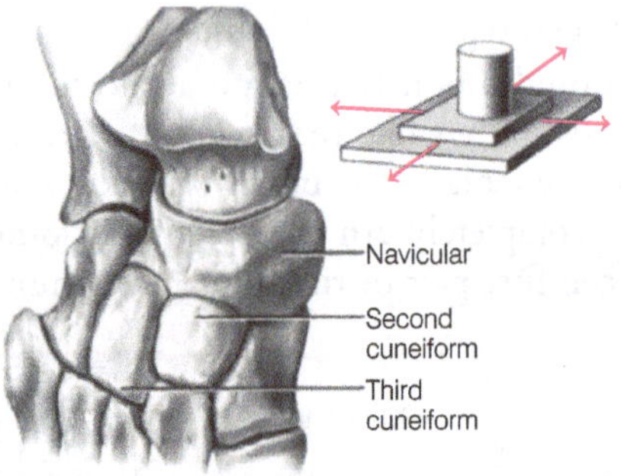


**Gliding Joint**

(ii) **Hinge Joints** In such joints, movement takes place on just one axis or direction, like a door on its hinges. One end of such joints has a concave shape while the other has convex, such that movement is possible only in one place.

The movements of these joints are called flexion and extension. Examples of such joints are joints present in elbow, fingers etc.

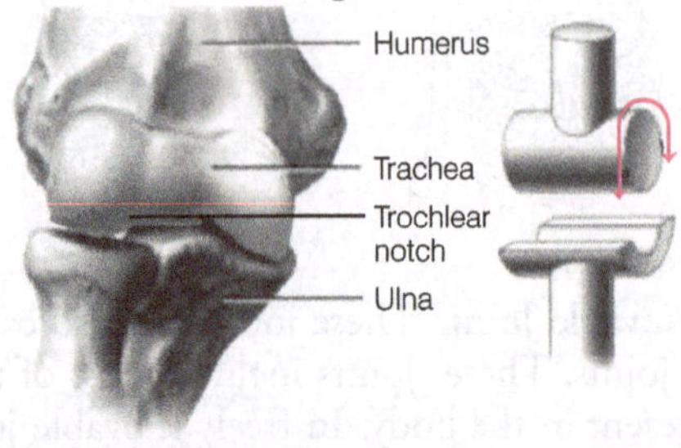


**Hinge Joint**

(iii) **Condyloid Joints** These joints are similar to hinge joints but they allow movement over two planes.

These joints permits flexion, extension and circular motion (adduction, abduction and circumduction)

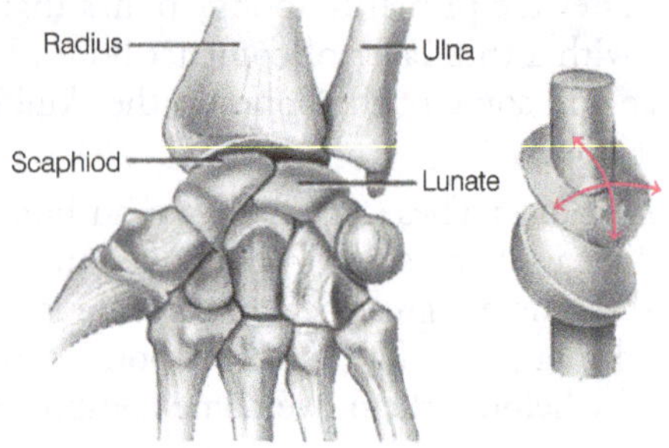


**Condyloid Joint**

(iv) **Saddle Joints** These joints allow for flexion, extension and other movements, but does not allow rotation.

An example is the thumb's saddle joint (between the carpal of the hand and metacarpal of the thumb). It lets the thumb cross over the palm and oppose the fingers.

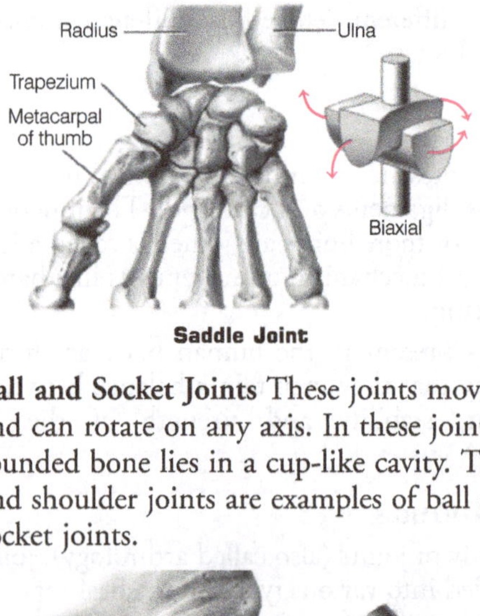


**Saddle Joint**

(v) **Ball and Socket Joints** These joints move freely and can rotate on any axis. In these joints, a rounded bone lies in a cup-like cavity. The hip and shoulder joints are examples of ball and socket joints.

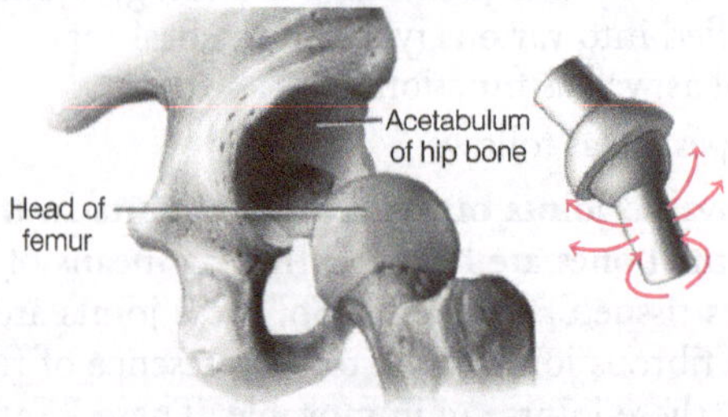


**Ball and Socket Joint**

(vi) **Pivot Joints** These are joints with a rotatory movement on one axis. In other words, a bone of cylindrical shape moves around a pivot within a ring made up of bone and cartilage.

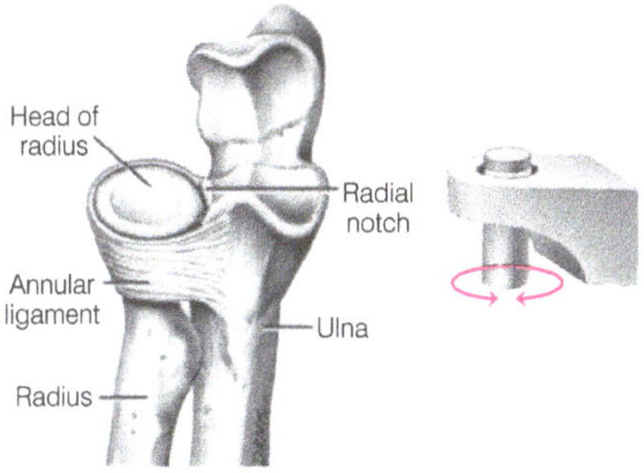


**Pivot Joint**

# Muscular System

Muscles are the soft tissues found in all living beings, which permit the movements of the body, maintains posture, and circulates blood throughout the body.

The human body comprises of mainly three types of muscles. These are as follows

1. **Smooth Muscles**

   These are the type of muscles that are not controlled by desire of a person and thus, are involuntary in nature.

   These muscles are found in the walls of our blood vessels, and in our hollow visceral organs such as stomach, urinary bladder, etc.

2. **Skeletal Muscles**

   These muscles move according to the will of an individual and thus, are voluntary in nature.

   These muscles are also called 'striated muscles' because of their appearance, which consists of light and darks bands visible under microscope.

   The muscles present in the abdomen are part of skeletal muscles.

3. **Cardiac Muscles**

   The muscles found only in the heart are known as cardiac muscles. These muscles forms the wall of the heart and help in pumping blood throughout the body while maintaining blood pressure. Such muscles are involuntary in nature.

## Properties of Muscles

Muscles present in the human body have some specific properties that enables them to perform various functions. These properties are as follows

1. **Contractility**

   Our muscles carry out a highly specialised function known as contraction. It is the ability to shorten and contract the muscle tissue when adequately stimulated. It leads to the opening of calcium channels.

2. **Excitability**

   It is the ability of the muscle cell to react to an electric stimulus. The stimulus activates the muscle so that it can contract. In other words, our muscles are enabled to respond to any kind of stimulus.

   Whenever a muscle recieves a stimulation, calcium is released into its cells which enables it to contract. If the muscular excitability in an individual is greater, its force, velocity and endurance properties will also be greater.

3. **Extensibility**

   It is the ability of the muscle to get stretched or extended. Muscles can be stretched even beyond their resting length when relaxed. This enables better mobility and range of motion.

4. **Elasticity**

   It is the ability of the muscle to return to its normal resting length after being stretched or contracted. This property enables the muscle to carry out its functions properly.

## Functions of the Muscles

The human body comprises of number of muscles categorised into the three main types *i.e.* smooth, skeletal and cardiac. Each type of muscle has its own specific function in our body.

Also, there are two types of skeletal muscle fibres, *namely,* red fibres and white fibres. They are also called slow twitch fibres and fast twitch fibres, respectively. These fibres also have different functions. The various functions that our muscles perform are as follows

1. **Allows Movement**

   The skeletal muscles in our body helps in the voluntary movement of the various body parts. While the bones act as levers, the muscles acts as the pulling force of as the levers.

2. **Maintains Posture**

   Muscles helps the tendons to take a proper shape and structure and thus helps to maintain posture.

3. **Smooth Functioning of the Organs**
The smooth muscles present in our bodies are essential for proper functioning of the organs. Therefore, the various processes in our body such as respiration, circulation, digestion, vision etc. are possible because of muscles.
4. **Protects Organs and Bones**
The muscles present in our abdomen and lower back help to protect vital organs such as the stomach, liver, etc. alongwith the bones with which they are attached.
5. **Regulates Temperature** Almost 85% of the heat that a person generates in their body comes from the high metabolic rate of digestive muscles. Hence, muscles are responsible for production and regulation of heat and energy.

# Respiratory System

The respiratory system is the body of organs that are involved in the process of breathing, commonly known as respiration.

In the process of respiration, we take Oxygen ($O_2$) from the environment and give out Carbon Dioxide ($CO_2$), a waste product, that is produced as a result of chemical changes within the cells of our body.

The process of respiration plays a vital role in our body. With oxygen going into our body cells, some chemical changes takes place which eliminates the carbon dioxide. Such a continuous inflow of oxygen and elimination of the $CO_2$ is essential for the normal functioning of our body.

In fact, respiration is a two fold process. It includes internal respiration and external respiration, which are as follows

1. **Internal or Cellular Respiration**
It is the process of exchange of respiratory gases between the blood and interstitial fluid surrounding the cells. Inside the cell, cellular respiration generates energy (ATP) using oxygen and glucose and produce $CO_2$.
2. **External Respiration**
It is the process of exchange of respiratory gases between the external environment and the lungs or between the alveoli of the lungs and the blood.
It consists of
   (i) **Pulmonary Ventilation** This is the process of the flowing of air into the lungs (inhalation) and out of the lungs (exhalation).
   (ii) **Gas Transport** This is carried out by the cardiovascular system by distributing the inhaled oxygen throughout the body, collecting $CO_2$ from the cells and returning it to the lungs.

## Structure of Respiratory System

There are three major parts of the respiratory system which play a vital role in respiration.

These are

- The **airways** (nose, mouth, pharynx, larynx etc.) allow air to enter the body and into the lungs.
- The **lungs** work to pass oxygen into the body and remove carbon dioxide from the body.
- The **muscles of respiration**, such as the diaphragm, work to pump air in and out of the lungs while breathing.

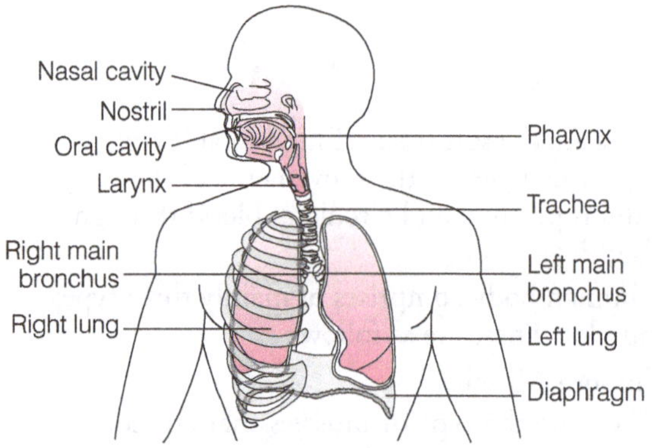


**Structure of Respiratory System**

The organs that take part in the process of respiration are

1. **Nose** The nose is the primary opening for the respiratory system made of bone, muscle and cartilage. It consists of two parts
   (i) **External Features** It is composed of a triangular framework of bone and cartilage covered by skin. On the inner side of the nose, there are two oval shaped openings called nostrils.
   (ii) **Internal or Nasal Cavities** These are two cavities separated by a septum or partition. At the entrance, each cavity or vestibule has numerous hair. The hair in the cavities serve as a filter to trap dust particles that may be taken in with the inhaled air.
2. **Mouth** It is the oral cavity and a secondary exterior opening for the respiratory system. Most commonly, the majority of respiration is achieved *via* the nose and nasal cavity, but the mouth can be used if needed.

3. **Pharynx** It is located in the back part of the nose. It is also called the throat. The pharynx is a funnel of muscle that opens through the larynx region into the trachea.

   The air that enters through the nasal cavity or the oral cavity, passes through the pharynx into the larynx by the epiglottis, so that the air enter the trachea.

4. **Larynx** It is the vocal sac or voice box located just below the pharynx, in the front portion of the neck. Mainly composed of cartilage and two pairs of membranes, the larynx is primarily a short section of airway that connects the pharynx with the trachea.

   As the air passes through the larynx, it vibrates the vocal chords which produces sound.

5. **Trachea** It is also called as wind pipe. It is a cylindrical tube made of hyaline cartilage rings. The length of the trachea is about 10-12 cm and diameter 2 to 2.5 cm. It lies in front of the oesophagus and extends from the larynx. Then it gets divided into two bronchi, one for each lung.

   The trachea is supported by 16-20 cartilaginous rings. These rings prevent the trachea from collapsing when no air is present in it and also provide flexibility and strength.

   There is a valve in the trachea on the side of the mouth known as epiglottis, which prevents the entry of food into the trachea.

6. **Bronchi** The bronchi are two tubes branching off the end of the trachea. Each tube is connected to a lung. The right bronchus is shorter, wider and more vertical than the left bronchus. Both the bronchi enter their respective lungs and then divide into smaller bronchi which are known as bronchioles or bronchial tubes.

   The main function of the Bronchi and the Bronchioles is to carry air from the trachea into the lungs.

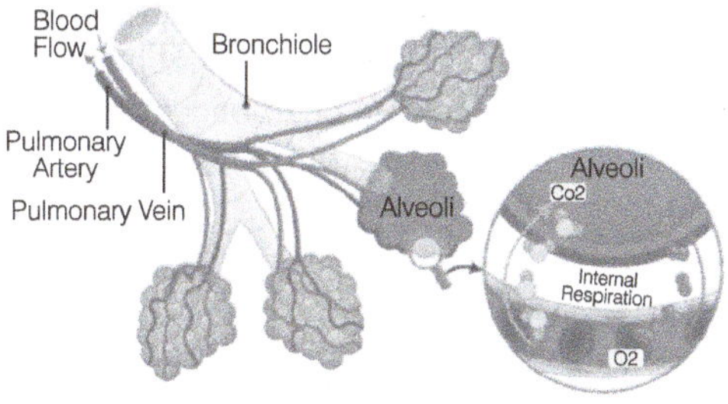


**Bronchi**

7. **Alveoli** The bronchioles end in blind air sacs called alveoli. Alveoli are hollow, individual cavities that are found within alveolar sacs. Oxygen and carbon dioxide easily diffuse across the tissue of the alveoli, thus making it the site of gaseous exchange.

8. **Lungs** These are the main organs of the respiratory system. Lungs are a pair of large, spongy organs that are located inside the thorax on both, left and right side.

   They are cone-shaped organs with the apex above. They are surrounded by a membrane that provides them with enough space to expand during inhalation.

   The Bronchi carry the air into lobes of the lungs. The lungs are divided into lobes by fissures. The left lung has two lobes and the right lung has three lobes. The base of the lungs lies resting on the floor of the thoracic cavity on the diaphragm.

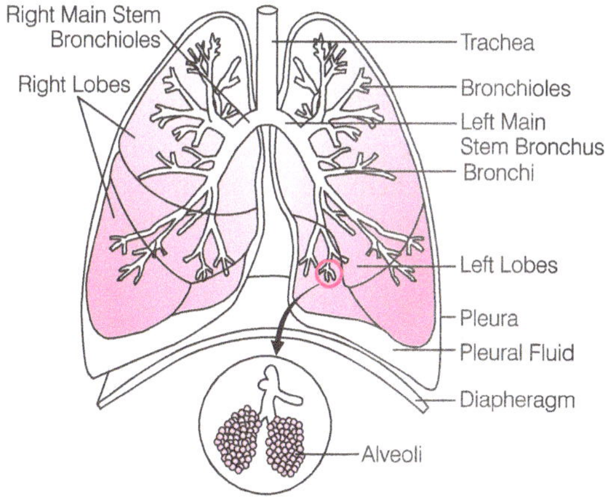


**Lungs**

9. **Diaphragm** The diaphragm is an important muscle of respiration which is situated beneath the lungs. It extends across the entire ribcage.

   The diaphragm separates the thoracic cavity (heart, lungs and ribs) from the abdominal cavity and performs an important function in respiration.

   When it contracts, the volume of the thoracic cavity increases and air is drawn into the lungs.

## Functions of Respiratory System

The primary function of the respiratory system is the exchange of gases, *i.e.* $O_2$ and $CO_2$ at both, internal and external levels.

The exchange of gases takes place through two process, namely inspiration or inhalation and expiration or exhalation of air.

Both these processes result in the process of oxygenation of blood and excretion of $CO_2$.

These processes are as follows

- **Oxygenation of the Blood** With inhalation, oxygen enters the lungs which supplies it to the organs of the body for usage.
- **Excretion of the Carbondioxide** ($CO_2$) $CO_2$ is a waste product for our body which is produced by the metabolic breakdown of carbohydrates.

  Excess of $CO_2$ in the body can be fatal, thus it needs to be excreted. So, when oxygenated blood comes to the cells, they exchange $CO_2$ for $O_2$. Then, the $CO_2$ is released by exhalation.

Apart from the primary function of breathing, respiratory organs are also used in some other processes.

These are as follows

- **Production of Sound** Vibration produced in the larynx during inhalation results in the production of sound.
- **Sense of Smell** The nasal cavities have olfactory fibres that sense certain chemicals in the inhaled air. These fibres then send a signal to the brain which identifies a particular smell.

# Circulatory System

The circulatory system is also known as the cardiovascular or the vascular system.

It is a group of organs that circulates bloods and transports nutrients such as amino acids, electrolytes, oxygen, carbon dioxide, hormones and blood cells to and from all the parts of the body.

It is a vast network of organs and blood vessels that acts both as a delivery and waste removal system for the body.

The circulatory system is divided into two seperate loops, that are as follows

1. **Pulmonary Circuit** It exchanges blood between the heart and lungs for oxygenation.
2. **Systematic Circuit** It distributes blood throughout all the other systems and tissues of the body.

## Structure of Circulatory System

The circulatory system consists of three main parts, *i.e.* the heart, the blood vessels and blood itself.

These are described as follows

### Heart

It is a hollow, muscular cone-shaped organ without which we cannot survive. As the only organ of the circulatory organ, the heart is responsible for pumping blood throughout the body.

Heart is located just under the rib cage, between the lungs, inclined towards the left, and is about the size of a closed fist which weighs about 300 gms. In a day, the heart beats about 15,200 times.

### Structure of the Heart

The heart is enclosed in an outer layer called the pericardium. Under this layer, the heart muscles called the 'myocardium' is situated.

The heart is divided into two sides/parts by a septum. Each side is further sub-divided into two chambers. The upper chambers are called atrium or auricles and the lower chambers are called ventricles.

Therefore, the heart is divided in four chambers.

They are as follows

1. **Right Atrium** It receives blood containing carbon dioxide from the veins and passes it to the right ventricle.
2. **Right Ventricle** It receives blood from the right atrium and pumps it to the lungs, where carbon dioxide is removed from it and it is loaded with oxygen.
3. **Left Atrium** It receives oxygenated blood from the lungs and passes it to the left ventricle.
4. **Left Ventricle** It is the strongest chamber and pumps oxygen-rich blood to the rest of the body. The left ventricle's vigorous contractions create what we know as the blood pressure.

It is to be noted here that the atriums have thin and less muscular walls than the ventricles. They are smaller and are the recieving chambers of the blood. Ventricles are large muscular pumping chambers that push the blood for circulation.

Further, the right atrium and the right ventricle are smaller than the adjacent chambers on the left. They have less muscle in their walls compared to the left side of the heart.

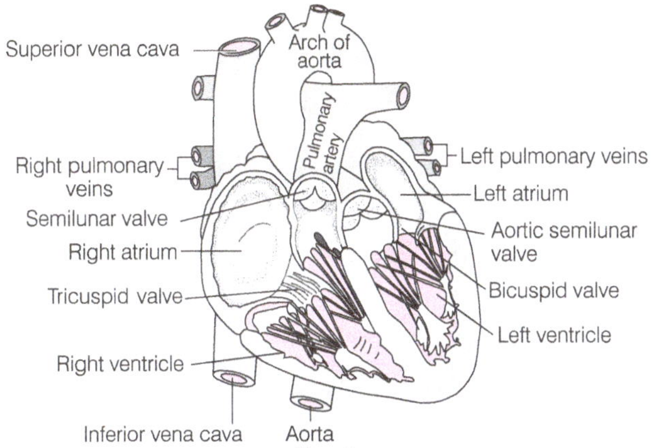

**Heart**

The difference in size is due to their functions. Blood from the right side of the heart goes for pulmonary circulation while blood from the left chambers is pumped to the rest of the body.

The communication between auricle/atrium and ventricle is controlled by atrio-ventricular valves. The heart consists of four values which allow the flow of blood in only one direction.

These valves are

1. **Right Atrioventricular Valve** It is also called tricuspid valve. This value is situated between the right auricle and right ventricle and allows the blood to flow from right auricle to right ventricle only.
2. **Left Atrioventricular Valve** It is also called the mitral valve and allows the blood to flow from left auricle to left ventricle only.
3. **Pulmonary Valve** It is situated between right ventricle and pulmonary artery and allows the blood to flow from right ventricle to lungs only.
4. **Aortic Valve** It is situated between the left ventricle and aorta and allows blood to flow from left ventricle to different parts of body only.

## Blood Vessels

These are the passages that allow blood to flow quickly from the heart to every region of the body and back again. The size of blood vessels corresponds to the amount of blood that passes through them. They contain a hollow area known as the lumen in which blood flows. The size of the lumen wall depends upon the type of the blood vessels.

Based on their structure and function, blood vessels are classified into three main categories, which are as follows

1. **Arteries** These are blood vessels that carry blood away from the heart. Blood carried by arteries is oxygenated, except pulmonary artery that carries deoxygenated blood.

   The walls of the arteries are thicker, elastic, and more muscular than other vessels to withstand this pressure. The largest arteries of the body contain a high percentage of elastic tissue that allows them to stretch and accommodate the pressure of the heart.

   The largest artery is the 'aorta' which is connected to the left ventricle. The aorta branches off into smaller, more muscular arteries.

   These smaller arteries contract or expand to regulate the flow of blood through their lumen. A smaller artery passes blood according to the requirement of the body. At the end of each artery, the smallest artery called arterioles are present. The arterioles are narrow arteries that carry blood to the capillaries.
2. **Veins** These are the blood vessels that carry blood from various body parts towards the heart. Very similar to arteries, veins are much thinner, less elastic and less muscular than the arteries. They tend to collapse when not filled with blood.

   The smallest veins are called venules. Venules collect blood from the capillaries of the organs and deposit it into the veins that gets larger near the heart.

The veins of the body have valves to prevent the blood from flowing backwards. The legs have more valves than the upper body.

3. **Capillaries** These are the smallest, thinnest and most common type of blood vessels in the body. Capillaries connect to arterioles on one end and venules on the other.

   They carry blood very close to the cells of the tissues of the body in order to exchange gases, nutrients and waste products. Capillaries consist of only a thin layer of endothelium which acts as a filter.

   The arteriole end of the capillaries have a smooth muscle called precapillary sphincters, that regulate the blood flow in the tissue. It makes sure that there is a free flow of blood into active tissues and limited flow into inactive tissues.

**Blood**

It is a specialised body fluid that actually performs the function of the circulatory system. It delivers the necessary nutrients and oxygen to the tissues and organs of the body. It is also responsible for carrying the waste products for excretion. There are four components of blood. They are as follows

- Red Blood Cells (RBCs) which carries oxygen to the tissues.
- White Blood Cells (WBCs) which fights all infections and diseases.
- Platelets which helps the blood to clot in case of wounds and injuries.
- Plasma carries the blood cells, nutrients and waste products.

## Functions of Circulatory System

The circulatory system is responsible for performing various functions. They are as follows

1. **Transportation** It transports blood to almost all of the body's tissues. The blood delivers essential nutrients and oxygen into the cells of the body. It removes wastes and carbondioxide from the body. Hormones are transported throughout the body via the blood's liquid plasma.

   This process of transportation takes place through two seperate circulatory processes as discussed below

   (i) **Pulmonary Circulation** It allows the oxygenation of the blood. The blood flows from right side of the heart through pulmonary artery to the lungs where the blood is oxygenated and $CO_2$ is removed.

   This blood then comes back to left side of the heart through pulmonary veins.

   (ii) **Systematic Circulation** It allows circulation of the oxygenated blood between heart and body's tissues. The left side of the heart, after receiving oxygenated blood, pumps it out through the aorta to all the body parts. After deoxygenation of blood, it goes back to the right side of the heart through superior and inferior vena cava.

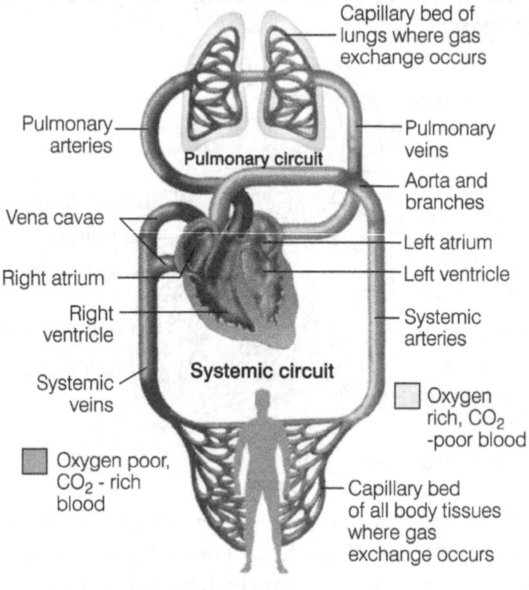


**Circulatory System**

2. **Protection** It protects the body from various diseases. The WBCs clean up cellular debris and fight pathogens that have entered the body. Platelets and red blood cells form scabs (known as 'blood clots') to seal wounds and prevent pathogens from entering the body and liquids from leaking out.
3. **Regulation** It is an instrument in the body to maintain homeostatic control of several internal conditions. Blood vessels help maintain a stable body temperature by controlling the blood flow to the surface of the skin.
4. **Nutrition** The circulatory system carries the nutrients and essential vitamins, minerals, amino acids as well as glucose to all parts of the body.

   As the blood goes through the small intestine, these nutrients enters the blood stream for its further use.

# CHAPTER PRACTICE

## OBJECTIVE TYPE QUESTIONS

### Multiple Choice Questions (MCQs)

**1** How many physiological systems are there in a human body?
(a) 4 (b) 9
(c) 6 (d) 10

*Ans* (b) 9

**2** Which of the following is a requirement for a long distance runner?
(a) Good cardiovascular endurance
(b) Good strength
(c) Good height
(d) All of the above

*Ans* (a) Good cardiovascular endurance

**3** Which of the following is not an Axial Skeletal bone?
(a) Ribs (b) Skull
(c) Upper limbs (d) Vertebral column

*Ans* (c) Upper limbs

**4** Which type of bone generally acts a lever?
(a) Short bones (b) Flat bones
(c) Sesamoid bones (d) Long bones

*Ans* (d) Long bones

**5** The joint found in our skull are
(a) Synarthrosis joints (b) Amphiarthrosis joints
(c) Synchrondrosis (d) Synovial joints

*Ans* (a) Synarthrosis joints

**6** The length of the trachea is about
(a) 14 cm (b) 9 cm
(c) 10-12 cm (d) 13 cm

*Ans* (c) 10-12 cm

**7** Which of the following is not a part of the circulatory system?
(a) Heart (b) Lungs
(c) Blood (d) Blood vessels

*Ans* (b) Lungs

**8** The weight of the heart is ......... .
(a) 100 gms (b) 300 gms
(c) 200 gms (d) 400 gms

*Ans* (b) 300 gms

### Fill in the Blanks

**9** Human skeletal system consists of ........... bones.

*Ans* 206

**10** The pelvis, the sternum and the scapulae are examples of ......... .

*Ans* flat bones

**11** The study of joints is called ......... .

*Ans* arthrology

**12** Synovial liquids helps in ......... .

*Ans* reducing friction between bones.

### State True or False

**13** Sutural bones are classified according to their shape.

*Ans* False. Sutural bones are classified according to their location.

**14** Intervertebral disc is a synarthroics joint.

*Ans* False. Intervertebral disc is a amphiarthrosis joint.

**15** Glycosis is a process of generating energy and $CO_2$.

*Ans* True

**16** Blood is responsible for maintaining the temperature of the body.

*Ans* True

**17** Identify the joint from the picture given below.

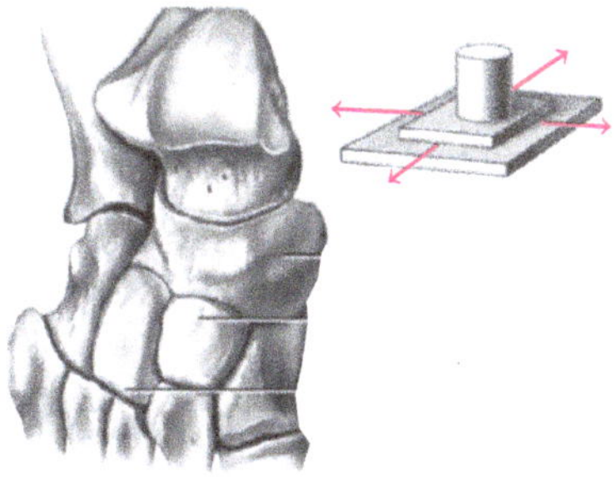

(a) Gliding joint (b) Hinge joint
(c) Condyloid joint (d) Saddle joint

*Ans* (a) Gliding joint

## Match the Following

**18**

| | List I (Name of Bone) | | List II (Number of Bone) |
|---|---|---|---|
| A. | Ribs | (i) | 26 |
| B. | Vertebral Column | (ii) | 1 |
| C. | Sternum | (iii) | 64 |
| D. | Upper limbs | (iv) | 24 |

**Codes**

| | A | B | C | D | | A | B | C | D |
|---|---|---|---|---|---|---|---|---|---|
| (a) | (iv) | (i) | (ii) | (iii) | (b) | (i) | (ii) | (iv) | (iii) |
| (c) | (i) | (iii) | (iv) | (ii) | (d) | (iv) | (i) | (iii) | (ii) |

*Ans* (a)

**19**

| | List I | | |
|---|---|---|---|
| A. | Short bone | (i) | Knee |
| B. | Irregular bone | (ii) | Femur |
| C. | Sesamoid bone | (iii) | Wrist |
| D. | Long bone | (iv) | Vertebrae |

**Codes**

| | A | B | C | D | | A | B | C | D |
|---|---|---|---|---|---|---|---|---|---|
| (a) | (i) | (ii) | (iii) | (iv) | (b) | (ii) | (iii) | (iv) | (i) |
| (c) | (iii) | (iv) | (i) | (ii) | (d) | (iv) | (i) | (ii) | (iii) |

*Ans* (c)

## Assertion-Reason

**20** **Assertion** (A) Human anatomy and physiology helps in the selection of proper sports person for different sports.
**Reason** (R) Human anatomy and physiology easily charaterises the body of an individual.

In the context of above two statements, which one of the following is correct?

**Codes**
(a) Both A and R are true and R is the correct explanation of A
(b) Both A and R are true, but R is not the correct explanation of A
(c) A is true, but R is false
(d) A is false, but R is true

*Ans* (a) Both A and R are true and R is the correct explanation of A

**21** **Assertion** (A) Human body is made up of 306 bones.
**Reason** (R) Skeletal system helps in production of Red blood cells.
In the context of above two statements, which one of the following is correct?

**Codes**
(a) Both A and R are true and R is the correct explanation of A
(b) Both A and R are true, but R is not the correct explanation of A
(c) A is true, but R is false
(d) A is false, but R is true

*Ans* (d) A is false, but R is true

**22** **Assertion** (A) Tendon, ligament and cartileges forms joints in the body.
**Reason** (R) Smooth muscles are not controlled by desire of a person.
In the context of above two statements, which one of the following is correct?

**Codes**
(a) Both A and R are true and R is the correct explanation of A
(b) Both A and R are true, but R is not the correct explanation of A
(c) A is true, but R is false
(d) A is false, but R is true

*Ans.* (b) Both A and R are true, but R is not the correct explanation of A

**23** **Assertion** (A) Heart is also part of circulatory system.
**Reason** (R) Veins are the smallest and most common type of blood vessels in the body.
In the context of above two statements, which one of the following is correct?

**Codes**
(a) Both A and R are true and R is the correct explanation of A
(b) Both A and R are true, but R is not the correct explanation of A
(c) A is true, but R is false
(d) A is false, but R is true

*Ans.* (c) A is true, but R is false

## C VERY SHORT ANSWER TYPE QUESTIONS

**24** What is anatomy?

*Ans* Anatomy is the branch of biology which is concerned with the study of the structure (mainly internal body structure) and shape of an organism or living being.

**25** What do you understand by physiology?

*Ans* Physiology is the branch of biology which deals with the functions and activities of living organisms and their mutual relationships. Infact, it is the study of the all mechanical, physical and biochemical processes that support the human body.

**26** What are short bones?

*Ans* Short bones are cube-like in shape, being approximately equal in length, width and thickness. They provide stability, support and some amount of motion. They are located in carpals of the wrists and tarsals of the ankles.

**27** Where are flat bones found?

*Ans* Flat bones are found as a covering of internal organs to protect them. For example, bones of the skull, the pelvis, the sternum and the scapulae.

**28** What do you understand by joints?

*Ans* Joints are the junctions between two or more bones or cartilages formed in such way that they maintain a balance between the movement, stability and strength of the human skeleton.

**29** What do you understand by synchrondosis?

*Ans* It is a temporary and almost immovable cartilaginous joint between bones bound by a layer of cartilage.

**30** How many types of joints are there?

*Ans* There are three types of joints

(i) Immovable joints
(ii) Slightly movable joints
(iii) Movable joints

**31** What do you mean by respiration?

*Ans* Respiration is a process to inhale oxygen and exhale carbon dioxide from our body.

**32** State what you know about the pharynx in the respiratory system in one sentence.

*Ans* The pharynx, also known as the throat, is a funnel of muscle that extends from the respiratory openings to the oesophagus and larynx.

**33** Where are alveoli found?

*Ans* Alveoli are hollow individual cavities that are found within alveolar sacs in the lungs.

**34** Write the name of the organs involved in respiration.

*Ans* The organs which are involved in respiration are nose, mouth, pharynx, larynx, trachea, bronchi, alveoli, diaphragm and lungs.

**35** What is the role of the mouth in the process of respiration?

*Ans* The mouth is an oral cavity which is a secondary exterior opening for the respiratory system. Most commonly, the majority of respiration is achieved *via* the nose and nasal cavity, but the mouth can also be used if needed.

**36** What is the function of the left atrium?

*Ans* The left atrium receives oxygenated blood from the lungs and sends it to the left ventricle.

**37** What are blood vessels?

*Ans* Blood vessels are the passages that allow the blood to flow quickly from the heart to every region of the body and come back to the heart again.

**38** What are precapillary sphincters?

*Ans* Precapillary sphincters are smooth muscle found at the arteriole end of capillaries. These muscle regulate the amount of blood that will go into active or inactive tissue.

## SHORT ANSWER TYPE QUESTIONS

**39** Briefly write any two reasons for the importance of anatomy.

*Ans* Two reasons for the importance of anatomy are

(i) **It Prevents Sports Injuries** Proper knowledge about the interrelated functioning of bones, muscles, tendons and ligaments helps in designing better protective equipment for the soft and delicate organs of the body.

Thus, sports related injuries like fracture, dislocation, contusion, sprain etc may be prevented by proper use of such equipment by sportspersons.

(ii) **It Speeds up Rehabilitation from Sports Injuries** Knowledge of the human anatomy helps in the speedy rehabilitation of sportspersons from injuries, if they occur. Initially, proper first-aid must be provided, for which knowledge of human anatomy is essential, otherwise the injury may worsen.

Further, knowledge of the physical structure, bones, joints, ligaments etc helps in design of better rehabilitation pro- grammes from injuries over the long-term.

**40** Explain in brief the Amphiarthrosis joints.

*Ans* Amphiarthrosis joints are slightly movable joints. A pad of cartilage lies between the bone surface and the fibrous capsule which holds the bone and the cartilage in place.

There are two types of such joints

(i) **Synchrondrosis** These are temporary form of joints that exist only while the skeleton is growing. It becomes a bone as the skeleton grows completely. For instance, the first pair of ribs and the sternum.

(ii) **Symphysis** These joints consists of a compressible fibro-cartilage pad that connects two bones allowing some movement. The hip bone is one example of such a joint.

**41** Write a short note on the respiratory system.

*Ans* The respiratory system is a body of organs that are involved in the process of breathing commonly known as respiration. Respiratory system includes various organs starting from the nose, mouth, trachea, bronchi, lungs etc. that work together for the proper and effective functioning of the body.

In the process of respiration, we take oxygen ($O_2$) from the environment and give out carbon dioxide ($CO_2$), a waste product.

Infact, the respiration is a part of a two-fold process as follows

(i) **Internal Respiration** It is the process of gas exchange between the blood and the interstitial fluids surrounding the cells. Inside the cell, cellular respiration generates energy (ATP) using $O_2$ and glucose and produces $CO_2$.

(ii) **External Respiration** It is the process of gas exchange between the atmosphere and the body tissues. In order to accomplish this task, the following events occur

(a) **Pulmonary Ventilation** It is the process of breathing, *i.e.* inhalation and expiration.

(b) **Gas Transport** It is carried out by the cardiovascular system. It is the process of distributing oxygen throughout the body and collecting carbon dioxide to return it to the lungs.

**42** Explain the three types of blood vessels in the human body.

*Ans* Blood vessels are the passages that allow blood to flow quickly from the heart to every region of the body and back again. They contain hollow area known as the lumen in which blood flows. The size of the lumen wall depends upon the type of the blood vessels. Based on their structure and function, blood vessels are classified into three main categories, which are as follows

(i) **Arteries** These are blood vessels that carry blood away from the heart. Blood carried by arteries is oxygenated, except pulmonary artery that carries deoxygenated blood. The walls of the arteries are thicker, elastic and more muscular than other vessels to withstand this pressure.

(ii) **Veins** These are the blood vessels that carry blood from various body parts towards the heart. Very similar to arteries, veins are much thinner, less elastic and less muscular than the arteries. They tend to collapse when not filled with blood.

(iii) **Capillaries** These are the smallest, thinnest and most common type of blood vessels in the body. Capillaries connect to arterioles on one end and venules on the other.

They carry blood very close to the cells of the tissues of the body in order to exchange gases, nutrients and waste products.

**43** Write a short note on blood as a part of circulatory system.

*Ans* Blood is one of the three parts of the circulatory system. It is a specialised fluid that actually performs the function of the circulatory system. It delivers the necessary nutrients and oxygen to the tissues and organs of the body. It is also responsible for carrying the waste products for excretion.

Blood is composed of four components that are

- Red Blood Cells or RBC's which carries oxygen to the tissues.
- White Blood Cells or WBC's which fights all infections and diseases.
- Platelets which helps the blood to clot in cases of wounds and injuries.
- Plasma which carries the blood cells, nutrients and waste products.

## LONG ANSWER TYPE QUESTIONS

**44** Elucidate five reasons for the importance of physiology.

*Ans* Five reasons for the importance of physiology are

(i) **Helps in Designing Better Training Sessions** A physical trainer can design better training sessions for sportspersons by knowing their physiological capacities and limitations. If training sessions are not designed keeping this knowledge in mind, it can even harm the sportsperson.

(ii) **Knowledge about Chemical Changes can Improve Performance** A number of chemical changes take place in our body during exercise or participating in sports. Human physiology provides detailed knowledge of these changes.

On the basis of this knowledge, a proper diet can be designed for the sportsperson concerned, so that his performance can be improved.

(iii) **Preventing Sports Injuries and Speedy Rehabilitation** Proper knowledge of the functioning of the bones, muscles, tendons and ligaments helps in designing better protective equipment for the soft and delicate organs of the body.

Knowledge of anatomy also helps in the speedy recovery of the sportspersons from injuries.

(iv) **Understanding Differences between Males and Females** With the knowledge of anatomy and physiology, and difference between males and females can be understood properly.

This knowledge of anatomical and physiological differences between males and females helps in designing proper sport and training programmes for both genders.

(v) **Understanding Environmental Effects on Sportspersons** To understand effect of the environment on sportspersons, we must have good knowledge of their physiology.

How and what type of problems a sportsperson is facing can be found by knowing the physiological changes that occur in their bodies.

For instance, when training or competing at a high altitude, where the air is rarefied, the red blood cell count goes up, unused air sacs in the lungs are activated and heart and respiratory rates go up.

The effects of these changes can be studied better with proper knowledge of human physiology.

**45** Highlight any five functions of the skeletal system in the human body.

*Ans* The functions of the skeletal system in the human body are

(i) **Support** Bones of the skeletal system provide structural support to the entire human body.

(ii) **Protection** The skeleton provides mechanical protection for internal organs of the body. It reduces the risk of injury to the body. Most of the soft tissues of the body are protected by bony structures.

For instance, cranial bones of the skull protect the brain, vertebrae protect the spinal cord and the ribcage protects the heart and lungs.

(iii) **Movement** Skeletal muscles are attached to bones. They bring about voluntary movement of the various body parts.

(iv) **Production of Blood Cells** The skeletal system assists in production of red blood cells in the bone marrows present in the long bones.

(v) **Storage of Minerals** Bone tissues store several minerals, including calcium and phosphorus. Bones release minerals into the blood whenever it is required to facilitate the balance of minerals in the body. These minerals are released into the bloodstream when needed by the body.

**46** Write notes on the following

(i) Long bones
(ii) Irregular bones
(iii) Sesamoid bones
(iv) Short bones
(v) Flat bones

*Ans* (i) **Long Bones** These bones are found mainly in the upper and the lower limbs, and act as a lever in our body which helps in making movements possible.

They are primarily compact and have a spongey material at the end. Long bones such as humerus and femur consists of a shaft and two extremities each. Some long bones present in our body are the femur, the tibia, the fibula etc.

(ii) **Irregular Bones** These bones have complicated shapes. They are primarily spongy bones that are covered with a thin layer of compact bone. The vertebrae and some of the bones in the skull are irregular bones.

(iii) **Sesamoid Bones** These are small, round bones shaped like a sesame seed. These bones are found in tendons where a great deal of pressure is generated in a joint.

The sesamoid bones protect tendons by helping them to overcome the compressive forces. They vary in number and placement from person to person, but are typically found in tendons associated with the feet, hands and knees.

(iv) **Short Bones** A short bone is one that is cube-like in shape, being approximately equal in length, width and thickness.

Short bones provide stability and support as well as some amount of motion. The only short bones in the human skeleton are in the carpals of the wrists and the tarsals of the ankles.

(v) **Flat Bones** Flat bones are thin, flattened and usually curved. They provide a large surface for muscle attachments and protect internal organs. Examples includes bones of the skull, the pelvis, the sternum and the scapulae.

**47** What are Diarthrosis joints of the human body? Explain their types briefly.

*Ans* Diarthrosis joints or synovial joints are freely movable joints that are most commonly present in a human body. These joints are covered by a hyaline cartilage which is a thin membrane filled with synovian fluid.

These joints are supported by ligaments that provide it with elasticity and prevents all injuries. The Diarthrosis joints are classified into further categories that are

(i) **Gliding Joints** These joints move against each other or glide on a single plane. The ends of one of the gliding joints are slightly concave and other is slightly convex. Bones of wrists and ankles are example of such joints.

(ii) **Hinge Joints** In such joints, movement takes place on just one axis or direction like a door on its hinges. One end of such joints has a concave shape while other has convex which allows movement only in one place. Such joints are present in elbow, fingers etc.

(iii) **Condyloid Joints** These joints allow for circular motion, flexion and extension. The wrist joint between the radius and the carpal bones is an example of a condyloid joint.

(iv) **Saddle Joints** These joints allow flexion, extension and other movements, but does not allow rotation. The joint between the carpal of the hand and the metacarpal of the thumb is one such joint.

(v) **Ball and Socket Joints** These joints move freely and can rotate on any axis. In these joints, a rounded bone lies in a cup-like cavity. The hip and shoulder joints are examples of ball and socket joints.

(vi) **Pivot Joints** These are joints with a rotatory movement on one axis. In other words, a bone of cylindrical shape moves around a pivot within a ring made of bones and cartilage.

**48** Elaborate the structure of the respiratory system with the help of a diagram.

*Ans* The various organs of respiratory system, which play a vital role in respiration are as follows

(i) **Nostrils** These are a pair of slits at the lower end of the nose which open into the nasal chamber through the nasal passage.

(ii) **Nasal Chambers** These are the pair of passages located at the back of nostrils just above the mouth cavity. Nasal septum is a median partition that separates the two chambers.

(iii) **Pharynx** It is a funnel of muscle that opens through the larynx into the trachea. The air that enters through the nose passes through the pharynx.

(iv) **Larynx** It is the voice box that is located just below the pharynx. It is the upper part of trachea that connects the pharynx to the trachea.

(v) **Trachea** It is a thin-walled tube, about 10-12 cm long and 2.5 cm wide. It extends up to the mid-thoracic cavity. It passes air to the alveoli in the lungs.

(vi) **Bronchi** The bronchi are two tubes branching off the end of the trachea. Each tube is connected to a lung. The right bronchus is shorter, wider and more vertical than the left bronchus.

Both the bronchi enter their respective lungs and then divide into smaller bronchi which are known as bronchioles or bronchial tubes.

(vii) **Alveoli** The bronchioles end in blind air sacs called alveoli. Alveoli are hollow, individual cavities that are found within alveolar sacs.

(viii) **Lungs** A pair of lungs are located inside the thorax on the left and right sides. They are surrounded by a membrane that provides them with enough space to expand when they fill with air.

(ix) **Diaphragm** The diaphragm is an important muscle of respiration which is situated beneath the lungs. It extends across the entire ribcage.

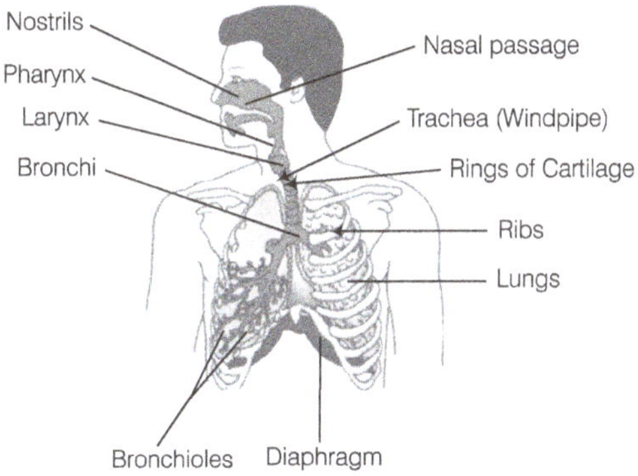


**Respiratory System**

**49** Explain the function of the respiratory system.

*Ans* The primary function of the respiratory system is the exchange of gases, *i.e.* $O_2$ and $CO_2$ at both, internal as well as external levels.

The exchange of gases takes place through two processes namely inspiration and expiration.

Both these processes result in the process of oxygenation of blood and excretion of the $CO_2$. These processes are as follows

(i) **Oxygenation of the Blood** With inspiration or inhalation, oxygen enters the lungs which supplies it to the organs of the body for usage.

(ii) **Excretion of the Carbon Dioxide** $CO_2$ is a waste product for our body which is produced by the metabolic breakdown of carbohydrates.

Excess of $CO_2$ in the body can be fatal, thus it needs to be excreted. So when oxygenated blood comes to the cells, they exchange $CO_2$ for $O_2$. Then, the $CO_2$ is released by exhalation.

Apart from this primary functions, the respiratory organs are also involved in performing other functions.

They are as follows

(i) **Production of Sound** The vibration produced in the larynx during inhalation results in the production of sound.

(ii) **Sense of Smell** The nasal cavities have some olfactory fibres that sense certain chemicals in the inhaled air. Then, it send a signal to the brain which recognises the chemical as a smell.

**50** Explain the functions of each of the four chambers and valves present in the heart.

*Ans* A human heart is divided into two sides by a Septum. Each of these sides are further divided into two chambers.

The upper chambers are called the atrium which are the parts of the heart with thin, less muscular walls. They are smaller and are the recieving chambers of blood while the lower parts are called ventricles.

Ventricles are the large muscular pumping chambers that push the blood for circulation.

Therefore, there are four chambers in the heart, which are as follows alongwith their functions

(i) **Right Atrium** It receives blood containing carbon dioxide from the veins and passes it to the right ventricle.

(ii) **Right Ventricle** It receives blood from the right atrium and pumps it to the lungs, where carbon dioxide is removed from it and it is loaded with oxygen.

(iii) **Left Atrium** It receives oxygenated blood from the lungs and passes it to the left ventricle.

(iv) **Left Ventricle** It is the strongest chamber of the heart. It pumps oxygen-rich blood to the rest of the body. The left ventricle's vigorous contractions create what we know as the blood pressure.

The communication between the atriums and the ventricles is controlled by four atrioventricular valves that allow the blood to flow in only one direction. These valves are

(i) **Right Atrioventricular Valve** It is also called as the triscupid valve. This valve is situated between the right auricle and right ventricle. It allows the blood to flow from right auricle to right ventricle only.

(ii) **Left Atrioventricular Valve** It is also called the mitral valve. It allows the blood to flow from the left auricle to left ventricle only.

(iii) **Pulmonary Valve** It is situated between right ventricle and pulmonary artery. It allows the blood to flow from right ventricle to lungs only.

(iv) **Aortic Valve** It is situated between the left ventricle and aorta. It allows the blood to flow from left ventricle to different parts of the body.

**51** Discuss the functions of the circulatory system.

*Ans* The circulatory system is responsible for performing various functions. They are

(i) **Transportation** It transports blood to almost all of the body's tissues. The blood delivers essential nutrients and oxygen into the cells of the body.

It removes wastes and carbon dioxide from the body. Hormones are transported throughout the body *via* the blood's liquid plasma.

This process of transportation takes place through two seperate circulatory process, which are as follows

(a) **Pulmonary Circulation** It allows oxygenation of blood. The blood goes to the lungs, from the right side of the heart, where the $CO_2$ is removed and the blood is oxygenated.

(b) **Systematic Circulation** It allows circulation of the oxygenated blood between heart and body's tissue. The left side of the heart after receiving oxygenated blood, pumps it out through the aorta to all the body parts. After oxygenation of body, it goes back to the right side of the heart through superior and inferior vena cava.

(ii) **Protection** It protects the body from various diseases. Its White Blood Cells (WBCs) cleans up cellular debris and fight pathogens that have entered the body.

Platelets and red blood cells form scabs (called 'clots') to seal wounds and prevent pathogens from entering the body and liquids from leaking out.

(iii) **Regulation** It is an instrument in the body to maintain homeostatic control of several internal conditions. Blood vessels help maintain a stable body temperature by controlling the blood flow to the surface of the skin.

(iv) **Nutrition** The circulatory system carries the nutrients and all the essential vitamins, minerals, amino acids as well as glucose to all parts of the body.

As the blood goes through the small intestine, the nutrients enter the blood stream for further use.

**52** In relation to the given pictures, answer the following questions.

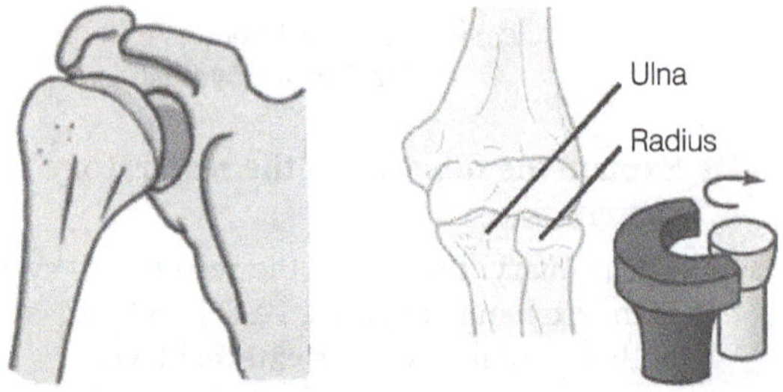


(i) Shoulder and hip joints are the examples of which joints?

(ii) Name the joint between 1st and 2nd cervical vertebrae.

(iii) .................. joints allow for flexion, extension and other movements, but does not allow rotation.

(iv) In which joints, movement takes place on just one axis or direction?

*Ans.* (i) Ball and socket joints

(ii) Pivot joints

(iii) Saddle

(iv) Hinge joints

CHAPTER PRACTICE

# SELF ASSESSMENT

## OBJECTIVE ANSWER TYPE QUESTIONS

1 How many bones are there in our lower limbs?
(a) 60 (b) 64
(c) 62 (d) 114

2 Which of the following is not a part of passage for respiratory system?
(a) Pharynx (b) Trachea
(c) Larynx (d) Diaphragm

3 Which of the following joints is not a freely movable joint?
(a) Hinge joints (b) Saddle joints
(c) Pivot joints (d) Symphysis joints

## VERY SHORT ANSWER TYPE QUESTIONS

4 What is a pivot joint? State with an example.

5 Why do the ventricles in the heart have thicker walls than the atria?

## SHORT ANSWER TYPE QUESTIONS

6 Elucidate about the lungs and trachea in the respiratory system.

7 Discuss about the function of arteries.

8 Briefly write three reasons for the importance of anatomy and physiology in physical education.

## LONG ANSWER TYPE QUESTIONS

9 Briefly describe blood vessels and its categories as a part of the circulatory system.

CHAPTER
08

# Fundamentals of Kinesiology and Biomechanics in Sports

## CHAPTER CHECKLIST

- Meaning of Kinesiology
- Meaning of Biomechanics
- Principles of Biomechanics
- Kinetics and Kinematics in Sports
- Types of Body Movements

## Meaning of Kinesiology

The word 'Kinesiology' has been derived from the Greek words, '*Kinesis*' which means 'movement' and '*ology*' meaning 'study'. Accordingly, kinesiology can be defined as a science that deals with the organisation system of information related to motion.

In other words, this field of science studies the mechanics and anatomy of a human body in relation to human motion.

Within this field, the experts study and assess how the human body moves and functions so as to understand how it affects our health and productivity.

With its various subdisciplines ranging from exercise psychology, biomechanics, athletic training sports medicine to fitness and health promotion, the field of kinesiology is central to sports and physical education.

Anatomy, physiology and kinesiology are fields that share a close and deep mutual relationship. While the fields of anatomy and physiology are closely inter-related, and help us to understand the functions and structures of the body, kinesiology helps us to understand how our body responds to a movement or physical activity.

### Importance of Kinesiology

The study and application of kinesiology is very important in the field of physical education. Its importance can be clearly understood from the following points

1. **Preparing Coaches and Physical Education Teachers** Kinesiology prepares coaches as well as physical education teachers to guide an individual towards success in their sport. They help students and athletes to stay mentally and physically fit by teaching them proper techniques of a sport as well as guiding them to make health choices.
2. **Promotion of Health and Fitness** The knowledge of kinesiology helps the trainers and physical education teachers to help a student or an athlete in improving their health, fitness and well-being.
3. **Preventing Injuries** With the knowledge of kinesiology, one can train properly and reduce the risk of injuries through movements.
4. **Rehabilitation** The treatment designed to facilitate the process of recovery from injury, illness or disease to as normal condition as possible is rehabilitation. Thus, if an individual is suffering from an injury, then an appropriate treatment in the form of therapeutic exercises can be developed with the knowledge of kinesiology.
5. **Developing New Equipments** Kinesiology helps to assess the suitability of the equipment. Also, its sub discipline, biomechanics helps in developing new equipments and tools for helping human movements.
6. **Helps in Developing Motor Skills** Kinesiology helps in developing motor skills and specialised sports skills that helps in efficient and effective movement.

   Through the knowledge of kinesiology, accuracy in direction, force and rhythm can be achieved.
7. **Improves Performance** Kinesiology helps in improving and correcting the movements of the body.

   This improvement further improves the performance of an athlete without wasting much energy.

## Meaning of Biomechanics

Biomechanics is derived from the combination of two words *i.e.* 'bio' means living thing and 'mechanics', which is a field of physics and the forces that act on bodies in motion.

Therefore, it can be defined as the study of the movement of living things using the science of mechanics. It is the branch of Kinesiology which deals with the precise information of human movements with scientific method. In sports and exercise, biomechanics refers to "the study of human movements, including the interaction between the athlete, sports equipment and the exercise environment."

Biomechanics not only provides proper and important techniques for the structure of bones and muscles and the movement they can produce, but also the mechanics of blood circulation, renal function, and other body function.

Basically, it is the application of mechanics in the human movements. In order to improve student's physical movement safely and effectively, biomechanical techniques are important and necessary.

According to the **American Society of Biomechanics**, "Biomechanics represents the broad interplay between mechanics and biological systems."

According to **Dworak LB**, "Biomechanics is the science of movement of a living body, including how muscles, bones, tendons and ligaments work together to produce movement."

Hence, biomechanics has a unique place in the field of Health Education, Physical Education and Sports. It helps trainers and coaches to improve the physical performance of students with the various biomechanical techniques of different games.

## Importance of Biomechanics in Sports

Biomechanics can play a crucial role in both injury prevention as well as performance enhancement. It is important for athletes of all ages and skill levels to understand the application of physics in sports, as physical principles like motion, resistance, momentum and friction play essential role in most sports events.

Thus, understanding of proper sports and exercise movements will allow the participant to be more efficient, technically sound and prone to good habits for long-term development.

Let us discuss in detail the importance of biomechanics in sports

1. **Technique Improvement** Biomechanics can be used by coaches to improve techniques of students or athletes.

   Coaches should make use of the methods of qualitative biomechanics analysis in their everyday practice to bring changes in the technique used by their students.

For example, if a gymnastics coach observes that his students has difficulties to turn a somersault, he can come up with three recommendations to help the gymnast execute this exercise correctly, *i.e.*

- To jump higher
- To curl up more tightly
- To fling arms with more energy before taking-off

**Somersault Technique**

All these recommendations can help to execute this task correctly and are based on the principles of biomechanics.

If the gymnast jumps higher, he has more time to finish the turn during the flight phase. To curl up more tightly means to increase the speed of rotation while keeping the same angular momentum.

To fling arms with more energy increases the angular momentum which helps the gymnast to rotate faster.

2. **Equipment Improvement** Use of biomechanics can also lead to better functioning of sports equipments. Sophisticated sports equipments gives advantage to both elite and recreational athletes.

   Biomechanics helps in improving design of the equipments used in various sports like sports shoes, clothes, etc. These equipments used by sportspersons may have an effect on the performance, either directly or indirectly.

   For example, Javelin Throw is a sport, where a basic application of mechanics to the equipment design changed the event dramatically.

   In 1952, **Frank 'Bud' Held** made the United States Olympics team in the javelin. At the 1952 Olympics in Helsinki, he placed ninth behind his American teammates, who won gold and silver medals.

   Upon returning to the United States, Bud met with his brother, **Dick Held** who designed and built a more aero- dynamic javelin. They increased surface area of their new javelin, gave it more lift, causing it to 'fly' farther.

   The Held brothers were not biomechanists, but their knowledge about mechanics enabled them to improve the design of javelin.

3. **Injury Prevention** Biomechanics is a tool that can be used in sports to identify forces and mechanical energy that causes injuries.

   It helps to understand how injuries originate, how to avoid them during sports performance and how to identify suitable exercise for injury prevention and rehabilitation.

   Biomechanics offers possibilities to create alternative techniques of executing specific movements, using new equipment and carrying out more effective training methods, which also contributes to injury prevention.

4. **Helps in Functioning of Human Body** Muscles strength can be improved by following the biomechanical principles.

   Actions such as kicking football by legs, throwing and catching ball, jumping long, lifting weight, etc. helps to maintain the elasticity in the muscles and build Biceps and Triceps, build joints that enhances the endurance, flexibility, etc.

   It also improves internal organ system with the help of several structural approach and techniques of biomechanics in sports.

5. **Improvement in Training** Biomechanics plays a significant role in improving training. With the help of biomechanics, training exercises can be modified which will help in improving sports performance of a player.

   Coaches can adapt effective techniques of biomechanics after proper analysis of technical deficiency of a player. Use of biomechanics in training, will enhance strength, flexibility, speed etc.

6. **Assist in Improving Coaching** Without biomechanics, it would have been difficult for coaches to provide right guidance to the players. It plays a critical role in learning process.

   By the use of biomechanics, coaches or teachers help in moving the body with precision or accuracy. For this, all the coaches must be well-trained with all the concepts and techniques of biomechanics.

7. **Enhances Performance** The main and ultimate objective of biomechanics in sports is to enhance performance of athletes.

A player who has trained itself with the techniques of biomechanics, will perform better than the other competitor who have not used techniques of biomechanics.

It enhances performance by utilising mechanical principles to improve an individual's technique, the equipment he/she uses and to modify the specific training method.

# Principles of Biomechanics

Issac Newton's laws of motion form the basic principles that are used in sports movements or biomechanics. A method of training that departs from these laws does not make sense mechanically.

These laws are divided into three parts, which are described as follows

## Newton's First Law of Motion

It is also known as Law of Inertia. This law states that "a body at rest will remain at rest and a body in motion will remain in motion at the same speed and in the same direction unless any external force is applied on it to change that state."

Newton's first law explains two fundamental concepts linked with motion and force

- It tells us that a stationary body will remain at rest until an external force is applied.
  For example, a golf ball will remain still unless a force, applied by the golf club, makes it move.
- It tells us that a moving body will continue to move with constant velocity unless acted upon by an external force.

For example, golf ball will continue to move at a constant velocity unless a force acts on it to slow it down or change its direction.

### Application in Sports

Newton's first law of motion is applicable in sports, like Equestrian. In this sport, the rider remains in motion along with the horse.

When the horse suddenly stops, the lower part of both the rider and the horse comes to rest but the rider's upper part remains in motion. Hence, he bends forward to avoid falling from the horse.

Some of the other applications in sports are given below

- **Softball** The ball is hit into the air. Eventually, gravity will act on the ball, pulling it down to the ground. Then, it will roll until friction between the ball and the grass stops it.
- **Soccer** When a soccer ball is kicked into the air, gravity will pull it back to the ground. Then, it will continue to roll until friction between the ball and the grass slows it down.
- **Dance** When a dancer leaps, he only stays in the air for a short period of time because air resistance and gravity work against him.
- **Basketball** When a basketball is shot, it takes a parabolic path due to gravity acting on it. Then it slows down due to air resistance and fluid friction.

Basketball

## Newton's Second Law of Motion

This law states that the "acceleration produced in an object due to extent force is directly proportional to the force producing it and inversely proportional to its mass."

When two unequal forces are applied to objects of equal mass, then the object to which greater force is applied, will move faster.

If equal force is applied to objects having different masses, the object having lighter mass will travel at a faster speed.

For example, a goal shooter who has received the ball at a strong position close to the goal, will only need to impart a relatively small amount of force in the direction of the ring. Whereas, a goal shooter who is at the edge of the shooting circle, before taking a shot, will need to impart a larger amount of force in the direction of the goal as the ball will need a greater change in momentum towards to its goal.

### Application in Sports

Newton's second law of motion can be applied in the sports like

- **Baseball** If a baseball player hits a ball with double the force, the rate at which the ball will accelerate (speed up) will be doubled.

- **Football** Football players can slow down, stop or reverse the direction of other players depending upon how much force they can generate and in which direction.
- **Sprints** In sprints (race) events, runners, running at top speed, pull themselves backward and slowly decrease their speed as sudden stop can lead to fall.

Sprints

## Newton's Third Law of Motion

This law states that "for every action, there is always an equal and opposite reaction." This law describes what happens to a body when it exerts a force on another body.

It is usual to call one of the forces involved *viz.* **action force** and the other as **reaction force.**

There are no strict rules that govern which force is in action, but for the purpose of sports mechanics, it is presumed that the athlete exerts the action force.

### Application in Sports

Newton's third law of motion is applicable in the sports mentioned below

- **High Jump** An athlete can jump higher off a solid surface because it opposes his body with as much force as he is able to generate, in contrast to sand or other unstable surface.
- **Sprints** When a sprinter (racer) pushes against the block, the block push back with the same force. The force through which block push, helps the sprinter to move forward with full energy.
- **Swimming** In swimming, we can relate this concept to the standard hand/arm stroke when the hand travels downward in the water and then backwards to propel the swimmer forward. In creating an equal and opposite reaction, the swimmer is kept afloat and propelled forward.

Swimming

## Kinetics and Kinematics in Sports

Kinetics is the study of the relationships between the forces acting on the body and how those forces affect motion.

Kinematics is the geometry of objects' motion, including displacement, velocity, and acceleration. In simple terms, kinetics studies the muscles that cause movement (gravity, friction, etc.), while kinematics describes the motion (velocity, acceleration, etc.)

Kinematics analyses motion in terms of time, displacement, velocity, or acceleration. Kinematics is the mechanics of motion without reference to the forces causing that motion. It is the displacement and velocity of your body's segments and joints.

Kinetics is useful in overcoming sports injuries as it is necessary to learn how to stretch and move the muscles in ways that promote healing. If you remain still the stiffness sets in your body and the injury may not heal at all.

An example of kinematics in sports is the study of golf swing. Kinematics focuses on details of the swing 'motion' such as the shape of the clubhead path, positions of the body and club at various swing events, velocities of the body parts and club, and the timing of slow-down of the body for speed-up of the club. In order to describe the swing motion objectively, it is important to accurately measure the motion first. This is why measurement of the motion is one of the central aspects of kinematics.

# Types of Body Movements

Physical activity is made possible by movements and motions. Every movement takes place in one plane and around one axis.

They are categorised by movement types as follows

1. **Flexion** It takes place when the angle decreases between the two bones attached to a joint.

   In other words, it refers to bending of parts at a joint such that it decreases the angle between them and brings the parts closer to each other.

   Flexion of the wrist joint is an important movement in many sports skills, especially racquet sports, as it provide stability and power to a sportsperson.

2. **Extension** It takes place when the angle increases between the two bones attached to a joint increases.

   In other words, it refers to extending or straightening the parts at a joint such that it increases the angle between them and moves the parts away from each other.

   For example, downward movement of the arm after a badminton shot has been made.

   Both flexion and extension occur in the sagittal plane (position of body) around a frontal axis.

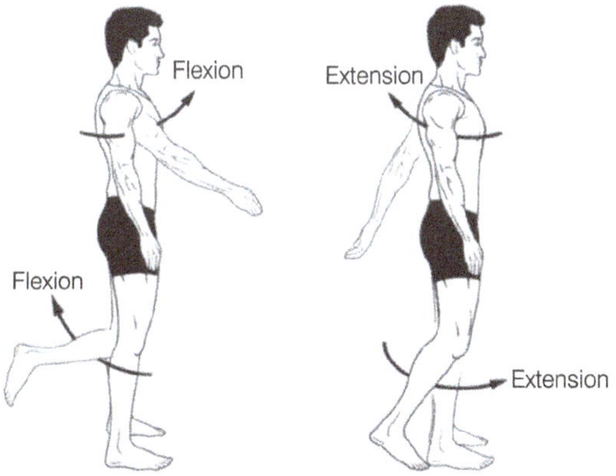


**Flexion** **Extension**

3. **Abduction** It means moving the body parts away from the midline of the body *i.e.* the axis.

   For example, moving legs, arms sideways to form a right angle with the side of the body. In sports, the act of abduction can be seen in cricket as performed by fielder to catch a ball which is above the head.

4. **Adduction** It is a movement towards the midline of the body. It means drawing the limbs closer to the body along the centre line.

   For example, shoulder adduction is a key movement in the performance of a golf swing. During a golf swing, the body segments work together in a coordinated sequence to maximise club head speed at ball impact.

   The lead arm accelerates into maximum adduction during the backswing which allows the golfer to attain a suitable position for the upcoming downswing and hence increases efficiency of the overall skill. Both adduction and abduction occur in the frontal plane about the sagittal axis.

5. **Circumduction** It is the movement of a body region in a circular manner, in which one end of the body region being moved stays relatively stationary while the other end describes a circle.

   It involves the sequential combination of flexion, extension, adduction and abduction at a joint. This kind of motion can be best seen in the shoulder and hip joints.

   For example, circumduction occurs at the shoulder during the execution of a cricket ball.

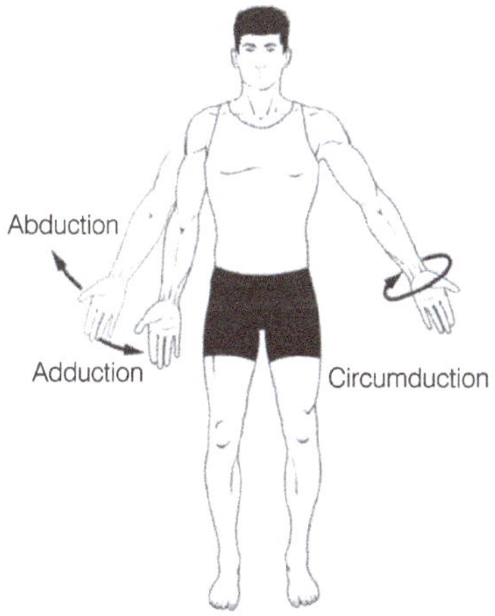


**Abduction, Adduction, Circumduction**

6. **External Rotation** This is a rotatory movement around the longitudinal axis of a bone away from the midline of the body.

   This movement occurs in a transverse plane and is also known as rotation laterally, outward rotation and lateral rotation.

   External rotation is evident during the tennis serve. During the wind-up of the tennis serve, the shoulder joint performs external rotation in order to store elastic potential energy that can be transferred into the forward motion of the serve, which will generate a tremendous amount of force and momentum.

7. **Internal Rotation** This is a rotatory movement around the longitudinal axis of a bone towards the midline of the body. It occurs in the transverse plane and is also known as rotation medially and inward rotation. Internal rotation is very common movement in the human body. The run up in javelin throw demonstrates internal rotation.

   The purpose of this movement is the production of momentum which can be transferred to the hand and wrist in order to maximise release speed of the javelin.

8. **Pronation and Supination** Prone is a person laying face-down on a surface. Supine is a person laying face-up on a surface.

   Pronation and supination generally refers to assuming prone or supine positions, but often they are used in a specific sense referring to rotation of the forearm or foot so that in the standard anatomical position the palm or sole is facing anteriorly (supination) or posteriorly (pronation).

   Pronation at the forearm is a rotational movement where the hand and upper arm are turned inwards. Pronation of the foot refers to turning of the sole outwards, so that weight is borne on the medial part of the foot.

   Supination of the forearm occurs when the forearm or palm are rotated outwards. Supination of the foot refers to turning of the sole of the foot inwards, shifting weight to the lateral edge.

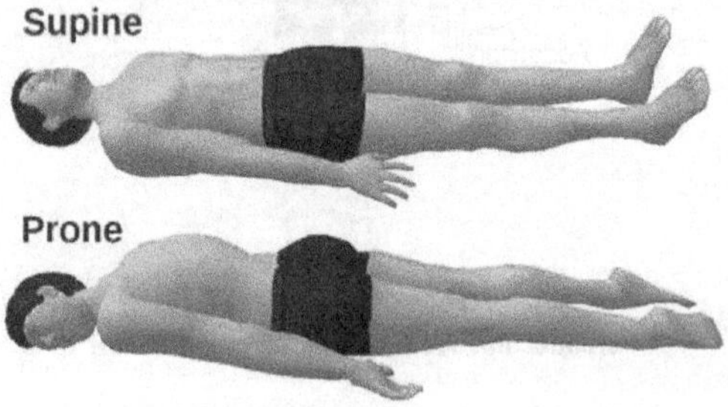


## Axis and its Application in Body Movements

An axis is an imaginary straight line around which an object rotates. Movement at a joint takes place in a plane about an axis. There are three axes of rotation

1. **Sagital Axis** The sagital axis passes horizontally from posterior to anterior and is formed by the intersection of the sagital and transverse planes.
2. **Frontal Axis** The frontal axis passes horizontally from left to right and is formed by the intersection of the frontal and transverse planes.
3. **Vertical Axis** The vertical axis passes vertically from inferior to superior and is formed by the intersection of the sagital and frontal planes.

## Plane and its Application in Body Movements

A plane is best described as an imaginary surface which divides the body into equal parts. The body moves through different 'planes of movement'.

Human movements are described in three dimensions based on a series of planes and axis. There are three planes of motion that pass through the human body

1. **The Sagital Plane** The sagital plane lies vertically and divides the body into right and left parts
2. **The Frontal Plane** The frontal plane also lies vertically and divides the body into anterior and posterior parts.
3. **The Transverse (horizontal) Plane** The transverse plane lies horizontally and divides the body into superior and inferior parts.

# CHAPTER PRACTICE

## OBJECTIVE TYPE QUESTIONS

### Multiple Choice Questions (MCQs)

**1** Which of the following is the study of a system of information related to Motion?
(a) Physiology (b) Anatomy
(c) Bio-mechanics (d) Kinesiology

*Ans* (d) Kinesiology

**2** Biomechanics can play a crucial role in ......... .
(a) injury prevention
(b) performance enhancement
(c) physical movement
(d) Both (a) and (b)

*Ans* (d) Both (a) and (b)

**3** Understanding of proper sports and exercise movements will allow the participant to be more ......... for long-term development.
(a) efficient (b) technically sound
(c) prone to good habits (d) All of these

*Ans* (d) All of these

**4** Coaches should make use of the methods of ......... biomechanics analysis in their everyday practice to produce changes in the technique used by their students.
(a) quantitative (b) qualitative
(c) effective (d) None of these

*Ans* (b) qualitative

**5** Sophisticated sports equipment gives advantage to ......... athletes.
(a) elite (b) recreational
(c) Both (a) and (b) (d) None of these

*Ans* (c) Both (a) and (b)

**6** This type of movement takes place when the angle decreases between the two bones attached to a joint. It is ........ .
(a) Adduction (b) Abduction
(c) Extension (d) Flexion

*Ans* (d) Flexion

**7** ......... means moving the body parts away from an imaginery centre line i.e. the axis.
(a) Adduction (b) Abduction
(c) Extension (d) External Rotation

*Ans* (b) Abduction

**8** This is a rotatory movement around the longitudinal axis of a bone away from the midline of the body. It is called ......... .
(a) External Rotation
(b) Internal Rotation
(c) Outward Rotation
(d) Both (a) and (c)

*Ans* (d) Both (a) and (c)

**9** ......... involves the sequential combination of flexion, adduction, extension and abduction at a joint.
(a) Internal Rotation
(b) External Rotation
(c) Circumduction
(d) None of the above

*Ans* (c) Circumduction

**10** Identify the human movement given in the picture below.

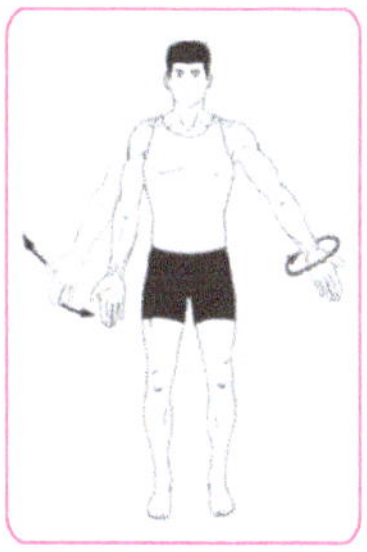

(a) Abduction (b) Flexion
(c) Adduction (d) Extension

*Ans* (a) Abduction

**11** **Assertion** (A) Biomechanics aims to achieve performance enhancement in sports.
**Reason** (R) Qualitative analysis helps in technique improvement and injury prevention.
In context of above two statements, which one of the following is correct?

**Codes**
(a) Both A and R are true and R is the correct explanation of A
(b) Both A and R are true, but R is not the correct explanation of A
(c) A is true, but R is false
(d) A is false, but R is true

*Ans.* (a) Both A and R are true and R is the correct explanation of A

**12** **Assertion** (A) Biomechanics is the study of forces and their effects on living system.
**Reason** (R) In swimming, 3rd law of motion (law of reaction) is utilised.

**Codes**
(a) Both A and R are true and R is the correct explanation of A
(b) Both A and R are true, but R is not the correct explanation of A
(c) A is true, but R is false
(d) A is false, but R is true

*Ans* (b) Both A and R are true, but R is not the correct explanation of A

## Fill in the Blanks

**13** ......... takes place when the angle between the two bones attached to a joint increases.

*Ans* Extension

**14** Newton's first law is also known as ......... .

*Ans* Law of Inertia

**15** Newton's ......... law is applied in football.

*Ans* first

**16** The ........... plane lies horizontally and divides the body into superior and parts.

*Ans* transverse

## State True or False

**17** Biomechanics helps in improving sports performance.

*Ans* True

**18** Extension takes place when angle decreases between two bones attached to a joint.

*Ans* False. Extension takes place when angle between two bones attached to a joint increases.

## VERY SHORT ANSWER TYPE QUESTIONS

**19** Which field of study in sports is called 'Biomechanics'?

*Ans* Biomechanics is the study of the movement of living things using the science of mechanics. It is the branch of kinesiology which deals with the precise information of human movements with scientific method.

**20** Define flexion.

*Ans* Flexion is a type of movement that takes place when the angle decreases between the two bones attached to a joint.

**21** What is the First Law of Newton?

*Ans* This law states that a body at rest will remain at rest and a body in motion will remain in motion at the same speed and in the same direction unless any external force is applied on it to change the state.

## SHORT ANSWER TYPE QUESTIONS

**22** Explain any three importance of biomechanics in brief.

*Ans* The importance of biomechanics is discussed below

(i) **Technique Improvement** Improvement of technique with the help of biomechanics can be used by teachers and coaches to correct motions of students or athletes.

Coaches should make use of the methods of qualitative biomechanics analysis in their everyday practice to produce changes in the technique used by their students.

(ii) **Equipment Improvement** Use of biomechanics can also lead to better functioning of sports equipments.
The equipments used by sportsperson may have an effect on the performance, either directly on indirectly.

(iii) **Injury Prevention** Biomechanics is a tool that can be used in sports medicine to identify forces and mechanical energy that causes injuries.

It helps to understantd how injuries originate, how to avoid them during sports performance and how to identify exercise suitable for injury pervention and rehabilitation.

**23** Discuss in detail about any two movements of the body.

*Or* Explain internal and external rotation in brief.

*Ans* The types of movements are discussed below

(i) **Internal Rotation** This is a rotatory movement around the longitudinal axis of a bone towards the midline of the body.
It occurs in a transverse plane and is also known as rotation medially and inward rotation.
The run up in the javelin throw demonstrates internal rotation. The purpose of this movement is the production of momentum which can be transferred to the hand and wrist in order to maximise release speed of the javelin.

(ii) **External Rotation** This is a rotatory movement around the longitudinal axis of a bone away from the midline of the body. This movement occurs in a transverse plane and is also known as rotation laterally, outward rotation and lateral rotation. External rotation is evident during the tennis serve.

**24** How kinesiology is important?

*Ans* Kinesiology is important because

(i) **Preparing Coaches and Physical Education Teachers** Kinesiology prepares coaches as well as physical education teachers to guide an individual towards success in their sport. They help students and athletes to stay mentally and physically fit by teaching them proper techniques of a sport as well as guiding them to make health choices.

(ii) **Promotion of Health and Fitness** The knowledge of kinesiology helps the trainers and physical education teachers to help a student or an athlete in improving their health, fitness and well-being.

**25** Explain the concepts of pronation and supination.

*Ans* **Pronation and Supination** Prone is a person laying face-down on a surface. Supine is a person laying face-up on a surface.

Pronation and supination generally refers to assuming prone or supine positions, but often they are used in a specific sense referring to rotation of the forearm or foot so that in the standard anatomical position of the palm or sole is facing anteriorly (supination) or posteriorly (pronation).

Pronation at the forearm is a rotational movement where the hand and upper arm are turned inwards. Pronation of the foot refers to turning of the sole outwards, so that weight is borne on the medial part of the foot.

**26** Briefly describe the concept of axis and plane.

*Ans* An axis is an imaginary straight line around which an object rotates. Movement at a joint takes place in a plane about an axis. There are three axes of rotation

(i) **Sagital Axis** The sagital axis passes horizontally from posterior to anterior and is formed by the intersection of the sagital and transverse planes.

(ii) **Frontal Axis** The frontal axis passes horizontally from left to right and is formed by the intersection of the frontal and transverse planes.

(iii) **Vertical Axis** The vertical axis passes vertically from inferior to superior and is formed by the intersection of the sagital and frontal planes.

A plane is best described as an imaginary surface which divides the body into equal parts. The body moves through different 'planes of movement'. Human movements are described in three dimensions based on a series of planes and axis. There are three planes of motion that pass through the human body

(i) **The Sagital Plane** The sagital plane lies vertically and divides the body into right and left parts.

(ii) **The Frontal Plane** The frontal plane also lies vertically and divides the body into anterior and posterior parts.

(iii) **The Transverse (horizontal) Plane** The transverse plane lies horizontally and divides the body into superior and inferior parts.

**27** Sohan, a new student in the school was very much interested in taking part in the school sports events. He was taught the latest rules and regulations of football game. In due course, he learnt biomechanical aspects of the game including various movements.

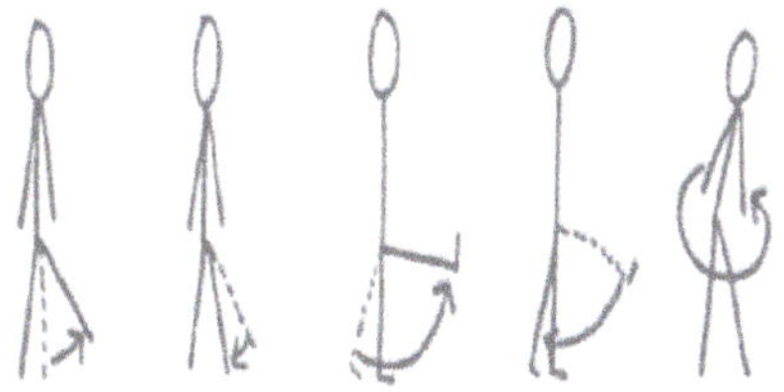

(i) The type of movement in which the angle between joint decreases is called

(a) Flexion (b) Extension
(c) Gliding (d) Sliding

(ii) Straightening parts of a joint so that the angle increases

(a) Flexion (b) Extension
(c) Abduction (d) Adduction

(iii) Moving a part away from mid line is

(a) Flexion (b) Extension
(c) Abduction (d) Adduction

*Ans* (i) (a) Flexion (ii) (b) Extension
(iii) (c) Abduction

CHAPTER PRACTICE

## LONG ANSWER TYPE QUESTIONS

**28** Describe different types of movements.

*Ans* A physical activity consists of different movements and motions. Every movement takes place in one plane and around one axis. They are categorised by movement type as follows

(i) **Flexion** It takes place when the angle decreases between the two bones attached to a joint.

(ii) **Extension** It takes place when the angle between the two bones attached to a joint increases. Both flexion and extension occur in the sagittal plane about the frontal axis.

(iii) **Adduction** It is a movement laterally towards the midline of the body like drawing limbs closer to the body.

(iv) **Abduction** It is a movement laterally away from the midline of the body like moving the body parts away from the body.

Both adduction and abduction occur in the frontal plane, around a sagital axis.

**29** Explain Newton's laws of motion and their application in sports.

*Ans* Newton's laws of motion have multiple application in sports. Each law and its application in sports in discussed below

(i) **Newton's First Law** It states that a body at rest will remain at rest and a body in motion will remain in motion at the same speed and in the same direction till any external force is applied on it to change that state.

This law is also known as 'Law of inertia'. This law has an application in many games such as soccer, in which when a soccer ball is kicked into the air, gravity will pull it back to the ground. Then, it will continue to roll until the frictional force of the ground on the ball ultimately slows it down.

(ii) **Newton's Second Law** It states that the acceleration produced in an object due to extent force is directly proportional to the force producing it and inversely proportional to its mass. It means the acceleration depends upon the force applied and the mass of an object.

This law has an application in many games such as baseball in which, if a batter hits the ball with double the normal force, the acceleration rate of the ball will be doubled.

(iii) **Newton's Third Law** It states that for every action, there is always an equal and opposite reaction. It describes what happens to a body when it exerts a force on another body.

This law has an application in sports such as swimming, in which a swimmer propels himself through the water because the water offers an equal counter force to oppose the action of the swimmer's hands and legs, push, thus, allowing him to move.

**30** In relation to the given picture, answer the following questions.

(i) The football player in the photo above is in motion. He will stay in motion unless players on the other team exert an unbalanced force against him.

(ii) A goalkeeper in a football game pulls his hands backwards after holding the ball shot at the goal. This enables the goalkeeper to____________ the rate of change of momentum.

(iii) When the football travels through the air, it always follows a curved path because the movement of the ball in the vertical direction is influenced by the__________.

(iv) An object at rest will remain at rest or an object in motion will remain at motion at constant velocity unless acted upon by a force. Identify the law of motion.

*Ans.* (i) Newton's First Law of Motion

(ii) decrease

(iii) force of gravity

(iv) Newton's First Law of Motion

CHAPTER PRACTICE

# SELF ASSESSMENT

## OBJECTIVE ANSWER TYPE QUESTIONS

1 .............. axis passes vertically from inferior to superior and is formed by the intersetion of the sagital and frontal planes.

(a) Vertical
(b) Frontal
(c) Sagital
(d) None of the above

2 **Which** is not a type of body movement?

(a) Flexion
(b) Extension
(c) Dynamic
(d) External Rotation

3 Biomechanics has a unique place in the field of

(a) health education
(b) sport
(c) physical education
(d) All of the above

## VERY SHORT ANSWER TYPE QUESTIONS

4 Explain any two types of body movements.

5 What is pronation?

6 What is supination?

## SHORT ANSWER TYPE QUESTIONS

7 Briefly write three reasons for the importance of kinesiology in physical education.

8 Discuss any five types of body movements with examples.

## LONG ANSWER TYPE QUESTIONS

9 Describe the principles of biomechanics.

10 Briefly discuss the importance of kinesiology in sports and physical education.

CHAPTER

# 09

# *Psychology and Sports*

A sport or a physical activity is essentially a mind game. It is a place where a small difference in mental powers often makes a big difference between success and failure. Thus, there came to be an understanding of importance of the inter-relatedness of sports and psychology.

In simple words, in physical education and sports, it is very important to understand the psychological aspects of an individual or sportsperson.

### CHAPTER CHECKLIST

- Meaning and Definition of Psychology
- Development Characteristics at Different Stages of Development
- Psychological Attributes
- Adolescent Problems and their Management
- Team Cohesion and Sports

## Meaning and Definition of Psychology

The word 'psychology' is derived from a Greek word 'Psyche' meaning 'soul' and 'logos' meaning 'scientific study'. Hence, psychology came to be understood as the scientific study of the soul. However, this definition of psychology was discarded and psychology was defined as 'science of mind'.

With time and further research, the definition of psychology kept on changing. It became the 'science of consciousness' and finally reached to its most accepted and latest definition as the, 'science of human behaviour'.

Various psychologists and scientists defined psychology in different ways. Some accepted definitions of psychology are

- According to **WB Pillsbury and JB Watson,** "Psychology is the science of human behaviour."
- According to **Woodworth,** "Psychology deals with the activities of the individual in relation to his environment."
- According to the **Oxford Dictionary,** "The scientific study of human mind and its functions, especially those affecting behaviour in a given context."
- According to **Crow and Crow,** "It is the study of human behaviour and human relationships."

## Meaning and Definition of Sports Psychology

The increasing importance of the field of psychology in sports and physical education lead to the emergence of a new discipline called Sports Psychology.

Sports psychology is the branch of applied psychology that deals with the performance and behaviour of an individual while performing sports and any other physical activity.

It is a multidisciplinary science that uses psychological knowledge and skills to address optimal performance and well-being of athletes, developmental and social aspects of sports participation, and systemic issues associated with sports settings and organisations.

In other words, sports psychology involves the study of how psychological factors, such as behaviour, arousal, motivation and aspiration, affect performance and how participation in sports and exercise affect psychological and physical factors.

Various eminent psychologists asserted such an understanding of sports psychology in different terms. Some of them are

- According to **RN Singer**, "Sports psychology is encompassing scholarly educational and practical activities associated with the understanding and influencing of selected behaviours of people in athletics, physical education, vigorous recreational activity and exercise."
- According to **Clark and Clark**, "Sports psychology is an applied psychology. It is more concerned with the personalities, emotional or motivational aspects of sports and physical activities. It employs many of the techniques used in psychology."
- According to **John Lauther**, "Sports psychology is an area which attempts to apply psychological facts and principles to learning performance and associated human behaviour in whole field of sports."
- According to **KM Burns**, "Sports psychology for physical education is that branch of psychology which deals with the physical fitness of an individual through his participation in games and sports."

## Importance of Psychology in Physical Education and Sports

In the present scenario, sports psychology is becoming increasingly important, particularly with respect to the improvement and maintenance of athletic performance. With its purpose being the modification of behaviour according to the needs of a situation, sports psychology helps to improve attitudes and mental skills to help sportspersons perform well.

It helps to identify limited beliefs, behaviours and attitudes that act as obstacles in good performance and helps to embrace a healthier philosophy during performance. Sports psychology also helps the coaches to make a good coaching technique that conditions and prepares a player to deal with stress situations while being mentally ready and confident.

The following points highlight the importance of sports psychology

1. **Enhancement of Physiological Capacities** Sports psychology plays a unique role in the enhancement of physiological capacities such as strength, speed, flexibility etc. Motivation and proper feedback plays a major role in the enhancement of physical capacity of sportspersons. It is an established fact that psychological capacity or power can increase physiological capacities of individuals.
2. **Learning Motor Skills** Sports psychology plays a major role in learning motor skills. Such a learning depends on the individual's level of readiness, *i.e.* both physiological and psychological readiness. Physiological readiness in children is development of the necessary strength, flexibility and endurance, while psychological readiness is related to the learner's state of mind, *i.e.* the desire and willingness to learn the particular skill.

   Sports psychology plays an essential part in understanding psychological readiness and interests as well as attitudes of an individual towards efficient learning and performance of a motor skill.
3. **Understanding Behaviour** Sports psychology helps in understanding the behaviour of athletes or sportspersons engaged in competitive sports. Coaches also come to know the interest, attitude towards a physical activity, instinct, drive and personality of a sportsperson.
4. **Controlling Emotions** Sports psychology plays an important role in controlling the emotions of sportspersons during practice as well as in competition. Spontaneous and uncontrolled outbursts of emotions such as anger, fear, negative self thinking etc. may lead to a decline in performance. Hence, it is essential to control emotions during sports competitions.

Sports psychology plays a vital role at such a juncture, as it helps in balancing the arousal of emotions, which further improves performance.

5. **Psychological Preparation for Competition** Sports psychology plays a significant role in the psychological preparation of an athlete.
   It focuses on improving mental abilities such as concentration, confidence, etc. reducing stress, and building the competitive spirit among the athletes. Owing to this feature, today, sports psychologist services are required for many national and international level games.
6. **Helps Solve Emotional Problems of Sportspersons** Stress, tension and anxiety are natural during competitions or tournaments as well as during practice/training.
   There may be some other emotional problems such as depression, frustration, anorexia, panic, etc. Knowledge of sports psychology is helpful in such situations. Techniques of relaxation and concentration for stress management can be applied by sportspersons who are facing such problems.

Thus, it can be said that sports psychology plays a vital role in enhancing the performance of sportspersons. It deals with various mental qualities such as concentration, confidence, emotional control, commitment etc, which are important for successful performance in sports and games.

## Developmental Characteristics at Different Stages of Development

The process of growing and developing begins on the cellular level and continues throughout life until death. As a result, all human beings around us belong to a certain stage of growth and development in which they show certain different and some similar characteristics. In order to understand growth and development easily, all growth and development have been divided into stages.

## Stages of Development

The scientific community divides human growth into stages according to the age and assesses their development as a human develops motor skills and reaches cognitive milestones.

Based on the age and certain characteristics, there are 7 stages of growth and development.

They are as follows

1. Pre-natal
2. Infancy or babyhood
3. Early childhood
4. Late childhood
5. Adolescence
6. Adulthood
7. Old age

In the field of physical education, the focus primarily lies on 5 of these stages, which are described below

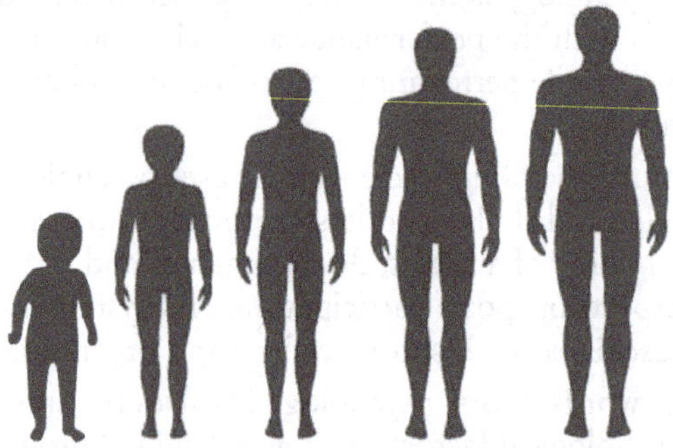


**Stages of Development**

## Infancy

This stage starts with the birth of a child and go upto 2 years of age. Shortest of all development periods, in this stage, growth and development is very progressive. Even though the child depends on its parents for even the basic of needs, a child very quickly grows.

### Physical Characteristics

- In this stage, physical growth is high with a considerable growth in height and weight. A baby's weight almost doubles within 6 months and triples within a year.
- In infancy, the muscular and nervous system along with other organ systems develops at a much faster rate.
- Children in this stage, learn motor skills like walking, jumping, catching, running, etc. easily and develop better bone and muscle coordination.
- Physical activities, at this stage, are spontaneous and individualistic. They are developed by imitation or hit and trail.

### Cognitive Characteristics

- At this stage, the brain of a child develops quickly. A child, in this stage, has great grasping power, his/her memory increases just like his/her thinking ability.
- A child, in this stage, starts understanding language. He/She develops a vocabulary of simple words.
- At this stage, the curiosity of a child is very high. He/She try to ask various questions and is easily satisfied by the answers of elder persons.

- Children are emotional in this stage and do not have control over their emotions. Social sentiments and emotions related to self-love become eminent in them. They do what they like and leave what they don't like.

## Early Childhood

This stage starts at the age of 2 years and goes upto 6 years. As the most important period of growth and development, in this period, the child is a pre-school going toddler.

### Physical Characteristics

- A child in this stage, gains height and weight rapidly. Three-year old pre-schooler may grow to be about 38 inches tall and weigh about 14 kg. In a year or two, the child will gain 2-3 inches of height and around 2 kgs of weight.
- The body proportions of the child changes and the baby look disappears.
- In this stage, the development of muscular systems and the nervous system is as dramatic as the previous stage.
- The motor skills that the child starts to learn at infancy keeps on continuing. In fact, they get more refined and graceful at this stage.
- Physical activities, in this stage, are not very rigorous. Children starts playing simple games with other children.

### Cognitive Characteristics

- A child's memory power increases considerably in this stage.
- At this stage, children start to communicate with ease. Their vocabulary increases, and they are able to form simple as well as complex sentences.
- Just like infancy, children at this stage are full of emotions that they cannot control.
- It is a stage of social development of a child. He/She is very keen to learn about his/her environment and surroundings. He/She not only learns to make new friends but also learns various good manners and social habits.
- Early childhood is also a period when some common interests develop. These include interest in play, human body, self, clothes, etc.

## Late Childhood

This stage lies between 6 to 12 years of age and is also referred to as troublesome age. It is also known as the gang age and children in this age are more influenced by their peers than anyone else.

### Physical Characteristics

- This period is characterised by a relatively slow physical growth. There are considerable variations due to gender, ethnic origin, genetics, hormones, nutrition, environment, or disease in growth patterns. While children of this age group follow the same basic developmental patterns, they do not necessarily mature at the same rate.
- Children, in this stage, typically acquire a leaner and a more athletic appearance.
- This stage is often also called as the pre-puberty stage. Children start experiencing certain changes in the body which will lead to puberty, a stage of sexual maturity.
- As school-age children grow physically, they become faster, stronger, and better coordinated. Consequently, during middle childhood, children become more adept at gross motor activities.
- Children, in this stage, make efforts to learn a skill regardless of ability. They develop a feeling of competence and are highly interested and motivated in many physical activities, especially related to teams.

### Cognitive Characteristics

- Child, at this stage, is expected to acquire the basic principles of knowledge that are considered essential for successful adjustment to adult life.
  This is a critical period as children start to form a habit. Habits formed in this period persist in adulthood.
- Children at this age become increasingly skilled at problem solving, critical thinking and creative thinking.
  They start applying reasoning and develop comprehending skills. Their power of memory, thinking and decision-making increases remarkably.
- With an enhanced interest in group activities, the child at this stage, develops vocabulary and comprehension ability. In contrast to the chatter box way of talking, the child talks less.
- Late childhood show changes from the previous stages as children are generally pleasant, although at times there are out bursts and the child suffers from anxiety and frustration.
- Another marked feature of late childhood is an increased need for peer acceptance and being with peer members. This results in improved socialisation in late childhood.

- By the end of this stage, children start to control their emotions and behaviours. The child becomes conscious of his/her self respect and self-esteem.

## Adolescence

Spanning between 13 to 19 years, adolescence is a stage, when the individual becomes integrated with the society of adults by undergoing marked intellectual and sexual transformations.

This is a stage of complex changes which brings us to the stage that will end the childhood and lead to adulthood.

### Physical Characteristics

- This stage marks the start of puberty *i.e.* a series of complex physical changes that marks the beginning of sexual maturity.
  It brings remarkable change in the shape of an individual such as breast development, muscular changes, bone hardening, change in voice, pimples, etc.
- Girls grow taller, their hips widen, their breasts become rounder and larger, hair grows on the body, their voice become sweet, soft and light.
  Around the age of 13 or 14, most girls today begin menstruating, or having menstrual periods and flow.
- Boys become taller, heavier and stronger, their voices deepen, their shoulders broaden, hair grows on the body, and reproductive organs enlarge.
- Motor coordination tends to improve rapidly in this stage. Due to development of strength as a result of physical changes, children enjoy participating in sports and physical education.

### Cognitive Characteristics

- Adolescents, in this stage, can consider future possibilities, search for answers, deal with problems of flexibly, test hypotheses, and draw conclusions about events they have not experienced firsthand.
- During adolescence, the ability to criticise, take decisions, and the eagerness or curiosity for novel thoughts and ideas are developed.
- Children, at this stage, are curious to know about the people, places and principles. Their memory power, attention and imagination reaches its maximum in this stage.

- Children, at this stage, demand self-respect, dignity and self-independence.
- The physical, social and emotional changes makes the children full of impatient, restless and worried. They remain under stress and tension and thus are constantly daydreaming.
- Adolescents are full of extreme emotions which they are not able to control properly. They become hyper and many a time aggressive. They do not like the guidance given by someone.
- Children, in this stage, enjoy the company of friends. Their loyalty towards their peers increases and they develop socially acceptable qualities. Children, in this stage, revolt against the traditions that stand in their way of life.

## Adulthood

Starting from 20 years and extending upto around 45 years of age, this stage is the longest span among all the stages of life. It is characterised by maturity in physical, emotional, intellectual and social relations.

The characteristics of this stage are as follows

- Physical development is complete in this stage. There is almost no natural change in height and weight of the body. Though, the weight of the body may change due to unhealthy lifestyle.
- Motor skills, endurance, strength, etc reach its maximum, but they can be improved with training.
- Cognitive development is also at its maximum at this stage. People start thinking rationally and intelligently.
- Adults know how to control emotions. They accept criticism gracefully and meet emergencies with poise.
- Adults become the acceptable members of the society. They accept their responsibilities and are usually open-minded.

# Adolescent Problems and their Management

Adolescence is a very important stage of development as it faces rapid and important physical developments.

The term 'Adolescence' is derived from a Latin word *'Adolescere'* meaning 'to grow to maturity'. It is a period which fills the gap between childhood and adulthood.

According to **Stanley Hall**, "Adolescence is a period of great stress and strain, storm and strife." In fact, it is a period of growth and development that acts as a bridge of transition from childhood to adulthood.

According to **Jersield**, "Adolescence is that span of years during which boys and girls move from childhood to adulthood mentally, emotionally, socially and physically."

This stage has been identified as a period of storm and stress. The adolescent undergoes extreme variations in emotions.

In a state of instability, as they are not sure of their capacities, interests and the treatment, they face intense emotions, confusion and rebellion nature between being independent and dependent in different situations.

Therefore, the lack of balance and understanding in the changes happening in their lives results in lot of problems that the adolescents face in their day-to-day lives.

Thus, the knowledge of these problems and how to manage them becomes crucial not only for educators but for parents as well. With this knowledge, they can help the children in laying a strong foundation for them and teach them to solve such problems for the future.

## Problems Faced by Adolescents

Due to the sudden and rapid biological, psychological and behavioural changes taking place in the body, an adolescent suffers through many problems.

The only source of comfort during these times, for them, are their peers with whom they might develop bad habits. Hence, it is essential to know these problems as well as the bad habits that an adolescent may develop.

The problems of adolescents are described below

1. **Physical and Biological Problems** In the stage of adolescence, both girls and boys go through immense bodily changes. Girls start menstruating and nightfall starts in boys. The lack of knowledge of such changes makes the adolescents feel restless and worried.

   As a result, they often go through the sleepless nights and are unable to rest leading to various health problems.
2. **Issues of Stability and Adjustment** Adolescents becomes highly conscious of themself and of the world around them. They try to find themselfs a place within this world.

   However, adolescents constantly go through the changes which makes them unstable. Their behaviour become erratic as they are not able to adjust themselves to such changes.

   Therefore, they find it difficult to coordinate and adjust easily with others. They feel that they are constantly under pressure and desire a free atmosphere.
3. **Aggression and Uncontrollable Emotions** Adolescents are very emotional and hyper. They go through sudden change of mood and outbursts almost every day.

   One aspect of this suddenness of change include the thoughts of suicide, self-hate, anxiety and depression that they may face.

   Adolescents also display aggressive behaviour. They overreact to minor situations and are rebellious towards criticism. This may get them into bad anti-social habits and also may land them into problems that may affect their future.
4. **Social Standing** Adolescents are very conscious of their social status and their personal identity. They want to make their own respectable place in the society while fitting into it. To fit perfectly, they come under peer pressure which sometimes leads them into wrong means of obtaining luxurious things.

   They feel themselves to be important and demand the same respect from others. They sometimes become overconfident and try to hide their mistakes. They put their blame on others and protect themselves.
5. **Problems Related to Sex** In contrast to the previous stages, adolescents now are more attracted to the opposite sex. Their urges related to this attraction is so strong that they become restless and may take wrong means to attain them.
6. **Mental Problems** At this stage, children suffer from immense stress, anxiety and tension. With a lot of things going on around them, their emotions are uncontrollable and their concentration power declines. This severely affects their studies and also results in many social problems.
7. **Drug Addiction** The imbalance and instability that the adolescents face lead them towards developing bad habits. In addition, the curiosity, lack of knowledge and peer pressure leads them towards the drugs and alcohol. This experimentation can turn into addiction which can spoil the entire future of the teenager.
8. **Criminal Activities** The desire to be accepted by the peers and the restlessness, as a result of changes occurring in their lives, makes them more inclined to participate in criminal activities. Adolescents indulge in criminal offences like thefts, stealing, violence, molestation, etc.

## Management of Adolescent Problems

The problems of adolescence should be managed and addressed promptly, otherwise it may spoil the life of the adolescents. They may be the victims of smoking, drug abuse, alcohol, unsafe abortions (girls) and other undesirable activities.

The following techniques may be used for the management of adolescent problems

1. **Proper Counselling** The problems of adolescence are the result of natural growth and development of the body. At this time, lack of experience develops shyness, introversion etc. in them. It prevents them from expressing their problems to their elders. This condition may increase their mental tension. Therefore, proper counselling and guidance by parents, teachers and elders is the best method for the management of adolescent problems.

Counselling

2. **Participation in Co-curricular Activities** Adolescence is an age of energy and dynamism. If the energy is utilised in activities other than academics *i.e.* sports, dance, social functions etc, their surplus energy is spent properly. As a result, emotional upheavals as well as instability will not occur. This helps in the development of their motor skills and in harmonising the personality of an adolescent.
3. **Mutual Understanding** Family members and all elders must try to understand the problems of adolecents. They should be symphathetic and affectionate towards them and must try to build a relationship with them.
   At the same time, adolescents must also understand that their parents are trying to help them for their betterment. With such a mutual understanding, teenagers feeling of instability can reduce and they may not get stressed and anxious.
4. **Recognition of Individuality** Adolescents are often disturbed by being treated as a small child. So, parents must recognise the opinions and views of such teenagers. They need respect and responsibility just like every other adult. Hence, parents must not constantly correct them and scold them.
5. **Sex Education** Adolescents must be educated about sex, just like any other lessons taught in school, in a straightforward way. Correct knowledge enables them to understand the changes occurring in the their body as well as their urges better.
   They must be properly guided to tackle all the problems related to sex as well as to channelise their drives towards constructive work.
6. **Religious and Moral Education** Religious and moral education is very important for managing adolescents.
   It will give them mental peace and some problems like indiscipline, anxiety and worry will be sorted out easily.
7. **Suitable Environment** Adolescents should be provided suitable environment for growth and development. They should be taught how to behave and live.
   Parents must look after the health and diet of adolescents and provide them a safe and healthy environment for growth and development.
8. **Adequate Independence** Adolescents value freedom and independence. They want to express their views and feelings independently.
   They desire to take their own decision and are irritated when any order or restriction is imposed on them. Hence, parents must give them adequate freedom and try to understand their sentiments.
   Therefore, it can be observed that adolescence is the age of struggle. It is very necessary to give proper attention to them, so that they are able to manage their problems during this crucial phase of growth and development.

## Team Cohesion and Sports

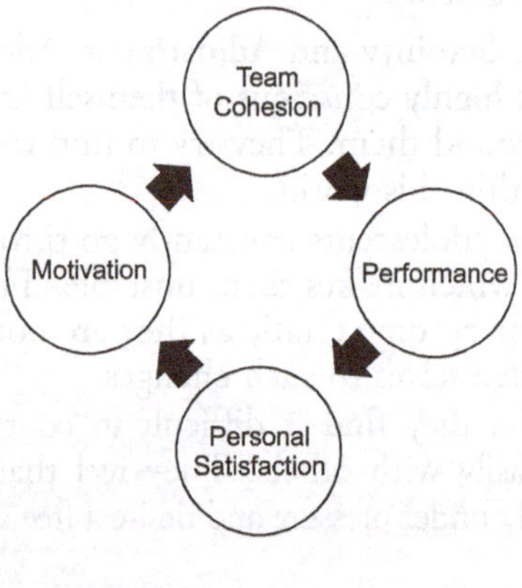

Team cohesion is a dynamic process which reflected in the tendency for a group to stick together and remain united in the pursuit of goals and objectives. It is essentially how well a team works together and is crucial for a sports team to be successful.

Successful team cohesion in sports is influenced by individuals view of their team and the objective set out to achieve. The success of football/soccer teams such as Liverpool, Manchester United or the success of New Zealand's rugby team and the tremendous success of Indian Cricket team is based on how well the individual athletes/players are performing as well as how successful the team are working together.

Team cohesion is useful as it can both improve performance and motivation of a team. If a team work well together, this improves their team cohesion, this in turn improves performance. This then improves personal satisfaction. Thus, improving team cohesion and then the cycle continues either on an upward or downward trend.

Tuckman, B.W. (1965) discusses the four main stages of team cohesion i.e. Forming, Storming , Norming and Performing.

### Steps to Improve Team Cohesion

Below are the key steps to what you can do to establish and improve team cohesion

- Set team goals
- Set individual goals
- Provide feedback to individuals as well as a team
- Listen to your athletes/players feedback
- Work together to achieve the goal
- Reward effort and performance
- Recognise improvement
- Establish an environment for success by setting expectations and professionalism.

### Factors affecting Team Cohesion

Many factors affect the cohesion that will develop on a team. Such factors include the environment (e.g. social and physical), personal factors (e.g. personality), team factors (e.g. norms), and leadership factors (e.g. styles).

Although each variable plays an essential role, the leadership factors may be the most important. This distinction is vital for coaches to know as they have a significant influence on how well team cohesion develops.

In fact, a practitioner's efforts to foster cohesion can be viewed as a performance in its own right. Athletes instinctively model their coach's behavior and an awareness of this can help coaches affect team cohesion in a positive way.

## Psychological Attributes

The different psychological attributes are discussed below.

### Attention

Attention in sports describes the focusing of his or her own role in relation to other teammates, set of situations, particular stimulus on the play field and its often accompanied by an increase in readiness to receive and respond to the situation involved.

It is interesting to understand that there are various types of attention focus and each type have specific utility for specific sports, this is referred as attention styles.

The attention styles can be classified of four types which is divided as per two independent dimensions, 'direction' and 'width'.

Attention style as per width can be narrow attention or broad attention focus, whereas attention style as per direction refers to external and internal attention focus.

### Mental Toughness

Mental toughness is having the natural or developed psychological edge that enables you to

- Cope better than your opponents with the many demands (competition, training, lifestyle) that sport places on a performer
- Be more consistent and better than your opponents in remaining determined, focused, confident, and in control under pressure.

  Mental toughness is important to sports psychology because it represents a culmination of what it takes to be an elite athlete at any level of competition. There are several important factors required for mental toughness
  - Ability to thrive through challenge
  - Sport awareness
  - Tough attitude
  - Desire for success

There are several characteristics of an individual which can be considered as attributes of mental toughness. These are

- Self-confident and self- assured
- Able to focus and concentrate
- Intrinsically motivated
- Strong work ethic
- Committed to excellence
- Persistent and determined

## Resilience

Resilience refers to one's ability to bounce back emotionally in the face of adversity. The one who has the ability to adapt to life's challenges by integrating a wide range of traits, habits, and skills is a resilient person.

The types of resilience are

- **Natural Resilience** It is a natural ability that is bestowed upon a person at conception. It is characterised by openness to new experiences, an eagerness to learn, and a want to have fun.
- **Adaptive Resilience** Adaptive resilience is when, as a result of adverse circumstances, one has to learn, adjust and adapt.
- **Restored Resilience** Restorative or "learned' 'resilience is the type of resilience, restored by learning skills that aid in coping with life's challenges. This can also aid in dealing with the past, present, and future traumas in a more effective manner.

# CHAPTER PRACTICE

## OBJECTIVE TYPE QUESTIONS

### Multiple Choice Questions (MCQs)

**1** According to its Greek meaning, psychology came to be understood as

(a) Scientific study of soul (b) Study of behaviour
(c) Study of mind (d) Study of consciousness

*Ans* (a) Scientific study of soul

**2** Which of the following is a problem faced by adolescents?

(a) Drug addiction (b) Social standing
(c) Aggression (d) All of the above

*Ans* (d) All of the above

**3** Children in adolescent age demand

(a) self worth (b) freedom
(c) money (d) All of these

*Ans* (b) freedom

**4** Which of the following are the stages of team Cohesion, according to Tuckman?

(a) Forming (b) Storming
(c) Norming (d) All of these

*Ans* (d) All of these

**5** Which of the following factors help in improving team cohesion?

(a) Set team goals (b) Set individual goals
(c) Reward effort and performance
(d) All of the above

*Ans* (d) All of the above

### Fill in the blanks

**6** ......... is the branch of applied psychology that deals with the performance and behaviour of an individual while performing sports.

*Ans* Sports psychology

**7** ......... is a dynamic process which reflected in the tendency for a group to stick together and remain united in the pursuit of goals and objectives.

*Ans* Team cohesion

### State True or false

**8** Adolescents are very conscious of their social status and their personal identity.

*Ans* True

**9** Sports psychology helps the coaches to make a good coaching technique.

*Ans* True

### Assertion-Reason

**10** **Assertion** (A) Psychology is the science of human behaviour.

**Reason** (R) Psychology is not related to sports. In the context of above two statements, which one of the following is correct?

**Codes**

(a) Both A and R are true and R is the correct explanation of A
(b) Both A and R are true, but R is not the correct explanation of A
(c) A is true, but R is false
(d) A is false, but R is true

*Ans* (c) A is true, but R is false

**11** **Assertion** (A) Sports psychology plays a major role in learning motor skills.

**Reason** (R) Growth refers to structural and physiological changes.

In the context of above two statements, which one of the following is correct?

**Codes**

(a) Both A and R are true and R is the correct explanation of A
(b) Both A and R are true, but R is not the correct explanation of A
(c) A is true, but R is false
(d) A is false, but R is true

*Ans.* (b) Both A and R are true, but R is not the correct explanation of A

**12** **Assertion** (A) Adolescent age period is quite dynamic in nature.

**Reason** (R) In this age group, both girls and boys go through the emotional and physical changes.

In the context of above two statements, which one of the following is correct?

**Codes**

(a) Both A and R are true and R is the correct explanation of A
(b) Both A and R are true, but R is not the correct explanation of A
(c) A is true, but R is false
(d) A is false, but R is true

*Ans.* (a) Both A and R are true and R is the correct explanation of A

## VERY SHORT ANSWER TYPE QUESTIONS

**13** Define psychology.

*Ans* According to the Oxford Dictionary, Psychology is the scientific study of the human mind and its functions, especially those affecting behaviour in a given context.

**14** How would you define sports psychology?

*Ans* Sports psychology is that branch of psychology which is intimately connected with human behaviour on the play field, both under practice and competitive situations, with a view to bring about qualitative improvement in performance and maintain the same even during the stresses of competition.

**15** Enlist some of the problems faced by adolescents.

*Ans* Adolescents face many problems including problems of social standing, lack of stability and adjustment, problems related to sex and problems of aggression and uncontrollable emotions.

**16** What may adolescents become victims of if their problems are not managed in time?

*Ans* Adolescents may become victims of smoking, drug abuse, alcohol, unsafe abortion (girls), and other undesirable activities if their problems are not managed in time.

**17** Write any two steps for improving team Cohesion?

*Ans* Below are the key steps to what you can do to establish and improve team cohesion:

- Set team goals
- Set individual goals

## SHORT ANSWER TYPE QUESTIONS

**18** Write a short note on sports psychology.

*Ans* Sports psychology is the branch of applied psychology that deals with the performance and behaviour of an individual while performing sports and any other physical activity.

It is a multidisciplinary science that uses psychological knowledge and skills to address optimal performance and well-being of athletes, developmental and social aspects of sports participation, and systemic issues associated with sports settings and organisations.

In other words, sports psychology involves the study of how psychological factors, such as behaviour, arousal, motivation and aspiration, affect performance and how participation in sport and exercise affect psychological and physical factors.

**19** Explain the physical, mental and adjustment problems of adolescents.

*Ans* These problems of adolescents are explained below

(i) **Physical Problems** In the stage of adolescence, both girls and boys go through immense bodily changes. Girls start menstruating and nightfall starts in boys.

The lack of knowledge of such changes makes the adolescents feel restless and worried. As a result, they often go through sleepless nights and are unable to rest leading to various health problems.

(ii) **Mental Problems** At this stage, children suffer from immense stress, anxiety and tension. With a lot of things going on around them, their emotions are uncontrollable and their concentration power declines.

This severely affects their studies and also results in many social problems.

(iii) **Issues of Adjustment** An adolescent becomes highly conscious of himself/herself and of the world around him/her. He/She tries to find himself/herself a place within this world.

However, adolescents constantly go through the changes which makes them unstable. Their behaviour become erratic as they are not able to adjust themselves to such changes. Therefore, they find it difficult to coordinate and adjust easily with others. They feel that they are constantly under pressure and desire a free atmosphere.

**20** Write a short note on the need to manage the problems faced by adolescents.

*Ans* Adolescence is a very important stage of development as it faces rapid and important physical developments.

In fact, it is a period of growth and development that acts as a bridge of transition from childhood to adulthood.

This stage has been identified as a period of storm and stress. The adolescent undergoes extreme variations in emotions.

In a state of instability as they are not sure of their capacities, interests and the treatment, they face intense emotions, confusion, etc.
Therefore, the lack of balance and understanding in the changes happening in their lives results in lot of problems that the adolescents face in their day-to-day lives.
The only source of comfort during these times, for them, are their peer with whom they might develop bad habits.
Thus, the knowledge of these problems and how to manage them becomes crucial not only for educators but for parents as well.
With this knowledge, they can help the children in laying a strong foundation for them and teach them to solve such problems for the future. Hence, it is essential to know these problems as well as the bad habits that an adolescent may develop.

**21** What is team cohesion? How can we Improve team cohesion?

*Ans* Team cohesion is a dynamic process which reflected in the tendency for a group to stick together and remain united in the pursuit of goals and objectives. It is essentially how well a team works together and is crucial for a sports team to be successful.

Successful team cohesion in sport is influenced by individuals' view of their team and the objective set out to achieve. The success of football/soccer teams such as Liverpool, Manchester United or the success of New Zealand's rugby team and the tremendous success of Indian Cricket team is based on how well the individual athletes/players are performing as well as how successful the team are working together.

Team cohesion is useful as it can both improve performance and motivation of a team. If a team work well together, this improves their team cohesion, this in turn improves performance. This then improves personal satisfaction. Thus improving team cohesion and then the cycle continues either on an upward or downward trend.

Below are the key steps to what you can do to establish and improve team cohesion:

- Set team goals
- Set individual goals
- Provide feedback to individuals as well as a team
- Listen to your athletes/players feedback
- Work together to achieve the goal
- Reward effort and performance
- Recognise improvement
- Establish an environment for success by setting expectations and professionalism.

**22** Praveen in his adolescence and he lives in society 'Y'. During a councelling session in his school he informs councellor about his bad habits.
Based on this case, answer the following questions.

(i) The adolescent age group lies between
(a) 10-15 (b) 12-20
(c) 13-14 (d) 13-122

(ii) What problems are faced by adolescents?
(a) Drugs abuse (b) Sex related issue
(c) Both (a) and (b) (d) None of these

(iii) Being a councellor, what you will suggest to Praveen, so that he can follow right path?
(a) Sex education
(b) Doing constructive activities
(c) Making good friends
(d) All of the above

*Ans* (i) (c) 13-14
(ii) (c) Both (a) and (b)
(iii) (d) All of the above

## LONG ANSWER TYPE QUESTIONS

**23** How is psychology important for sportspersons?

*Ans* Sports psychology plays a very important role in improving the performance of a sportsperson. Its importance is clearly highlighted below

(i) **Enhancement of Physiological Capacities** Sports psychology plays a unique role in the enhancement of physiological capacities such as strength, speed, flexibility etc.

Motivation and proper feedback plays a major role in the enhancement of physical caoacity of a sportsperson.

(ii) **Learning Motor Skills** Sports psychology plays a major role in learning motor skills. Such a learning depends on the individual's level of readiness, *i.e.* both physiological and psychological readiness.

It plays an essential role as well as attitudes of an individual towards in understanding psychological readiness and intrerests efficient learning and performance of a motor skill.

(iii) **Psychological Preparation for Competition** Sports psychology plays a significant role in the psychological preparation of an athlete. It focuses on improving mental abilities, reducing stress, and building the competitive spirit among athletes.

(iv) **Understanding Behaviour** Sports psychology helps in understanding the behaviour of athletes or sportspersons engaged in competitive sports.

Coaches also come to know the interest, attitude towards physical activity, instinct, drive and personality of a sportsperson.

(v) **Controlling Emotions** Sports psychology plays an important role in controlling the emotions of sportspersons during practice as well as in competition.

Spontaneous and uncontrollable outbursts of emotions such as anger, fear etc. may lead to decline in performance. Hence, it is important to control emotions during competitions.

Sports psychology plays a vital role at such a juncture, as it helps in balancing the arousal of emotions, which further improves performance.

(vi) **Helps to Solve Emotional Problems of Sportspersons** Stress, tension and anxiety are natural during competitions or tournaments as well as during practice/training.

There may be some other emotional problems such as depression, frustration, anorexia, panic etc. Knowledge of sports psychology is helpful in such situations.

Techniques of relaxation and concentration for stress management can be applied by sportspersons who are facing such problems.

**24** Briefly explain the problems faced by adolescents.

*Ans* Due to the sudden and rapid biological, psychological and behavioural changes taking place in the body, an adolescent suffers through many problems.

The only source of comfort during these times for them are their peer with whom they might develop bad habits.

The problems of adolescents are described below

(i) **Aggression and Uncontrollable Emotions** Adolescents are very emotional and hyper. They go through sudden change of mood and outbursts almost every day. One aspect of this suddenness of change include the thoughts of suicide, self-hate, anxiety and depression that they may face.

Adolescents also display aggressive behaviour They overreact to minor situations and are rebellious towards criticism. This may get them into bad anti-social habits and also may land them into problems that may affect their future.

(ii) **Social Standing** Adolescents are very conscious of their social status and their personal identity. They want to make their own respectable place in the society while fitting into it.

To fit perfectly, they come under peer pressure which sometimes leads them into wrong means of obtaining luxurious things.

They feel themselves to be important and demand the same respect from others. They sometimes become overconfident and try to hide their mistakes. They put their blame on others and protect themselves.

(iii) **Problems Related to Sex** In contrast to the previous stages, adolescents now are more attracted to the opposite sex. Their urges related to this attraction is so strong that they become restless and may take wrong means to attain them.

(iv) **Drug Addiction** The imbalance and instability that the adolescents face lead them towards developing bad habits.

In addition, the curiosity, lack of knowledge and peer pressure leads them towards the drugs and alcohol.

This experimentation can turn into addiction which can spoil the entire future of the teenager.

(v) **Criminal Activities** The desire to be accepted by the peers and the restlessness as a result of changes occurring in their lives, makes them more inclined to participate in criminal activities.

Adolescents indulge in criminal offences like thefts, stealing, violence, molestation, etc.

**25** How can the problems of adolescence be managed? Explain in detail.

*Ans* Problems of adolescence can be managed by using the five techniques mentioned below

(i) **Proper Counselling** The problems of adolescence are the result of natural growth and development of the body

At this time, lack of experience develops shyness, introversion, etc in them.

It prevents them from expressing their problems to their elders. This condition may increase their mental tension. Therefore, proper counselling and guidance by parents, teachers and elders is the best method for management of adolescent problems.

(ii) **Participation in Co-curricular Activities** Adolescence is an age of energy and dynamism. If the adolescents' energy is utilised in activities other than academics i.e. sports, dance, social functions etc. their surplus energy is spent properly.

As a result, emotional upheavals as well as instability will not occur. This helps in the development of motor skills and in harmonising the personality of an adolescent.

(iii) **Mutual Understanding** Family members and all elders must try to understand the problems of adolescents. They should be symphathetic and affectionate.
At the same time, adolescents must also understand that their parents are trying to help them for their betterment.

(iv) **Sex Education** Adolescents must be educated about sex, just like any other lessons taught in school, in a straightforward way. Correct knowledge enables them to understand their urges better.
They must be properly guided to tackle all the problems related to sex as well as to channelise their drives towards constructive work.

(v) **Adequate Independence** Adolescents want adequate freedom in behaviour. They wish to express their views independently. They must be provided a proper platform to express their feelings.

They should be allowed recreational and creative activities. Orders and strict instructions should not be imposed on them. Parents should try to understand the sentiments of adolescents and cooperate with them.

**26** Aditya is a councellor in a school 'X' of Uttar Pradesh. During parent teacher, meeting, some parents approached Aditya and briefed him various problem being faced by their adolescent children. Now, what advise Aditya will give to teachers and concerned parents to solved the problems.

*Ans* In order to solve the problems of parents, Aditya should given following suggession.

- Adolescent children should be given proper counselling. The guidance by parents, teachers and elders is the best method for the managements of adolescent problems.
- The energy of adolescent should be utilised activities other than academics i.e. sports, dance, social function etc. This helps in the development of their motor skills and in harmonising the personality of an adolescent.
- Family members and all elders must try to understand the problems of adolescent. They should be symphathetic and affectionate towards them and must try to build a relationship with them.
- Parents must recognise the opinions and views of adolescent. Parents should not scold them in front of others.
- Adolescent should be provided proper sex education, so that they deal with all the sex related issues.
- Moreover, religious and moral education is very important for managing adolescents.
- Adolescent should be provided suitable environment for growth and development.

**27** Describe the steps team cohesion. What are the factors that affect team cohesion?

*Ans* The key steps to improve team cohesion are

- Set team goals
- Set individual goals
- Provide feedback to individuals as well as a team
- Listen to your athletes/players feedback
- Work together to achieve the goal
- Reward effort and performance
- Recognise improvement
- Establish an environment for success by setting expectations and professionalism.

Many factors affect the cohesion that will develop on a team. Such factors include the environment (e.g. social and physical), personal factors (e.g. personality), team factors (e.g. norms), and leadership factors (e.g. styles). Although each variable plays an essential role, the leadership factors may be the most important. This distinction is vital for coaches to know as they have a significant influence on how well team cohesion develops. In fact, a practitioner's efforts to foster cohesion can be viewed as a performance in its own right. Athletes instinctively model their coach's behavior and an awareness of this can help coaches affect team cohesion in a positive way.

**28** Elucidate upon the developmental characteristics of early childhood.

*Ans* The early childhood stage starts at the age of 2 years and goes up to 6 years. As the most important period of growth and development, in this period the child is a preschool-going toddler. Some of the common characteristics seem in a child in this age are as given below

**Physical Characteristics**

- A child in this stage gains height and weight rapidly. Three-year-old preschoolers may grow to be about 38 inches tall and weigh about 14 kg. In a year or two, this child will gain 2-3 inches of height and around 2 kgs of weight.
- The body proportions of the child changes and the baby look disappears.
- In this stage, the development of muscular systems and the nervous system is as dramatic as the previous stage.
- The motor skills that the child starts to learn at infancy keeps on continuing. In fact, they get more refined and graceful at this stage.
- Physical activities in this stage are not very rigorous. Children starts playing simple games with other children.

**Cognitive Characteristics**

- A child's memory power increases considerably in this stage.
- At this stage, children start to communicate with ease. Their vocabulary increases, and they are able to form simple as well as complex sentences.
- Just like infancy, children at this stage are full of emotions that they cannot control.
- It is a stage of social development of a child. He/She is very keen to learn about his/her environment and surroundings. He/She not only learns to make new friends but also learns various good manner and social habits.
- Early childhood is also a period when some common interests develop. These include interest in play, human body, self, clothes, etc.

# SELF ASSESSMENT

## OBJECTIVE ANSWER TYPE QUESTIONS

1 How is psychology defined today?
(a) The science of behaviour and mental processes
(b) The science of human behaviour and mental processes
(c) The science of mind
(d) The study of motivation, emotion, personality, adjustment and abnormality

2 What is the meaning of development?
(a) Change in structure of body organ
(b) Change in size
(c) Change in maturity
(d) All of these

3 **Assertion** (A) Sports psychology helps coaches in guiding the sportpersons.
**Reason** (R) The knowledge of growth and development is essential for physical education teachers as well as parents.
In the context of above two statements, which one of the following is correct?
(a) Both A and R are true and R is the correct explanation of A
(b) Both A and R are true, but R is not the correct explanation of A
(c) A is true, but R is false
(d) A is false, but R is true

## VERY SHORT ANSWER TYPE QUESTIONS

4 Define sports psychology.

5 Mention the importance of sports psychology.

## SHORT ANSWER TYPE QUESTIONS

6 Describe any two developmental characteristics of adolescence.

7 How team cohesion can be improved?

## LONG ANSWER TYPE QUESTIONS

8 Discuss methods adopted for management of adolescent problems in detail.

9 Explain the importance of sports psychology.

CHAPTER

10

# Training and Doping in Sports

Today, sports and physical education are specialised fields. All sports and physical activities require a specific, scientific and systematic set of skills and techniques that leads to a successful performance of a player.

A sportsperson also needs special types of physical fitness components. These set of skills, techniques and components are achieved by training that further improves the performance of an individual. Hence, training is essential in the field of sports and physical education.

### CHAPTER CHECKLIST

- Meaning and Definition of Sports Training
- Training Load
- Warming-up
- Limbering Down
- Skill, Technique, Tactics and Strategies
- Concept of Doping

## Meaning and Definition of Sports Training

The word 'training' means the process of preparation for some task. It is a process by which one gains practical and theoretical knowledge.

Training in sports means the preparation of a sportsperson based on the scientific principles for giving the highest level of performance. It is a specialised process of all-round physical strengthening aimed at improving an athlete's fitness in a selected activity.

Various definitions of sports training as given by scholars are as follows

- According to **Thiess and Schnabel**, "Sports training is a scientifically based and pedagogically organised process which, through planned and systematic effort, affects performance ability and performance readiness, aims at sports perfection and performance improvement as well as the contest in sports competitions."
- According to **Martin**, "Sports training is a planned and controlled process of achieving goals in which the changes of motor performance and behaviour are made through measures of content, methods and organisation."

- According to **D Harre**, "Sports training, based on scientific knowledge, is a pedagogical process of sports perfection which, through systematic effect on psycho-physical performance ability and performance readiness, aims at leading the sportsman to high and highest performance. Through active and conscious interaction with the given demands in sports training, the sportman's personality develops according to the norms and standards of socialist society."

Training is a long-term, systematic and a continuous process that recognises an individual's needs and capabilities to develop exercises based on scientific knowledge that enhances sports performance.

It develops basic and advanced skills, techniques, tactics, strategies, etc. for all sports activities and competitions.

Often, the concept of training and preparation coincide but they are not identical. While preparation is a broader and a complex term including training, nutrition, competitions, etc. training is one part of preparation that includes fitness, safety, individual care, exercise, etc.

## Concept of Sports Training

Sports training is a concept whose practice is spread over many years. Training method for a particular sport consists of training periods which are split into sessions and schedules.

These sessions and schedules are progressive in nature and training continues till mastery over a skill is achieved.

All training programmes are divided into three parts as discussed below

1. **Preparatory Period** This is the basic training programme wherein stress is given on basic fitness and skill for competitions. It is further divided into number of phases as follows
   - **Phase I** It includes various conditioning programmes that develops general abilities such as endurance, speed, strength, etc. taking about 6-12 weeks of practice. Training techniques include weightlifting, circuit training, running, etc.
   - **Phase II** In this phase, training focuses on mastery of advanced skills which continues for 4-8 weeks. Various techniques of specific games are also introduced in this phase.
   - **Phase III** In this phase, a player develops the tactics and strategies to be used under difficult situations like that of a competition. This phase continues over 2-5 weeks.
2. **Competition Period** In this period, the player achieves its top form and can participate in competitions to achieve top performance. Training, in this period, has maximum intensity. Sportspersons are trained fully technically and tactically with main focus on speed.
3. **Transitional Period** This period comes after the competition. In this period, a player relaxes and rests to recover from stress. The main purpose of this period is the maintenance of physical abilities for next competition.

## Objectives of Sports Training

Training improves an individual's physical, psychological, intellectual and technical capacities and capabilities.

Training techniques have the following objectives

1. **Physical Preparation** Athletes need a holistic physical development as a training base as well as overall physical fitness. The purpose is to increase endurance and strength, develop speed, improve flexibility, and refine coordination, thus achieving a harmoniously developed body.
2. **Technical Preparation** Technical training involves developing the capacity to perform all technical actions correctly, perfecting the required technique, performing specific techniques and improving the technique of related sports while ensuring the ability to perform all movements correctly.
3. **Tactical Preparation** Tactical factors include improving strategy by studying the tactics of opponents, expanding the optimal tactics within athletes' capabilities, perfecting strategies, and developing a strategy considering future opponents.
4. **Psychological Preparation** Psychological preparation is also necessary to ensure enhanced physical performance. Psychological training improves discipline, perseverance, willpower, confidence, and courage.

# Principles of Sports Training

Sports training is based on certain scientific principles which guides the coaches, trainers and sportspersons to develop and implement suitable training programmes. These principles are generally agreed upon guidelines that are grounded in sport science and hold true in practice and competition.

The key sports training principles are

1. **Principle of Continuity** Training should be a continuous process, as any break in training will reduce physiological capacity of the sportsperson. Training should be carried out on a regular basis without any long period of inactivity. However, there should be intervals of rest and recovery between training sessions.
2. **Principle of Balanced Training** This principle suggests that the right mix of training activities, diet and healthy lifestyle habits are required for optimal functioning.
   Going to extremes can result in poor performance, illness and injury. Overtraining, consuming too much of certain foods and nutrients (including water), or adopting crash diets are examples of imbalance.
3. **Principle of Individual Differences** It concerns adjustments in training based on differences between individual athletes. As different persons respond differently to exercise and load, their training programmes should be modified to take care of their differences.
4. **Principle of Overload** It provides guidance about intensity of workloads and increasing the workload after the body has adapted to the previous load. It means that the training loads should be increased for improving the performance of sportspersons. Once the load is adapted, it is no longer efficient. Hence, the load must be increased after a passage of time for continuous improvement.
5. **Principle of Rest and Recovery** It concerns rest and recovery between exercises and time gap between workouts. The body regenerates between training sessions and so intervals between them should be planned accordingly.
6. **Principle of Reversibility** It provides guidance about detraining when athletes stop working out. It says that sportspersons lose the beneficial effects of training when they stop working out.
   The physiological effects of fitness training diminishes over time, causing the body to revert to its pre-training condition. Conversely, it also means that detraining effects can be reversed when athletes resume training.
7. **Principle of Specificity** It tells how workouts change sportspersons' bodies to prepare for the demands of their sports. To become better in a particular skill, the sportsperson must train in that particular exercise or skill required in it. For example, Gymnasts require more flexibility training.
8. **Principle of Transfer** It provides guidance on how workout activities can speed up the athlete's results in competitive performances. It says that learning and performing one activity affects the performance of related skills and activities.
   This principle is essential for designing practice strategies that have the greatest positive impact on competitive performance. Correctly applying this principle saves valuable training time besides accelerating results.
9. **Principle of Variation** It provides direction about variations in exercises, rest time, intensity and other variables.
   As training occurs over a long period of time, it tends to become boring for both the sportsperson and the coach.
   Varying the training programmes helps maintain the interest and motivation of the sportsperson. Further, introduction of new activities and including fun games into the session can prevent problems such as plateaus in performance and overtraining effects.
10. **Principle of Progression** According to this principle, the overload should not be increased too slowly or too rapidly as it may result in injury or muscle damage. Exercising above the target zone can be dangerous.
    The principle of progression also makes us realise the need for proper rest and recovery. The constant overload can lead to exhaustion and injury.
11. **Principle of General and Specific Preparation** For the improvement of performance, both the general and specific preparations are significant. General preparation serves as the base for specific preparation.
    The general preparation increases the functional capacity of all the body systems and organs while, specific preparation is required to improve those systems and organs, on which the performance of sportspersons directly depends.

12. **Principle of Active Involvement** The principle of active involvement means that for an effective training programme, the athlete must participate actively and willingly.

    Various experts list and describe sports training principles in different ways but the underlying concepts in all of them are essentially the same.

    All of these principles work together in coordination with each other during sports training to effectively improve the performance.

# Training Load

In sports training, the load is a major concern. Efforts should be made so that possible work can be done with minimum effort. Load is defined as the amount of work done by an individual's body. It is the psychological and phsiological demand put on the body parts through motor stimuli resulting in improvement and maintenance of higher performance capacity. Sports training consists of physical exercises.

## Overload

During training of sports persons, load is given to the players according to their capacity. Whenever this load goes beyond the capacity of an individual, the physiological and psychological functions get disturbed. Though this increased load does not affect the sports person immediately, if the administration of the overload continues for a longer period, it results in decrease of his/her performance.

The important signs and symptoms of over load are fatigue, decline in performance, loss of interest in sports, loss of concentration, lack of motivation, sleep disorder, loss of appetite and prone to injuries.

## Adaptation Process and Training Load

Adaptation is defined as the adjustment of physical and psychological functional systems to the training load. Adaptation to a load results in the enhancement of performance capacity. Thus, a sports person is able to increase his/her performance as a result of adaptation process.

Adaptation process demands that a sportsperson maintains regularity in training. If a sportsperson is exposed to new and unfamiliar load in a systematic planned way the adaptation process will be faster.

## Recovery

Recovery is the ability to meet or exceed performance in a particular activity. Recovery may include an active component (such as a post-workout walk) and/or a passive component (such as a post-workout hydrotherary treatment).

## Types of Recovery

- **Immediate Recovery** The most rapid form of recovery, is immediate recovery which occurs during exercise itself. With this phase of recovery, energy regeneration occurs with the lower extremities between strides. As each leg recovers more quickly, the walker will be able to complete the striding task more efficiently.
- **Short Term Recovery** It involves recovery between sets of a given exercise or between interval workouts. Short-term recovery is the most common form of recovery in training.
- **Training Recovery** It is used to describe the recovery between workout sessions or athletic competition. If consecutive workouts occur (such as within the same day) without appropriate recovery time, the individual may be improperly prepared for the next training session.

## Factors of Recovery

The following factors are involved in the ability of a person to recover

- Muscle soreness and weakness
- Poor exercise performance
- Decrease in appetite
- Increased infection
- Quality and quantity of sleep
- Gastrointestinal abnormalities

# Warming-up

Before performing any sports activity, a preliminary preparatory activity is performed for the physiological and psychological preparation of an athlete. This preparation is called warming-up.

Warming-up is a process of heating the body muscles through certain short-term exercises such that an activity is performed in most refined and efficient way.

Some definitions of warming-up given by scholars are

- "Warming-up consists of a series of preparatory exercises either before a training session or competition."

- "Warming-up is a preliminary exercise of physical and mental preparation for a strenuous exertion."
- According to **De Vries**, "Warming-up increases temperature of blood, and muscles improve the performance."

Warm-up consists of light cardiovascular exercises which are combined with stretches to help the sportsperson prepare physically, mentally, and physiologically for any type of training.

It makes the muscles ready to respond efficiently to exercises such as jogging, running, etc.

The intensity of the warm-up should begin at a low level, gradually building to the level of intensity required during training or competition.

The warm-up aims to

- Prepare the body and mind for the activity.
- Increase the body's core temperature.
- Increase heart rate.
- Increase breathing rate.

*Warming-up*

## Types and Methods of Warming-up

The types and methods of warming-up are described as below

### Psychological Warming-up

This type of warming-up prepares the mental attitude of a sportsperson towards a competition. It makes an athlete mentally ready to bear stress and anxiety.

This includes motivation, feedback, behavioural changes, etc.

### Physiological Warming-up

This type of warming-up makes a sportsperson physically ready for all trainings and competitions. It is categorised into two types, which are described below

1. **Active Warming-up**

   In active warming-up, an athlete participates in various physical activities to improve the efficiency of body and to tone up the muscles.

   It is performed for a duration of 10 to 30 minutes and the activities involved in this warming-up does not make the person feel tired.

   Active warming can be subdivided into two types that are

   - **General Warming-up** Exercises in general warming-up are performed for all sports. It consists of simple exercises such as

     ***Jogging/Running*** An athlete should jog or run for about 5 to 10 minutes with a slow intensity which should increase with time.

     ***Simple Exercises*** After jogging, simple exercises should be performed in a relaxed position starting from simple exercises moving to complex ones.

     ***Striding*** It means covering a distance in long strides. It should be done for 60 metres with 6 to 8 repetitions.

     ***Stretching Exercises*** It is the most critical part of warming-up. It involves stretching the joints and muscles so that they are stronger, healthier and more flexible.

   - **Specific Warming-up** Exercises in specific warming-up are different for different sports. It tones the muscles that are used in different sports and improves the mobility of smaller joints. This type of warming-up is also known as formal activity and is performed after general warming-up.

     Specific warm-up for some games and sports are

     ***For Badminton*** Jumping, tossing shuttle, high and low clears, smashing etc.

     ***For Cricket*** Bowling, batting action, catching, net practice, etc.

     ***For Football*** Ball dribbling, juggling, kicking, etc.

     ***For Hockey*** Stick rotation, dribbling, taping, hitting, etc.

     ***For Tennis*** Service, knocking, passing shots, volley clear, slice clear, etc.

*For Basketball* Shuttle running, dribbling, shooting, dodging etc.

Dribbling Drill

2. Passive Warming-up
   The main aim of passive warming-up is to increase the body temperature without any expenditure of energy in the process of warming-up.
   This type of warm-up does not include any physical activity or exercise. It includes external sources such as body massage, sunbath, steam bath, hot drinks etc.

## Importance of Warming-up

Many scholars all around the world have different opinions regarding the importance and use of warming-up exercises.

Some scholars believe that warming-up is not essential for any sports. However, at large, most eminent educationists and physiologists believe that warming-up is important. The following points clearly describe the importance of warming-up

1. **Increases the Body Temperature**
   A proper warming-up exercises increase the body and muscle temperature. As the muscles are warmed-up, the speed with which the muscles functions is increased which ultimately improves the performance of an athlete.
2. **Improves the Functioning of Muscular and Nervous System**
   Warming-up increases the rate at which muscles relax and contract. It increases the speed of the nerve impulses and decreases resistance in muscle capillaries. Further, the neuromuscular coordination improves which increases the efficiency of sportspersons.
3. **Increased Metabolism and Circulation**
   Warming-up increases the speed of transfer of oxygen and fuel of tissues. It increases the metabolic rate which leads to higher energy levels. An increase in 0.5°C increases the metabolic rate by 7%.
4. **Improves Sports Skills**
   Warm-up increases flexibility, strength, speed and endurance of a sportsperson.
5. **Reduces the Chance of Injuries**
   Warming-up ensures that the muscles are well prepared for any competition. Further, an efficient nervous system improves and sharpens the reaction time. This reduces the risk of wear and tear as well as any injury.
6. **Improves Performance**
   Warming-up increases the concentration power of athletes which, alongwith efficient skills, makes one perfect the skills, techniques and tactics that helps in attaining success in sports.

# Limbering Down

After training or any sport competitions, the body is required to cool down. It is also called as warming down, and includes exercises that brings the body in the normal state.

The limbering down exercises allows the body to transit gradually from the exertional state of the body to a near-resting state.

As a necessary procedure after every rigorous activity, limbering down includes exercises such as jogging and stretching.

Jogging for 5 to 10 minutes is suggested to lower the body temperature. After jogging, static exercises are performed for 5 to 10 minutes.

Stretching exercises focusing on all major muscle groups should be performed to help the muscles relax, realign and re-establish the normal range of movements.

Limbering Down

### Types and Methods of Limbering Down

- **Stretching** Static stretching is the appropriate form of stretching to aid in the cooling down procedure. It aids in decreasing the body's temperature, removing lactic acid from the muscles and increasing flexibility. Each stretch should be held for a minimum of 10–20 seconds and stretched to the point of mild discomfort but not pain. Each muscle used in mid-high intensity exercise should then be stretched during the cool-down.
- **Half-time Cooling Down** It involves using either ice vests, cooling products or manually cooling down the body through gentle light intensity exercise to cool down the body during half time or breaks in an activity or sport. Half-time cooling down has proven to decrease body temperature and increase aerobic performance.

## Importance of Limbering Down

Just as warming-up is essential before any sports activity, limbering down is also important after any sports activity, especially after vigorous exercise.

However, it is often ignored by sportspersons.

As a matter of fact, it offers many advantanges that are described below

1. **Normalises Body Temperature**
   During strenuous training or competition, the body temperature increases. Limbering down helps in gradually reducing this temperature to normal.
2. **Removes Waste Products**
   During training or competition, waste products like lactic acid, uric acid, sulphates, chlorides, phosphates and carbon dioxide get accumulated in the muscles. Limbering down gradually removes these waste products from the muscles so that the muscles can work efficiently.
3. **Reduces Tension and Dizziness**
   Muscular and mental tension reduces during limbering down. If it is not done, the heart rate reduces suddenly and blood tends to pool in the legs and feet, which may cause dizziness and even fainting.
4. **Improves Oxygen Supply**
   As the amount of oxygen in the body is less during training or competition, the oxygen level needs to be restored. This restoration takes place during limbering down.
5. **Decreases Adrenaline Level**
   Limbering down reduces adrenaline level in the blood which normalises the blood flow in the body.
6. **Reduces Muscle Stiffness**
   Limbering down prevents muscles from getting stiff, as they gradually relax to their normal state.
7. **Returns Heart Rate to Normal**
   After finishing training or competition, the heart rate will come down very quickly if limbering down is not carried out, which is not good for blood flow. Limbering down gradually reduces the heart rate over a period of time, thus gradually normalising the blood flow.

Thus, limbering down is an important step in aiding recovery after training or competition. It should occur immediately after completion of the activity and should last 5 to10 minutes.

# Skill, Technique, Tactics and Strategies

### Meaning of Skill

Skill is basically the ability to perform a whole movement. It is the amount of effectiveness with which any motor action is performed. If any action required for fulfilling a purpose in any form of physical activity is done automatically, it is termed as a skill.

In other words, a skill in an action that is learnt for purpose and is needed so that an individual is able to participate in various activities related to it.

Instances of skills in sports are shooting in basketball, serving in tennis, heading in football etc.

### Classification of Skill

In the field of physical education and sports, skills play an essential role, as every sport requires a specific set of skills which allows an individual to play that sport. Owing to many different characteristic of skills, it is very difficult to categorise them in a clear cut manner. However, generally some types of skills are accepted. These are as follows

1. **Open**
   These skills are not fully under our control and are thus unpredictable. For example, in badminton, performing any skill depends upon the position of the opponent.
2. **Closed**
   These skills take place in a stable environment where the sportsperson knows exactly what to do, and when to do like serving in tennis.

3. **Simple**
   These skills are straightforward, easy to learn and not difficult to perform, like an underarm service in badminton, etc.
4. **Complex**
   These skills are complicated and difficult to perform. They can sometimes result in injury if not done carefully, like handspring in gymnastics.
5. **Gross**
   These skills involve large muscle movements involving fundamental patterns like walking, running and jumping. Putting the shot is an instance of a gross skill.
6. **Fine**
   Such skills involve complex precise movements using small muscle groups and a high level of hand-eye coordination. Shooting in snooker is an instance of a fine skill.
7. **Discrete**
   These skills are brief and have a clearly defined start and finish, like a penalty flick in hockey.
8. **Serial**
   This is a group of skills performed in a particular order one after another, like the triple jump in athletics.
9. **Continuous**
   Such skills do not have a clearly defined start or end. The end of one cycle of movement act as a beginning of the next skill. Swimming and cycling are some instances of continuous skills.
10. **Individual**
    These skills are performed in isolation, like high jump and long jump.
11. **Coactive**
    These skills are performed at the same time as other sportspersons but not in a confrontation, like rhythmic swimming.
12. **Interactive**
    These skills are performed where other participants are directly involved, like playing basketball or football.

## Meaning of Technique

A technique is the basic movement of a sport or event. It involves scientific and economical methods that tell a sportsperson how an action is performed so as to achieve top performance.

In other words, a technique in a sport is a sequence of movements that makes the performance better.

For example, in soccer, there are many techniques such as dribbling, passing, shooting, etc. that are used to achieve success.

**Soccer Technique**

As there are a number of techniques that a player can use, a particular technique is selected by a player to suit his/her level. Any technique is selected by a player on the following basis

- Improves his/her performance
- Suites the skill level of player
- Be within the rules
- Be the best in the given circumstances

## Meaning of Tactics

Tactics are actions and strategies planned to achieve an overall objective and, in the sport, that objective is predominantly to win.

Tactical preparation enables athletes to make the most effective utilisation of their motor and technical abilities in competitions.

The factors affecting tactics are

- Opposition – including their strengths and weaknesses
- Players available for selection
- The importance of the match
- Weather

## Meaning of Strategies

Strategy is something like, having the goal to win the season or win the match as well as making a plan to achieve this, such as developing an athlete's power or selecting the right players, etc.

Strategy often requires a SWOT (strengths, weaknesses, opportunities, and threats) analysis.

Strategising is a great way to improve the team's synchronicity. The process involves aligning each member to the same end goal. Each of the players' motivations are combined and the team's morale consequently, improves. Having the same focus and end goal will have them work as a unit in the game. Formulating strategies will involve open conversations and lots of set planning of techniques and tactics. As a result, players will be more confident about what is expected of them on the field. Every player will have a better understanding of their input in the team's performance and will be more motivated.

## Concept of Doping

The word 'doping' refers to the use of drugs in the field of sports to enhance the physical capacity of sportspersons. In general, it is the use of performance enhancing substances by the athletes or sportspersons to gain an advantage over competitors.

The concept of doping is not new in sports. In ancient Greece, there were specialists who would offer nutritional ingredients such as mushrooms, opium and other herbal beverages that enhanced sports performance. Even Gladiators are known to use various substances that aimed at enhancing strength.

In the modern times, the use of doping first came out in 1904 Olympics, when Thomas Hicks won the marathon race. He had taken injections of strychnine.

The increase in doping increased so much that in 1928, the International Athletic Association Federation banned doping followed by other sport federations.

With the introduction of synthetic hormones, the problem of doping worsened. As a result, sports federations all-round the globe, banned doping and emphasised on blood testing.

The International Olympic Committee started considering the "presence in the human body of substances which are prohibited according to the list published by the IOC and/or the international organisation" as illegal.

Soon, the World Anti-Doping Agency (WADA) was formed in 1999 which defined doping as "the occurrence of one or more of the anti-doping rule violations set forth in Article 2.1 through Article 2.8 of the code." They set some anti-doping rules that identified doping as

- The presence of prohibited substances and methods.
- Use or attempted use of a prohibited substance or prohibited method by an athlete.
- Refusing or failing to submit sample collection after notification by the authority.
- Possession of prohibited substances or prohibited methods.
- Tampering or attempting to tamper with any part of the doping control process.
- Trafficking or attempted trafficking in any prohibited substance or prohibited methods.
- Failure to inform an athlete's whereabouts after being notified.
- Administering, or attempting to administer a prohibited substance or method to an athlete.

Therefore, doping refers to the substances that are prohibited by the authority.

Doping

## Disadvantages of Doping

### Physiological Effects of Doping

- Acne
- Male pattern baldness
- Liver damage
- Premature closure of the growth centres of long bones (in adolescents) which may result in stunted growth
- Increased aggressiveness and sexual appetite, sometimes resulting in abnormal sexual and criminal behaviour, often referred to as 'Roid Rage'
- Withdrawal from anabolic steroid use can be associated with depression, and in some cases, suicide.

### Gender Specific Effects (Males)

- Breast tissue development
- Shrinking of the testicles
- Impotence
- Reduction in sperm production

### Gender Specific Effects (Females)

- Deepening of the voice
- Cessation of breast development
- Growth of hair on the face, stomach and upper back
- Enlarged clitoris
- Abnormal menstrual cycles

# CHAPTER PRACTICE

## OBJECTIVE TYPE QUESTIONS

### Multiple Choice Questions (MCQs)

1 Which period of training comes after competition?

(a) Preparatory (b) Competition
(c) Transitional (d) Technical

*Ans* (c) Transitional

2 Which of the following is/are the signs of over load?

(a) fatigue
(b) decline in performance
(c) loss of appetite (d) All of these

*Ans* (d) All of these

3 What is defined as the amount of work done by an individual's body?

(a) Load (b) Stress
(c) Fatigue (d) Fracture point

*Ans* (a) Load

4 Which of the following is not a disadvantage of Doping in females?

(a) Deepening of the voice
(b) Abnormal Menstrual cycles
(c) impotence
(d) Growth of hair on the face

*Ans* (c) impotence

### Fill in the Blanks

5 .............. provides guidance about detraining when the athletes stop working out.

*Ans* Principle of reversibility

6 ........... skills are performed when competitors are directly involved in a sport.

*Ans* Interactive

### State True or False

7 Adaptation is defined as the adjustment of physical and psychological functional systems to the training load.

*Ans* True

8 Recovery is the ability to meet or exceed performance in a particular activity.

*Ans* True

### Assertion-Reason

9 **Assertion** (A) Sports training is planned and controlled process.
**Reason** (R) Training is essential in the field of sports and physical education.
In the context of above two statements, which one of the following is correct?

**Codes**

(a) Both A and R are true and R is the correct explanation of A
(b) Both A and R are true, but R is not the correct explanation of A
(c) A is true, but R is false
(d) A is false, but R is true

*Ans* (b) Both A and R are true, but R is not the correct explanation of A

10 **Assertion** (A) After training or any sports competitions, the body is required to cool down.
**Reason** (R) Technique is basically the ability to perform a whole movement.
In the context of above two statements, which one of the following is correct?

**Codes**

(a) Both A and R are true and R is the correct explanation of A
(b) Both A and R are true, but R is not the correct explanation of A
(c) A is true, but R is false
(d) A is false, but R is true

*Ans* (c) A is true, but R is false

## VERY SHORT ANSWER TYPE QUESTIONS

11 What is sports training?

*Ans* Sports training means 'the process of preparation for some task in sports'. The training process normally extends to a number of days, months and even years (like preparations for Olympic Games).

12 Why coaches rely on the principles of sports training?

*Ans* Coaches rely on well-established sports training principles to build fitness training programmes and develop sports skills.

These principles are generally agreed upon guidelines that consistently apply for training sportspersons successfully.

**13** Define in short, the concept of training load.

*Ans* Load is defined as the amount of work done by an individual's body. It is the psychological and physiological demand put on the body parts through motor stimuli resulting in improvement and maintenance of higher performance capacity.

**14** What is overload?

*Ans* During training of sports persons, load is given to the players according to their capacity. Whenever this load goes beyond the capacity of an individual the physiological and psychological functions get disturbed, it is called overload.

**15** What is adaptation process?

*Ans* Adaptation is defined as the adjustment of physical and psychological functional systems to the training load.

**16** What is recovery?

*Ans* Recovery is the ability to meet or exceed performance in a particular activity. Recovery may include an active component (such as a post-workout walk) and/or a passive component (such as a post-workout hydrotherary treatment).

**17** What are the disadvantages of doping? (any two)

*Ans* The disadvantages of doping are

(i) Acne

(ii) Liver Damage

**18** What do you understand by doping?

*Ans* Doping means the use of drugs in the field of sports to enhance the physical capacity of the athletes.

## C SHORT ANSWER TYPE QUESTIONS

**19** Enlist the principles of sports training.

*Ans* The principles of sports training are

- Continuity
- Balanced training
- Individual differences
- Overload
- Recovery
- Reversibility
- Specificity
- Transfer
- Variation
- Progression
- General and specific preparation
- Active involvement

**20** Explain any three principles of sports training.

*Ans* Three principles of sports training are

(i) **Principle of Balanced Training** It concerns achieving the right proportions between training activities and rest. It also relates to the body's tendency to return to normalcy or homeostasis.

(ii) **Principle of Individual Differences** It concerns adjustments in training based on differences between individual sportspersons.

(iii) **Principle of Overload** It provides guidance about intensity of workloads and increasing the workload after the body has adapted to the previous load.

**21** Define training load.

*Ans* In sports training, the load is a major concern. Efforts should be made so that possible work can be done with minimum effort. Load is defined as the amount of work done by an individual's body. It is the psychological and physiological demand put on the body parts through motor stimuli resulting in improvement and maintenance of higher performance capacity. Sports training consists of physical exercises.

**22** Explain the concept of overload.

*Ans* During training of sports persons, load is given to the players according to their capacity. Whenever this load goes beyond the capacity of an individual, the physiological and psychological functions get disturbed. Though this increased load does not affect the sports person immediately, if the administration of the overload continues for a longer period, it results in decrease of his/her performance. The important signs and symptoms of over load are: (i) fatigue, (ii) decline in performance, (iii) loss of interest in sports, (iv) loss of concentration, (v) lack of motivation, (vi) sleep disorder and (vii) loss of appetite (viii) prone to injuries.

**23** Explain the concept of adaptation.

*Ans* Adaptation is defined as the adjustment of physical and psychological functional systems to the training load. Adaptation to a load results in the enhancement of performance capacity. Thus, a sports person is able to increase his/her performance as a result of adaptation process. Adaptation process demands that a sports person maintains regularity in training. If a sports person is exposed to new and unfamiliar load in a systematic planned way the adaptation process will be faster.

**24** What are two reasons for the requirement of an effective training programme in sports? What is the result if they are not conducted?

*Ans* Two reasons for the requirement of an effective training programme in sports are

(i) Producing skilful high performers for success in major international competitions.

(ii) Development of healthy participants.

If such training programmes are not conducted, a sportsperson's potential will never be fulfilled.

**25** "Doping has been a part of the field of sports since time immemorial." Justify the statement.

*Ans* Doping refers to the use of drugs to enhance physical performance. The concept of doping is not new in sports.

In ancient Greece, there were specialists who would offer nutritional ingredients such as mushrooms, opium and other herbal beverages that enhanced sports performance.

Even Gladiators are known to use various substances that aimed at enhancing strength.

In the modern times, the use of doping first came out in 1904 Olympics, when Thomas Hicks won the marathon race. He had taken injections of strychnine.

After that the increase in doping increased so much that in 1928, the International Athletic Association Federation banned doping followed by other doping federations.

Soon, the International Olympic Committee started considering the "presence in the human body of substances which are prohibited according to the list published by the IOC and/or the international organisation" as illegal.

Hence, it can be said that doping has been a part of the field of sports since time immemorial.

## LONG ANSWER TYPE QUESTIONS

**26** Explain in brief the meaning and concept of sports training.

*Ans* Training in sports means the preparation of a sportsperson based on the scientific principles for giving the highest level of performance.

It is a specialised process of all-round physical strengthening aimed at improving an athlete's fitness in a selected activity.

Training is a long-term, systematic and a continuous process that recognises an individual's needs and capabilities to develop exercises based on scientific knowledge that enhances sports performance.

It develops basic and advanced skills, techniques, tactics, strategies, etc for all sports activities and competitions.

Sports' training is a concept whose practice is spread over many years. Training method for a particular sport consists of training periods which are split into sessions and schedules. These sessions and schedules are progressive in nature and training continues till mastery over a skill is achieved.

All training programs are divided into three parts as discussed below

(i) **Preparatory Period** This is the basic training program wherein stress is given on basic fitness and skill for competitions.

(ii) **Competition Period** In this period, the player achieves its top form and can participate in competitions to achieve top performance.

(iii) **Transitional Period** This period comes after the competition. In this period, a player relaxes and rests to recover from stress.

**27** Briefly describe any five skills required in the field of physical education and sports.

*Ans* Owing to many different characteristics of skills, it is very difficult to classify them, however, some types of skills are generally accepted. Few of these are as follows

(i) **Open** These skills are not fully under our control and are thus unpredictable. For example, in badminton, performing any skill depends upon the position of the opponent.

(ii) **Closed** These skills take place in a stable environment where the sportsperson knows exactly what to do, and when to do like serving in tennis.

(iii) **Gross** These skills involve large muscle movements involving fundamental patterns like walking, running and jumping. Putting the shot is an instance of a gross skill.

(iv) **Fine** Such skills involve complex precise movements using small muscle groups and a high level of hand-eye coordination. Shooting in snooker is an instance of a fine skill.

(v) **Coactive** These skills are performed at the same time as other sportspersons but not in a confrontation, like rhythmic swimming.

**28** What is 'Warming-up'? What are its benefits?

*Ans* Before performing any sports activity, a preliminary preparatory activity is performed for the physiological and psychological preparation of an athlete. This preparation is called warming-up.

Warming-up is a process of heating the body muscles through certain short-term exercises such that an activity is performed in most refined and efficient way.

Warming-up brings the body to a condition at which it safely responds to nerve signals for quick and efficient action.

Its benefits are as follows

- Increased speed of contraction and relaxation of warmed muscles.
- Reduced muscle stiffness due to exercises.
- Greater economy of movement because of lowered viscous resistance within warmed muscles.
- Facilitated nerve transmission and muscle metabolism at higher temperatures; specific warming-up can facilitate a motor unit required in subsequent competition activity.
- It focuses the body on the training or competition.

**29** Enumerate the methods of warming-up in detail.

*Ans* The methods of warming-up can be described as

(i) **Psychological Warming-up** This type of warming-up prepares the mental attitude of a sportsperson towards a competition. It makes an athlete mentally ready to bear stress and anxiety. This includes motivation, feedback, behavioural changes, etc.

(ii) **Physiological Warming-up** This types of warming-up makes a sportsperson physically ready for all training and competitions.

It is categorised into two types which are described below

(a) **Active Warming-up** In active warming-up, an athlete participates in various physical activities to improve the efficiency of body and to tone up the muscles. It is performed for a duration of 10 to 30 minutes.

Active warming can be sub-divided into two types *viz.* General and Specific warming-up. Exercises in general warming-up are performed for all sports. It tones the muscles that are used in different sports and improves the mobility of smaller joints.

While, exercises in specific warming-up are different for different sports. Specific warming-up is also known as formal activity and is performed after general warming-up.

(b) **Passive Warming-up** This type of warm-up does not include any physical activity or exercise. It includes external sources such as body massage, sunbath, steam bath, hot drinks etc. The main aim of passive warming-up is to increase the body temperature without any expenditure of energy in the process of warming-up.

# SELF ASSESSMENT

## OBJECTIVE ANSWER TYPE QUESTIONS

**1** Taking of prohibited or banned substances is called ............ .

(a) Steroids (b) Alcohol
(c) Doping (d) Autologos doping

**2** During phase III of preparatory period, the training volume is

(a) Decreased (b) Increased
(c) Not changed (d) None of these

## VERY SHORT ANSWER TYPE QUESTIONS

**3** What do you mean by preparatory period?

**4** What is psychological preparation?

## SHORT ANSWER TYPE QUESTIONS

**5** What are the objectives of training in sports ?

**6** Explain the objectives of sports training.

## LONG ANSWER TYPE QUESTIONS

**7** Explain the principles of sports training.

**8** Briefly discuss the concept of doping.

**9** Explain the process of recovery.

# Part B
# Practical

# SAI KHELO INDIA FITNESS TEST

Fitness defines the ability to perform physical activity and encompasses a wide range of abilities. Each activity and sports requires a specific set of skills, and so being fit for an activity or a sport does not necessarily make a person fit for another. Fitness is generally divided into specific fitness categories or components, and each can be tested and trained individually.

SAI Khelo India Fitness Test measure the ability and physical fitness of the children of age group 5-8 years and age group 9-18+ years.

## AGE GROUP 5-8 YEARS/ CLASS 1 to 3

At Primary class 1-3, children should acquire Fundamental Movement Skills (FMS) leaving the learning of specific physical activities to later stages. FMS provide the building blocks for many physical activities, such as playing games, dance, and sport. Locomotor, Manipulative & Body Management abilities are key to success in most sports and physical activities. Following are the abilities of children in class 1-3 which need to be measured and tracked and are important for controlling the body in various situations

- Body Composition (BMI)
- Coordination (Plate Tapping)
- Balance (Flamingo Balance)

## AGE GROUP: 9-18+ YEARS/ CLASS 4 to 12

For Class 4 to 12, it is important for students to have an overall physical fitness. The following components are to be considered in Physical Health and Fitness Profile

- Body Composition (BMI)
- Strength
  - a. Abdominal (Partial Curl-up)
  - b. Muscular Endurance (Push Ups for Boys, Modified Push Ups for Girls)
- Flexibility (Sit and Reach Test)
- Cardiovascular Endurance (600 Meter Run/Walk)
- Speed (50 mt. Dash)

## Test Description

The following are the Khelo India Fitness Tests which can be done in schools

### Body Composition (BMI)

Body Composition refers primarily to the distribution of muscle and fat in the body. Body size such as height, lengths and girths are also grouped under this component. The test performed is Body Mass Index (BMI), which is calculated from body Weight (W) and Height (H) such as:

BMI=W/(HxH)

Where W = body weight in kilograms and

H = height in meters.

The higher score usually indicating higher levels of body fat.

### Equipments Required

- Flat and clean surface
- Weighing Machine,
- Stadiometer/Measuring Tape pasted on a wall

### Procedure

#### Measuring Height Accurately

- Remove the participant's shoes, bulky clothing, and hair ornaments, and unbraid hair that interferes with the measurement.
- Take the height measurement on flooring that is not carpeted and against a flat surface such as a wall with no molding.
- Have the participant stand with feet flat, together and back against the wall. Make sure legs are straight, arms are at sides and shoulders are level.
- Make sure the participant is looking straight ahead and that the line of sight is parallel with the floor.
- Take the measurement while the participant stands with head, shoulders, buttocks, and heels touching the flat surface (wall). Depending on the overall body shape of the participant, all points may not touch the wall.

- Use a flat headpiece to form a right-angle with the wall and lower the headpiece until, it firmly touches the crown of the head.
- Make sure the measurer's eyes are at the same level as the headpiece.
- Lightly mark where the bottom of the headpiece meets the wall.
- Then, use a metal tape to measure from the base on the floor to the marked measurement on the wall to get the height measurement.
- Accurately record the height to the nearest 0.1 centimeter.

### Measuring Weight Accurately

- Use a digital scale. Avoid using bathroom scales that are spring loaded. Place the scale on firm flooring such as tile or wood rather than carpet.
- Have the participant remove shoes and heavy clothing, such as sweaters.
- Have the participant stand with both feet in the center of the scale.
- Record the weight to the nearest decimal fraction e.g. 30.6 kilograms.

## Plate Tapping Test

It measures speed and coordination of limb movement of children.

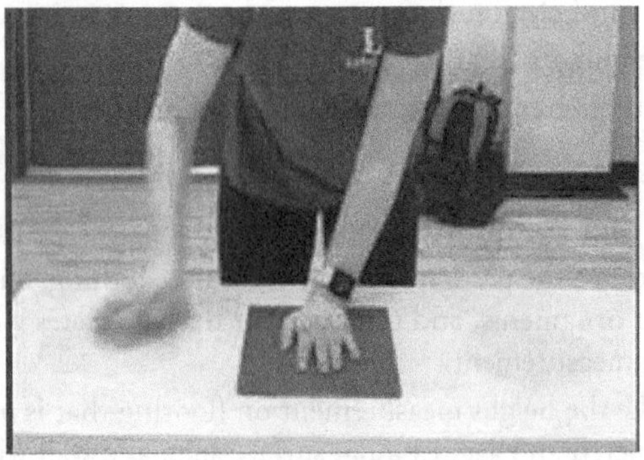

Plate Tapping Test

### Equipments Required

- Table (adjustable height)
- 2 yellow discs (20cm diameter)
- Rectangle (30 x 20 cm)
- Stopwatch

### Procedure

- If possible, the table height should be adjusted so that the subject IS standing comfortably in front of the discs. The two yellow discs are placed with their centers 60 cm apart on the table. The rectangle is placed equidistant between both discs.
- The non-preferred hand is placed on the rectangle. The subject moves the preferred hand back and forth between the discs over the hand in the middle as quickly as possible.
- This action is repeated for 25 full cycles (50 taps).

### Suggestions

- Participants should be encouraged to stand in a balanced posture, feet apart to shoulder width.
- Results are usually better, if the participant can maintain constant pace during most of the run.

## Flamingo Balance Test

It measures ability to balance successfully on a single leg. This single leg balance test assesses the strength of the leg, pelvic, and trunk muscle as well as static balance.

### Equipments Required

- Non- Slippery even surface
- Stopwatch

### Procedure

- Stand on the beam. Keep balance by holding the instructor's hand (if required to start).
- While balancing on the preferred leg, the free leg is flexed at the knee and the foot of this leg held close to the buttocks.
- Start the watch as the instructor lets go of the participant/subject.
- Pause the stopwatch each time the subject loses balance (either by falling off the beam or letting goes of the foot being held).
- Resume over, again timing until they lose balance. Count the number of falls in 60 seconds of balancing.
- If there are more than 15 falls in the first 30 seconds, the test is terminated.

### Suggestion

Participants should be encouraged to eyes focused on stationary object straight ahead.

## Partial Curl Up (30 seconds)

It measures abdominal muscular strength and endurance of the abdominals and hip- Flexors, important in back support and core stability.

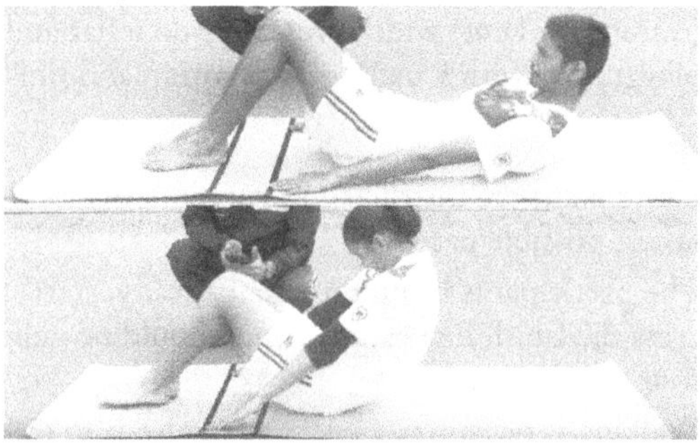

**Partial Curl Up**

### Equipments Required

- Flat clean cushioned surface with two parallel strips (6 inches apart)
- Stopwatch
- Recording sheets
- Pen

### Procedure

- The subject lies on a cushioned, flat, clean surface with knees flexed, usually at 90 degrees, with hands straight on the sides (palms facing downwards) closer to the ground, parallel to the body.
- The subject raises the trunk in a smooth motion, keeping the arms in position, curling up the desired amount (at least 6 inches above/along the ground towards the parallel strip).
- The trunk is lowered back to the floor, so that the shoulder blades or upper back touch the floor.

### Suggestions

- Participants should be encouraged to keep normal breathing rate.
- Results are usually better if the participant can maintain constant pace during the activity.

## Push Ups (Boys)/Modified Push Ups (Girls)

It measures upper body strength endurance and trunk stability.

### Equipment Required

Flat clean cushioned surface or Gym mat

### Procedure

- A standard push up begins with the hands and toes touching the floor, the body and legs in a straight line, feet slightly apart, the arms at shoulder width apart, extended and at a right angles to the body.
- Keeping the back and knees straight, the subject lowers the body to a predetermined point, to touch some other object, or until there is a 90-degree angle at the elbows, then returns back to the starting position with the arms extended.
- This action is repeated and test continues until exhaustion, or until they can do no more in rhythm or have reached the target number of push-ups.
- For Girls: push-up technique is with the knees resting on the ground.

### Suggestions

- Participants should be encouraged to emphasis to keep the back straight.
- Results are usually better if the participant can maintain constant pace during the activity.

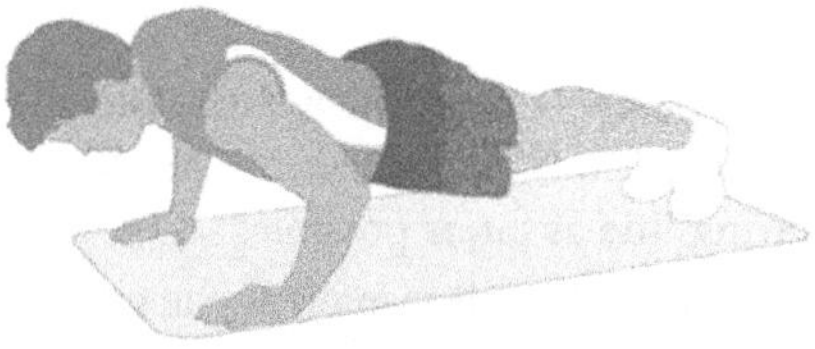

**Push Ups (Boys)**

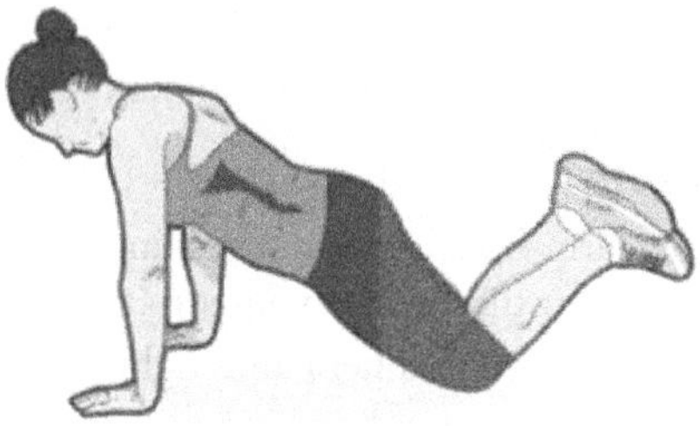

**Push Ups (Girls)**

## Sit and Reach

It specifically measures the flexibility of the lower back and hamstring muscles. This test is important as because tightness in this area is implicated in lumbar lordosis, forward pelvic tilt and lower back pain.

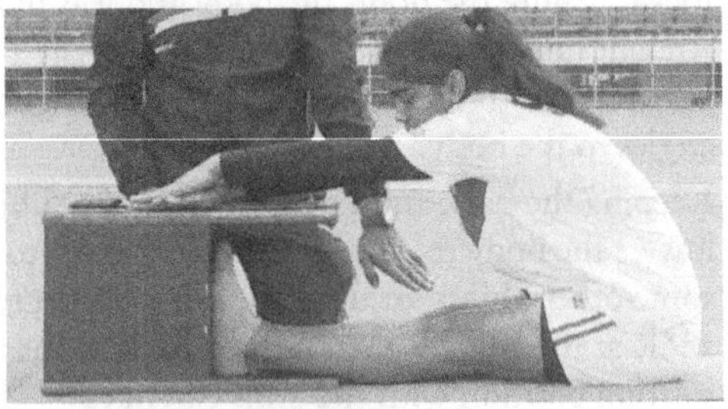

Sit and Reach

### Equipments Required

- Sit and Reach box with dimensions 12" x 12" (sides), 12" x 10" (front and back), 12" x 21" (top)
- Flat clean cushioned surface or gym mat

### Procedure

- This test involves sitting on the floor with legs stretched out straight ahead. Shoes should be removed. The soles of the feet are placed flat against the Sit and Reach box. Both knees should be locked and pressed flat to the floor - the tester may assist by holding them down.
- With the palms facing downwards, and the hands on top of each other, the subject reaches forward along the measuring line as far as possible.
- Ensure that the hands remain at the same level, not one reaching further forward than the other. After some practice reaches, the subject reaches out and holds that position for at one-two seconds while the distance is recorded. Make sure there are no jerky movements.

### Suggestions

- Proper warm-up and static stretching of the lower back and posterior thighs is very important for this test.
- A partner placing his/her hands lightly across knees can prevent the flexing of knees.
- Keep the hands over each other (fish pose). Besides in order to prevent the test apparatus from sliding away from the participants during the test, it should be placed against a wall or a similar immovable object.

## 600 Mtr Run/Walk

It measures cardiovascular fitness or cardiovascular endurance.

### Equipments Required

- Stopwatch Whistle
- Marker powder
- Measuring tape, 200 or 400 mts with 1.22 mt (minimum 1 mt) width preferably on a flat and even playground with a marking of starting and finish line.

### Procedure

- Participants are instructed to run 600 mts. in the fastest possible pace.
- The participants begin on signal, "ready, start" as they cross the finish line elapsed time should be announced to the participants.
- Walking is permitted but the objective is to cover the distance in the shortest possible time.

### Suggestions

- Participants should be encouraged to practice running with emphasis placed on the concept of pace.
- Results are usually better if the participant can maintain constant pace during most of the run and perhaps using a strong closing effort.

## 50 Mtr Dash (Standing Start)

It measure acceleration and speed.

### Equipments Required

- Measuring tape or marked track
- Stopwatch
- Cone markers
- Flat and clear surface of at least 60 meters

### Procedure

- A thorough warm up should be given, including some practice starts and accelerations.
- Start from a stationary position, with one foot in front of the other. The front foot must be on or behind the starting line. This starting position should be static (dead start).
- The tester should provide hints for maximising speed (such as keeping low, driving hard with the arms and legs) and encouraged to continue running hard through the finish line.

### Suggestions

- Participants should be encouraged to practice running with emphasis placed on the concept of pace.
- Results are usually better if the participant can maintain constant pace during most of the run and perhaps using a strong closing effort.

# VIVA-VOCE

**1** What do you mean by fitness?

***Ans*** Fitness defines the ability to perform physical activity and encompasses a wide range of abilities.

**2** What is the importance of FMS for the children of age group 5-8 years?

***Ans*** FMS provide the building blocks for many physical activities, such as playing games, dance, and sport.

**3** Mention the abilities of children in class 1-3 which need to be measured and tracked.

***Ans*** The abilities of children in class 1-3 which need to be measured and tracked are Body Composition (Body Mass Index, BMI), Coordination (Plate Tapping Test) and Balance (Flamingo Balance Test).

**4** Define Body Composition.

***Ans*** Body Composition refers primarily to the distribution of muscle and fat in the body.

**5** How the Body Mass Index is calculated?

***Ans*** BMI is calculated from body Weight (W) and Height (H) such as:

$BMI = W/(H \times H)$

Where W = body weight in kilograms and H = height in meters.

**6** What equipments are required in BMI?

***Ans*** The equipments required in BMI are

- Flat and clean surface
- Weighing Machine
- Stadiometer/Measuring Tape pasted on a wall

**7** What does Plate Tapping Test measures?

***Ans*** Plate Tapping Test measures speed and coordination of limb movement of children.

**8** How Flamingo Balance Test is important?

***Ans*** Flamingo Balance Test is important as it measures ability to balance successfully on a single leg. This single leg balance test assesses the strength of the leg, pelvic, and trunk muscle as well as static balance.

**9** Mention the equipments required in Partial Curl Up test.

***Ans*** The equipments required in Partial Curl Up test are

- Flat clean cushioned surface with two parallel strips (6 inches apart)
- Stopwatch
- Recording sheets
- Pen

**10** What does Sit and Reach test measures?

***Ans*** Sit and Reach test measures the flexibility of the lower back and hamstring muscles. This test is important as because tightness in this area is implicated in lumbar lordosis, forward pelvic tilt and lower back pain.

# BROCKPORT PHYSICAL FITNESS TEST

The BPFT (Brockport Physical Fitness Test) is a criterion-referenced test of health-related fitness. In a criterion-referenced approach, test scores obtained by youngsters are compared to standards that are thought to be associated with some index of positive health.

This schematic, which is modified from a model described by Bouchard and Shephard (1994), helps to understand how and why test items and standards on the BPFT were selected. In this conceptual framework, health that impacts or relates to physical activity, provides the basis for indices and criteria for the evaluation of physical fitness.

## Project Target

Between 1993 and 1998, the U.S. Department of Education Office of Special Education and Rehabilitative Services funded 'Project Target', a research study designed to develop a health-related, criterion-referenced physical fitness test for youngsters aged 10 to 17 with disabilities. The project was entitled 'Project Target: Criterion- Referenced Physical Fitness Standards for Adolescents with Disabilities.' Project Target was centered at the State University of the Brockport.

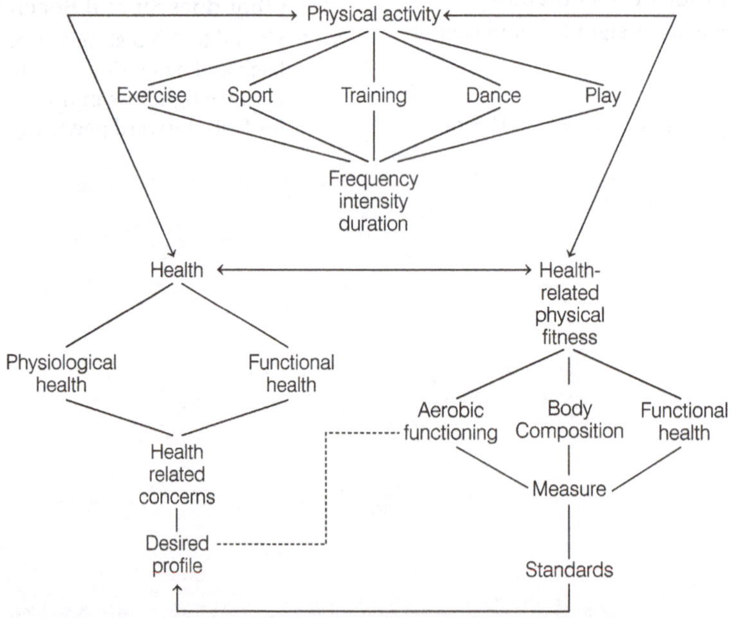


**Relationship among Health, Physical Activity and Health-related Physical Fitness from the Brockport Physical Fitness Test Manual**

## Target Group

The Brockport Physical Fitness Test is designed for and is suitable for use with both able-bodied youngsters and those with disabilities such as mental retardation, spinal cord injuries cerebral polsy, blindness, congenital anomalies, amputation. The BPFT includes 27 different test items under three components of health-related physical fitness, aerobic functioning, body composition and musculoskeletal functioning.

## Aerobic Functioning

Aerobic functioning is a term that encompasses both aerobic capacity (maximum oxygen uptake) and aerobic behaviour (the ability to perform aerobic activity at specified levels of intensity and duration.

The tests for aerobic functioning are

- **Target Aerobic Movement Test** It test the ability to sustain a moderate intensity of (any) physical activity by maintaining a heart rate between 70 and 85 percent of maximal predicted heart rate for 15 minutes.
- **One-mile Run/Walk** Run or walk as fast as possible over a one-mile distance.

## Body Composition

Body composition provides an indication of the degree of leanness/fatness of the body.

The tests for body composition are

- **Skinfold Measures** Calipers are used to measure the thickness of the skin at the triceps, subscapular, and calf measurement sites.
- **Body Mass Index** It is calculated by taking a person's weight and dividing by their height squared.
- **Bioelectrical Impedance Analysis** It measure the resistance of body tissues to the flow of a small electrical signal, and from that the proportion of body fat is calculated.

## Musculoskeletal Functioning

Musculoskeletal functioning is a component that combines measures of muscular strength, muscular endurance and flexibility/range of motion.

Strength/Endurance exercises and tests for musculoskeletal functioning are

- **Trunk Lift** While lying face down, lift the upper body off the floor as high as you can using the muscles of the back.
- **Grip Strength** A measure of hand and arm strength, using the dominant hand to grip a dynamometer with as much force as possible.
- **Bench Press** Perform as many bench presses as possible using a 35lb (15.9kg) barbell.
- **Isometric Push-up** Hold a raised push-up position for upto 40 seconds.
- **Push-up** Complete as many push-ups as possible at a rate of 1 push-up every 3 seconds.
- **Seated Push-up** Extend the arms and raise the body out of a chair and hold this position for as long as possible.
- **Dumbbell Press** Lift a 15lb (6.8kg) dumbbell as many times as possible at a specific cadence while sitting on a chair.
- **Reverse Curl** A measure of hand, wrist, and arm strength. While sitting on a chair, the subject must perform one repetition of bringing a 1lb (0.5kg) dumbbell from the thigh to the flexed-arm position, holding it there for 2 seconds, then returning it to the thigh in a controlled manner.
- **Push/Walk (40m)** Walk or push a wheelchair at a comfortable speed for 40 min, with a 5 min start zone. It is not a race, participants are encouraged to travel at the speed they usually use for mobility. To pass, they must cover the 40 meters distance in less than 60 seconds while keeping the heart rate below 120 bpm (walkers) or 114 bpm (wheelchair users).
- **Wheelchair Ramp Test** A test of upper-body strength and endurance, in which participants attempt to push their wheelchairs up a standard wheelchair ramp. The ramp must be at least 8 feet (2.4 meters) long, at a gradient of 8.3%.
- **Curl-Up** Complete upto 75 curl-ups at a rate of 1 every 3 seconds. The hands slide 4.5 inches along the ground for a complete repetition.
- **Curl-Up (modified)** The curl-up test, though with the hands resting on the thighs rather than by the side.
- **Extended-Arm Hang** Hanging from an overhead bar with straight arms for upto 40 seconds.
- **Pull-Up** Grasp an overhead bar and pull-up the body so the chin raises above the bar, then return to arms fully extended position.
- **Pull-Up (modified)** With the horizontal body, grasp a bar set just out of reach, and pull-up towards the bar.

Flexibility tests for musculoskeletal functioning are

- **Back-Saver Sit and Reach** It is performed with one leg bent. It is designed to measure the flexibility of the left and right legs separately.
- **Shoulder Stretch** Touch the fingertips together behind the back by reaching over the shoulder and down the back with one arm and across the back with the other arm.
- **Apley Scratch Test (modified)** Attempt to reach overhead with one hand and touch the top of the opposite shoulder blade.
- **Thomas Test (modified)** It requires the subject to sit at the very edge of a bench, then roll back onto the bench while pulling both knees to the chest. Measures hip flexibility.

## General Recommendations for Administering BPFT

Although the BPFT includes 27 test items, testers generally administer only 4 to 6 items to a particular individual. The following list provides general recommendations for administering the BPFT

- Practice administering test items and be confident of mastery in administering them before taking formal measurements.
- Develop forms for selecting test items and recording scores, or use materials developed as part of the Brockport Physical Fitness Test.
- Describe the test to participants and explain what it is intended to assess.
- Ensure that individuals being tested dress appropriately, exercise clothing and sneakers (where appropriate) are recommended.
- Plan and provide general and specific warmups, as appropriate.
- Provide cool-down activities after testing. This is especially important after aerobic-functioning test items.
- Provide a positive testing atmosphere. Encourage individuals being tested to try their best and continually provide positive reinforcement for effort.
- Compare participants' performances with criterion-referenced standards rather than with other individuals' performances.
- Administer not more than half of the items on a particular day. If fatigue appears to be influencing performance, provide longer rest intervals between test items.
- Administer aerobic-functioning tests in last.
- Administer running items on a surface that is flat and hard yet resilient.
- Give participants who are blind, the opportunity to become clearly oriented to a test station or testing area. This is particularly important for tests that involve running.
- Provide careful demonstrations for participants with hearing impairment. Give instructions in writing or manually (e.g. signing, finger spelling). Use hand signals to start and stop activities.
- Administer the following test items individually to one participant at a time- Target Aerobic Movement Test (TAMT), percent body fat, skinfolds, extended-arm hang, flexed-arm hang, modified pull-up, pull-up, dominant grip strength, bench press, curl-up, modified curl-up, 40 meter push/walk, reverse curl, seated push-up, trunk lift, wheelchair ramp test, and most flexibility or range-of-motion test items (except shoulder stretch).
- The PACER, one-mile run/walk, and shoulder stretch may be administered to small groups of subjects at once. However, it may be necessary or most appropriate to provide partners for assistance.
- The following items can be administered to groups of two or three- dumbbell press, isometric push-up, and push-up. For the dumbbell press, provide spotters.

## Equipment Required For Conducting BPFT

Relatively inexpensive material are required for conducting the BPFT such as a stopwatch, ruler, grip dynamometer, 35lb, barbell, seated push-up blocks, 11lb weight, ramp, curl-up strip, pull-up bars, skinfold caliper, height weight scale, sit and reach apporatus, heat range monitor, 15lb dumbbell and calibrated tapes.

## Safety Guidelines and Precautions

Test items used in connection with the BPFT(including non-traditional ones) are typical of those used elsewhere in physical education or physical fitness programmes. Some have appeared on disability-specific tests of physical fitness or tests classifying athletes with disability or are associated with activities of daily living. Although the BPFT is considered safe, one must recognise that accidents are possible. Use the following guidelines and precautions when administering test items

- Personnel who administer the test should be qualified and knowledgeable about physical fitness testing and disability.
- Maximise the safety of all youngsters. Professionals using this test should follow the policies of their school or agency regarding medical information, records, and clearance for activity. Any others should administer this test only following approval by a physician who is aware of the health status of the individual taking the test.
- Avoid administering tests under conditions of unusually high or low temperature or humidity or when windy. Youngsters with spinal cord injury may be especially prone to problems with thermoregulation including overheating.
- Be sure that individuals being tested understand test instructions. Provide opportunities for students to practice test items.

- Terminate the test item if the individual being tested experiences dizziness, pain, or disorientation.
- Avoid comparing individuals' performances with each other.
- Spot youngsters where necessary and appropriate.
- Incorporate warm-up and cool-down periods as appropriate for test items.

## General Brockport Physical Fitness Test Form

Student name: ............................. Sex: ...... M ...... F ................. Age (yr): .........

Height : ............................. Weight: .............. .............. Date: .............................

Classification: ............................. Subclassification: .............................

This form identifies all test items on the Brockport Physical Fitness Test (BPFT). It can be used as a resource for developing a fitness test for a particular student, recording results, and matching results to fitness zones. The BPFT typically includes four to seven test items: one for aerobic functioning, one for body composition, and at least two for musculoskeletal functioning. (The Target Stretch Test items are considered as a single test for this purpose). It is recommended that an individualised specific test form for each student consisting only of the items taken on the test be subsequently developed for each student and be used for reporting results to students, parents, and guardians.

### Aerobic Functioning

| **Test item** | **Units of measure** | **Test scores** | **Adapted fitness zone (if applicable)** | **Healthy fitness zone** |
|---|---|---|---|---|
| AEROBIC CAPACITY | | | | |
| Mile run or walk | min/sec | | | |
| 20 m (laps) | # | | | |
| 15 m (laps) | # | | | |
| AEROBIC BEHAVIOUR | | | | |
| TAMT | P/F | | None | |

### Body Composition

| **Test item** | **Units of measure** | **Test scores** | **Adapted fitness zone (if applicable)** | **Healthy fitness zone** |
|---|---|---|---|---|
| Percent body fat | % | | No AFZ for body composition | |
| Triceps | (mm) | | | |
| Triceps + subscapular | (mm) | | | |
| Triceps + calf | (mm) | | | |
| Body mass index | | | | |

### Musculoskeletal Functioning

| **Test item** | **Units of measure** | **Test scores** | **Adapted fitness zone (if applicable)** | **Healthy fitness zone** |
|---|---|---|---|---|
| STRENGTH AND ENDURANCE | | | | |
| Reverse curl | # | | | |
| 40 m push/walk | P/F | | | |
| Ramp test | feet | | | |
| Push-ups | # | | | |
| Seated push-ups | # | | | |
| Pull-ups | # | | | |
| Modified pull-ups | # | | | |
| Dumbbell press | # | | | |
| Bench press | # | | | |

| Test item | Units of measure | Test scores | Adapted fitness zone (if applicable) | Healthy fitness zone |
|---|---|---|---|---|
| Grip strength | kg. | | | |
| Isometric push-ups | sec. | | | |
| Extended arm hang | sec. | | | |
| Flexed arm hang | sec. | | | |
| Curl-ups | # | | | |
| Modified curl-ups | # | | | |
| FLEXIBILITY OR RANGE OF MOTION | | | | |
| Trunk lift | # | | | |
| Shoulder stretch, right | P/F | | | |
| Shoulder stretch, left | P/F | | | |
| Back-saver sit-and-reach, right | in. | | | |
| Back-saver sit-and-reach, left | in. | | | |
| Modified thomas test | 0-3 | | | |
| Modified apley test | 0-3 | | | |
| Target stretch test | 0-2 | | | |
| Wrist extension, right | 0-2 | | | |
| Wrist extension, left | 0-2 | | | |
| Elbow extension, right | 0-2 | | | |
| Elbow extension, left | 0-2 | | | |
| Shoulder extension, right | 0-2 | | | |
| Shoulder extension, left | 0-2 | | | |
| Shoulder abduction, right | 0-2 | | | |
| Shoulder abduction, left | 0-2 | | | |
| Shoulder external rotation, right | 0-2 | | | |
| Shoulder external rotation, left | 0-2 | | | |
| Forearm supination, right | 0-2 | | | |
| Forearm supination, left | 0-2 | | | |
| Forearm pronation, right | 0-2 | | | |
| Forearm pronation, left | 0-2 | | | |
| Knee extension, right | 0-2 | | | |
| Knee extension, left | 0-2 | | | |

Interpretation : ..........................................................................................................

Needs : ......................................................................................................................

# VIVA-VOCE

**1** What is test?

***Ans*** The process of collecting the data about a specific skill, strength, endurance, knowledge and behaviour is generally known as test.

**2** What is measurement?

***Ans*** The process of administrating a test in order to obtain a quantitative data is called as measurement.

**3** What is BPFT?

***Ans*** The Brockport Physical Fitness Test (BPFT) is a criterion-referenced test of health-related fitness test.

**4** How many tests have been included in the BPFT?

***Ans*** 27 tests have been included in the BPFT.

**5** How many components of health have been included in BPFT?

***Ans*** There are 3 components of health related to physical fitness have been included in BPFT.

**6** Which type of indication provided by the body composition test in BPFT.

***Ans*** Body composition provides an indication of the degree of leanness/fatness of the body.

**7** Which type of test is done for measure of muscular strength in Brockport Physical Fitness Test (BPFT)?

***Ans*** Musculoskeletal functioning is a component of BPFT that combine measures of muscular strength, muscular endurance and flexibility range of motion.

**8** Who has modified Brockport Physical Fitness Test?

***Ans*** Bouchard and Shephard modified the Brockport Physical Fitness Test.

**9** Who has conducted the Project Target?

***Ans*** The U.S. Department of Education Office of Special Education and Rehabilitative Service has funded and conducted the Project Target.

**10** Does expensive material required for administrating BPFT?

***Ans*** No, relatively inexpensive material are required for conducting the BPFT.

**11** What does AAHPERD stands for?

***Ans*** AAHPERD stands for American Alliance for Health, Physical Education, Recreation and Dance.

**12** For which purpose, partial curl-up test is used?

***Ans*** The strength and endurance of abdominal muscles is measured with the help of curl-up test.

**13** Which test is also called as Harvard Step?

***Ans*** Aerobic fitness test is also called as Harvard Step.

| GAME 1 |

# BOCCE

Throwing balls toward a target is the oldest game known to mankind. As early as 5000 BC the Egyptians played a form of Bocce with polished rocks. From this early objective, the basic rules of Bocce were born. From Egypt, the game made its way to Greece around 800 BC. The Romans learned the game from the Greeks, and then introduced it throughout the Roman empire. The Roman influence in Bocce is preserved in the game's name; Bocce is derived from the Latin word bottia, meaning boss.

Bocce frequently lost and gained popularity throughout the ages. It was Giuseppe Garibaldi, who, while unifying and nationalising Italy, popularised the sport as it is known today.

## History

In 1896 the first Bocce Olympiad was held in Athens, Greece. Bocce has been a part of international sports ever since. In modern times, the first Bocce clubs were organized in Italy. Notably the first Italian League was formed in 1947 by fifteen teams in and around the town of Rivoli (Torino). 1947 also marks the beginning of the yearly Bocce World Championships. This Championship event continues today with participants from over thirty nations.

## Basic Rules of the Game

Various versions of the game are played across the world with different rules. We will consider the version known as Bocce *Volo*, which is played in European countries and is the most popular version internationally.

1. The game of bocce consists of:
   - *Punto* throws
   - *Raffa* and *volo* throws which are allowed provided the player has first declared the item (ball or *pallino*) the player wishes to hit.
   - Continuing to throw one's balls for the duration of a frame until one has scored one or more points.
   - Trying to be the first to attain the maximum number of points to win the game.
2. The teams may consist of:
   - Singles: one against one with four balls per player
   - Doubles: two against two with two balls per player
   - Triples: three against three with two balls per player
3. The *Pallino* is spherical ball with a dimension of 4±1 cm diameter and weighs 60±5 grams. All team balls are of 10.7 cm (10.6 for women) diameter and weigh 920 grams (900 for women). The balls of any team must be of the same colour and differ sharply in colour from those of the opposing team.
4. The game begins by placing the *pallino* on point 'p' at the centre of the court's playing area, equidistant from the sides
5. The object of the game is to roll the bocce balls closer to the pallino than your opponent.
6. The right to throw the first ball or choose which end to start is determined by the toss of a coin.
7. The ball may be played by making a *punto*, *raffa*, or *volo* throw. *It is explained as follows*:
   - *Punto* throws are those which aim at getting one's ball as close as possible to a reference point on the court.
   - A *raffa* throw is one that aims at hitting, with or without bouncing, any given ball, either the opponents' or one's own ball, or the *pallino*, after having declared to the referee the item to be hit.
   - A *volo* throw is one that aims at hitting, either directly or with the support of some part of the court surface, either the opponents' or one's own ball, or the *pallino*, after having declared the item to the referee.
8. This 'nearest ball' rule governs the sequence of thrown balls. The team whose ball is the closest to the *pallino* is called the 'in' ball and the opposing side ball the 'out' ball. Whenever a team gets 'in', it steps aside and allows the 'out' team to bowl.
9. A team has the option of rolling, throwing, bouncing, banking etc its ball down the court provided it does not go out of bounds or the player does not violate the foul markers.
10. The place where each ball comes to rest must be marked by the referee using a different marking for each team.
11. A player also has the option of 'spocking' or hitting out any ball in play in trying to obtain a point, or decreasing the opposing team's points.
12. At the end of each frame (when both teams have exhausted 4 balls each), the referee will determine the points scored.
13. Scoring points are all those balls of one team closer to the *pallino* 1 opint for 1 ball than the closest ball of the opposing team, which can be determined by viewing or by mechanical measurement.
14. A ball has completed its run whenever
    - It has been played by the *punto* throw, comes to a rest, and its position has been marked, or
    - It has been played by either a *raffa* or *volo* throw, hit the declared item (ball or *pallino*) and has surpassed the latter.
15. If a ball should be considered invalid, the team who threw it at the beginning of the game or in any subsequent frame must throw another ball until they succeed in making a valid throw.
16. One point is assigned to each of one's team's own balls that rest closer to the *pallino* than that of the opposing team. The game is won by the first team to attain a total of 15 points (In some competitions this may be 12 points).

## Dimensional Diagrams of the Equipment Used in Bocce

### Diagram and other details of Bocce Volo Court

1. The game's playing area is a flat and perfectly levelled surface subdivided into courts enclosed by wooden planks or other non-metallic sides.
2. The court must be 26.50 metres long (variation from 27.5 to 24.5 metres is allowed) and between 4.00 and 4.50 metres wide.
3. The ends of the court must be made with swinging headboards, possibly of synthetic rubber, hinged on the upper part of the sideboards. The headboards should not be fastened to either the sideboards or the

court surface in order to prevent the balls or jack from bouncing back.

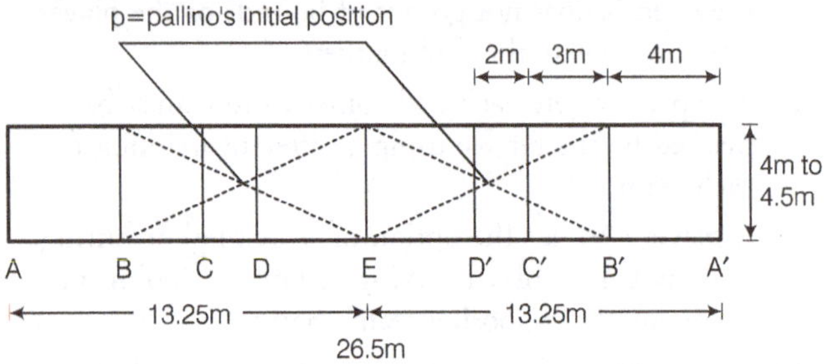


## Terminology

**Advantage** The team throwing the *pallino* is said to have a "*pallino* advantage" because they can place the *pallino* where they want it on the court and have a clear shot to place the first bocce ball.

**Backboards** The shorter court walls at each end of the court. Also called endboards or backwalls.

**Banking** Throwing the bocce ball such that it hits and bounces off the sideboards towards the *pallino*.

**Foul** An act committed by a thrower that violates the game rules. A team/ player is penalised as specified in the rules for committing a foul.

**Hitting or Spocking** A declared underhand bowling type hard throw directly at the balls on the court to purposely hit and move an opponent's ball or the *pallino*. Sometimes called shooting, bombing or *raffa*.

**Illegal Movement** This occurs when a legally thrown ball is moved from its resting position by a player or referee.

**In-bound Lines** Lines marked on the sideboards/ backboards/ court surface to define the 12 inch boundary for the initial *pallino* throw.

**Interference** A legally thrown ball is interfered with while moving by someone or something not on the playing surface before the throw.

**No Point or Tie** This occurs when the closest balls of both teams are equidistant from the *pallino*. The team delivering the last ball must throw again, or if all balls have been played, no points are awarded for that frame.

**Out Team** The team which does not have the closest ball to the *pallino*.

**Pointing Foul Line** The first foul line marked on the sideboards/ court surface near each backboard behind which the *pallino* and balls rolled for points must be released. Sometimes called the lagging, throwing, pitch, *punto*, or *puntata* foul line.

**Referee** An independent official that enforces all game rules, directs play, determines in the team, makes measurements and determines team points for each frame.

**Scoreboard** Numbers 1 through 12 arranged similar to a clock face with an arrow pointing to the score for the red or green team. The scoreboard can be a single set of numbers with a red and green arrow or a separate set of numbers for each colour.

**Sideboards** The longer court walls parallel to the direction of throwing.

## Fundamental Skills & Techniques Used

*Some basic techniques are*

1. **Playing first** If a player plays first, he should try to place his first ball as close as possible in front of the *pallino*. This forces the opposing player to play around this ball.
2. **Getting around blocking balls** On a regular tournament court it will be possible to bounce balls off the sidewall. This can aid in getting a ball around blocking balls. But remember, tournament rules stipulate that balls hitting the backboard first are removed from play and their effects are reversed.
3. **Maintaining your advantage** When both teams have a ball close to the *pallino*, but yours is slightly closer, it is sometimes wise to not risk hitting your own ball and losing the advantage. This can be accomplished simply by tossing the ball considerably short.

4. **Hitting opponent's balls** Throwing the ball in the air past the centre point is not legal; so lobbing the ball over the opponent's blocking balls becomes problematic. Often the best way to improve the position of a side is to either hit an opponent's ball or to strike the *pallino*.
5. **Ball placement technique** Getting points is dependent on getting balls closer to the *pallino* than the opponents. To do this requires accuracy. But it also requires discretion in placement. It is therefore better to toss the balls slightly short of the *pallino* than slightly beyond or beside because this will help in blocking opponent's shots.
6. **Gripping the ball and throwing** Before tossing a ball, hold it in the front portion of your palm, spreading your fingers out evenly beneath the ball, supporting the weight. Don't apply any pressure with your thumb because the purpose of your thumb is to simply provide some guidance and stability. Then throw the ball with your palm facing up, or try a palm down throw to try to create a good back-spin.

## Important Tournaments

### International

- Special Olympics
- World Bocce Championships
- Oberto Bocce Tournament, Italy

### National

None, as this game is not officially played in India

### Current Awardees

None, as this game is not officially played in India

# VIVA-VOCE

**1** The word "bocce" comes from which language?
*Ans* Italian

**2** The small white or yellow ball, which is thrown first to start the game is called what?
*Ans* Pallino or Jack

**3** When throwing to start the game, the white ball should cross what part of the court?
*Ans* The middle

**4** A Bocce ball is considered dead when it hits what?
*Ans* The back wall or backboard.

**5** What is a *raffa* shot in international Bocce?
*Ans* A ground throw at another ball to move that ball out of the way.

**6** What is an acceptable way to use a measuring device to decide points?
*Ans* The most common method used is an extendable pointer that can be placed between the ball and the pallino to measure the distance.

**7** How do you score points in Bocce?
*Ans* By getting your balls closer to the pallino than the opponent's balls.

**8** Where did the primitive game of Bocce originate?
*Ans* Egypt

**9** How many points would a side score if they had 2 balls closest to the pallino?
*Ans* Two

**10** When and where was the first Bocce olympiad held?
*Ans* **1896 in Athens, Greece.**

**11** Who popularised the Bocce sport in Italy?
*Ans* Giuseppe Garibaldi

**12** How long is a standard Bocce ball court?
*Ans* 26.5 metres

**13** How far is the foul line marked out from each backstop?
*Ans* 6 metres

**14** What other sport is Bocce closely related to?
*Ans* Lawn bowls

GAME 2

# SITTING VOLLEYBALL

Volleyball is one of the popular sports in the world. Volleyball is a team sport in which two teams of six players are separated by a net. Each team tries to score points by grounding a ball on the other team's court under organised rules. It is very easy and relatively an inexpensive game that can be played on very small levelled ground. Sitting volleyball is a discipline of the sport in which athletes play in a seated position.

## History

In Germany Athletics and Sitzball were the main sports. Sitzball, which is played sitting down on the floor, was too passive. In 1956, the Dutch Sports Committee introduced a new game called Sitting Volleyball, a combination of sitzball and volleyball. Sitting volleyball is played with six players per team on a smaller volleyball court with lowered nets.

Sitting volleyball for disabled was invented by William G. Morgan. He introduced a simple game which would be suitable for participants with different abilities. A classification system was set up where each player received points according to the degree of disability. Volleyball for the disabled was accepted as an official event at the Paralympic Games for the first time in Toronto (Canada) in 1976 as a demonstration sport where four standing volleyball teams took part. It was then introduced as a medal sport in Arnhem (Netherlands) during 1980.

### Eligibility

Athletes with the following disabilities are eligible to compete in sitting volleyball-athletes with amputations, spinal cord injuries, cerebral palsy, brain injuries and stroke.

Classifications of these athletes by disability are placed into two categories i.e. MD and D. MD stands for 'Minimally Disabled' and D stands for 'Disabled.' Minimally Disabled athletes have lost only a fraction of their muscular strength and flexibility in a joint preventing them from successfully playing standing volleyball. On the other hand, Disabled athletes have lost all of their muscular strength and flexibility in that joint. Only two MD players are allowed on the roster for the Paralympic Games and only one is allowed on the court at a time to keep the fair competition between rival teams. The rest of the team must be classified as D players.

## Terminology

**Ace** — A serve that lands in the opponent's court without being touched.

**Attack** — An attempt by a player to win a point by hitting the ball over the net.

**Attack Line** — In indoor volleyball, it is a line three metres from the net which marks the limit for where a back-row player may advance to hit a ball from above the net.

**Back-row Player** — In indoor volleyball, any of three players positioned at the back of the court.

**Block** — To block an opposing player from spiking the ball by jumping at the net with arms in the air.

**Centre Line** — In indoor volleyball, the imaginary line running directly under the net and dividing the court in half.

**Chuck** — To push or throw the ball rather than hit it (slang).

**Court** — The playing area.

**Crossing Space** — The zone above the net and between two antennae through which the ball must pass during a rally.

**Dig** — A defensive move in which both arms are placed together in an attempt to bounce a hardhit ball up into the air.

**End Line** — A back boundary line of the court.

**Facial** — A boom or spike that hits an opponent in the face (slang).

**Fault** — A foul or error which results in the loss of the rally.

| | |
|---|---|
| **Front-row Player** | In indoor volleyball, any of three players positioned closest to the net. |
| **Front Zone** | In indoor volleyball, the area between the net and the attack line. |
| **Ground** | To hit the ball to the ground, preferably on the other team's court. |
| **Heater** | A hard-hit or spiked ball (slang). |
| **Hit** | To touch the ball as an offensive player, one of three 'hits' allowed a team in getting the ball back over the net. |
| **Hold** | To let the ball settle into the hands briefly on a shot instead of releasing it immediately. |
| **Kill** | To smash the ball overarm into the opponent's court. |
| **Kong** | A one-handed block, named after King Kong's style of swatting biplanes in the original King Kong movie (slang). |
| **Libero** | In indoor volleyball, a substitute defensive player especially adept at digging. |
| **Lip** | A good dig (slang). |
| **Match** | A series of sets to determine a winner. |
| **Mintonette** | The original name for volleyball. |
| **Missile** | A spike or serve hit out of bounds (slang). |
| **Pass** | The attempt by a team to properly handle the opponent's serve or any form of attack. |
| **Rally** | The exchange of plays that decides each point. |
| **Rotate** | In indoor volleyball, to move to the next position on the floor in a clockwise manner. |
| **Screen** | To impede the opponent's view of the ball during the serve. |
| **Serve** | The stroke used to put the ball in play at the start of each rally. |
| **Set** | The part of a match completed, when one side has scored enough points to win a single contest. |
| **Setter** | A player who excels in setting up teammates to attack. |
| **Sideline** | A side boundary line on a court. |

## Measurements and Specification for Sitting Volleyball

- **Playing Court** The court is rectangular measuring 10 × 6 m, surrounded by a free zone which is minimum of 3m wide on all sides and 7m in height from the playing surface.
- **Playing Surface** The surface must be flat, horizontal and uniform. It is forbidden to play on rough or slippery surfaces.
- **Line of the Court** All lines are 5 cm wide.
- **Boundary Line** Two side lines and two ends lines mark the playing court. Both side lines and end lines are drawn inside the dimensions of the playing court.
- **Centre Line** The axis of the centre line divides the playing court into two equal courts measuring 6 m × 5 m each.
- **Attack Line** It is drawn 2 m back from the axis of the centre line marks the front zone.
- **Front Zone** On each court the front zone is limited by the axis of the centre line and the rear edge of the attack line.
- **Service Zone** The service zone is a 6 m wide area behind each end line.
- **Substitution Zone** The substitution zone is limited by the extention of both attack lines upto the scorer's table.
- **Libero-Replacement Zone** The Libero Replacement Zone is a part of the free zone on the side of the team benches, limited by the extension of the attack line up to the end line.
- **Warm up Area** 3 × 3 m area is located in both of the bench-side corners.
- **Penalty Area** Size 1 × 1m equipped with two chairs is located in the control area.
- **Net** Height 1.15 m for men and 1.05 m for women. The net is 0.80 m wide and 6.50 to 7 m long.
- **Antennae** 1.60 m long and 10 mm in diameter.
- **Post** The posts supporting the net area placed at a distance of 0.5 – 1.00 m outside the side lines. Maximum height is 1.25 m.

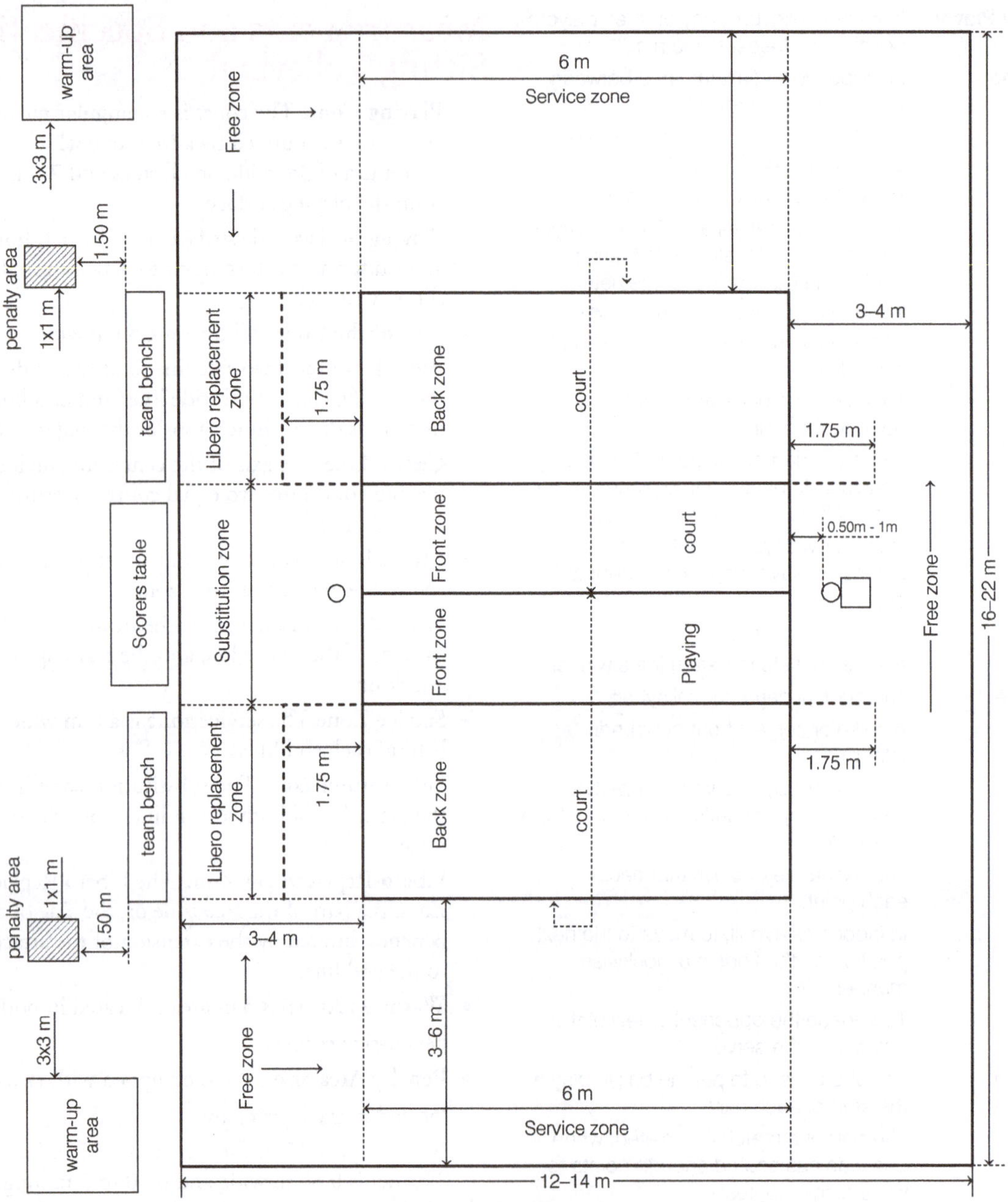


**Sitting Volleyball Court**

## Basic Rules of Sitting Volleyball

- Sitting volleyball is played with six players per teams.
- The rules are the same as the orignial form of volleyball with the exceptions that player must have at least one buttock in contact with the floor and block the serve.
- This game is faster than standing volleyball. It is played in a best-of-five set format and the first to reach 25 points with at aleast a 2 point lead wins the set.
- The court is smaller and the net is lower as the players hit the ball over the net sitting down.

- Unlike standing volleyball, blocking of the serve is allowed and teams can hit the ball no more than three times in succession.
- Similar to standing volleyball, the ball must be touched a maximum of three time before being sent over the net.
- The team can score points by sending the ball on to the other team's half of the court in a way that is impossible to return.
- If a front row player is hitting or attacking the ball, the pelvis of the player in the front zone must be touching the ground.
- Players on defense that are making any defensive plays must be touching the ground in some way with any part of the body.
- Each team in sitting volleyball is allowed to have a defensive specialist called the Libero, responsible for making sure that no balls drop in any part of the court.
- Players are required to remain in contact with the ground, failure to do so will result in a loss of point and service.
- During each possession of the ball, a team can only have these contacts with the ball knonw as a pass, a set and a hit, three are also called as bump, set and spike.
- In this game, the position of each player rotates. Positions are numbered from one to six, starting with the server in the back right corner and going in an anti-clockwise direction.
- There is a special player called Libero in the team and these are separate set of rules for him which are
  - He is a player of backline, who plays as a specialised defensive player and is not allowed to attack from the attacking area.
  - He can not do service neither block the ball or smash it.
  - A diffrent coloured T-Shirt (other than the players) should be worn by a Libero. The word Libero must be printed on the backside of his T-Shirt.
  - His position is fixed during the game and he does not take part in rotation.
- Touching the opponent's court beyond the centre line with a hand is permitted.
- The player is not allowed to lift his/her bottom from the court when executing any type of attack-hit.
- The back row player may perform any type of attack hit from any height.
- The player must have contact with the court with some part of the upper part of the body at all times when playing the ball, except when making a defensive free zone play.
- The referee's official hand signal of 'Lifting from the court' is raising the upper hand and forearm positioned parallel to the floor.
- Referees in sitting volleyball must stand to the sides of the court because of the height of the net and the fact that the players are in an seated position.

## Duties of Officials

### Duties of Referee

- He is responsible for fair play in the match.
- He is the final authority on the rules and regulations from the start to the end of the match.
- Referee performs toss before the start of the match.
- He has the final say on every decision of the match.

### Duties of Scorer

- He takes notes of all the proceedings of the match in a chronological order, alongwith the points gained, time and substitutions made.
- He makes a record of all the fouls made by each player of each team.
- He records personal and technical fouls separately.
- He maintains a score sheet with all the details of each player.

### Duties of Linesmen

- There are 4 to 6 linesmen in a match.
- They basically are responsible for assisting the referee in case of infringement of boundary line rules.
- However, their assistance may be overruled by referee.

## Fundamental Skills and Techniques

These may be divided into the following major categories

### Serving

Each point starts with a serve. There are many techniques of serving. The underhand serving is done by beginners. Another technique is overhead serve where the ball is tossed in the air about 2 feet above the head. Topspin and jump serve are other overhead techniques.

### Passing

This is the first part in a three part sequence. The players need to pass the ball to the setters. The passers use their fingers to pass the ball with both hands using forearms.

### Setting

Setting is the second contact of the ball. In a 'set', the player uses the finger pads to launch the ball high in the air towards the hitters. The fingers should be in a diamond shape to start and they should finish outwards. It is also termed as tip or lift.

### Hitting/Spiking/Attacking

Attacking the ball is all about timing and precision. The 'goal' of the third hit or 'spike', is to make the ball difficult for the opposing team to return. Players spiking should have excellent judgement to perceive the direction of the ball and balance the body to lift it while hitting the ball forcefully. The aim is to land the ball on the floor of the opponent's team.

### Blocking

This is a defensive technique where the players block the offensive shots and try it to shot them back to the opponent. The blocking can be done by one, two or three players according to the standard of match. For one man blocking, the player standy close to the net, face towards it. The player should try to interrupt the ball by taking a jump and raising his hands above the net.

## Important Tournaments

### International

- World Paravolley Sitting Volleyball Championship.
- European Sitting Volleyball Championships for Men and Women.
- Sitting Volleyball Champions Cup.

### Nation

- Sitting Volleyball Senior National Championships.
- National Paralympic (Sitting) Volleyball Tournament.

# VIVA-VOCE

**1** Which of the two games are the combination of sitting volleyball?

***Ans*** Sitzball and volleyball.

**2** Who invented the sitting volleyball game?

***Ans*** Sitting volleyball was invented by William G. Morgan.

**3** When was sitting volleyball game accepted as an official event at the Paralympic Games?

***Ans*** Toronto (Canada) in 1976.

**4** When was sitting volleyball introduced as a medal sport?

***Ans*** Arnhem (Netherlands) during 1980.

**5** Which type of disabilities are eligible to compete in sitting volleyball?

***Ans*** Athletes with amputations, spinal cord injuries, cerebral palsy, brain injuries and stroke.

**6** What is the length and width of the sitting volleyball net?

***Ans*** The length of the sitting volleyball net is 6.50 to 7 m and 0.80 m wide.

**7** What is the length of Antennae in sitting volley ball?

***Ans*** 1.60 m long and 10 mm in diameter.

**8** Who introduced a new game called sitting volley ball?

***Ans*** In 1956, the Dutch Sports Committee introduced a new game called sitting volleyball.

**9** How many players are in sitting volleyball game?

***Ans*** A sitting volleyball team consists of 12 players.

**10** What is the specialised defensive player in sitting volleyball called?

***Ans*** Libero.

**11** Which line divides the playing court into two equal courts?

***Ans*** Centre line.

**12** What is a yellow card in sitting volleyball?

***Ans*** A yellow card shown by an offical indicates that a player or coach has been warned by the official.

**13** What is underhand serve? What kind of player use this serve?

***Ans*** A serve in which ball is given a slight underhand toss from about waist height is called underhand serve.

**14** How many players as substitutes are allowed in a sitting volleyball match?

***Ans*** A maximum of 6 substitutes are allowed in sitting volleyball match.

**15** What does the rotation rule in sitting volleyball regulate?

***Ans*** The rotation rule in volleyball regulate the clockwise movement of players around the court.

**16** Is tossing of the ball necessary in the game of sitting volleyball?

***Ans*** Yes, tossing of the ball is necessary in the sitting volleyball game.

**17** When was the women's sitting volleyball introduced in the Paralympic games?

***Ans*** The women's sitting volleyball event introduction followed in the 2004 in the Paralympic Games.

**18** A player drignated as 'Libero' is not allowed to do what and why?

***Ans*** A player drignated as Libero is not allowed to serve, block or make any attempt to smash as he is the specialised defensive player.

**19** What are the types of passing in sitting volleyball?

***Ans*** There are two types of passing i.e. underhand pass and overhead pass.

**20** What is the weight of the ball used in sitting volleyball match?

***Ans*** Weight of the ball used in sitting volleyball match should be between 260 and 280 gm.

| GAME 3 |

# WHEELCHAIR BASKETBALL

Basketball is a sport that is played by two teams of five players on a rectangular court. The objective is to shoot a ball through a hoop or a basket (18 inches in diameter) which is mounted at a height of 10 feet (3.048) to backboards at each end of the court.

Wheelchair basketball is played by people with varying physical disabilities that disqualify them from playing a non-disabled sport. It is played by people with different level of physical disabilities that prevents running, jumping and pivoting. These include spina bifida, birth defects, cerebral palsy, paralysis due to accident, amputations (of the legs, or other parts) and many other disabilities.

The sport is very similar to regular basketball. The court, the hoop and the backboard are all of the same dimension. Each team has 12 players and only five on court at any point of time. Players use small and lightweight wheelchairs and usually comes with one or two smaller wheels at the front, this is to provide balance and stability. The objective of the game is to score the most points in the opposing team's basket. The team with the most points by the time the clock end, wins.

## History

World War II veterans developed the sport in 1945 as part of rehabilitation in the USA. Riding on a wheelchair, a game of basketball is played among two teams of five players each. Men's wheelchair basketball has featured at first time in Paralympic Games in 1960 in the city of Rome. Women's competition was introduced in 1968.

The sport is governed by the International Wheelchair Basketball Federation (IWBF). It is recognised by the International Paralympic Committee (IPC) as the sole competent authority in Wheelchair Basketball Worldwide. Wheelchair Basketball World Championship is played within two years after every Paralympic Games.

## Wheelchair

Wheelchairs are an essential element in the playing of sports, therefore some rules have been made for wheel chair, such as

- The chair must have 3 to 4 wheels and the rear 2 must be large.
- The rear tires should be a maximum of 66 cm in diameter and should have hand support.
- The maximum accent height should be 53 inches from the floor and the footrest should be at 11 inches.
- Players may have a cushion in the accent upto 10 cm except for players rated 3.0 or higher, which have a maximum of 5 cm.
- Black tires, steering equipments and brakes are prohibited.
- Mechanised or motorised wheelchairs are not allowed at all.
- Wheelchair basketball rules and regulations allow pivoting. The technique gets performed by turning the wheels in opposite directions.
- There is no game law violation to the regulations providing the pivot gets conducted in one spot and not in a certain direction.
- A protective horizontal bar at the front side of the wheelchair must be 11 cm from the floor at its most forward point and throughout its whole length .
- Such a bar may be straight, angled or curved between the two front castors. Where the angle is made up of two or more straight bars joined, the external angle of the joined bars should not be more than 2000 degrees:
- The large wheels including the tyres, may have a maximum diameter of 69 cm. Wheel hubs must be of round outer construction with no sharp points, edges or protrusions.

- In the case of the 3-wheel wheelchair, the small wheel (or castor) must be located at the centre and inside of the horizontal bar at the front of the wheelchair.
- A second small wheel (or castor) may be added to the single small wheel at the front of the wheelchair. Lighting that reflects or flashes, is not permitted on the wheels, the chair or the castors. There must be 1 hand rim on each wheel.
- No steering devices, brakes or gears are allowed on the wheelchair.
- Arm rests and other upper body supports hat are attached to the wheelchair should not project beyond the line of the player's legs or trunk in the natural sitting position.
- During a game, it is possible to have a problem with the wheelchair that causes the wheelchair to no longer be functional or become unsafe. The referee will stop the game at an appropriate time to allow the team to complete the repair. If the repair cannot be completed in 50 seconds or less from the time, the game was stopped and the player must be substituted.
- It is possible that a player may fall out of the wheelchair without a foul occurring. The referee should pay careful attention to the need to protect the player when determining the appropriate time to stop the play.

## Measurement and Specification

- The court dimensions = 28 × 15 m
- Dimension of lower edge of board = 2.90 m from floor
- Thickness of background = 3 cm
- Playing time = 4 × 10 minutes and
- Radius of centre circle = 1.80 m
- Dimension of background = 1.8 m × 1.05 m
- Basket height = 3 cm
- Number of players on court= 5.

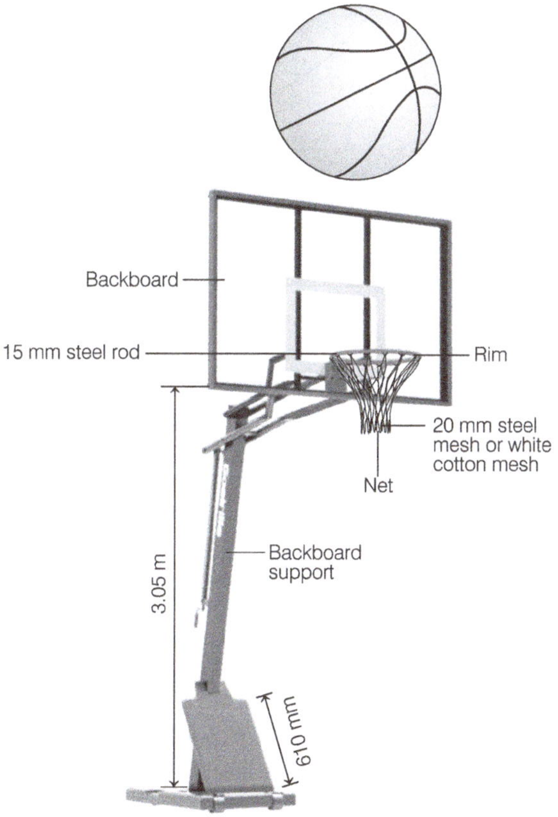


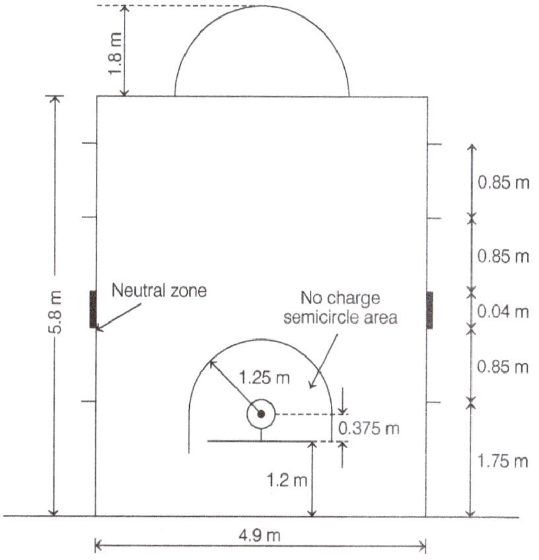


Specification of Restricted Area

**Wheelchair Basketball**

- Diameter of basket ring = 45 ern
- Length of net of basket = 60 ern
- Circumference of ball = 75-78 ern
- Weight of ball = 600 gm to 650 gm
- Number of players of a team = 5 + 7 (extra) = 12
- Number of officials = 5 (1-Referee, l-Umpire, 1-Scorer, 1-Timekeeper, 1-24 second operator)

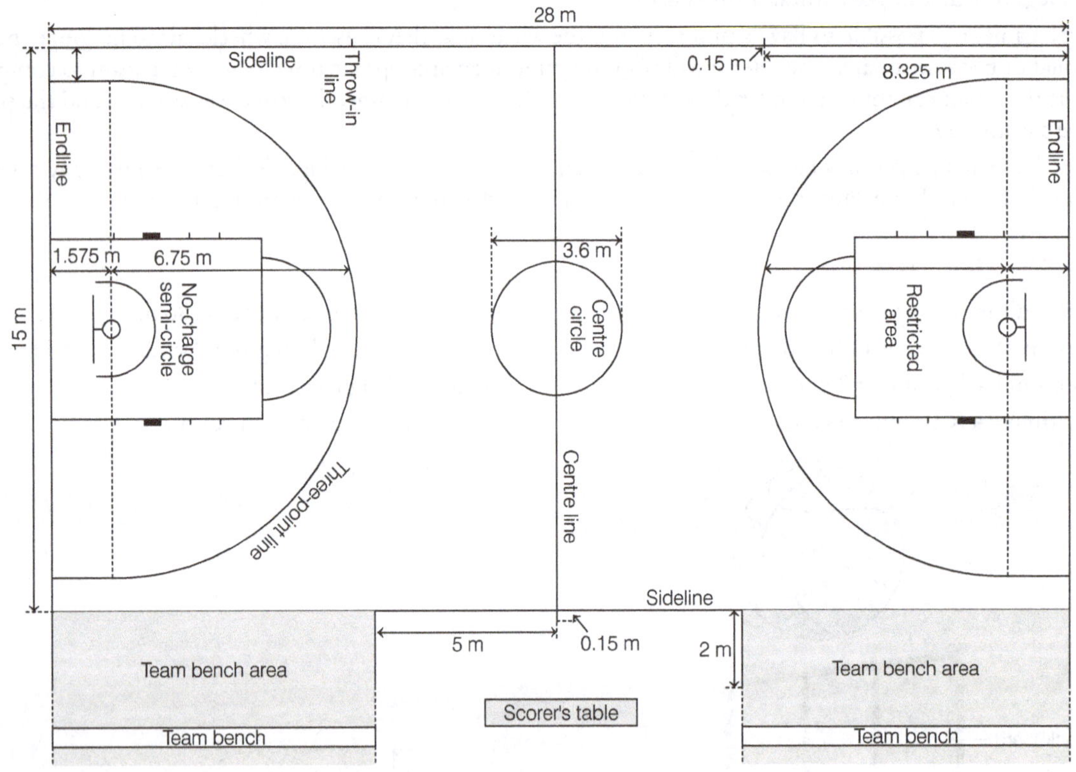


**Wheelchair Basketball Playing Court**

## Terminology

| | |
|---|---|
| **Axle** | The part that attaches the wheel to the chair and allows the wheel to spin. |
| **Backdoor** | Baiting an opponent into overplaying a defensive position and then making an offensive move in the opposite directions towards the basket for a scoring opportunity. |
| **Backpick** | A pick set on a defender who is caught in transition from offense to defense (this usually takes place in their front court) keeping them out of the play giving the offense a numerical advantage. |
| **Banana Cut** | Utilising a curved path when moving into a picking position. |
| **Bounce Stop** | The use of a high bounce to create enough time to stop the chair with both hands and still maintain ball control. |
| **Caster** | Small wheels located on the front and rear of the wheelchair, typically made of hard polyurethane. |
| **Classification** | System used to determine eligibility to play wheelchair basketball at the national level may be used in the schools to create equitable play. |
| **Crossing** | In transition, moving from sideline to sideline in order to create space and picking angles. |
| **Cross Pick** | Pick that is executed horizontally (parallel to the baseline) on the floor. |
| **Dive** | Setting an offensive position in the low post. |

| | |
|---|---|
| **Dump** | The height difference between the front and rear of the seat on a wheelchair. Creates a stable pocket for athletes with higher level injuries and less function. |
| **Flat** | In transitional defense, maintaining position at ball level or lower i.e. the ball should not be further up court than the last defender. In one-on-one defense, maintain proper defensive angle. |
| **Hand Position** | The thumb pads should be places on the tire, not the push rim, with the thumb extended forward and slightly outward to prevent the thumb hitting the chair side guards. The action makes a D-shape and should resemble the wheels of an old time train locomotive. |
| **Help Position** | On defense, the middle of the free throw lane. |
| **Hi-Lo/Lo-Hi Pick** | Pick that is executed vertically (parallel to the sideline) on the floor. |
| **Hook** | Impeding movement of an opponent by illegally utilising the wheelchair to hold the opponent in a static position. |
| **Integrated** | Individuals with disabilities participate in sport alongside students without disabilities. |
| **Lifting** | Raising the buttocks off of the seat cushion during play. |
| **Over** | In defending a pick, moving over the top of the person attempting to set the pick. |
| **Physical Advantage Foul** | Penalty for utilising a functional movement of the lower extremities to gain an advantage during a competition. |
| **Screen Shooter** | Utilises a dive person as a screen in the low post. |
| **Seal** | Technique used in the low post to create a positional advantage for the offense. |
| **Strapping** | Various types of straps utilised to create snug fit between the chair and the athlete. |
| **Threat(s)** | Person(s) on opposing team most likely to score. |
| **Tilting** | Balancing the chair on one front caser and one rear wheel in order to gain a height advantage for shooting, rebounding or defending. |
| **Travelling** | A travelling violation occurs when a person with possession of the ball makes more than two pushes or pulls on the rear wheel(s) that create forward or rearward movement without dribbling the ball. A pivot or turn is allowed after the two pushes or pulls as long as the player does not impart an impulse on the wheels. |
| **Triple Switch** | Defensive technique to maintain position in the low post and point positions. |
| **Turning** | 90 Degree Turn = a square corner. 45 Degree Turn = 1/2 of a square corner. 180 Degree Turn = turn to face the total opposite direction. 360 Degree Turn = turn in a full circle. |
| **Volume of Movement** | The area in which an athlete can repeatedly and successfully catch, pass and shoot a ball. The volume of movement will be different for each athlete based on the disability and functional ability. |
| **Yo-Yo** | On defense, working in tandem in the low post to prevent the offense from gaining a positional advantage. |

## Rules

The rules of wheelchair basketball are very similar to running basketball. In 1964, basic international rules were adopted which included minor adjustments to meet the needs of the game in a wheelchair. Wheelchair basketball is played in accordance with the International Wheelchair Basketball Federation (IWBF) rules.

### Basic Rules

- To start the game, the ball is tossed and players jump for collecting the ball. They are not allowed to push or hit the opposing player.
- Players cannot travel with the ball and are required to throw or bounce after every two touches on their wheelchair.
- Unlike regular basketball, double dribble is not considered a violation. It is allowed to dribble again after picking up one's dribble.
- For the sport to be more equal and fair, players have a rating system based on their degree of motor impairment, which from 1.0 to 4.5.
- Each team gets 24 seconds from taking possession of the ball to complete an attempted shot at the basket.
- One point gets scored for a successful free-throw. Player get two points for a normal field basket score. Three points occurs for a successful shot made from behind the arc of the three-point line.
- Players should throw or bounce the ball after every two pushes of the wheels on their chairs. This avoids getting penalised for wheelchair basketball travelling rule.

- There is no double dribble rule in wheelchair basketball.
- Any player committing 5 personal fouls in the game must get replaced by another player.
- Wheelchair basketball rules and regulations consider the chair as part of the player's body. This relates to any case of charging, blocking, or going out of bounds. Adjusting to this rule is usually the most difficult for seated chair players.
- If player pick up the ball or place it on their lap they can only push twice before they must shoot, pass, or dribble the ball again.
- Player advantage fouls may get called if an athlete uses their legs to raise themselves in their seats. The same applies for steering their chairs or balancing themselves to gain advantage.
- Travel violation called when player in possession pushes more than twice without dribbling.
- Foul is an infraction of the rules concerning illegal personal contact with an opponent.

### Time Limits

- An offensive player cannot remain more than 3 seconds in the free throw lane while the player's team is in possession of the ball.
- If the offensive player is trapped in the lane and attempting to leave the lane, the 3 seconds count will cease and a violation will not be called as long as the player exits the lane as soon as it is possible.
- If the trapped player is in the lane for more than 3 seconds and chooses to become an offensive threat by calling for a pass then the 3 seconds violation will be called.
- If a shot attempt is made by another player, the player trapped in the lane may rebound the ball without a 3 seconds violation be called.

### Other Rules

- **Dribble** A player in possession of the ball may not push more than twice in succession or both hands in either direction without dribbling the ball to the floor again. Taking more than two consecutive pushes constitutes a travelling violation. A player may, however, wheel the chair and bounce the ball simultaneously just as a non-disabled player runs and bounces the ball simultaneously in stand up basketball. There is no double dribble violation in wheelchair basketball.
- **Loss of the Ball** If a player in possession of the ball makes any physical (bodily) contact with the floor or tilts the chair so that the footplate or wing touch the floor, it is a violation and the ball is a warded to the other team.
- **Out-Of-Bounds** A player is considered out-of-bounds when any part of the player's body or wheelchair touches the floor on or beyond the boundary.
- **Physical Advantage Foul (PAF)** Because of the varying causes and manifestations (degrees) of disability among participants, a basic rule of keeping firmly seated in the wheelchair at all times and not using a functional leg or leg stump to gain a physical advantage over an opponent, is strictly enforced. An infraction of this rule constitutes a Physical Advantage Foul (PAF). Examples of a PAF include lifting the buttocks off of the chair seat to rebound, shoot, block a shot, pass, or to tap a jump ball using a foot in contact with the floor to stop/move the chair, or to use a lower limb to manipulate the rear wheels. The foul is so recorded in the official scorebook. Three such fouls disqualify a player from the game. Two free throws are awarded and the ball is given to the opposing team, out of bounds.
- **Falling** If a player falls out of the chair during play, the officials will immediately suspend play if there is any chance of danger to the fallen player. If not, the officials will withhold their whistles until the particular play in progress has been completed. If a player falls out of the chair to gain possession of the ball or by falling keeps opponents from gaining possession of the ball, the ball is awarded to the opposing team.
- **Lines** For free throw and 3 point shooting attempts, the shooter need only have their rear wheels behind the shooting line. The shooters allowed to have the front caster cross the line. For free throws, players lined up on the blocks must have the whole chair behind the lane lines.

## Duties of Officials

### Duties of Referee and Umpire

- He is responsible for fair play in the match.
- He is the final authority on the rules and regulations from the start to the end of the match.
- Referee performs toss before the start of the match.
- He has the final say on every decision related of the match.

### Duties of Scorer

- He takes notes of all the proceedings of the match in a chronological order, alongwith the points gained, time and substitutions made.
- He makes a record of all the fouls made by each player of each team.
- He records personal and technical fouls separately.
- He maintains a score sheet with all the details of each player.

### Duties of Timekeeper

- He notifies and assists the referee regarding the issues of the game.
- He is responsible for notifying referee about the time at which each part of the match has to begin. This needs to be done atleast three minutes before the actual start of the game.
- The timekeeper also keeps record of the various times and situations when the match was paused and resumed.

### Duties of 24 Second Operator

- His main duty is to check the 24 second rule.
- He keeps a record of every time when possession of ball changes.

## Important Tournaments

### International

- Wheelchair Basketball World Championship
- Paralympic Games
- Asian Para Games

### National

- Wheelchair Basketball National Championship

## Important Personalities

### Indian

- Geeta Chouhan

### International

- Patrick Anderson, Canada
- Matt Scott, USA
- Brian Bell, USA
- Michael Paye, USA
- Joshua Turek, USA
- Barbara Grob, Germany

# VIVA-VOCE

**1** **How many players are on court at one time in wheelchair basketball?**

***Ans*** Five (5).

**2** **What is the total number of classification points in one team on court at any time?**

***Ans*** 14 points.

**3** **How long does each period last in wheelchair basketball game?**

***Ans*** 10 minutes.

**4** **When was men's wheelchair basketball first introduced in the Olympic Games?**

***Ans*** Men's wheelchair basketball was introduced in 1960 in the city of Rome.

**5** **What is dribbling?**

***Ans*** Dribbling is when a player repeatedly bounces the ball of the floor so that it returns to his/her possession.

**6** **When does a team score 3 points?**

***Ans*** A basket scored from beyond the 3 point line give 3 points to them.

**7** **What is man-to-man defence?**

***Ans*** Man-to-man defence is a team defence in which each player is assigned to guard a particular opponent.

**8** **When is a 'Jump ball' necessary?**

***Ans*** A 'Jump ball' is necessary to start a game, to start all overtime periods and sometimes to restart play.

**9** **How long is each team allowed to stay in possession of the ball before they must shot?**

***Ans*** Each team is allowed for maximum of 24 seconds to stay in possession of the ball before they must shot.

**10** **How many periods are there in a game of wheelchair basketball?**

***Ans*** There are total of 4 periods with intervals between each period in the game of wheelchair basketball.

**11** **What happens if a player fails to dribble while moving with the ball?**

***Ans*** The possession of the ball is given to the opposing team when a player fails to dribble while moving with the ball.

**12** **When was the wheelchair basketball game begun?**

***Ans*** Wheelchair basketball began in 1946 by young men returned from World War II, paralysed and used wheelchairs for mobility.

**13** **How high is the goal for wheelchair basketball?**

***Ans*** The height of the hoop in wheelchair basketball is the same as in the running game i.e. 3.05 m.

**14** **How long is a game of wheelchair basketball?**

***Ans*** In accordance with IWBF, a wheelchair basketball game consists of four periods of 10 minutes. If the score is tied at the end of four quaters, an overtime period of 5 minutes is played.

**15** **What is the aim of wheelchair basketball?**

***Ans*** The object of the game is to score the most points in the opposing team's basket.

**16** **Where was the first wheelchair basketball game played?**

***Ans*** The first game were played at Veteran's Administration Hospital in California and Massachusetts.

**17** **What are the measurements of a basketball court?**

***Ans*** The measurements of a basketball court are 28 m × 15 m.

**18** **How many points is a shot worth when inside the opponent's semi-circle?**

***Ans*** A shot is worth 2 points when inside the opponent's semi-circle.

| GAME 4 |

# UNIFIED BADMINTON

Unified Sports are team sports that bring people together. Here people with and without intellectual disabilities together form the same team to compete. Special Olympics Badminton provides athletes who participate with the opportunity to compete in meaningful competitions.

Badminton is a sport that is enjoyed all around the world by millions of people of a wide range of ages. It is a sport that explores speed changes, reaction time demands, muscular strength and endurance challenges, and is heart-pumping fun. This newly identified Olympic Sport offers benefits to all who pick up a racket and a shuttle for a test outing on the court.

## History

Unified Sports are also an integral part of Special Olympics Unified Champion Schools, which was founded in 2008 and funded by the US Department of Education. The Special Olympic Movement was founded in USA in 1968 by Late Eunice Kennedy Shirer, sister of President John F Kennedy. She believed that Olympic ideals of sports could give confidence and new hope to people with intellectual (learning) disabilities as well as to those who cared for them. In 1989, Unified Sports were adopted by Special Olympics International.

Since 1995, badminton has been a part of the Special Olympics World Games. In badminton, reaction time, muscle strength and endurance are the most important factors. The goal of the players is to hit the shuttlecock over the net in such a way that the other side cannot hit it back.

Special Olympics Badminton includes the following events

- Singles
- Target Serve
- Unified Sports Doubles
- Unified Sports Mixed Doubles
- Doubles
- Mixed Doubles
- Individual Skills Competition

Special Olympics also have meaningful competitions for athletes who have lower abilities levels. These competitions include Return Volley and Return Serve.

## Rules

- The rules of competitions include some various modifications. For example, Special Olympics wheelchair athletes have the option of serving an overhead serve from either the left or right serving area.
- The serving area is shortened to half the distance for Special Olympics wheelchair athletes.
- In Unified Sports Doubles, each Unified Sports Doubles team consists of one athlete and one partner. Each team determines their own order of service, as well as their selection of courts, add or deuce.
- Where Hand Feeding is concerned in relation to the Individual Skills Competition, the feeder usually the coach holds a number of shuttles on their arm and throws the shuttles to the athlete in the same manner, a dart would be thrown. The athlete attempts to hit the shuttles with their racket and receives one point every time when they hit the shuttle.

- Racket Feeding for overhead strokes involves the feeder holding four or five shuttles at one time. The feeder hits the shuttle to the athlete using an underhand stroke. The athlete receives one point if they hit the shuttle. If the athlete misses the shuttle, the feeder immediately throws another one and the count continues.
- In the, 'Ups,' Contest the shuttle is repeatedly hit into the air by the athlete. The athlete receives a point for each time they hit the shuttle within a thirty-second time frame. If the shuttle hits the floor, another shuttle is given and the count continues.
- The forehand stroke requires a Special Olympics athlete to stand two feet from the net with the feeder, who is positioned on the opposite side of the net. The feeder uses an underhand serve to hit a shuttle to the forehand side of the athlete. The athlete has five tries to hit the shuttle and receives one point for each successful forehand stroke.
- Backhand stroke, in Special Olympics Badminton, is served and scored the same way as the forehand stroke, with the exception that the feeder hits the shuttle to the backhand side of the athlete. During the serve, an athlete has five attempts to serve from either side of the service court. If the athlete is unable to serve the underhand serve, they may use the overhand serve. Athletes receive ten points for each serve that lands in the correct service box. No points are awarded for any serve that lands outside of the service box.
- Athletes are given ten attempts to serve the shuttle anywhere within the bounds of their opponent's singles court. The athlete serves from behind the service line. Athletes are given one point for each successful target serve.
- Where Return Volleys are concerned, athletes are also given ten tries to return the shuttle. A feeder, from the opponent's mid-court, hits the shuttle into the athlete's court.
- The athlete then attempts to send the shuttle back into their opponent's single court. Athletes are awarded one point for every successful hit into their opponent's single court.
- During the Return Serve, athletes are given ten attempts to return a served shuttle. A feeder, from the athlete's opponent's service area, serves a shuttle into the athlete's court, five serves from each side of the court. The athlete attempts to return the serve. Athletes are awarded one point for each successfully returned serve.
- The final score is determined by adding all of the scores together for each of the six individual skills competitions.

## Terminology

| | |
|---|---|
| **Alley** | Side-extension of the court by 1½ feet on both sides that is used for doubles play. |
| **Back Alley** | Area between the back boundary line and the long service line for doubles. |
| **Baseline** | Back boundary line at each end of the court that runs parallel to the net. |
| **Bird or Birdie** | Another name for the shuttlecock. |
| **Carry** | An illegal tactic, also called a sling or throw, in which the shuttle is caught and held on the racket and then slung during the execution of a stroke. |
| **Center Line** | Line perpendicular to the net that separates the left and right service courts. |
| **Clear** | A shot hit deep to the opponent's back court. |
| **Court** | Area of play, as defined by the outer boundary lines. |
| **Drive** | A fast and low shot that makes a horizontal flight over the net. |
| **Fault** | A violation of the playing rules, either in serving, receiving, or during play. |
| **Flick** | A quick wrist and forearm rotation that surprises an opponent by changing an apparently soft shot into a faster passing one, used primarily on the serve and at the net. |
| **Hairpin Net Shot** | Shot made from below and very close to the net with the shuttle rising, just clearing the net, and then dropping sharply down the other side. The shuttle's flight approximates the shape of a hairpin. |
| **Halfcourt Shot** | A shot hit low and to midcourt, used effectively in doubles against the up-and-back formation. |
| **Kill** | Fast, downward shot that cannot be returned. |
| **Let** | A legitimate cessation of play to allow a rally to be replayed. |
| **Match** | A series of games, to determine a winner. |
| **Mid-court** | The middle third of the court, halfway between the net and the back boundary line. |
| **Net Shot** | Shot hit from the forecourt that just clears the net and drops sharply. |

| | |
|---|---|
| **Push Shot** | Gentle shot played by pushing the shuttle with little wrist motion, usually from net or mid-court to the opponent's mid-court. |
| **Racket** | Instrument used by player to hit shuttlecock. |
| **Rally** | This occurs when the players hit the bird back and forth several times before one side scores a point. |
| **Serve or Service** | Players put the shuttlecock into play for points by serving it to opponents, hitting it over the net into a special part of the court near their opponent. |
| **Service Court** | Area into which the serve must be delivered. Different for singles and doubles play. |
| **Short Service Line** | The line 6½ feet from the net which a serve must reach to be legal. |
| **Shuttlecock** | The name for the object that players hit, made of a ball of cork or rubber with a crown of feathers in an open conical shape. |
| **Smash** | When a shuttle is floated high into the air, a player has time to unleash a powerful overhand shot straight to the floor of the opposing court |
| **Wood Shot** | A shot that results when the base of the shuttle is hit by the frame of the racket. Once illegal, this shot was ruled acceptable by the International Badminton Federation in 1963. |

# Equipments Required

## Racket

The racket shall be a frame not exceeding 680 mm in overall length and 230 mm in overall width consisting of the main parts. The handle is the part of the racket intended to be gripped by a player. The stringed area is the part of the racket with which it is intended that a player hits the shuttle. The stringed area shall be flat and consist of a pattern of crossed strings either alternately interlaced or bonded where they cross. It shall not exceed 280 mm in overall length and 220 mm in overall width. The width of the extended stringed area does not exceed 35 mm. The overall length of the stringed area does not exceed 330 mm. The head bounds the stringed area.

- The shaft connects the handle to the head
- The throat (if present) connects the shaft to the head.

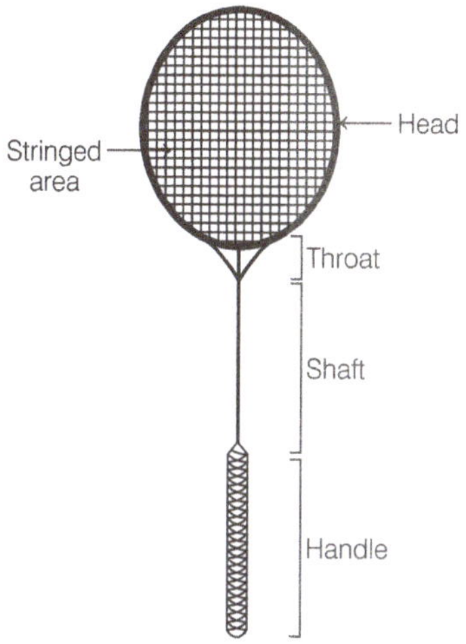

Racket

## Shuttle

The shuttle shall be made of natural and/or synthetic materials. From whatever material the shuttle is made, the flight characteristics generally shall be similar to those produced by a natural feathered shuttle with a cork base covered by a thin layer of leather.

### Feathered Shuttle

The shuttle shall have 16 feathers fixed in the base. The feathers shall have a uniform length between 62 mm to 70 mm when measured from the tip to the top of the base. The tips of the feathers shall lie on a circle with a diameter from 58 mm to 68 mm. The feathers shall be fastened firmly with thread or other suitable material. The base shall be 25 mm to 28 mm in diameter and rounded on the bottom. The shuttle shall weight from 4.74 to 5.50 grams.

### Non-Feathered Shuttle

The skirt, or simulation of feathers in synthetic materials, shall replace natural feathers.

Measurements and weight shall be same as feathered shuttle. However, because of the difference in the specific gravity and other properties of synthetic materials in comparison with feathers, a variation of upto 10 per cent shall be acceptable.

# VIVA-VOCE

**1** When was Unified Sports first adopted by Special Olympics International?

***Ans*** In 1989, Unified Sports was first adopted.

**2** What is Unified Sports?

***Ans*** In Unified Sports, people with and without intellectual disabilities together form the same team to compete.

**3** What is the significance of unified badminton?

***Ans*** The significance of unified badminton is that it explores speed changes, reaction time demands, muscular strength and endurance challenges.

**4** From which year badminton has been part of the Special Olympics World Games?

***Ans*** Since 1995, badminton has been part of the Special Olympics World Games.

**5** What is the goal of players in this sport?

***Ans*** The goal of players in unified badminton game is to hit the shuttlecock over the net in such a way that the other side cannot hit it back.

**6** Unified badminton double team consists of how many players?

***Ans*** Each unified sports double team consists of one athlete and one partner.

**7** How hand feeding is done?

***Ans*** Hand feeding is done in such a manner that the feeder (usually the coach) holds five shuttles at one time in his/her arm and throws the shuttles, one at a time, to the athlete like a dart would be thrown.

**8** What is the procedure of racquet feeding?

***Ans*** Racquet feeding (for overhead strokes) is done in such a way that the feeder (coach) holds five shuttles and hits the shuttle (one at a time) high to the athlete using an underhand stroke.

**9** The athlete has how many attempts to serve from either side of the service court?

***Ans*** The athlete has five attempts to serve from either side of the service court.

**10** How is final score determined?

***Ans*** Final score is determined by adding all the scores together for each of the six individual skills competition.

**11** What do you understand by baseline?

***Ans*** Baseline is the back boundary line at each end of the court, parallel to the net.

**12** What is centre line?

***Ans*** Centre line is the line perpendicular to the net that separates the left and right service courts.

**13** What is flick?

***Ans*** Flick is a quick wrist and forearm rotation that surprises an opponent by changing an apparently soft shot into a faster passing one, used primarily on the serve and at the net.

**14** What do you understand by wood shot?

***Ans*** Wood shot is a shot that results when the base of the shuttle is hit by the frame of the racquet.

**15** In which year wood shot became acceptable?

***Ans*** Wood shot was ruled acceptable by the International Badminton Federation in 1963.

**16** What is the length and width of a racket?

***Ans*** The length of the frame of a racket should be no longer than 680 mm or wider than 230 mm.

**17** What is the length and width of an stringed area?

***Ans*** The dimension of the stringed area must not exceed 280 mm in length or 220 mm in width.

| GAME 5 |

# UNIFIED BASKETBALL

Unified Basketball is one of the Unified Sports in the world. The game partners students with developmental disabilities and students without developmental disabilities to train, compete and represent their school.

*Unified Basketball*

## Measurements and Specifications

- **Basketball Court** 28 m by 15m (84 ft × 50 ft)
- **Half court** 12.5 m by 15m
- **Radius of center circle** 1.80 m
- **Height of lower edge of board** 2.90 m from floor
- **Dimensions of backboard** 1.8 m × 1.05m
- **Thickness of backboard** 3 cm
- **Number of players** 5 (3 athletes i.e. students without disability + 2 student partners i.e. students with disability)
- **No. of players in half court basketball** 3 (2 athletes + 1 student partner)
- **Uniform** Same colour shorts and shirt with number on front and back written 3/4 inch wide. Only these numbers can be written on shirt 0, 5, 10, 20, 25, 30, 35....
- **No. of officials** 1 Referee, 2 Assistant Referee
- **Type of events** All the events classified as above and below 12 years

### Age 12 years and above

- **Height of basket from the ground** 3.05 m (10 ft) above the floor
- **Ball size** 7 for males and 6 for females
- **Circumference of the ball** 74.9 mm (29.5 in)- 78.0 mm (30.7 in) for males, 72.4 m (28.5 in) 73.7 mm (29 in) for females
- **Weight of the ball** 567 - 650 gm for males, 510 - 567 gm for females

## Age below 12 years

- **Height of basket from the ground** 2.44m (8 ft) above the floor
- **Ball size** 5 (for both boys and girls)
- **Circumference of the ball** 68.6 mm (27 in) - 72.4 mm (28.5 in)
- **Weight of the ball** 397 - 454 gm.

## Terminology

| | |
|---|---|
| **Baskets** | The baskets shall comprise the backboard, rings and nets. For competition, the basket ring is normally 3.05 metres (10 ft) above the floor. |
| **Blocks** | The first lane spaces underneath the basket. |
| **Bounce Pass** | A pass that strikes the floor just more than halfway to the receiver. |
| **Coach** | Coach makes the strategy and directs the team or individual basketball player. |
| **Dead Ball** | When a ball is considered dead such as in foul, a foul shot or when the ball is out of bounds. |
| **Defense** | The ball is moved down the court towards the basket by passing or dribbling. The team with the ball is called the offense. The team without the ball is called the defense. |
| **Double Dribble** | Dribbling the ball twice or using both hands before passing the ball. Latest General Rules. |
| **Dribble** | Ball movement caused by a player in control who throws or taps the ball in the air or onto the floor and then touches it. The dribble ends when the player touches the ball with both hands simultaneously, permits it to come to rest while he is in contact with it, or loses control. |
| **Field Goal** | It refers to basket scored on any shot or tap other than a free throw. It is worth either 2 or 3 points. |
| **Free Throw** | An unimpeded attempt at a goal awarded to a player following a foul or other infringement. |
| **Jump Ball** | A method of putting the ball into play by tossing it up between two opponents in one of the three circles. |
| **Perimeter Players** | The offensive players who play outside the lane and face the basket. |
| **Pivot** | It takes place when a player who is holding the ball steps once or more than once in any direction with the same foot, the other foot called the pivot foot, being kept at its point of contact with the floor |
| **Post Players** | The offensive players who play near the lane and have their backs to the basket. |
| **Rebound** | A term usually applied when the ball bounces off the backboard or basket. |
| **Referee** | A person who has the responsibility to enforce the rules and maintain the order of the game. |
| **Screen** | An attempt to protect a teammate's play by shutting off an opponent's approach without personal contact. |
| **Shooting** | It is the most important skill in basketball. To win, you have to score points. All the other skills are tools a team user to get the ball and its players into position to score. If your athletes can develop confident, accurate shooting skills, they will be hard to stop on the court. |
| **Student Partners** | Those players that have intellectual disabilities. They play in wheelchairs. |
| **Technical Foul** | A penalty for improper behaviour such as using foul language or arguing with the referee. |
| **Three-second Area** | Area inside the 'Key' below the free throw line. |
| **Throw in** | A method of putting the ball in play from out of bounds. Must be done in 5 seconds. |
| **Time Outs** | Four time outs per game is allowed. substitution is made during time outs. |
| **Timeouts** | Two 60-second and one 30-second timeout per team for entirety of game. Referee may call timeouts as needed for injury without using team timeouts. |

## Rules

- A team may have no more than 22 individuals on their bench. This includes coaches and student assistants. Teams are encouraged to have an equal number of athletes and partners if possible.
- There must be 3 Unified Student Athletes and 2 Unified Student Partners on the floor at all times. The game will end if a team is not able to have the correct number of athletes and partners.

- There must be two athletes and one partner from each team on the court at all times.
- Length of the game is adjusted but usually it lasts for 20-24 minutes each. A 24 minute game consists of 2 halves of 12 minutes each. These halves are further divided into 6 minutes with a 3 minute interval in between 2 halves.
- The aim is to catch the ball, throw it accurately to the next team member till the ball reaches the player who is supposed to put the ball in the basket.
- The positions of all the members are fixed before the starting of the match. The round ends after the attempt of field goal is made.
- The next team begins in the same way.
- Substitutes are allowed after a round ends.
- Team receives 1 point for each correct pass and for each successful catch.
- Team receives 2 points for each successful field goal.
- Unified athletes must score at least 75% of the points in a given game.
- Each game will begin with a jump ball between two athletes.
- One basket within the 3 point arc equals 2 points. One basket outside the 3 point arc equals 3 points. Free throws equals 1 point.
- Pushing, tripping, dominate, improper shooting attempts result in fouls. Seven team fouls during a period results in 1 team foul penalty. Five personal fouls result in expulsion from the game. Personal fouls are the fouls that are counted for improper behaviour, using abusive language, showing aggression towards others or trying to hurt other players deliberately.

## Rules (Half Court)

- Each team must have 3 players i.e. 2 athletes and 1 student partner.
- The game is played for 20 minutes or till one team scores 20 points.
- If there is a tie, then overtime is given. A 1 minute interval is given between each overtime period.

## Individual Skills

Unified basketball is played as a team game. Individual skills like dribbling, pass, shot are also accounted.

Unified Basketball measures the individual skills of the student partners in two levels i.e. Level 1 and Level 2. In Level 1 there are 3 events - Passing, Dribbling and Shooting. Level 2 consists of 3 events - 12 m Dribble, Catch and Pass and Perimeter Shooting.

The scores of all the individual events are added. Then the score is converted according to conversion chart and individual points are awarded to each player.

# Fundamental Skills and Techniques

The game depends on teamwork and inclusion of everyone. The student partners or partners are expected to facilitate game by bringing the ball up the court, creating scoring opportunities for athletes, rebounding and setting plays. The athletes are expected to shoot and score, steal the ball or block shots. It should be done strictly in coordination with the partners.

## Team Game

When Unified Basketball is played, then the position of all the players (athletes and partners) are marked on the floor of the court beforehand. They are marked to 2-1-2 zone with players positioned 4 m apart from each other.

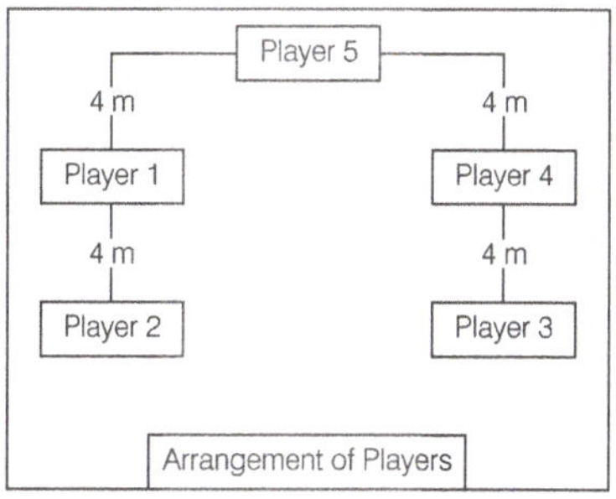


**Team Game**

The official hands the ball to the player no. 1 to begin each round. Each player attempts to catch the ball and then throws it accurately to the player stationed at next position. The throwing is sequential i.e. from player 1 to 2 till 5.

In position 5, one athlete is positioned who attempts to score. Coaches remain on the sideline and give verbal or signed instructions. A team score points on every successful catch, pass and field goal.

## Individual Game

The skills and techniques required in unified basketball in individual game category are

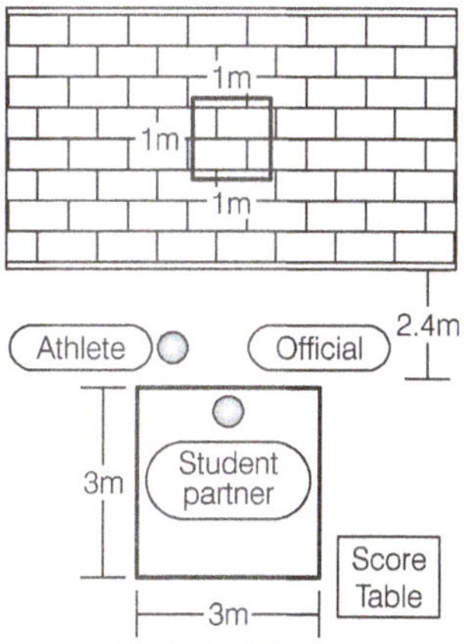


**Individual Game**

- **Passing** The individual stands 3 metres the wall and bounces on the 1 m by 1m box marked on the wall. The student partner receives 1 point for hitting the target and catching the ball on its return.
- **Dribbling** There are two events in it. They are dribbling the ball for a distance of 10 metre i.e. 10 metre dribble. Individual Game and speed dribble

i.e dribble for 60 seconds and score points based on how many times they dribble. The scoring is done by counting the number of dribbles and converting it into points.

| Seconds | Points | Seconds | Points |
|---|---|---|---|
| 0-2 | 30 | 2.1-3 | 28 |
| 3.1-4 | 26 | 4.1-5 | 24 |
| 5.1-6 | 22 | 6.1-7 | 20 |
| 7.1-8 | 18 | 8.1-9 | 16 |
| 9.1-10 | 14 | 10.1-11 | 12 |
| 12.1-14 | 10 | 14.1-16 | 08 |
| 16.1-18 | 06 | 18.1-20 | 04 |
| 20.1-22 | 02 | 22.1 and over | 01 |

Conversion Chart

- **Shooting / Spot Shot** In this, the individual shoots twice from 6 different spots along both sides of the free throw lane. The spots are marked from no. 1 to 6. They are 1.5 m apart from each other. The players attempt 2 field goals from each of six spots. The attempt is made from spots 2, 4 and 6, and then from spots 1, 3 and 5.

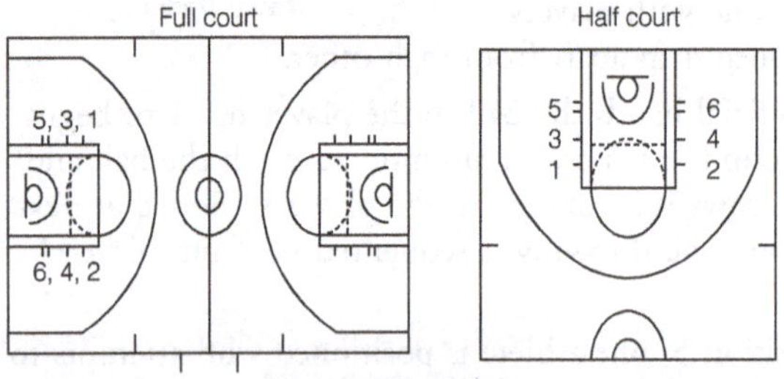


**Shooting Positions**

- **12 Metre Dribble** Here an individual dribbles the ball for 12 metres and scores points based on how fast they go. Scoring is done according to the conversion chart. Time is 60 seconds and the player dribbles the ball while passing alternately to the right and left of the six obstacles placed 2 metres apart.

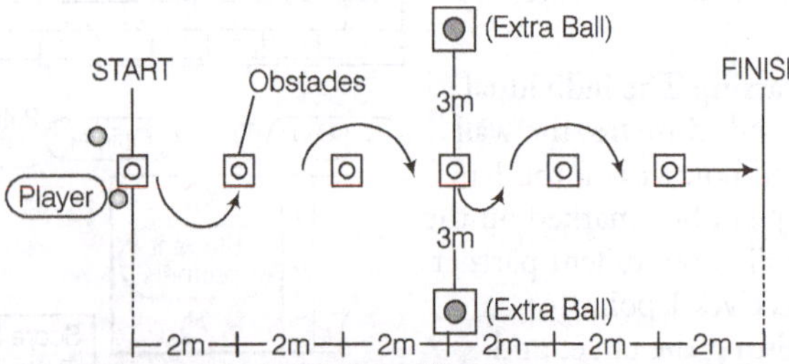


**12 Metre Dribble**

- **Catch and Pass** Here it means to catch the ball in any manner like with hands only, bounce pass in arms and chest, catch with bounce pass in hands only or attempt to catch a pass while moving. After catching the ball, moving or passing it by putting a step forward to increase power is pass. Hands are used excessively to ensure accuracy.
- **Perimeter Shooting** Here a player stands at the juncture of a free throw line either to the left or right. The player dribbles towards the goal and attempts a field goal of his/her choice outside the 2.75 m arc. The player then rebounds the basketball and dribbles anywhere outside the arc before attempting another field goal. The time limit is 2 minutes and the player can make as many trials.

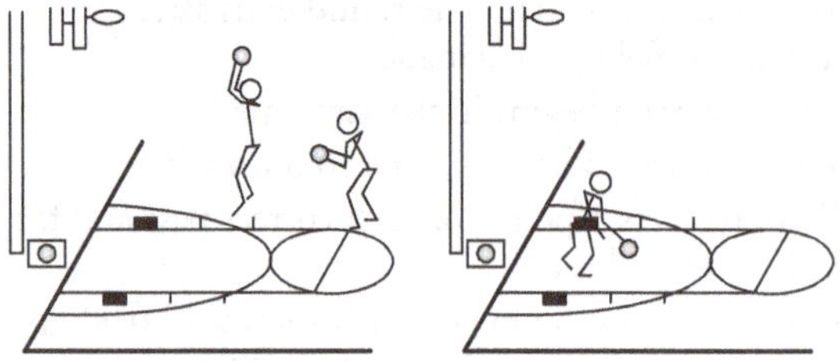

*Perimeter Shooting*

## Important Tournaments

### National

- National Federation of High Schools (NFHS)
- National Intramural- Recreational Sports Association
- National Championship Basketball
- National Basketball Association (NBA)

### International

- Special Olympics Unified Sports
- International Unified Basketball Tournament
- Unified Basketball Match
- National Basketball Association Tournaments
- FIBA- Federation International Basketball Association

## Important Personalities

Joelyn Jweedy, Stephen Curry, Isabel Gomez, Ryan Shaughnessy

## Important Venues

- Thyagraj Stadium, New Delhi
- Rajiv Gandhi Indoor Stadium Puducherry
- Kansas and Washburn Rural High School, Kansas city (upcoming event on 15th October, 2017)
- Hall Holleschbierg- Trassen, Luxembourg
- Galen Center- University of Southern California (USC)
- Torontos Enercare Centre
- Madison Square Garden, New York

# VIVA-VOCE

**1** How many players are there in Unified Basketball team?

***Ans*** Game should be played between two teams each consisting of 5 players.

**2** Which equipments are required to play the game basketball?

***Ans*** Basketball and nets are required to play basketball.

**3** What do you mean by Unified Basketball?

***Ans*** It is a game where students with developmental disabilities and students without developmental disabilities play together as a team.

**4** What should be the size of the basketball court?

***Ans*** The court should be 28 m $\times$ 15 m (84 ft $\times$ 50 ft) and marked accordingly.

**5** What should be the size of ball in female competition?

***Ans*** It should be size 6.

**6** What is the circumference of the ball in male competition?

***Ans*** It is between 749 mm (29.5 in) and 780 mm (30.7 in)

**7** What does the basket comprise in Unified Basketball?

***Ans*** The basket comprises backboard, rings and nets.

**8** Who are student partners?

***Ans*** Student partners are those players that have intellectual disabilities.

**9** What is Rebound?

***Ans*** Rebound is a term usually applied when the ball bounces off the backboard or basket.

**10** What is defense in basketball?

***Ans*** The ball is moved down the court towards the basket by passing or dribbling. The team without the ball is called defense.

**11** What is shooting in basketball?

***Ans*** It is a collection of best practice used in Unified Sports.

**12** What is Screen?

***Ans*** Screen is an attempt to protect a teammate's play by shutting off an opponent's approach without personal contact.

**13** Which international organisation conducts tournaments in Unified Basketball?.

***Ans*** Special Olympics Unified Sports conducts tournaments in Unified Basketball.

**14** How many points are received by a team for attempting a successful field goal?

***Ans*** A team receives two points for a successful field goal.

**15** What is the minimum requirement of players in the basketball court at all times?

***Ans*** The minimum requirement is two athletes and 1 partner at all times.

**16** Name 2 events that measure the individual skills in Unified Basketball.

***Ans*** 2 events that measure the individual skills in Unified Basketball are passing and 12 m dribbling.

**17** Mention 2 instances when a team gets a foul.

***Ans*** 2 instances when a team gets a foul is pushing between players and some players dominating other players.

**18** Are the coaches allowed to give instructions during the game?

***Ans*** Yes, the coaches are allowed to instruct the players verbally or using sign language.

**19** In which event, players dribble while passing between obstacles?

***Ans*** They do this in the '12 m dribble' event.

**20** What is the main purpose of playing Unified Basketball?

***Ans*** The main purpose is inclusion of everyone and promoting team work.

# UNIFIED FOOTBALL (SOCCER)

Unified football has players with and without intellectual disabilities playing together on the same team at the same time, against other teams with the same make up.

Special Olympics Kansas has created the rules for unified football based upon National Federation of High School (NFHS) rules for soccer. NFHS rules shall be employed except when they are in conflict with these rules. In such cases, these rules shall apply. Special Olympics Kansas offers 5-a-side team outdoor for Unified soccer.

## The Field of Play and the Ball

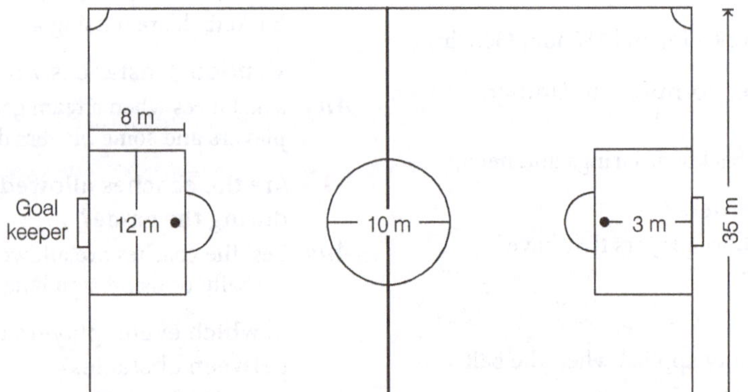


- The 5-a-side field shall be in rectangular form with a maximum dimensions of 50 meters by 35 meters, minimum dimensions of 40 meters by 30 meters. The smaller field is recommended for lower ability teams.
- The goal size shall be between 4 meters by 2 meters and 3 meters by 2 meters.
- The goal/penalty area shall be 8 meters by 12 meters.
- The penalty mark shall be at 7 meters or 6 meters for smaller goals.
- The recommended playing surface is grass.
- Size of the ball should not more than 70 cm (28 inch) and not less than 68 cm (27 inch).

## Players and Substitutions

- The game is played between two teams, each consisting of five players, one of whom shall be the goalkeeper.
- A team is allowed to play with a maximum of five and a minimum three players during competition. Only the following lineups are allowed
  - 3 athletes and 2 partners
  - 2 athletes and 2 partners
  - 2 athletes and 1 partner

  Failure to adhere to the required ratio results in a forfeit.
- If at any time a team is not in compliance with the athlete-partner ratio, the opposing team coach shall notify the referee. If the referee determines non-compliance, the team shall make adjustments to reach compliance and the referee shall award the opposing team a Penalty Kick.
- In Level 3, an additional non-playing partner may be on the field to assist a specific athlete for safety concerns. This non-playing partner will wear a pinny to distinguish as non-playing, and must refrain from participating in the game play.
- Players who utilise wheelchairs, or similar adaptive equipment, may only participate in Level 3.
- A unified partner may play the goalkeeper position. Unified partners may score.
- The roster shall contain a proportionate number of athletes and partners.
- Substitutions are unlimited in number (players may return to the field after being substituted). Substitutions can be made any time like the ball is out of bounds, between periods after a goal is scored, or during a timeout. The coach shall signal the referee or linesman in order to make a substitution. A substituted player can only come on to the field when given a signal by the referee.

## Player's Equipment

- Teams should wear uniforms with colours to distinguish them from the opposing team and referees.
- Shirts shall be numbered.
- Shin guards are required.
- No metal studs are allowed.
- No hats or jewellery are allowed.

## Coaches and Referees

- A non-playing bench coach shall be designated at the beginning of the match.
- The coach may not enter the field during play, even to provide instruction.
- Each match is controlled by one referee who has full authority to enforce the Laws of the Game in connection with the match to which he has been appointed.
- Two assistant referees are appointed to each match for Regional and International Competitions. For Local Programmes and National Competitions, it is recommended to have two referees if there are not enough assistant referees.

## Duration of the Game

- The duration of the game shall be two equal periods of fifteen minutes with a halftime interval of five minutes.
- The referee should be responsible for keeping the playing time.
- In the case of extreme heat, the official representative from the Competition Committee (e.g., Field Manager) may signal to the referee to introduce a water break (maximum of three minutes) at a natural break in play, approximately halfway through each half.
- Overtime is used to break a tie (see Rule 18) during tournament play.

## Fundamentals and Techniques

- **Kickoff** A kickoff will start play at the start of each period and after a goal has been scored. A ball shall be kicked from the center spot in any direction. A goal may be scored directly from a kickoff.
- **Ball in and Out of Play** Ball over the sideline results in a throw in. Ball over the end line results in a goal clearance or a corner kick. The ball shall be completely over the line to be considered out of play.
- **Method of Scoring** The whole of the ball shall have completely crossed the goal line between the posts and underneath the crossbar to count as a goal.
- **Fouls and Misconduct** Tripping, pushing, handball or charging result in a direct free kick from the spot of the foul. In Level 2, handball will result in re-do and in Level 3, only handball with significant advantage will result in re-do.
- Obstruction or dangerous play results in an indirect free kick from the spot of the foul.

- If there are five players playing against three or four against three and the team with the larger number scores a goal, the team with three players may be increased by one more player only.
- If both teams are playing with three players and a goal is scored, both teams may add one more player.
- If the team scoring the goal is the one with fewer players, the game shall continue without changing the number of players.
- The player who enters the game as a substitute after two minutes may only do so with the consent of the referee and when the ball is out of bounds.

- **Free Kick** When an indirect free kick is awarded to the attacking team inside the penalty area, within 5 meters from the goal line, the referee shall place the ball at 5 meters from the goal line. A goal may be scored directly from a Direct Free Kick, but an Indirect Free Kick must first be touched by another player. Any free kick that is awarded to the defending team inside their own penalty area will be restarted with a goal clearance.
- **Penalty Kick** A penalty kick is awarded against a team that commits one of the offences for which a direct free kick is awarded, inside its own penalty area and while the ball is in play. A penalty kick is taken from the 7 meter line (6 meter line for smaller goals). All players except the kicker and the goalkeeper shall retire outside the penalty area and arc. The goalkeeper shall stand on his/her goal line until the penalty kick is taken.
- **Throw in** When the whole of the ball passes over a sideline, it shall be thrown back into the game, from the place where it crossed the line (on the sideline), by a player from the opposing team to that of the player who last touched it. The player shall be stationary before throwing with both feet on the ground. The players from the opposing team shall retire at least 5 meters from the spot where thrown. It shall be deemed in-play immediately after it has left the players hands. The ball cannot be played again by the thrower until it has been touched by another player. A goal cannot be scored directly from a throw in.
- **Corner-Kick** It is awarded to the attacking team when a player from the defending team kicks the ball over the goal line (not in the goal).
- **Overtime** In regular league play, ties are considered final. In tournament play, if overtime is used to break a tie, a 5-minute 'sudden-victory' period shall be played. If the game is still tied after the overtime period, penalty kicks shall be used to decide the game.

# VIVA-VOCE

**1** Which organisation has created Unified Soccer rules?

*Ans* Special Olympics Kansas has created Unified Soccer rules.

**2** Special Olympics Kansas (SOKS) offers which team outdoor for Unified Soccer?

*Ans* Special Olympics Kansas (SOKS) only offers 5-a-side team outdoor for Unified Soccer.

**3** On which basis Unified Teams will be divisioned?

*Ans* Unified Teams will be divisioned based on the SOKS Soccer Team Assessment Form.

**4** What is the size of the 5-a-side field?

*Ans* The 5-a-side field shall be in rectangular form with a maximum dimensions of 50 meters by 35 meters, minimum dimensions of 40 meters by 30 meters.

**5** What is the goal size of the 5-a-side field?

*Ans* The goal size shall be between 4 meters by 2 meters and 3 meters by 2 meters.

**6** What is the size of the ball?

*Ans* The size of the ball is not more than 70 cm (28 inch) and not less than 68 cm (27 inch).

**7** State about player's equipments.

*Ans* The player's equipments required are

- Teams should wear uniforms with colours to distinguish them from the opposing team and referees.
- Shirts shall be numbered.
- Shin guards are required.
- No metal studs are allowed.
- No hats or jewellery are allowed.

**8** What is the duration of the Unified football game?

*Ans* The duration of the Unified football game is two equal periods of fifteen minutes with a half-time interval of five minutes.

**9** What is penalty kick in Unified football?

*Ans* A penalty kick is awarded against a team that commits one of the offences for which a direct free kick is awarded, inside its own penalty area and while the ball is in play.

**10** When is a corner kick awarded?

*Ans* Corner-Kick is awarded to the attacking team when a player from the defending team kicks the ball over the goal line (not in the goal).

**11** What happens when a player is expelled from the game?

*Ans* If a player is expelled from the game (receives two yellow cards or a red card), he may not re-enter the game. His team shall play a player down for two minutes, unless a goal is scored before the two minutes have elapsed.

**12** What happens if both teams have taken five kicks, both have scored the same number of goals, or have not scored any goals,?

*Ans* If both teams have taken five kicks, both have scored the same number of goals, or have not scored any goals, kicks continue to be taken in the same order until one team has scored a goal more than the other from the same number of kicks.

| GAME 7 |

# BLIND CRICKET

Blind cricket is a version of the sport of cricket adapted for blind and partially sighted players. It has been governed by the World Blind Cricket Council (WBCC) since 1996. So far, five Blind World Cups have been held: New Delhi, India (1998), Chennai, India (2002), Islamabad, Pakistan (2006), and India (2018). In 2012, the first Blind World Cup T20 was held in Bangalore, India. Blind cricket relies on common use of the 'sweep shot', in order to provide maximum chance of the bat hitting the ball.

## History

Blind cricket was invented in Melbourne in 1922 by two blind factory workers who improvised the game using a tin can containing rocks. The Victorian Blind Cricket Association was founded shortly after, in 1922, and the first sports ground and clubhouse for blind cricket was built at Kooyong, Melbourne in 1928.

The world's first Test Cricket Match for the blind was played between Pakistan and South Africa in which Pakistan defeated South Africa by 94 runs in the year of 2000.

South Africa won first Blind Cricket World Cup (BCWC) in 1998 defeating Pakistan in the finals, while Pakistan consecutively won next two BCWC by defeating South Africa and India in the finals in 2002 and 2006. In 2014, championship was won by India by defeating the two-time winner Pakistan.

## Rules

The rules of blind cricket are based on the standard laws of cricket with some essential modifications. WBCC international playing rules are codified in 25 clauses, first ratified in 2005. The rules are

- There are a total number of 11 players in each team: at least four players who are totally blind (classified as B1) and three partially blind players (B2), and upto four partially sighted players (B3).
- In terms of playing equipment, the major adaptation is the ball, which is significantly larger than a standard cricket ball and filled with ball bearings to provide audible clues. The size allows partially sighted players to see the ball and the contents allow blind players to hear it.
- The wicket (stumps) is also larger, made of metal tubes painted in fluorescent colours, to allow partially sighted players to see and blind players to touch it in order to correctly orient themselves when batting or bowling.
- Verbal signals are widely used both by umpires and players. In particular, the bowler must shout 'Play!' as he releases the ball.
- Totally blind batsmen cannot be out due to being stumped, and must be found to be LBW twice before going out.
- Totally blind fielders are allowed to take a catch on the bounce.
- The bowling has to underarm. At the point of delivery the arm has to be below the shoulder. Failure of this will result in a no ball being called. The delivery is required to pitch at least twice when bowled to a batsman, but must not be rolling.

## Players

The players in blind cricket include B1 (Totally blind players), B2 (Partially blind) and B3 (Partially sighted players).

### Team Composition

There are total 11 players including a minimum of 4 B1 players, 3 of B2 players and a maximum of 4 B3 players.

There are runners for batsmen. B1 shall have a runner, B2 has the option of a runner Batsman who has opted for a runner cannot act as a runner for another batsman.

A 'one bounce' catch by a B1 player will result in the batsman being given out.

### Sight Classification

- **B1** No light perception in either eye up to light perception, but inability to recognise shape of a hand at any distance or in any direction
- **B2** From ability to recognise the shape of the hand up to a visual acuity of 2/60 or visual field of less than five degrees in the better eye after correction.
- **B3** From visual acuity above 2/60 up to visual acuity of 6/60 or a visual field of less than 20 degrees in better eye after correction.

### Identifying Classification of the Players on the Field

B1 players will be distinguished on the field of play by a white wrist band to be worn on the right wrist or by one white stripe on the right upper arm of the playing shirt.

B2 players will be distinguished on the field of play by a red wrist band to be worn on the right wrist or by two white stripes on the right upper arm of the playing shirt.

B3 players will be distinguished on the field of play by a blue wrist band to be worn on the right wrist or by three white stripes on the right upper arm of the playing shirt.

### How they Play

The bowler has to say 'ready?' to the batsman when he is set to bowl, to which the batsman has to respond by calling out "yes". At the point of delivery, the bowler must say "play". Failure to do so will result in a no ball being called. A no ball will also be called if the call of "play", is in the opinion of the umpire, early or late.

## Equiptments

- **The Ball** The ball is considerably larger than the standard cricket ball and filled with ball bearings. The audible ball helps the player to sense the direction of the ball and play the game.
- **The Stumps** Wooden stumps or plastic are used, if the match is being played on an artificial surface. The colour of the stumps shall be fluorescent orange or yellow. No bails are used.
- **The Bat** The regular cricket bat to be used with standard specifications.
- **The Pitch and Boundary** The pitch is of 22 yards and made of turf or synthetic grass surfaces. Boundary is minimum of 45 yards to a maximum of 55.

### World Blind Cricket Council (WBCC)

The WBCC was established in 1996 during an international cricket meeting held in New Delhi, India in September 1996. The WBCC was set up with the objective of promoting and administering the game of blind cricket globally.

Today the WBCC has 10 full members namely Australia, Bangladesh, England, India, New Zealand, South Africa, Sri Lanka, Pakistan, West Indies and Nepal. George Abraham of India is the founding Chairman of the WBCC. Under his leadership, the inaugural Blind Cricket World Cup was held in New Delhi in November 1998 in which seven countries participated.

## Blind Cricket World Cup

- **1998 (Winner - South Africa)** The first World Cup Cricket for the blind competition was held in New Delhi, India. The tournament was named and designated as, 'Kanishka World Cup Cricket for the Blind.'
- **2002 (Winner - Pakistan)** The second World Cup was held in Chennai, India in December. Pakistan defeated South Africa in the finals.
- **2006 (Winner - Pakistan)** The third World Cup was held in Islamabad, Pakistan defeated India, under the leadership of Aga Shaukat Ali, the founder of Pakistan Blind Cricket Council.
- **2014 (Winner - India)** On 7th December 2014, India defeated Pakistan in the final at Cape Town, South Africa .
- **2018 (Winner - India)** On 20th January 2018, India defeated Pakistan in the final at Sharjah.
- **T20 Blind Cricket World Cup 2012 (Winner-India)** The first T20 Blind Cricket World Cup was held at Aditya Academy Ground in Bangalore, India in 2012. India defeated Pakistan by 29 runs in the final.

## Important Personalities

Sunil Ramesh Kumar, Ajay Kumar Reddy (Captain of Indian Blind Cricket Team), Rury Field, etc.

# VIVA-VOCE

1 Which organisation governs blind cricket sport?

**Ans** World Blind Cricket Council governs blind cricket sport.

2 How many Blind Cricket World Cups have been organised since its inception?

**Ans** About five Blind Cricket World Cups have been organised since its inception.

3 The first Blind World Cup was held in which place?

**Ans** The first blind World Cup was held in New Delhi.

4 The first Blind T20 World Cup was held at which place of India?

**Ans** The first Blind T20 World Cup was held at Bangalore in Karnataka.

5 Blind cricket was invented at which place?

**Ans** Blind cricket was invented at Melbourne.

6 The world's first Test Cricket match for the blind was played between which two countries?

**Ans** The world's first Test Cricket match for the blind was played between Pakistan and South Africa.

7 Which country won the championship of BCWC in 2014?

**Ans** India won the championship of BCWC in 2014.

8 How many players are there in a blind cricket team?

**Ans** There are a total number of 11 players in each team: at least four players who are totally blind (classified as Bl) and three partially blind players (B2), and upto four partially sighted players (B3).

9 What is the major feature of a cricket ball used in blind cricket?

**Ans** The cricket ball used in blind cricket is significantly larger than a standard cricket ball and filled with ball bearings to provide audible clues.

10 In which year the World Blind Cricket Council was established?

**Ans** The World Blind Cricket Council was established in 1996.

11 Which countries are the members of WBCC?

**Ans** The WBCC has 10 full member countries namely Australia, Bangladesh, England, India, New Zealand, South Africa, Sri Lanka, Pakistan, West Indies and Nepal.

12 What was the name of the first World Cup Cricket for the blind competition tournament?

**Ans** The name of the first World Cup Cricket for the blind tournament was "Kanishka World Cup Cricket for the Blind."

13 Who is the captain of Indian Blind Cricket Team?

**Ans** Ajay Kumar Reddy is the captain of Indian Blind Cricket Team.

14 What is the role of audible ball in blind cricket?

**Ans** The audible ball helps the player to sense the direction of the ball and play the game.

15 What is the specification of pitch and boundary for blind cricket?

**Ans** A pitch should be of 22 yards and made of turf or synthetic grass surfaces. Boundary should be minimum of 45 yards to a maximum of 55.

| GAME 8 |

# GOALBALL

Goalball is a team sport specifically for athletes with a vision impairment. Two teams of three blindfolded players throw a bell-ball towards their opponent's goal, using their body to protect their own goal. Games consist of 12-minute halves, played indoors, usually on a volleyball court. Teams alternate throwing or rolling the ball from one end of the playing area to the other. Players remain in the area of their own goal in both defence and attack. The sport is for people who experience visual impairment, the ball makes noise when it is in motion, so the players may locate it audibly. For this reason, silence at events is crucial.

The game is played on a court with tactile markings, so the players can determine their location on the court and which direction they are facing.

Athletes with a visual field of a maximum diameter of less than 40 degrees are eligible to compete in goalball. In order to ensure fair competition between teams, all players must wear eyeshades during the game.

The International Blind Sports Federation (IBSA) is responsible for a range of sports for blind and partially sighted people, including goalball. To compete internationally, players must be classified as B1, B2 or B3 (varying degrees of visual impairment), but domestically everybody can play-blind players, partially sighted players and fully sighted players.

The aim of goalball is for each team to score as many goals as possible while trying to use their bodies to block and save any shots from their opponents. Each game is made up of two halves of 12-minutes. Goalball is played inside in a sports hall with minimal background noise.

**Goalball**

## History

Goalball was originally developed in 1946 by the Austrian Hans Lorenzen and German Sepp Reindle. Goalball originated as a rehabilitative sport for veterans who lost their sight following World War II.

Goalball gradually evolved into a competitive game during the 1950s and 1960s. It was eventually nominated as a demonstration sport at the 1972 Summer Paralympics in Heidelberg, West Germany and became a Paralympic Games sport at the 1976 Summer Paralympics in Toronto.

The sport's First World Championship was held in Austria in 1978. In 2011, the long-standing IBSA Goalball Sub-committee sought to separate from IBSA and form a new international body, the World Goalball Association.

## Goalball Court

The court is the same size as a volleyball court and has tactile markings to allow the players to 'feel' where they are. A goalball court is a standard gymnasium volleyball court measuring 9m wide by 18m long.

There are two team areas at either end of the court which measure 3m wide by 9m long. Inside the team areas there are player orientation marks consisting of two 1.5m wing lines and one 0.50 m centre line.

The court is divided into six even sections, 3 by 9 m (9.8 by 29.5 ft). At either end, just in front of the goal, is the team area. Beyond that, is each team's landing zone. The middle two sections are collectively referred to as the neutral zone. The remaining 9m × 6m area, between the two landing areas, is called the neutral area, which is divided into two parts by the centre line. With the exception of the final lines, all court markings are tactile to help players orientate themselves on the court. Starting from the final lines, where the goalposts are placed, a 9m × 3m team area and a 9m × 3m landing area for each team are marked. Goals measure 9m (equal to the length of the court) x 1.3m.

In preparing the court, use of standard duct tape is necessary. It is general practice to make the court two layers thick, one layer one top of the other, giving the court a superior tactile feel permitting players to easily find their positions.

The taped lines are the entire team areas with the players orientation lines. The over throw lines, centre line and the outside lines of the neutral area only have to be taped if they do not exist on the volleyball court. The lines only have to be one layer thick because they are used mainly by the referees.

## Ball

The ball contains internal bells so, players are able to track its movement by its sound. Its specifications are

- It is 24.25 cm in diameter / 75-78.5 cm circumference.
- It weighs 1.250 g
- It has 4 sounds holes in upper hemisphere and 4 sounds holes in lower hemisphere.
- It has 2 pieces of bells / is made of natural rubber.
- It is Blue in colour.

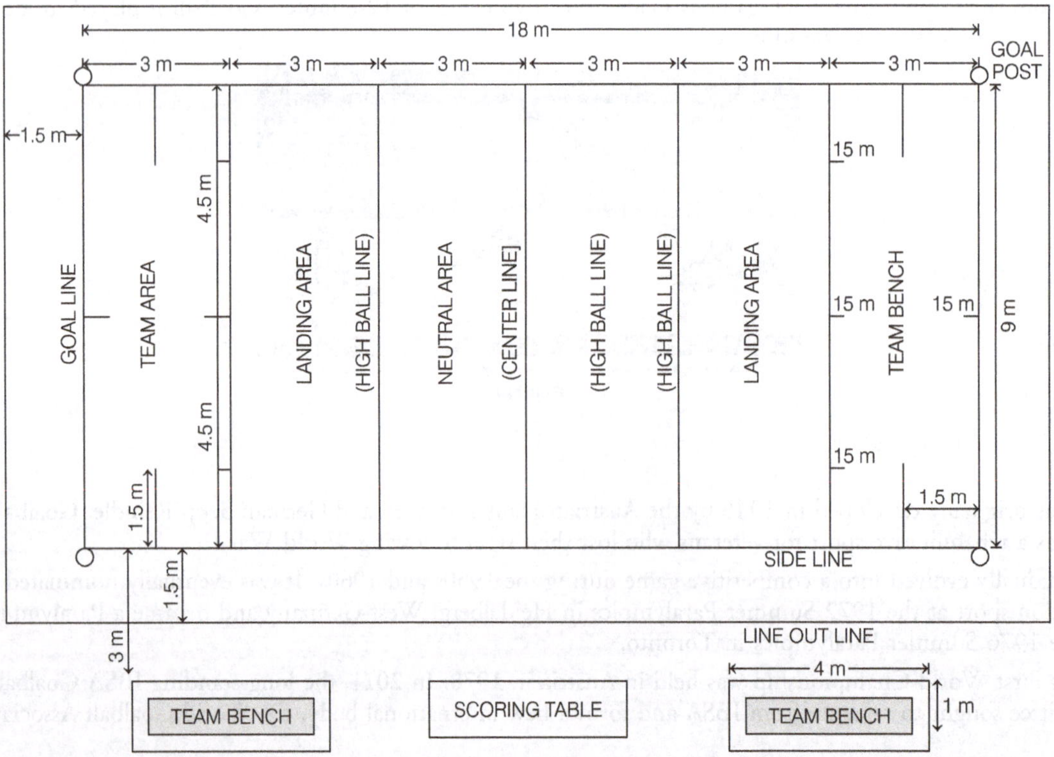

## Terminology

| | |
|---|---|
| **Time Limits** | After receiving control of the ball, a team has only ten seconds to throw the ball back at the opposing team, if not, it is considered a team penalty. |
| **Ten Second Penalty** | A team takes more than ten seconds to throw the ball back over the centre line. |
| **Game Time** | A regular goalball game is twenty minutes consisting of two 10-minute halves. There is a three minute half time in order for the teams to switch ends of the court. |
| **Defending** | Players must stay within the team area while defending. When stopping the ball, some part of the player's body must be touching the team area or it is called illegal defense and constitutes a penalty. |
| **Play** | The audible command, 'Play' must be called by the referee to begin or restart the game. After any official stoppage of the game, 'Play' must be called to restart it. |
| **Throwing** | The ball must be rolled on the floor. When throwing the ball, it must touch the floor before the over throw line or it is considered to be a 'high ball'. A high ball would constitute a penalty and nullifies any goal scored from that particular throw. |
| **Eyeshades** | In order to maintain an equal advantage, every team member must wear eyeshades at all times during the game. Once the game has begun, a player may only adjust their eyeshades by raising their arm up into the air and calling 'eyeshades.' Only then, after a referee tells the player to turn around, the player may adjust their eyeshades. |
| **Delay of Game** | This can be caused by many different things. A coach reporting the wrong numbers for substitutions, a team not arriving in time for the coin toss that precedes the game, or too many or too few players taking the court. |
| **Illegal Defence** | This is called, if a defender makes contact with the ball while no part of the body is touching the team area. |
| **Short Ball** | The ball fails to reach the opponent's team area when thrown. |
| **High Ball** | The ball does not touch the thrower's landing zone when thrown. |
| **Long Ball** | The ball does not touch the neutral zone when thrown. |
| **Unsportsman like Conduct** | This can be a variety of things, from arguing with an official to pounding the floor and swearing. |
| **Noise** | Unnecessary noise by the offensive team that prevents the defence from tracking the ball while the ball is travelling down the court. |

## Fundamental Skills and Technique

### The Game

- Each goalball game consists of two 12-minute halves. Throughout the game, players on each team roll the ball from inside their respective zones toward the opposing team's goal.
- The defending team attempts to defend their goal by blocking the ball with their bodies.
- Each ball is filled with bells so that defenders can locate it as it approaches them.
- Crowd noise is prohibited for goalball games so that players can hear the bells on the ball. Once a shot is blocked, the other team gains possession of the ball and tries to score.

### Positions

- The three main positions in goalball include centre, right wing and left wing.
- The centre, who plays in the middle of the zone, is the main defensive player of the team. They are responsible for defending most of the court.
- The wing players are the main offensive players of the team and do most of the throwing.
- Although, focused on scoring the wing players also play defense behind the centre on each side of the court.

### Losing Possession

There are few ways to lose possession of the ball

- **Premature Throw** A premature throw occurs when a player throws the ball earlier than they are allowed to. This may be before the beginning of the game or after a penalty before play resumes.
- **Ball Over** When a defender blocks a shot, but the ball rolls over the centre line back to the other side of the court.
- **Pass-out** When a player attempts to pass the ball to a teammate, but the ball goes out of bounds.

### Types of Shots

In goalball, there are a few different types of shot

- A quick throw is done when a defense stops a shot and immediately shoots the ball back down the court in hopes that the players from the other team are not back in their defensive positions.

- A defense player may also attempt other shots that differ in direction and velocity such as curve balls and off speed balls.

### Scoring

- When shooting the ball, players have a 10 second shot clock in which they must roll the ball for the time, to count.
- As the ball travels down the court, it must bounce at least once before crossing the highball line or else a highball penalty is called.
- If the ball passes successfully over the other team's goal line and into the goal, the offensive team is awarded one point. If the score ends up tied at the end of the game, an overtime period will occur followed by a shootout if the score is still even.

## How Goalball is Played

- Team has three players on the court at a time, with one to three substitute players on the bench.
- At an international level, including the Paralympic Games, the competition is divided into two categories for male and female.
- It goalball, the centre player is most responsible player for defence. The player typically lines up at the centre orientation mark at the front of the orientation area (the 3.0 m (9.8 ft) line forward of the goal post).
- The centre player is the most defensive position simply because the player is able to move both to the left and right to defend, covering a greater proportion of possible attacking shot lines.
- When a member of the defensive team touches the ball, they have 10 seconds to throw it back without being penalised. Penalties normally result in a penalty shot, during which the penalised player has to defend the entire nine-metre net alone.

## Game Protocols

- The referee will call 'quiet please' before calling 'centre', and throwing the ball to the team. The referee will throw the ball to the player who is closest to the centre position. The referee will then blow their whistle three times and call 'play'.
- The main clock and the ten second clock will start on the call 'play'. The referee will complete any half by whistling once and calling 'half time', 'game', 'overtime', 'extra throws' or 'sudden death extra throws'. This is a signal that players may touch their eyeshades and is to ensure that a penalty situation did not occur before the end of the half.
- During extra throws and between extra-throws and sudden-death extra throws players are not allowed to touch their eyeshades.
- The game clock and the ten second clock will be stopped whenever the referee blows their whistle and started again on the call 'play' except during a penalty situation. The game clock is stopped during a penalty situation.
- At a time the ball needs to be put back into play, it will be dropped by a referee or goal judge at the side line 1.5 m in front of the goal post closest to the side it exited the court. The referee will then call 'quiet please', blow their whistle once and call 'play'.
- In case of the ball goes over the centre line then after the goal the team can keep the ball. If, in the act of throwing, a ball is thrown out over the side line without touching the defending team, the referee will blow their whistle once and call "out". The game clock will stop.
- The ten second clock will also be stopped and reset. Any time the ball needs to be put back into play it will be dropped by a referee or goal judge. The referee will say 'quiet please', whistle and say 'play'. The game clock and the ten second clock will both restart on the call 'play'.
- No additional orientation aids are permitted on court. Failure to comply will result in personal penalty i.e. delay of game.
- Following a penalty situation, players may be re-orientated to the goal post by a referee or goal judge. If at any other time, a referee must re-orientate a player, a personal delay of game penalty will be called.
- When a thrown ball comes to rest in the Team Area of the defending team, without a defending player touching it, this will be called a 'Dead Ball'. The referee will blow the whistle and call 'dead ball.' The ball will be given to the defending team by an official as per rule.
- A team member will only be allowed to leave the field of play during an official stoppage in play after receiving permission from the referee. That team member may not return until the end of that half of the game.

## Offence

- To score, a player must roll or bounce the ball down the length of the court, past the opposing defenders, and into the opponents' goal.
- Typically, the player with the ball will stand, orient themselves using the tactile lines, sounds from teammates and/or the crossbar of their own goal. The player will then stride forward, lean low and roll or side arm the ball down the court.
- The ball must hit in the player's own landing zone and anywhere in the neutral zone. So long as it hits each zone, the style of throw is entirely up to the player in question.
- Many players will take several strides and release the ball as close to their own high ball line as possible, leaning low to ensure a legal throw.
- Some players will throw after spinning, transferring the momentum of the spin into additional velocity. Others are able to throw the ball so that it will bounce just once in each of the required zones. Most elite players are effective when using multiple types of throws.

## Defence

- The defending players stay within the team area, generally in somewhat staggered positions to avoid collisions. When they hear the other team throw the ball, they 'lay out', that is slide on their hips and stretch their arms above their heads and extend their legs in order to cover as much distance as possible.
- Some players prefer to block the ball with their chests and absorb the impact. Others like to block with their legs so the ball will roll up their bodies into their hands. Regardless of method, the players will always try to make themselves as long as possible to block the greatest area.

### Officials

For competitive games, the following set of officials are on the court

- **Two Referees** Each referee remains along the sideline at one half of the court. One referee is 'table-side', the other is 'off-table side'.
- **Four Goal Judges** They positioned to the side of each goal edge. The goal judge raises their hand to confirm to the referee when a ball crosses the goal line. Goal judges are also crucial to the game's speed since they retrieve a ball going off court and drop it at the side hash mark of the Team Area so play can resume.
- **Two Ten-second Timers** They keep track of the time between when a defending player contacts the ball and when the ball is thrown, calling '10 second' penalties when applicable.
- **Scorer** This technical official keeps track of the number of time-outs and substitutions taken by a team and as the term suggests, keeps score.
- **Game Timer and Back-up Timer** Usually, as with a basketball scoreboard, the period's time counts down to zero. It is stopped and started by the referee's whistle. A back-up timer is used in case of power failure to the venue.

## Important Tournaments

- World Goalball Championship (both for men and women)
- Paralympic Games
- Asia-Pacific Youth Championship
- Asian Youth Para Games.

# VIVA-VOCE

**1** Who developed the goalball game?

***Ans*** Goalball was developed by Australian Hans Lorenzen and German Sepp Reindle in 1946.

**2** Where is the neutral zone in goalball?

***Ans*** Goalball court is split into six zones along its width. Two zone on either ends are allocated for each team and the middle two zones are the neutral area.

**3** How long is a goalball game?

***Ans*** The game consists of two 12-minute halves and takes about an hour to play a full game.

**4** What is the main goal of goalball?

***Ans*** The object of the game is to throw a ball part the opponents and into their net to score points.

**5** What is illegal defense in goalball?

***Ans*** When defending a shot in goalball, players must be inside of their respective team areas. If a defender blocks a shot and no part of them is touching the team area and illegal defense penalty is called illegal defense.

**6** What is the difference between a short and long ball?

***Ans*** A short ball occurs when a player rolls the ball across the court, but it stops short of the opposing team's area. Long ball occurs when a player throws the ball and it fails to bounce at least once in the central area on the court.

**7** Can players be penalised for touching their eyeshades?

***Ans*** Yes, goalball player can be penalized for touching or adjusting their eyeshades without permission from a referee.

**8** Who is eligible to compete in goalball?

***Ans*** Only athletes with a vision impairment affecting both eyes are eligible to compete in goalball at an international level.

**9** What are the classes?

***Ans*** Athletes are classified into one of three classes depending on their level of vision. The international classes in goalball are B1, B2 and B3.

**10** What type of ball is used in goalball?

***Ans*** The ball used for goalball is made up of rubber, weighs 1.25 kg and has a circumference of approximately 76 cm. It has eight holes and there are noise bells inside.

**11** What are the two skills used in the goalball?

***Ans*** The skills used in the goalball are
- **Blocking** Blocking are typically made from a horizontal lying position with arms and legs fully extended.
- **Throwing** An underhand technique is used to throw a goalball.

**12** How many players are in goalball?

***Ans*** In goalball, two teams of three players face each others across a court.

**13** How many referees are in goalball?

***Ans*** For every game of goalball, two referees (one per half) are required to use their judgement. The referee is suppressed by four goal judges who are positioned to the side of the goals to ensure all balls are retrieved and placed back at the designated area.

**14** What is high ball?

***Ans*** If the ball touches the ground after the first high ball line, it is a high ball which results in a penalty shot.

**15** What is the goalball court measurement?

***Ans*** The measurement of goalball court is 18 m long and 9 m wide.

**16** What is the diameter of ball in goalball?

***Ans*** The ball is 24-25 cm in diameter.

**17** What is pre-mature throw?

***Ans*** A pre-mature throw occurs when a player throws a ball earlier than they are allowed to the goalball.

**18** When was the goalball inducted in Paralymic Game?

***Ans*** The goalball was inducted in 1976 Summer Paralympics in Toronto.

**19** Who is responsible for making rule for the goalball game?

***Ans*** The International Blind Sports Federation (IBSF) is responsible for making rule for the goalball.

**20** What is ball over?

***Ans*** When a defender blocks a shot, but the ball rolls over the centre line back to the other side of the court, it is called ball over.

# FLOORBALL

Floorball is a type of floor hockey with five players and a goalkeeper in each team. Men and women play indoors with sticks and a plastic ball with holes. For players with disabilities, wheelchair floorball has been developed which is played with exactly the same rules as regular floorball.

Wheelchair Floorball

## History

Floorball was invented in Sweden in the late 1960s.

Floorball is most popular where it has been developed the longest, such as the Czech Republic, Denmark, Estonia, Finland, Latvia, Norway, Sweden, and Switzerland. It is gaining popularity in Australia, New Zealand, India, Canada, Germany, Ireland, Japan, Singapore, Malaysia, the United States and the United Kingdom.

Floorball was formally organised as an international and more organised sport in the late 1970s in Gothenburg, Sweden. The basic rules were established in 1979 when the first floorball club in the world, Sala IBK from Sala, was founded in Sweden. Official rules for matches were first written down in 1981. The sport began as something that was played for fun as a pastime in schools. After a decade or so, floorball began showing up in Nordic countries where the former schoolyard pastime was becoming a developed sport. Formal rules were soon developed, and clubs began to form. After some time, several countries developed national associations, and the IFF was founded in 1986. The sport is organised internationally by the International Floorball Federation (IFF).

### Measurements

Floorball is played indoors on a rink whose size can officially vary from 18-20 m (59-66 ft) wide to 36-40 m (118-131 ft) long, and which is surrounded by 50 cm (20 in) high enclosed boards with rounded corners.

The goals are 160 cm (63 in) wide and 115 cm (45 in) high. Their depth is 65 cm (26 in) and they are 2.85 m (9 ft 4 in) from the end of the nearest boards. Face-off dots are marked on the center line.

Dots are also marked 1.5 m (4 ft 11 in) from both sides of the rink on the goal lines imaginary extensions. The dots don't exceed 30 cm (12 in) in diameter. They do not have to be dots, they can also be crosses.

## Equipments

Typical equipment for a floorball player consists of a stick, a pair of shorts, a shirt, socks, and indoor sport shoes. Players may wear skin guards, eye protectors and protective padding for vital areas. Protective eyewear is in some countries compulsory for junior players.

### Stick

A floorball stick is short compared with one for ice hockey, the maximum size for a stick is 114 cm. A stick cannot weigh more than 350 grams. Floorball sticks are often made of carbon and composite materials. The blade of the stick can either be right or left which indicates which way stick is supposed to be held from the players point of view. A player who is right-handed will often use a left blade, since he/she will be holding the stick to left and the other way around for left-handed people.

### Ball

A floorball ball is a plastic precision type ball, characterised by 1,516 tiny dimples that reduce air resistance, as well as friction on the floor. A floorball weighs 23 g (0.81 oz) and its diameter is 72 mm (2.8 in). It has 26 holes in it, each of which are 10 mm (0.39 in) in diameter. Many of these balls now are made with aerodynamic technology, where the ball has over a thousand small dimples in it that reduce air resistance. There have been several times where a ball has been recorded to have travelled at a speed of approximately 200 km/h (120 mph).

## Goalkeepers

Goalkeepers do not use sticks and may use their hands to play the ball when they are within the goalkeeper's box. They are allowed to throw the ball out to their teammates provided that the ball touches the ground before the half court mark. When they are completely outside the box, goalkeepers are considered field players and are not allowed to touch the ball with their hands.

Goalkeepers wear limited protection provided by padded pants, a padded chest protector, knee pads and a helmet. Some goalkeepers like to wear gloves and/or wristbands The goalkeeper may also wear other protective equipment such as elbow pads and jock straps, but bulky padding is not permitted.

## Rules

- Each team can field six players at a time on the court, one player being a goalkeeper. But the coach can take the goalkeeper off and substitute them for a field player whenever they like, although it usually only happens in the end to increase the chances of scoring with one more outfield player. This can bring an advantage for the attacking side of the team, but also disadvantages when it comes to their own defense.
- Both teams are also allowed to change players any time in the game, usually, a change comprises the whole team. Individual substitution happens sometimes, but usually only when a player is exhausted or hurt.
- A floorball game is officially played over three periods lasting 20 minutes each (15 minutes for juniors). The clock is stopped in the case of penalties, goals, time-outs and any situation where the ball is not considered to be in play. The signal of a timeout is a triple honking sound an intermission of 10 minutes (or maximum 15 minutes in some competitions) takes place between each period, where teams change ends and substitution areas. Each team is allowed one timeout of 30 seconds, which is often used late in matches.

## Competitions

In addition to the Floorball World Championships, there are other IFF events for club teams such as the Champions Cup which is for the national competition winners from the Top-4 ranked nations, and the Euro Floorball Cup for the national competition winners from the 5th and lower ranked nations. There are also many international floorball club competitions such as

### Asia Pacific Floorball Championship

The Asia Pacific Floorball Championships are played every single year in New Zealand, Australia, Singapore or Japan. The event was created by the Singapore Floorball Association together with the Cooperation of the Asia Oceania Floorball Confederation (AOFC). Members of the AOFC get together during this tournament to play for the Asia Pacific Floorball Championship every year.

### Canada Cup

The Canada Cup is an international club tournament that is held every year in Toronto, Ontario, Canada. It is the largest floorball club tournament outside of Europe and attracts 55+ clubs from worldwide, every year.

### Czech Open

The world's largest club team tournament, the Czech Open is a traditional summer tournament held in Prague, Czech Republic. It is famous not only for its on-court activities, but also for off-court activities. The tournament attracts 200+ clubs every year from 20 countries.

## Champions Cup

The Champions Cup was played for the first time in 2011. It is now the premier IFF event for Men's and Women's Club teams. The national championship winners from the Top-4 ranked nations compete in the event.

## Euro Floorball Cup

The Euro Floorball Cup (formerly European Cup) is an IFF organised club event for both men's and women's teams. It has taken place every single year since 1993, and in 2000, it changed its format to a 2 year event (i.e. 2000-01). In 2008, the tournament switched back to its one-year format. In 2011, it underwent another change when the Champions Cup was introduced for the first time.

## North American Floorball League

The North American Floorball League is the first and only semi-professional floorball league outside of Europe. It is not affiliated with any federation, so it has players from around the world. The inaugural set of teams are entirely based in the United States, though, there is potential for expansion into Canada.

## Special Olympics

Floorball at the Special Olympics is slightly modified from the 'regular' form of floorball. Matches are played 3-on-3 with a goaltender, on a smaller court that measures 20 metres (66 ft) long by 12 m (39 ft) wide. This form of floorball was developed for the intellectually disabled, and has yet to be played at the Special Olympics. Floorball was played as a demonstration sport at the 2013 Special Olympics World Winter Games, and was played as an official sport at the games in 2017.

# VIVA-VOCE

**1** Floorball is a type of which game?

***Ans*** Floorball is a type of floor hockey.

**2** How many players are there in a floorball game?

***Ans*** There are five players in a floorball game.

**3** In which country floorball game was invented?

***Ans*** The floorball game was invented in Sweden in the late 1960s.

**4** In which year the first football club was set up in Sweden?

***Ans*** In 1979, the first floorball club in the world, Sala IBK from Sala, was founded in Sweden.

**5** In which year official rules for floorball matches were first written down?

***Ans*** Official rules for floorball matches were first written down in 1981.

**6** Name the organisation which organises floorball internationally.

***Ans*** The floorball sport is organised internationally by the International Floorball Federation (IFF).

**7** In which countries floorball is most popular?

***Ans*** Floorball is most popular in countries like the Czech Republic, Denmark, Estonia, Finland, Latvia, Norway, Sweden, and Switzerland.

**8** What is the measurement of floorball rink?

***Ans*** Floorball is played indoors on a rink whose size can officially vary from 18-20 m (59-66 ft) wide to 36-40 m (118-131 ft) long, and which is surrounded by 50 cm (20 in) high enclosed boards with rounded corners.

**9** What is the dimension of the goals of floorball rink?

***Ans*** The goals of floorball rink are 160 cm wide and 115 cm high. Their depth is 65 cm and they are 2.85 m from the end of the nearest boards.

**10** What is the size of floorball stick and from which material it is made?

***Ans*** A floorball stick is short compared with one for ice hockey. The maximum size for a stick is 114 cm. A stick cannot weigh more than 350 grams. Floorball sticks are often made of carbon and composite materials.

**11** Why about thousand dimples are made on a floorball?

***Ans*** The floorball has over a thousand small dimples in it that reduce air resistance.

**12** What is the period of floorball game?

***Ans*** A floorball game is officially played over three periods lasting 20 minutes each (15 minutes for juniors).

**13** The Asia Pacific Floorball Championships are played every single year in which places?

***Ans*** The Asia Pacific Floorball Championships are played every single year in New Zealand, Australia, Singapore, or Japan.

**14** Name the world's largest club team tournament.

***Ans*** The world's largest club team tournament, the Czech Open is a traditional summer tournament. It is held in Prague, Czech Republic.

**15** What is the name of Champions Cup premier?

***Ans*** The name of Champions Cup premier is IFF event for Men's and Women's Club teams.

GAME 10

# WHEELCHAIR RACING

Wheelchair racing is the racing of wheelchairs in track and road races. Wheelchair racing is open to athletes with any qualifying type of disability, amputees, spinal cord injuries, cerebral palsy and partially sighted (when combined with another disability). Athletes are classified in accordance with the nature and severity of their disability or combinations of disabilities. Like running, it can take place on a track or as a road race.

The main competitions take place at the Summer Paralympics which wheelchair racing and athletics has been a part of since 1960. Competitors compete in specialized wheelchairs which allow the athletes to reach speeds of 30 km/h (18.6 mph) or more. It is one of the most prominent forms of Paralympic athletics.

**Wheelchair Racing**

## History

The British government opened the Spinal Injuries Centre at Stoke Mandeville Hospital in Aylesbury, England, in 1944. Sir Ludwig Guttmann, director of this center, introduced competitive sports for disabled. With Guttmann's guidance, the first Stoke Mandeville Games for the Paralyzed were held in 1948.

In 1952 the first international competition for athletes in wheelchairs was organized between the British and the Netherlands. In 1960, the International Stoke Mandeville Wheelchair Sports Federation (ISMWSF) was formed to allow all international competitions for individuals with spinal cord injuries. In the 1960s international sports competitions were expanded to include other disability groups who were not eligible for the World Games. In addition, the International Sports Organisation for the Disabled (ISOD) was officially formed in Paris in 1964, to provide international sports opportunities for the blind, amputees and persons with other loco motor disabilities.

## Events

The distances involved in wheelchair racing include sprint distances of 100 m (109.4 yards), 200 m (218.7 yards) and 400 m (437.4 yards), middle distances of 800 m (874.9 yards) and 1500 m (1640.4 yards), long distances of 5000 m (3.1 miles) and 10,000 m (6.2 miles) and relay races of 4 × 100 m (109.4 yards) and 4 × 400 m (437.4 yards). There is also a road event which is the wheelchair marathon.

## Equipment Needed

Wheelchairs are a necessary piece of equipment for athletes competing in wheelchair racing and track and field events. Many of the wheelchairs tend to be very lightweight, with pneumatic tires, and with the dimensions and features on the wheelchairs clearly specified in the IPC Athletics rules.

## Rules

- The wheelchair shall have at least two large wheels and one small wheel.
- No part of the body of the chair may extend forwards beyond the hub of the front wheel and be wider than the inside of the hubs of the two rear wheels. The maximum height from the ground of the main body of the chair shall be 50 cm (1.6 ft).
- The maximum diameter of the large wheel including the inflated tyre shall not exceed 70 cm (2.3 ft). The maximum diameter of the small wheel including the inflated tyre shall not exceed 50 cm (1.6 ft).
- Only one plain, round, hand rim is allowed for each large wheel. This rule may be waived for persons requiring a single arm drive chair, if so stated on their medical and Games identity cards.
- No mechanical gears or levers shall be allowed, that may be used to propel the chair.
- Only hand-operated, mechanical steering devices will be allowed.
- In all races of 800 metres or over, the athlete should be able to turn the front wheel(s) manually both to the left and the right.
- The use of mirrors is not permitted in track or road races.
- No part of the chair may protrude behind the vertical plane of the back edge of the rear tyres.
- It will be the responsibility of the competitor to ensure the wheelchair conforms to all the above rules, and no event shall be delayed whilst a competitor makes adjustments to the athletes chair.
- Chairs will be measured in the Marshalling Area, and may not leave that area before the start of the event. Chairs that have been examined may be liable to re-examination before or after the event by the official in charge of the event.
- It shall be the responsibility, in the first instance, of the official conducting the event, to rule on the safety of the chair.
- Athletes must ensure that no part of their lower limbs can fall to the ground or track during the event.

# VIVA-VOCE

**1** Where is the main competition of wheelchair racing takes place?

***Ans*** Summer Paralympics

**2 How much speed can an athlete reach with specialised wheelchair?**

***Ans*** An athlete can reach speeds of 30 km/h or more with specialised wheelchair.

**3 Who introduced competitive sports for disabled persons?**

***Ans*** Sir Ludwig Guttman introduced competitive sports for disabled persons.

**4 When did the first international competition for athletes in wheelchairs organised?**

***Ans*** The first international competition for athletes in wheelchairs organised in 1952.

**5 What is the aim of International Sports Organisation for the Disabled?**

***Ans*** The aim of International Sports Organisation for the Disabled is to provide international sports opportunities for the blind, amputees and persons with other loco motor disabilities.

**6 How much sprint distance is involved in wheelchair racing?**

***Ans*** The distances involved in wheelchair racing include sprint distances of 100 m (109.4 yards), 200 m (218.7 yards) and 400 m (437.4 yards).

**7 How much wheels a wheelchair shall have in wheelchair racing?**

***Ans*** The wheelchair shall have at least two large wheels and one small wheel.

**8 What is the maximum diameter of the large wheel in the wheelchair?**

***Ans*** The maximum diameter of the large wheel including the inflated tyre shall not exceed 70 cm.

**9 How are athletes classified in wheelchair racing?**

***Ans*** In wheelchair racing, athletes are classified in accordance with the nature and severity of their disability or combinations of disabilities.

GAME 11

# WHEELCHAIR THROWS

Paralympic athletics include four seated or wheel chairs throwing sports, which are shot put, discus, club throw and javelin. While both ambulatory and seated athletes participate in all throws, this section focuses on the seated thrower or classifications F31-34 and F51-58. The term "seated throws" refers to athletes who compete from a seated position, either from a specially designed piece of equipment called a throws chair/throwing frame or from the athlete's day chair (either manual chair or power chair).

## Equipment Needed

- **Throwing Chair** The throwing chair is tied down to the ground to provide stability for the thrower. Without tie-downs, the chair can move out from under the thrower as he/she applies a large amount of force on the chair.
- **Tie-downs** Tie-downs are ratchet straps and metal stakes that should be used at a minimum on all four corners. Concrete stakes put into the ground at an angle work well, if the ratchet strap has a circle just ahead of the hook. It is not advisable to use aluminum stakes, as a very sharp edge will form on the top.
- **Sledge Hammer** A sledge hammer is used to hammer stakes into the ground at a 60 degree angle and angled away from the athlete. The ground should be level.
- **Alternative** An alternative is a portable ring made of angle irons with holes that the ratchet strap hooks will fit into, to secure the chair.

Wheelchair Throws (Shot Put)

## Specification of Equipment

| | Description |
|---|---|
| **Chair Dimensions** | • Max height (with cushion) = 75 cm<br>• Minimum side lengths = 30 cm long<br>• Seat of chair must be square or rectangular; it can be level or inclined backwards (i.r. the front of the chair can be higher than the back chair, but not the other way around)<br>• Footplates can be used as long as they are used for stability or support. |
| **Backrest** | • Can have side, front or back rest for stability and safety<br>• Has to be rigid part of chair frame or made of non-elastic fabric<br>• If backrest has cushioning, cannot be more than 5 cm thick<br>• Backrest cannot block the view of the official in judging a "lifting" fault |
| **Pole** | • Must be rigid, one piece, vertical bar that's circular or square in nature (not oval or rectangular)<br>• Can have layers of tape (or something similar) to assist with grip<br>• Pole cannot flex to the naked eyes during an attempt; spirit of this rule is to prevent an unfair advantage by helping propel the body forward while the athlete pulls on the bar<br>• Rules state that most materials will flex/distort to some degree' a fault will be called if it's clearly flexing and is going against the spirit of the rule<br>• No part of the throwing frame (including the pole) can moved during the throwing action (except for incidental movement that can't be reasonably eliminated) |
| **Strapping** | • All strapping used secure the athlete to the throwing frame must be made of non-elastic fabric. Weight lifting belts and snowboard binding are most commonly use |

# Techniques and Rules for Seated Throws

- Athlete must sit so that both legs are in contact with the seat surface from the back of the knee to the back of the buttock (Ischial Tuberosity).
- Sitting position must be maintained throughout the throwing action until throw marked.
- Strapping of the legs and hips is encouraged.
- The rule changes are being made to minimise the contribution of the legs.
- The athlete starts his/her trial from stationary seated position.
- The athlete cannot touch the straps outside the throwing ring.
- The throw is considered a failure if the athlete moves from the seated position from the time the athlete takes to implement into the starting position of trial until the throw has been marked.
- The feet may not be on the ground.

## Shot Diameters

Shots come in a variety of sizes, in both weight and diameter. Paralympic Sport classes use different size weights. The track and field rules at all levels allow for a variation in the diameter in each weight. The larger diameter is a good starting point for most athletes. The larger diameter enables the athlete to apply force over a larger surface and it reduces the tendency for the shot to 'roll' in the hand. Those shots can be found in track and field speciality catalogues. If the athlete is a high school athlete, check the high school equipment requirements before purchasing. The chart below illustrates the IPC requirements.

| Class | Weight | Diameter |
|---|---|---|
| Female - 33, 34, 53, 54, 55, 56, 57 | 3kg | 85mm-110mm |
| Male - 52 | 2kg | 85mm-100mm |
| Male - 33, 53 | 3kg | 85mm-100mm |
| Male - 34, 54, 55, 56, 57 | 4kg | 95 mm-110 mm |

## Type of Wheelchair Throws

We know that there are 4 types of seated throws these are discussed below:

## Club Throw

Club throw requires athletes to propel the club as far as possible into the designated throwing sector. It can be thrown in any manner (forward, sideways, or backwards). It should be thrown from a circle within a caged circle or portable platform. Distance is measured from the first point of contact the club makes in the sector.

Club Throw

### Techniques used in Club Throw

**Start/Entry** The club is either grasped in the palm of the hand or held between the fingers (depending on the athlete's hand function and the direction they are throwing). Athletes will typically start the throw by bringing it forward over their lap or by swinging it away from their legs. This motion all depends on the direction they are throwing. Strong body position should be emphasized from the start to ensure athlete is sitting as tall as possible.

**Drawback** The club is slowly swung back until they are at their most rearward position. It is important the club is not swung back abruptly as the weight on the end of the club will cause it to swing upwards, resulting in the club coming out of the hand too early during the release. Athletes may use an adhesive spray to help secure the club in their hand (as long as it can be easily removed from the implement without leaving a residue). If athlete is using a pole, the body will typically move in a similar direction as the club to create length in their throw.

**Release** The club is swung forward and released. It can fly out of their grasp at either the highest point (facing forward or back) or slide out of their grasp at the point of greatest speed (facing sideways). While the club is brought forward the athlete will pull into their pole (if using one) for increased speed and/or stability. Ideally the athlete's arm will stay as straight as possible during this motion to create length in the throw and increase the speed of the club at the release point. Timing as to when the arm flexes will vary by athlete and will impact how the club is released from the hand. Temperature, humidity and other weather conditions can all contribute to the timing of the release.

**Follow through** After the club is released the arm continues along the same path. Depending on chair set up the athlete may be falling forward or rotating at the waist due to momentum. Ensure that strapping is providing proper support for the athlete.

**Safety** Make sure the clubs are not damaged, splintered, or cracked. Check to ensure the weight on the end is not loose; it may dislodge when thrown. If athlete is throwing club for the first time start at a slow pace as the club may get stuck in the athlete's hand and swing back towards them.

## Shotput

Shot Put requires athletes to push the shot as far as possible in the designated throwing sector. The shot shall be put from the shoulder with one hand only. The shot shall touch or be in close proximity to the neck or chin and the hand shall not be dropped below this position during the action of putting. The shot shall not be taken behind the line of the shoulders.

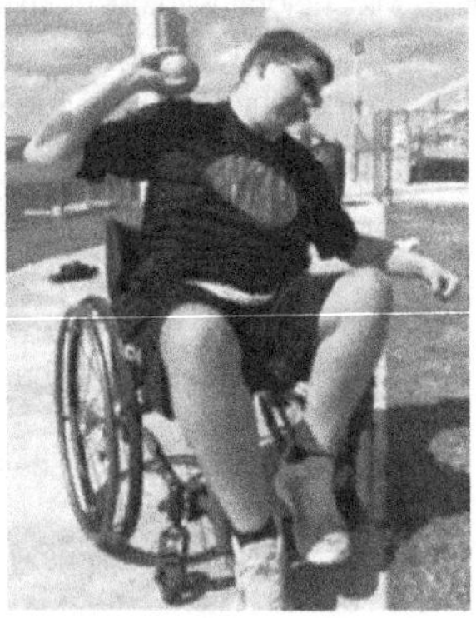

Shotput

### Techniques used in Shotput

**Start** Athlete begins in a tall upright position. Similar to able-bodied throwers, the athlete may hold the shot over the head until it is in the right position of the hand. Shot is then tucked under the chin/jawline. Lower functioning athletes will tend to turn the palm completely upwards in fear of losing the shot through their hands due to poor hand/finger function. The non-throwing hand is positioned at the top of the pole with the back of the wrist slightly turned outwards. This enables the pull during the release to feel natural and the body to come forward. Elbow of the non-throwing hand should be held between 45 to 90 degrees from the athlete's side to allow for an optimal pull. Degree will be based on athlete preference and coach feedback on how the body is being pulled forward.

**Entry** The athlete leans forward to initiate the throw. Athletes should be cautioned not to lean too far forward as it may be difficult for them to extend back (particularly for the lower functioning athletes). Ensure the elbow does not drop too much during this motion or the athlete will tend to rock back into a poor position during the drawback.

**Drawback** Athlete transitions backward to one of two positions: Athlete moves straight back, keeping their shoulders square to the sector or Athlete rotates at the waist, leads back with the elbow of their throwing arm, and rotates head back (as depicted in the picture). Style of drawback is individualized and should be selected on the position the athlete feels most comfortable and powerful.

**Release** Athlete pulls with non-throwing arm on the pole, bringing the body back to an upright position. If athlete is in the rotated position this pull is critical in bringing the shoulders square to the sector. if athlete rotates at waist before pulling themselves upright they will lose power in the throw. During the pull action the athlete will also begin to rotate their head forward to allow for clearance of the shot. The shot is pushed forward as the athlete reaches their maximum upright position. At the end of the explosive push of the shot, the wrist will flex causing the shot put to flick off the end of the fingers.

**Follow through** Momentum from the pull and body movement should cause the athlete to bend forward at the waist. if an athlete is not following through they are slowing their body (and therefore the shot) down before it has left the hand. Head either maintains an upright position or continues to rotate towards the side of the non-throwing arm, ensuring the shot clears and no fault is called.

**Safety** Take caution when handing an athlete the shot put. Some athlete's hand function and/or fatigue levels make it difficult to hold on to the shot put every time and they may potentially drop it on their legs or feet.

## Discus Throw

Discus is "flung" as far as possible within a designated sector. All discus throws should be attempted from either a portable or permanent cage for safety.

Discuss Throw

### Techniques used in Discus Throw

**Start** Athlete begins in a tall upright position with the discus in their hand. If using a pole, hand position is approximately shoulder height or slightly above; this position will cue the angle of the throwing arm during the drawback and release phase of the throw.

**Entry** The discus is brought forward in a circular motion while maintaining an upright position. Athletes without a pole will be able to rotate at the waist towards their non-throwing arm whereas athletes using a pole will bring the discus to the front of their body.

**Drawback** The discus is swung back with the palm of the throwing hand facing down. Cues such as "come around a barrel" will help athletes bring arm out and around rather than straight by their side. If using a pole, athlete leans away from pole until arm has a slight bend in it and is able to draw a straight line from the non-throwing hand to the discus Head is turned back to elongate the throw for greater momentum.

**Release** With no pole, the non-throwing arm is swung up and around, causing the chest to open and creating separation. Momentum is maintained as the throwing arm comes around with the discus. If using a pole, the non-throwing arm will pull, bringing the body into an upright position. This will also cause the shoulders to be square with the sector, causing the chest to open and creating separation. In both motions the head is turned to help create separation and the discus is released at the optimum angle.

**Follow through** As the body finishes its rotation it should be in an upright position. The head should keep turning as the throw is completed. The throwing arm finishes high; cueing the athletes to "pat themselves on the back" will maintain the throwing arm speed and reinforce follow through.

## Javelin Throw

Athletes must sling the javelin and have it land correctly in the designated throwing sector. Athletes must sling the implement over the shoulder using one hand. It cannot be "cartwheeled" or spun. It must land nose first and must be gripped by the cord.

Javelin Throw

## Techniques used in Javelin Throw

**Start** Athlete begins in a tall upright position with the javelin either above the head or at shoulder height. The non-throwing hand is positioned at the top of the pole (shoulder height or slightly higher) with the back of the wrist slightly turned outwards. This enables the pull during the release to feel natural and the body to come forward. Elbow of the non-throwing hand should be held between 45 to 90 degrees from the athlete's side to allow for an optimal pull. Degree will be based on athlete preference and coach feedback on how the body is being pulled forward.

**Entry** Some athletes will move from the start position right into drawback position. This can help the athlete maintain the optimal angle of the javelin. Some athletes will bring the javelin and arm forward; this movement will be created by bending forward at the waist. Hand position on the pole remains the same during this motion.

**Drawback** The javelin is brought back until the arm is straight. Athlete leans away from pole until the non-throwing arm has a slight bend. Majority of throwers will maintain their head position forward, looking towards the angle of release. Athletes should be cautious that the javelin does not hit the back of the circle as the body leans back.

**Release** Athlete pulls with non-throwing arm on the pole, bringing the body back to an upright position. The javelin is propelled forward using the same whip like action as able-bodied throws where the elbow leads the throw as high as possible, followed by the forearm and eventual flick/rotation of the wrist at the release point.

**Follow through** The throwing arm follows the javelin through the release, where the wrist flicks/rotates and results in a downward thumb position. The body continues forward with a similar follow through as shot put. If an athlete is pulling on an angle into the pole, they will fall as far forward as they can without hitting the pole.

**Safety** When carrying javelins back to the athlete, make sure to carry them vertically as the athlete will not be able to move if they are approached with a javelin held horizontally.

# VIVA-VOCE

**1 Which sports are included in Paralympic athletics?**

*Ans.* Paralympic athletics include four throwing sports which are shot put, discus, club throw and javelin.

**2 In which circumstance is a throw considered a failure?**

*Ans.* The throw is considered a failure if the athlete moves from the seated position from the time the athlete takes to implement into the starting position of trial until the throw has been marked.

**3 How does an athlete start his/her trial?**

*Ans.* An athlete starts his/her trial from stationary seated position.

**4 How is the shot held in seated shot put?**

*Ans.* The shot is really not held. The shot rests on the base of the fingers with the thumb and the little finger providing the lateral support and the other three fingers spread out over the surface of the shot.

**5** What is a sledge hammer used to do?

*Ans.* A sledge hammer is used to hammer stakes into the ground at a 60 degree angle and angled away from the athlete.

**6** What does finger flick mean?

*Ans.* The last action applied to the shot is a finger flick. The wrist is leading the shot until the last minute when the fingers push the shot up and forward with a forceful flick of the fingers.

**7** What is the shot diameter for male class-34?

*Ans.* The shot diameter for male class-34 is 85mm-100mm.

**8** What is the shot diameter for female class-57?

*Ans.* The shot diameter for female class-57 is 85mm-110mm.

**9** How is the throwing chair used in the seated shot put?

*Ans.* The throwing chair is tied down to the ground to provide stability for the thrower. Without tie-downs, the chair can move out from under the thrower as he/she applies a large amount of force on the chair.

**10** What is an alternative used in seated shot put?

*Ans.* An alternative is a portable ring made of angle irons with holes that the ratchet strap hooks will fit into, to secure the chair.

| GAME 12 |

# ATHLETICS (400 M TRACK AND FIELD)

The word *athletics* is derived from Greek word *athlon* which means *competition*. Athletics is considered to be mother of all games and is in fact a way of living and not just a sport. It is an exclusive collection of sporting events that involve competitive running, jumping and throwing. An athlete is the person who participates in any sort of competition involving physical activity.

### Ancient Olympic

The first olympic in ancient Greece dates back to 8th or 9th century BC. In 776 BC in Olmpia, Greece only one event was contested which was the stadion footrace. The first olympic winner of this event was Koroibos. In later years, further running competitions were added.

### Modern Olympic

Modern competition in athletics, took place for the first time in the 19th century. The establishment of the Modern Olympic Games in Athens in 1896 marked a new era for track and field events. For the first time, fourteen nations participated in one sporting event.

## HISTORY

In **1912**, the International Amateur Athletic Federation (IAAF) was established and it became the international governing body for athletics. In the **1928** Summer Olympics, women competed for the first time.

In **1960**, the major athletics competitions for disabled athletes were first introduced in Summer Para Olympics. From the **1960s**, athletics gained more exposure through television coverage. In the late **1970s**, the amateur status of the sport began to be displaced by growing professionalism.

In **1982**, the IAAF abandoned amateurism and later changed its name to International Association of Athletics Federations.

## STANDARD TRACK WITH ALL SPECIFICATIONS

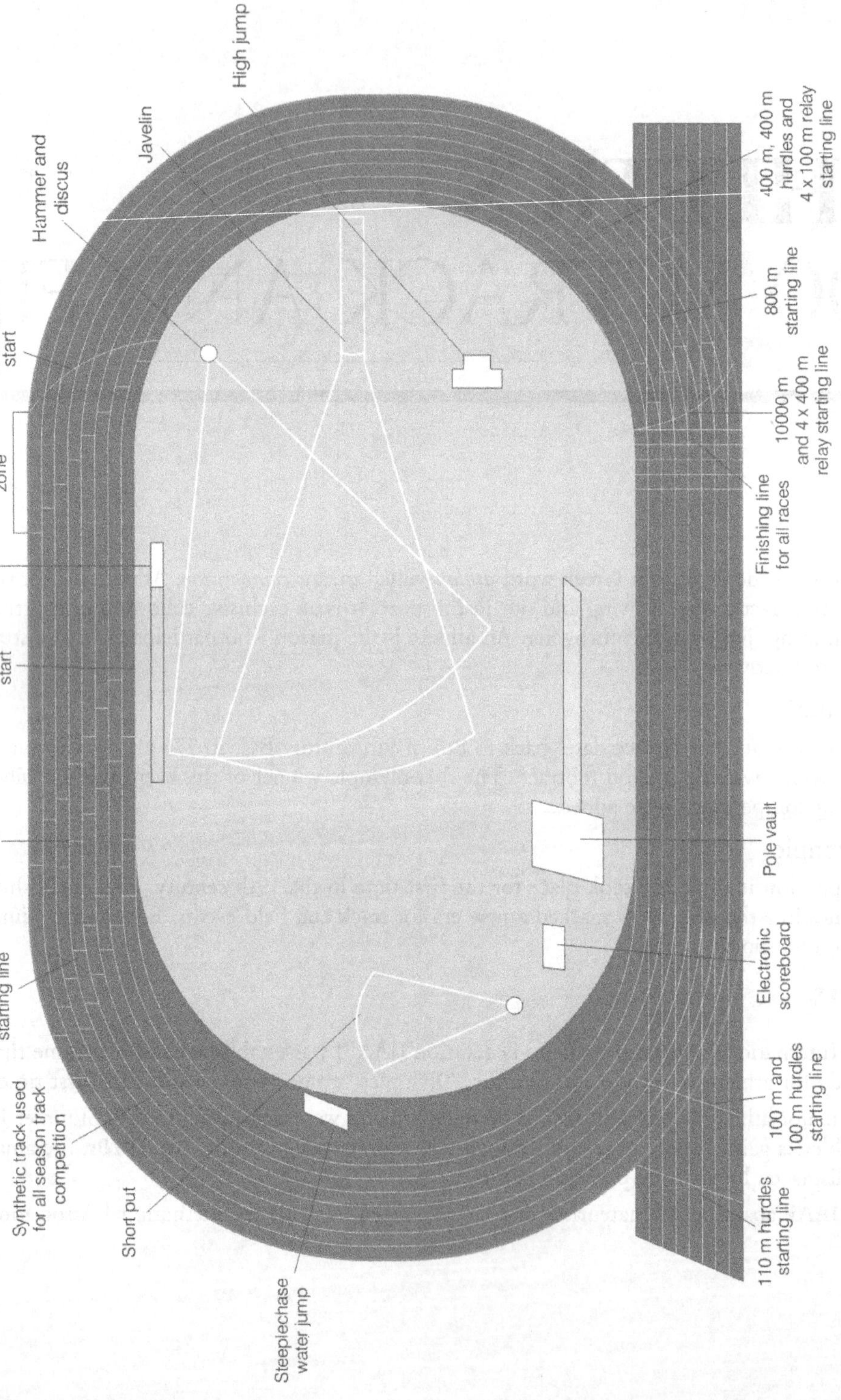

## A Standard Track

In athletics, a proper track is the most essential thing. A standard track (400 m) consists of 2 straight paths and 2 curves (making one circle). The straight paths of the track should be in parallel to each other and the curves connecting them.

The straight paths of a standard track may be from 70 to 90 m, but in international competitions, straight path of 84 m is preferred.

Standard track (400 m) = 2 straight + 2 curves

= 2 straight + circumference of circle ($2\pi R$)

In standard track, a straight path is 84 m.

$\therefore$ 2 straight $= 84 + 84 = 168$ m

$\therefore$ Circumference of circle

$$(2\pi R) = 400 - 168 = 232 \text{ m}$$

$$\text{Radius } (R) = \frac{232}{2\pi} = \frac{232}{2 \times 3.14}$$

$$= 36.90 \text{ m}$$

This is known as Running Radius (RR).

$\therefore$ Running Radius (RR) = 36.90 m

The track is marked 30 cm inside the running radius to avoid fouls.

$\therefore$ Marking Radius (MR) = $36.90 - 0.30$

$= 36.60$ m

All lines over the track are marked 5 cm thick.

### Staggers

There are lanes 8-9 in an athletic track. Each lane has minimum width of 1.22 m and maximum width of 1.25 m. Stagger is the arrangement of the runner in lanes or a running track at the start of a race, so that, the runner in the inside lane is positioned behind those in the next lane and so on till, the outside lane. Staggers are marked so that no athlete is at advantage or disadvantage while running in different lanes. *Stagger for different lanes is calculated by the formula*

$$[w(n-1) - 10 \text{ cm}] \times 2\pi$$

where, $w$ = width of lane (1.22 m),

$n$ = number of lanes,

$\pi = \frac{22}{7}$ or 3.14

| Stagger for 400 m race (on 400 m track) | Lane No. | Stagger for 200 m race (on 400 m track) |
|---|---|---|
| 0 | 1st Lane | 0 |
| 7.04 metres | 2nd Lane | 3.52 metres |
| 14.71 metres | 3rd Lane | 7.35 metres |
| 22.38 metres | 4th Lane | 11.19 metres |
| 30.05 metres | 5th Lane | 15.02 metres |
| 37.72 metres | 6th Lane | 18.86 metres |
| 45.38 metres | 7th Lane | 22.69 metres |
| 53.05 metres | 8th Lane | 26.52 metres |

# VIVA-VOCE

**1** What does the word 'athletics' mean?

*Ans.* The word 'athletics' is derived from the Greek word 'athlon' which means competition.

**2** When did the first recorded organised athletics event happen?

*Ans.* The first recorded organised athletics event happened in 776 BC in Olympia, Greece.

**3** Where was the first modern athletic competition started?

*Ans* The first modern athletic competition started in Athens in 1896 as Modern Olympic games.

**4** How many nations participated in it?

*Ans.* Fourteen nation participated in that event.

**5** When was the International Amateur Athletic Federation (IAAF) established?

*Ans.* The International Amateur Athletic Federation (IAAF) was established in 1912.

**6** In which Olympics, women competed for the first time?

*Ans.* In Summer Olympics of 1928, women competed for the first- time.

**7** When did the IAAF abandon amateurism and change its name?

*Ans.* In 1982, the IAAF abandoned amateurism and changed its name to the International Association of Athletics Federations.

**8** Generally, how many types of events are there in athletics?

*Ans.* Athletics mainly has two types of events–Track events and Field events.

**9** What are regarded as track events?

*Ans.* A variety of running events, *viz.*, sprint races, hurdle races, relay races, steeplechase races are held on the track and these are known as track events.

**10** What do you mean by sprint race?

*Ans.* A sprint race is a short distance running race, it is generally of three types i.e. 100 m, 200 m and 400 m.

**11** What is a hurdle race?

*Ans* A hurdle race is one in which obstacles are placed at intervals along the track that runners must jump over on their way to the finishing line.

**12** Which factors are necessary for winning hurdle race?

*Ans* Timing, footwork and jumping techniques are key factors for winning hurdle races.

**13** What is a standard track?

*Ans.* 400 m track is called a standard track.

**14** How many lanes are permitted in international level competitions?

*Ans.* 9 lanes are permitted in international level competitions.

**15** What is the minimum and maximum width of a lane?

*Ans.* Lane should be minimum 1.22 m wide and maximum 1.25 m wide for all races.

**16** Which lane is allotted to the topmost runner?

*Ans.* Fourth lane is allotted to the topmost runner.

**17** What are staggers?

*Ans.* Staggers are the arrangement of the runners in different lanes of a running track.

# SAMPLE
# QUESTION PAPERS (1-3)

# SAMPLE QUESTION PAPER 1

**A Highly Simulated Sample Question Paper for CBSE Class XI Examination**

# PHYSICAL EDUCATION

## General Instructions

- The question paper consists of 5 sections and 37 questions.
- **Section-A** consists of question 1-18 carrying 1 mark each and is Multiple Choice Questions. All questions are compulsory.
- **Section-B** consists of question 19-24 carrying 2 marks each and are Very Short Answer Type Questions and should not exceed 60-90 words. Attempt any 5.
- **Section-C** consists of question 25-30 carrying 3 marks each and are Short Answer Type Questions and should not exceed 100-150 words. Attempt any 5.
- **Section-D** consists of question 31-33 carrying 4 marks each and are Case Studies. There is internal choice available.
- **Section-E** consists of question 34-37 carrying 5 marks each and are Long Answer Type Questions and should not exceed 200-300 words. Attempt any 3.

***Time : 3 hours*** ***Max. Marks : 70***

FULLY SOLVED

## SECTION A

**1** Identify the given asana. (1)

(a) Vajrasana
(b) Dhanurasana
(c) Bhujangasana
(d) Halasana

**2** When an individual starts to think, imagine, contemplate and recollect, the state is called .................. . (1)

(a) Dharana
(b) Ishvara Pranidhana
(c) Samadhi
(d) Dhyanavastha

**3** The foundation of physical education was laid in (1)

(a) England (b) Greece (c) USA (d) Italy

**4** Career options through physical education are (1)

(a) Sports Departments
(b) Sports Facilities Management
(c) Sports Journalism
(d) All of the above

**5** Which of the following is not the component of wellness? (1)

(a) Physical
(b) Emotional
(c) Muscular strength
(d) Nutritional

**6** Which one of the following is not a component of physical fitness? (1)

(a) Speed
(b) Flexibility
(c) Strength
(d) Cardiovascular endurance

**7** Biomechanics can play a crucial role in ... . (1)

(a) injury prevention
(b) performance enhancement
(c) physical movement
(d) Both (a) and (b)

**8** A physical education teacher can provide leadership opportunities by (1)

(a) recognising the leaders
(b) providing leadership courses
(c) giving leadership roles
(d) All of the above

**9** Given below are the two statements labeled Assertion (A) and Reason (R). (1)

**Assertion** (A) Yoga unites the individual's soul with the divine soul.

**Reason** (R) The word 'Yoga' is derived from the Sanskrit word 'Yuj' which means 'to unite'.

In the context of above two statements, which one of the following is correct?

(a) Both A and R are true and R is the correct explanation of A
(b) Both A and R are true, but R is not the correct explanation of A
(c) A is true, but R is false
(d) A is false, but R is true

**10** How many physiological systems are there in a human body? (1)

(a) 4 (b) 9 (c) 6 (d) 10

**11** What are the benefits of bringing traditional games back to life? (1)

(a) Bunging together of indigenous and non-indigenous people.
(b) Help reconnect urban indigenous youth to their culture.
(c) Enhance physical health
(d) All of the above

**12** Which of the following is not a disadvantage of doping in females? (1)

(a) Deepening of the voice
(b) Abnormal menstrual cycles
(c) Impotence
(d) Growth of hair on the face

**13** Test is generally used to measure (1)

(a) a specific body type
(b) the level of skill
(c) a specific skill
(d) the abilities of a sportsperson

**14** Which of these is/are the functions of International Olympic Committee? (1)

(a) It sets the general guidelines, rules and regulations of the different sporting events.
(b) It fights against doping practices in sports
(c) It decides the host country where Olympic Games will be held.
(d) All of the above

**15** According to whom "Yoga is attaining the pose"? (1)

(a) Patanjali (b) Maharishi Ved Vyas
(c) Agam (d) None of these

**16** Match the following diseases to the lack of nutrient which causes them. (1)

| List I | | List II | |
|---|---|---|---|
| A. | Vitamin C | (i) | Bleeding disorders |
| B. | Vitamin B | (ii) | Scurvy |
| C. | Vitamin A | (iii) | Beri Beri |
| D. | Vitamin K | (iv) | Night Blindness |

**Codes**

| | A | B | C | D |
|---|---|---|---|---|
| (a) | (i) | (iii) | (iv) | (ii) |
| (b) | (ii) | (iii) | (iv) | (i) |
| (c) | (iv) | (iii) | (ii) | (i) |
| (d) | (iii) | (iv) | (i) | (ii) |

**17** Match the following. (1)

| **List I** (Health Related Components) | | **List II** (Characteristics) | |
|---|---|---|---|
| A. | Muscular Strength | (i) | It refers to the range of motion around a movement. |
| B. | Cardiovascular Endurance | (ii) | It is the percentage of lean body mass in comparison to body fat. |
| C. | Body Composition | (iii) | It refers to the ability of muscle to exert force during an activity. |
| D. | Flexibility | (iv) | It refers to the physical activity of an individual to indulge in aerobic exercises. |

**Codes**

| | A | B | C | D |
|---|---|---|---|---|
| (a) | (i) | (ii) | (iii) | (iv) |
| (b) | (iii) | (iv) | (ii) | (i) |
| (c) | (ii) | (i) | (iv) | (iii) |
| (d) | (iv) | (ii) | (iii) | (i) |

**18** What is the role of physiotherapist? (1)

(a) To manage special needs children with movement disorder.
(b) To help special needs children to develop fine and gross motor skills.
(c) To build communication of children with special needs.
(d) To work for the overall development of children with special needs.

## Section B (1 × 2 = 2)

**19** Describe any two components of the wellness. (2)

**20** How can an occupational therapist help a child with special needs? (2)

**21** What were the winners awarded within the ancient Olympic Games? (2)

**22** How kinesiology is important? (2)

**23** Discuss the short and long-term courses available in the field of physical education in India by giving examples. (2)

**24** How does physical education develop the ability and capacity of an individual? (2)

## Section C

**25** Briefly write about Special Olympic symbol and Olympic flame. (1.5 + 1.5 = 3)

**26** What do you mean by Yama? What are the five basic virtues mentioned in it? (1 + 2 = 3)

**27** Enlist the reasons, why the practice of Yoga is important for us. (3)

**28** Explain in brief the Amphiarthrosis joints. (3)

**29** Discuss the role of a special educator in the overall development of children with special needs. (3)

**30** "Doping has been a part of the field of sports since time immemorial." Justify the statement. (3)

## Section D

**31** In relation to the picture given below, answer the following questions. (4 × 1 = 4)

(i) What is the motto of the Paralympics?
(a) Spirit in Motion (b) Together We Can
(c) Citius, Altius, Fortius (d) One World, One Dream

(ii) Where is the headquarters of the Paralympics?

(iii) The first Indian woman to win a medal at the Paralympics is
(a) Deepa Malik (b) Devika Malik
(c) Shashi Kiran (d) Aruna Tanwar

(iv) The first Paralympic Games took place in Rome in the year ............... .

*Or* The Motto of Tokyo Paralympics Games was ................ .

**32** In relation to the picture given below, answer the following questions. (4 × 1 = 4)

(i) What do you mean by the Olympic Motto 'Citius, Altius, Fortius'?
(a) Faster, Higher, Stronger
(b) Together, United, Strong
(c) Peace, Unity, Strength
(d) Excellence, Honor, Victory

(ii) The five rings of the Olympic symbol are in five different colors i.e. Red, Green, Yellow, Blue and .................. .

(iii) Olympic Games were held in ancient Greece in the honour of Greek God ................ .

(iv) .................. is the first city in the world to be awarded both Summer and Winter Olympics.

**33** Biomechanics and Newton's laws of motion find tremendous application in modern sports. Not only is their knowledge important to enhance performance, it also helps prevent sports injuries. In relation to the pictures given below, answer the following questions. **(4 × 1 = 4)**

(1) 

(2) 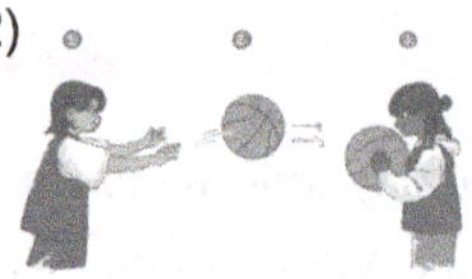

(i) When a swimmer applies force on the water, the reaction force acts on the man due to water. The force on the man drives the man forward in the water. The force being referred here is
(a) Gravitational force
(b) Frictional force
(c) Buoyant force
(d) Thrust force

(ii) Among the above given pictures, Newton's First Law is depicted in ............ .

(iii) The study of the human body and various forces acting on it is known as
(a) Anatomy
(b) Physiology
(c) Biomechanics
(d) Psychology

(iv) Newton's First Law is also known as ............... .



## Section E

**34** Explain five strategies to make physical activities accessible for children with special needs. **(1 × 5 = 5)**

**35** Describe the five components of health related fitness. **(1 × 5 = 5)**

**36** Discuss the functions of the circulatory system. **(5)**

**37** How can the problems of adolescence be managed? Explain in detail. **(5)**

# Answers

**1** (c) Bhujangasana
**2** (d) Dhyanavastha
**3** (b) Greece
**4** (d) All of the above
**5** (c) Muscular strength
**6** (d) Cardiovascular endurance
**7** (d) Both (a) and (b)
**8** (d) All of the above
**9** (b) Both A and R are true, but R is not the correct explanation of A
**10** (b) 9
**11** (d) All of the above
**12** (c) Impotence
**13** (c) a specific skill
**14** (d) All of the above
**15** (b) Maharishi Ved Vyas
**16** (b) ii, iii, iv, i
**17** (b) iii, iv, ii, i
**18** (a) To manage special needs children with movement disorder.

**19** The three components of the wellness are as follows

(i) **Physical Wellness** It refers to physical appearance which can be achieved by taking nutritious food, doing regular exercises, getting in shape, having a glowing skin and a youthful appearance.

(ii) **Emotional Wellness** It is the ability to control stress, manage anger and anxiety, and express feelings appropriately. It also lays stress on getting more out of every day with laughter and enjoyment.

(iii) **Social Wellness** It refers to the ability to work with different people, to communicate well and interact with the community.

**20** An occupational therapist is a professional who can help a child with special needs by developing its fine and gross motor skills. This is done by teaching simple activities like grasping, reaching, picking, dressing, etc. These activities increase physical coordination among such children. When the child is able to do simple activities independently, it builds confidence in the child. The occupational therapist also arranges for any special equipment needed by the child.

**21** In the ancient Olympic Games, till the sixth games, the winners were awarded cattle and corn. Afterwards, the winners were awarded a wreath made of wild olive leaves from a sacred tree near the temple of Zeus.

**22** Kinesiology is important because

(i) **Preparing Coaches and Physical Education Teachers** Kinesiology prepares coaches as well as physical education teachers to guide an individual towards success in their sport. They help students and athletes to stay mentally and physically fit by teaching them proper techniques of a sport as well as guiding them to make health choices.

(ii) **Promotion of Health and Fitness** The knowledge of kinesiology helps the trainers and physical education teachers to help a student or an athlete in improving their health, fitness and well-being.

**23** Short-term courses are for a duration of a few months to 1-2 years. Diploma and certificate courses are short-term courses.

There are many such courses like Diploma in Physical Education, Diploma in Adaptive Physical Education etc. Certificate courses are available in Aerobics, Yoga Science, Coaching, Sports Administration etc.

Long-term courses available in physical education are degree courses like Bachelor of Arts in Physical Education, Master of Arts in Physical Education, M.Phil. in Physical Education etc.

**24** Physical education tells us about the benefits of physical activities. Regular physical activities ensure smooth working of the internal organs of the body like heart, lungs, liver and kidney.

Physical activity also ensures smooth functioning of all the different systems working in our body such as digestive system, circulatory system, respiratory system, nervous system and muscular system. When these systems work smoothly, our body works in a better way and develops our ability and capacity to work.

**25** The Special Olympic Symbol (logo) is based on the sculpture i.e. 'Joy and Happiness to all Children of the World'. The logo is a symbol of growth, confidence, and joy among children and adult with disabilities who are learning coordination, mastery skill, participating in competitions and preparing themselves for richer and more productive lives. Its Olympic flame is known as the 'Flame of Hope'. It is carried to and lit at Special Olympic Games. It is used in the same spirit as the Olympic flame in the Olympic Games.

**26** Yama is the first element of Yoga, which teaches that we should not corrupt our souls by indulging in wrongful activities. It contains five basic virtues which everyone should have. These are as follows

(i) Ahimsa (non-violence)

(ii) Satya (truthfulness)

(iii) Asteya (non-stealing)

(iv) Brahmacharya (celibacy) (v) Aparigraha (non-possessiveness)

**27** The practice of Yoga is important for us due to some reasons, they are as follows:

- It brings about physical purity.
- It prevents and cures diseases by providing immunity to the body.
- It reduces mental tension.
- It reduces obesity and beautifies the body. . It relaxes the body and mind.
- It corrects and maintains posture.
- It increases flexibility.
- It develops people spiritually.
- It improves moral and ethical values.

**28** Amphiarthrosis joints are slightly movable joints. A pad of cartilage lies between the bone surface and the fibrous capsule which holds the bone and the cartilage in place.

There are two types of such joints

(i) **Synchrondrosis** These are temporary form of joints that exist only while the skeleton is growing. It becomes at bone as the skeleton grows completely. For instance, the first pair of ribs and the sternum.

(ii) **Symphysis** These joints consists of a compressible fibro-cartilage pad that connects two bones allowing some movement. The hip bone is one example of such a joint.

**29** The role of a special educator is to work for the overall development of children with special needs. This is done by developing teaching aids and instructional materials as well as through remedial teaching. Special educators are concerned with the overall success of children with special needs. Their role is to improve a student's ability to function in social, emotional and behavioural capacities.

Another role of special educator is to encourage family involvement, working with other school staff to better understand the needs of the specific child, etc. For this purpose, collaborating with school and community professionals is also required.

**30** Doping refers to the use of drugs to enhance physical performance. The concept of doping is not new in sports. In ancient Greece, there were specialists who would offer nutritional ingredients such as mushrooms, opium and other herbal beverages that enhanced sports performance. Even Gladiators are known to use various substances that aimed at enhancing strength.

In the modern times, the use of doping first came out in 1904 Olympics, when Thomas Hicks won the marathon race. He had taken injections of strychnine. After that the increase in doping increased so much that in 1928, the International Athletic Association Federation banned doping followed by other doping federations. Soon, the International Olympic Committee started considering the "presence in the human body of substances which are prohibited according to the list published by the IOC and/or the international organisation" as illegal. Hence, it can be said that doping has been a part of the field of sports since time immemorial.

FULLY SOLVED

**31** (i) (a) Spirit in Motion (ii) Bonn, Germany
(iii) (a) Deepa Malik (iv) 1960

*Or*

United by Emotions

**32** (i) (a) Faster, Higher, Stronger (ii) Black
(iii) Zeus (iv) Beijing

**33** (i) (d) Newton's Third Law of Motion
(ii) the 2nd picture
(iii) (c) Biomechanics
(iv) Law of Inertia

**34** The five strategies to make physical activities accessible for children with special needs are as follows

(i) **Medical Check-up** If we want to make physical activities accessible for the children with special needs, we need to understand the type of disabilities of children and for this purpose complete medical check-up of the children is required.

(ii) **Assistive Technology** It refers to creating devices, tools or equipments that help children with special needs to participate in learning activities like bigger balls, balls with bells, balls attached to strings etc. This kind of new technology makes physical activities accessible for children with special needs.

(iii) **Adaptive Physical Education** Adapted physical education means developing, implementing and monitoring a carefully designed physical education instructional programme for a learner with a disability.

(iv) **Creating Specific Environment** This means making a friendly atmosphere by keeping in mind the specific needs of the children with disability. In this way, it shows that they are also wanted in society and like other children of their age, they can also play.

(v) **Activities based on Interests** Physical activities must be based on interest, aptitudes, abilities, previous experience and limitations of children with special needs, The teachers of physical education should have deep knowledge of limitations, interests and aptitudes of children.

**35** The five components of health related fitness are

(i) **Cardiovascular Endurance** It refers to the physical activity of an individual to indulge in aerobic exercises for longer period of time.

It can also be referred to as the ability of heart, lungs and blood vessels to supply oxygen and nutritients to the working muscles and the ability of those muscles to allow sustained exercise.The endurance system can be improved through the activities like cycling, walking, etc.

(ii) **Muscular Strength** This refers to the ability of the muscles to exert force during an activity.
Muscular strength of the different muscles can be improved by lifting weights, rapidly climbing the stairs, etc.

(iii) **Muscular Endurance** This refers to the ability of the muscles to continue to perform repetitive exercises without fatigue. Muscular endurance can be improved by doing cardio-respiratory activities like walking, cycling, jogging, dancing, etc.

(iv) **Body Composition** It refers to the relative amount of muscles, fat, bone and other vital parts of the body. It is basically the percentage of lean body mass i.e. bones, tendons, muscles, ligaments, etc. in comparison to body fat.

This percentage differs from person to person. A fit person has relatively low percentage of body fat one can have good body composition by having proper diet and exercise. For reducing percentage of body fat one can do jogging, climbing stairs, etc.

(v) **Flexibility** It refers to the maximum range of movements possible at a joint. It depends on the structure of joints, muscles length, tendons, ligaments and other factors. An individual having a good flexibility will be able to move his/her joints through a full range of motion while performing activities. Flexibility can be improved through regular yoga, gymnastics and basic stretching exercises.

**36** The circulatory system is responsible for performing various functions. They are

(i) **Transportation** It transports blood to almost all of the body's tissues. The blood delivers essential nutrients and oxygen into the cells of the body. It removes wastes and carbon dioxide from the body. Hormones are transported throughout the body via the blood's liquid plasma.

This process of transportation takes place through two seperate circulatory process which are as follows

(a) **Pulmonary Circulation** It allows oxygenation of blood. The blood goes to the lungs from the right side of the heart, where the $CO_2$ is removed and the blood is oxygenated.

(b) **Systematic Circulation** It allows circulation of the oxygenated blood between heart and body's tissue. The left side of the heart after receiving oxygenated blood, pumps it out through the aorta to all the body parts. After deoxygenation of body, it goes back to the right side of the heart through superior and inferior vena cava.

(ii) **Protection** It protects the body from various diseases. Its White Blood Cells (WBCs) cleans up cellular debris and fight pathogens that have entered the body. Platelets and red blood cells form scabs (called 'clots') to seal wounds and prevent pathogens from entering the body and liquids from leaking out.

(iii) **Regulation** It is an instrument in the body to maintain homeostatic control of several internal conditions. Blood vessels help maintain a stable body temperature by controlling the blood flow to the surface of the skin.

(iv) **Nutrition** The circulatory system carries the nutrients and all the essential vitamins, minerals, amino acids as well as glucose to all parts of the body. As the blood goes through the small intestine, the nutrients enter the blood stream for further use.

**37** Problems of adolescence can be managed by using the five techniques mentioned below

(i) **Proper Counselling** The problems of adolescence are the result of natural growth and development of the body. At this time, lack of experience develops shyness, introversion, etc in them. It prevents them from expressing their problems to their elders. This condition may increase their mental tension.

Therefore, proper counselling and guidance by parents, teachers and elders is the best method for management of adolescent problems.

(ii) **Participation in Co-curricular Activities** Adolescence is an age of energy and dynamism. If the adolescents' energy is utilised in activities other than academics i.e. sports, dance, social functions etc. their surplus energy is spent properly. As a result, emotional upheavals as well as instability will not occur. This helps in the development of motor skills and in harmonising the personality of an adolescent.

(iii) **Mutual Understanding** Family members and all elders must try to understand the problems of adolescents. They should be sympathetic and affectionate.

At the same time, adolescents must also understand that their parents are trying to help them for their betterment.

(iv) **Sex Education** Adolescents must be educated about sex, just like any other lessons taught in school, in a straightforward way. Correct knowledge enables them to understand their urges better. They must be properly guided to tackle all the problems related to sex as well as to channelise their drives towards constructive work.

(v) **Adequate Independence** Adolescents want adequate freedom in behaviour. They wish to express their views independently. They must be provided a proper platform to express their feelings. They should be allowed recreational and creative activities. Orders and strict instructions should not be imposed on them. Parents should try to understand the sentiments of adolescents and cooperate with them.

# SAMPLE QUESTION PAPER 2

**A Highly Simulated Sample Question Paper for CBSE Class XI Examination**

# PHYSICAL EDUCATION

## General Instructions

- The question paper consists of 5 sections and 37 questions.
- **Section-A** consists of question 1-18 carrying 1 mark each and is Multiple Choice Questions. All questions are compulsory.
- **Section-B** consists of question 19-24 carrying 2 marks each and are Very Short Answer Type Questions and should not exceed 60-90 words. Attempt any 5.
- **Section-C** consists of question 25-30 carrying 3 marks each and are Short Answer Type Questions and should not exceed 100-150 words. Attempt any 5.
- **Section-D** consists of question 31-33 carrying 4 marks each and are Case Studies. There is internal choice available.
- **Section-E** consists of question 34-37 carrying 5 marks each and are Long Answer Type Questions and should not exceed 200-300 words. Attempt any 3.

UNSOLVED

***Time : 3 hours*** ***Max. Marks : 70***

## Section A

**1** Identify the given asana. (1)

(a) Chakrasana (b) Pranayama
(c) Matsyasana (d) Trikonasana

**2** Career options through physical education are (1)

(a) Sports Departments
(b) Sports Facilities Management
(c) Sports Journalism
(d) All of the above

**3** When did revival of Olympic games took place? (1)

(a) 1895 (b) 1896
(c) 1899 (d) 1892

**4** Which of the following terms is defined as "a blip in the usual functioning of a person" ? (1)

(a) Disability
(b) Impulsive
(c) Disorder
(d) None of the above

**5** Which of the following is/are the signs of overload? (1)

(a) Fatigue
(b) Decline in performance
(c) Loss of appetite
(d) All of the above

**6** Where is the Headquarters of Indian Olympic Association? (1)

(a) Kolkata
(b) New Delhi
(c) Chandigarh
(d) Mumbai

**7** When an individual starts to think, imagine, contemplate and recollect, the state is called (1)

(a) Dharana
(b) Ishvara Pranidhana
(c) Samadhi
(d) Dhyanavastha

**8** The board whose length is less than 7 feet is called (1)

(a) long board
(b) mat board
(c) knee board
(d) short board

**9** Given below are two statements labeled as Assertion (A) and Reason (R). (1)

**Assertion** (A) Psychology is the science of human behaviour.

**Reason** (R) Psychology is not related to sports.

In the context of above two statements, which one of the following is correct?

(a) Both A and R are true and R is the correct explanation of A
(b) Both A and R are true, but R is not the correct explanation of A
(c) A is true, but R is false
(d) A is false, but R is true

**10** Who said that "Physical fitness is the capacity to meet the present and potential physical challenges of life with success"? (1)

(a) Don Hoskins (b) Kroles
(c) D R Lamb (d) Harre

**11** Which of the following is not an Axial Skeletal bone? (1)

(a) Ribs (b) Skull
(c) Upper limbs (d) Vertebral column

**12** .......... involves the sequential combination of flexion, adduction, extension and abduction at a joint. (1)

(a) Circumduction (b) External rotation
(c) Internal rotation (d) None of these

**13** Understanding of proper sports and exercise movements will allow the participant to be more ......... for long-term development. (1)

(a) efficient
(b) technically sound
(c) prone to good habits
(d) All of the above

**14** Which among the following movements take place when the angle decreases between the two bones attached to a joint? (1)

(a) Abduction (b) Extension
(c) Flexion (d) Adduction

**15** According to its Greek meaning, psychology came to be understood as (1)

(a) Scientific study of soul
(b) Study of behaviour
(c) Study of mind
(d) Study of consciousness

**16** Match the following. (1)

| | List I | | List II |
|---|---|---|---|
| A. | Sprain | (i) | Bone |
| B. | Dislocation | (ii) | Skin |
| C. | Laceration | (iii) | Joint |
| D. | Fracture | (iv) | Soft tissues |

**Codes**

| | A | B | C | D |
|---|---|---|---|---|
| (a) | (iv) | (iii) | (i) | (ii) |
| (b) | (iv) | (iii) | (ii) | (i) |
| (c) | (iii) | (i) | (ii) | (iv) |
| (d) | (i) | (iv) | (ii) | (iii) |

**17** Match the following. (1)

| | List I | | List II |
|---|---|---|---|
| A. | Santosh | (i) | Non-possessiveness |
| B. | Brahmacharya | (ii) | Purity |
| C. | Saucha | (iii) | Contentment |
| D. | Aparigraha | (iv) | Celibacy |

**Codes**

| | A | B | C | D |
|---|---|---|---|---|
| (a) | (iv) | (iii) | (i) | (ii) |
| (b) | (iii) | (iv) | (ii) | (i) |
| (c) | (iii) | (i) | (ii) | (iv) |
| (d) | (i) | (iv) | (ii) | (iii) |

**18** .............. is defined as the amount of work done by an individual's body. (1)

(a) Fatigue
(b) Stress
(b) Fracture point
(d) Load

## Section B

**19** Who selects the sites and dates of the Olympic Games? (2)

**20** Describe the ceremonies associated with the Olympic flame. (2)

**21** Why does the Olympic flag have five rings?

**22** What are the six yogic kriyas and what are the functions of these kriyas? (1+1)

**23** Explain the major objective of the Khelo India Programme. (2)

**24** Who started the Modern Olympics? What was his aim behind it? (1+1)

UNSOLVED

## Section C

**25** Discuss social, spiritual and intellectual wellness.

**26** Why is flexibility essential in sports, games and other physical activities? (1+1+1)

**27** What do you understand by pranayama? Describe its three parts in detail. (1 + 2)

**28** Explain internal and external rotation in brief. (1.5 + 1.5)

**29** Discuss the importance of test and measurement in sports. (1.5 + 1.5)

**30** What are the values promoted by organising the Olympic event? (3)

## Section D

**31** In relation to the pictures given below, answer the following questions. (4 × 1 = 4)

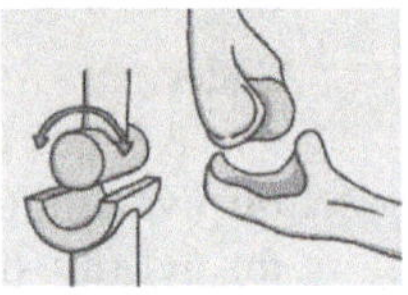

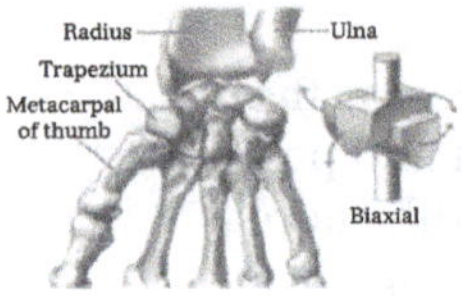


(i) The joint in our elbow is an example of
- (a) Ball and socket joint
- (b) Hinge joint
- (c) Pivot joint
- (d) Saddle joint

(ii) In which joint, the articulating surface of bone is saddle shaped and the articulating surface of another bone fits into it?

(iii) The joint in the bones of the wrist is an example of which joint?
- (a) Ball and socket joint
- (b) Pivot joint
- (c) Gliding joint
- (d) Hinge joint

(iv) In........... joints, a rounded bone lies in a cup-like cavity.

*Or* .................. are joints with a rotatory movement on one axis.

**32** The teachers as well as coaches always make their best efforts to improve performance of their students in various competitive games and sports. They help to improve the performance of students if they have adequate knowledge of biomechanics.

In relation to the above pictures, answer the following questions. (4 × 1 = 4)

(i) In cricket, the ball is hit by the batsman; the ball after being struck by the bat goes away from the batsman. What law explained by Newton is working between the ball and the bat?
- (a) Newton's First Law of Motion
- (b) Newton's Second Law of Motion
- (c) Newton's Third Law of Motion
- (d) Law of Universal Gravitation

(ii) Which Newton's law is applied when an athlete is in the running position?

(iii) In Equestrian, which law of motion is applicable?

(iv) Study of the structure, function and motion of the mechanical aspects of biological systems is called as............ .

**33** In relation to the given picture, answer the following questions. (4 × 1 = 4)

(i) What is the Motto of Khelo India Youth Games?

(a) Play for India (b) Kheloge Kudoge Banoge Lajawaab

(c) Unity in Diversity (d) Strength Through Sports

(ii) Khelo India program launched in the year ............ .

(iii) Where were the first Khelo India Games held?

(a) Ranchi (b) Pune

(c) Guwahati (d) New Delhi

(iv) ................ won the first Khelo India.

## Section E

**34** What are the main features of Olympic flag? (5)

**35** Write any three steps for improving team cohesion. (5)

**36** What is intellectual wellness? How can it be a measure of being healthy? (2 + 3)

**37** What are Diarthrosis joints of the human body? Explain their types briefly. (2 + 3)



# Answers

**1** (b) Pranayama

**2** (d) All of the above

**3** (b) 1896

**4** (c) Disorder

**5** (d) All of the above

**6** (d) Mumbai

**7** (d) Dhyanavastha

**8** (d) Short board

**9** (c) A is true, but R is false

**10** (c) D R Lamb

**11** (c) Upper limbs

**12** (a) Circumduction

**13** (d) All of the above

**14** (c) Flexion

**15** (a) Scientific study of soul

**16** (b) A-(iv), B-(iii), C-(ii), D-(i)

**17** (b) A-(iii), B-(iv), C-(ii), D-(i)

**18** (d) Load

**31** (i) (b) Hinge joint (ii) Saddle joint
(iii) (c) Gliding joint (iv) ball and socket joint
*Or* Pivot joints

**32** (i) (c) Newton's Second Law of Motion
(ii) Newton's Second Law of Motion
(iii) Newton's First Law of Motion
(iv) Biomechanics

**33** (i) (b) Kheloge Kudoge Banoge Lajawaab
(ii) 2017-18
(iii) (d) New Delhi
(iv) Haryana

# SAMPLE QUESTION PAPER 3

**A Highly Simulated Sample Question Paper for CBSE Class XI Examination**

# PHYSICAL EDUCATION

UNSOLVED

### General Instructions

- The question paper consists of 5 sections and 37 questions.
- **Section-A** consists of question 1-18 carrying 1 mark each and is Multiple Choice Questions. All questions are compulsory.
- **Section-B** consists of question 19-24 carrying 2 marks each and are Very Short Answer Type Questions and should not exceed 60-90 words. Attempt any 5.
- **Section-C** consists of question 25-30 carrying 3 marks each and are Short Answer Type Questions and should not exceed 100-150 words. Attempt any 5.
- **Section-D** consists of question 31-33 carrying 4 marks each and are Case Studies. There is internal choice available.
- **Section-E** consists of question 34-37 carrying 5 marks each and are Long Answer Type Questions and should not exceed 200-300 words. Attempt any 3.

***Time : 3 hours*** | ***Max. Marks : 70***

## Section A

**1** Identify the given asana. (1)

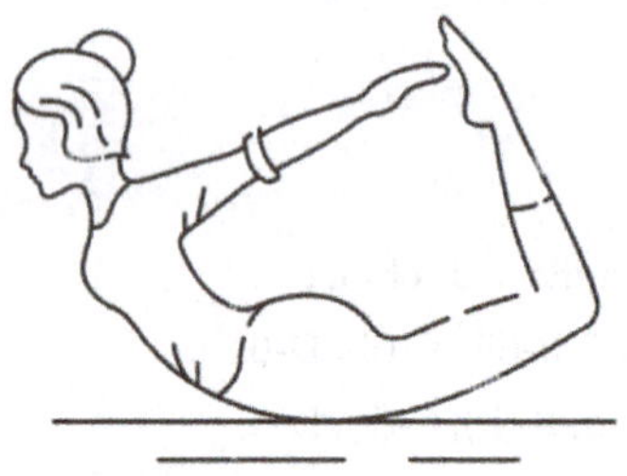

(a) Bhujangasana (b) Dhanurasana
(c) Makarasana (d) Padmasana

**2** According to JB Nash, the objectives of physical education are (1)

(a) Neuromuscular development
(b) Organic development
(c) Interpretative development
(d) All of the above

**3** The Olympic flag displays how many interlocking rings in the centre? (1)

(a) Three (b) Five
(c) Two (d) Six

**4** The first Modern Olympic Games were held in Athens, Greece in which year? (1)

(a) 1893 (b) 1894
(c) 1896 (d) 1861

**5** Which of the following is not a characteristic of static strength? (1)

(a) It is also called isotonic strength
(b) It can be measured by dynamometer
(c) It is not usually applied in sports
(d) This strength is not experienced directly

**6** Which component of wellness refers to "As the ability to work with different people, to communicate well and interact with the community"? (1)

(a) Emotional Wellness
(b) Intellectual Wellness
(c) Social Wellness
(d) Environmental Wellness

**7** Which of the following is/are the indigenous sports of India? (1)

(a) Kho-Kho (b) Kabaddi
(c) Archery (d) All of these

8 What is the role of physiotherapist? (1)
(a) To manage special needs children with movement disorder.
(b) To help special needs children to develop fine and gross motor skills.
(c) To build communication of children with special needs.
(d) To work for the overall development of children with special needs.

9 Given below are two statements labeled as Assertion (A) and Reason (R). (1)
**Assertion** (A) Special educators work is to work for the overall development of children with special needs.
**Reason** (R) In inclusive education, students with special needs spends most of their time with normal student.
In the context of above two statements, which one of the following is correct?
(a) Both A and R are true and R is the correct explanation of A
(b) Both A and R are true, but R is not the correct explanation of A
(c) A is true, but R is false
(d) A is false, but R is true

10 What does person require to maintain physical fitness? (1)
(a) Efficient motar mechanism
(b) Efficient organic mechanism
(c) Efficient mental functioning
(d) All of the above

11 .......... is a type of movement that takes place when the angle decreases between two bones attached to a joint. (1)
(a) Flexion (b) Adduction
(c) Abduction (d) None of these

12 Which of the following is not a part of the circulatory system? (1)
(a) Heart (b) Lungs
(c) Blood (d) Blood vessels

13 According to its Greek meaning, psychology came to be understood as (1)
(a) Scientific study of soul
(b) Study of behaviour
(c) Study of mind
(d) Study of consciousness

14 The weight of the heart is (1)
(a) 100 gms (b) 300 gms
(c) 200 gms (d) 400 gms

15 What among the following does regular physical exercise results in? (1)
(a) Improved functional status
(b) Improved quality of life
(c) Improved cognitive abilities
(d) All of the above

16 Match the following (1)

| | List I | | List II |
|---|---|---|---|
| A. | Short bone | (i) | Knee |
| B. | Irregular bone | (ii) | Femur |
| C. | Sesamoid bone | (iii) | Wrist |
| D. | Long bone | (iv) | Vertebrae |

**Codes**

| | A | B | C | D | | A | B | C | D |
|---|---|---|---|---|---|---|---|---|---|
| (a) | (i) | (ii) | (iii) | (iv) | (b) | (ii) | (iii) | (iv) | (i) |
| (c) | (iii) | (iv) | (i) | (ii) | (d) | (iv) | (i) | (ii) | (iii) |

17 Match the following. (1)

| | List I (Name of Bone) | | List II (Number of Bone) |
|---|---|---|---|
| A. | Ribs | (i) | 26 |
| B. | Vertebral column | (ii) | 1 |
| C. | Sternum | (iii) | 64 |
| D. | Upper limbs | (iv) | 24 |

**Codes**

| | A | B | C | D | | A | B | C | D |
|---|---|---|---|---|---|---|---|---|---|
| (a) | (i) | (ii) | (iii) | (iv) | (b) | (ii) | (iii) | (iv) | (i) |
| (c) | (iii) | (iv) | (i) | (ii) | (d) | (iv) | (i) | (ii) | (iii) |

18 Which of the following is/are a requirement for a long distance runner? (1)
(a) Good cardiovascular endurance
(b) Good strength
(c) Good height (d) All of these

## Section B

19 What may adolescents become victims of if their problems are not managed in time? (2)

20 Briefly discuss the concepts of pronation and supination. (2)

21 Write a short note on blood as a part of circulatory system. (2)

22 Discuss the short and long-term courses available in the field of physical education in India by giving examples. (1 + 1)

23 How does physical education develop the ability and capacity of an individual? (2)

UNSOLVED

**24** Describe the ceremonies associated with the Olympic flame.

## Section C

**25** Explain coordinative abilities in detail. (3)

**26** What are asanas and how are they beneficial? (1.5 + 1.5)

**27** Explain any three points of importance of biomechanics in brief. (1 × 3 = 3)

**28** Write the procedure for performing push-ups for men. (3)

**29** Explain the three types of blood vessels in the human body. (1 × 3 = 3)

**30** Explain the physical, mental and adjustment problems of adolescents. (1 + 1+ 1)

## Section D

**31** Biomechanics and Newton's laws of motion find tremendous application in modern sports. Not only is their knowledge important to enhance performance, it also helps prevent sports injuries.

In relation to the pictures given below, answer the following questions. (4 × 1 = 4)

(1)

(2)

(i) While catching a fast-moving cricket ball, a fielder in the ground gradually pulls his hand backward with the ball, to reduce

(a) impulse force
(b) acceleration
(c) friction
(d) speed

(ii) In the second picture, what kind of force is applied when throwing a ball?

(iii) Among the above two pictures, Newton's second law is applied on ................

(a) Picture 1
(b) Picture 2
(c) Both Picture 1 and 2
(d) None of these

(iv) A cricketer pulls his hands back while catching a fast moving cricket ball. He is using the Newton's ........... law.

*Or* If cricket player stops a fast moving ball suddenly,then large momentum of ball will be reduced to zero in a very short time. Name the law used in this.

**32** In relation to the picture given below, answer the following questions. (4 × 1= 4)

(i) ................ is an ethical practice that is related to the individual's body and senses.

(a) Karma
(b) Samadhi
(c) Dhyana
(d) Niyama

(ii) Which among the above Yoga involves controlled breathing?

(iii) Which Yoga means to control our mind and sense?

(iv) ................ is the ultimate union of an individual's soul with God.

*Or* ................ is a process of complete constancy of mind.

**33** In relation to the given picture, answer the following questions. (4 × 1 = 4)

(i) When did the Fit India Movement launch?

(a) 2017 (b) 2018
(c) 2019 (d) 2020

(ii) The mission of the Fit India Movement was .................. .

(iii) What is the main Motto of Fit India Movement?

(a) To reduce obesity in children (b) To promote fitness as easy, fun and free
(c) Fitness First (d) Fitness for All

(iv) .............. had launched the Fit India Movement in India.

## Section E

**34** Elucidate five reasons for the importance of physiology. (1 × 5 = 5)

**35** Explain Newton's laws of motion and their application in sports. (2 + 3 = 5)

**36** Briefly describe any five skills required in the field of physical education and sports. (1 × 5 = 5)

**37** Describe the steps of team cohesion. What are the factors that affect team cohesion? (2 + 3 = 5)



# Answers

**1** (b) Dhanurasana

**2** (d) All of the above

**3** (b) Five

**4** (c) 1896

**5** (a) It is also called isotonic strength

**6** (c) Social Wellness

**7** (d) All of these

**8** (a) To manage special needs children with movement disorder.

**9** (b) Both A and R are true, but R is not the correct explanation of A

**10** (d) All of the above

**11** (a) Flexion

**12** (b) Lungs

**13** (a) Scientific study of soul

**14** (b) 300 gms

**15** (d) All of the above

**16** (c) A (iii), B (iv), C (i), D (ii)

**17** (d) A (iv), B (i), C (ii), D (iii)

**18** (a) Good cardiovascular endurance

**31** (i) (a) impulse force
(ii) Muscular force
(iii) (a) Picture (1) (iv) second
*Or* Newton's Second Law of Motion

**32** (i) (d) Niyama (ii) Pranayama
(iii) Pratyahara (iv) Samadhi

**33** (i) (c) 2019
(ii) to bring about behavioural changes and move towards a more physically active lifestyle
(iii) (b) To promote fitness as easy, fun and free
(iv) Narendra Modi

# NEW
# PATTERN QUESTIONS

# New Pattern Questions

## Match the Following

**1.** Match the following List I with List II.

| | List I | | List II |
|---|---|---|---|
| I. | Physical fitness | 1. | The ability to perform daily tasks without fatigue. |
| II. | Physical education | 2. | A state of complete physical, mental, and social well-being. |
| III. | Exercise | 3. | An educational program promoting holistic development. |
| IV. | Health | 4. | Planned, structured, and repetitive physical activity. |

**Options**

(a) I-1, II-3, III-4, IV-2 (b) I-3, II-1, III-4, IV-2
(c) I-4, II-2, III-1, IV-3 (d) I-2, II-3, III-4, IV-1

**2.** Match the following List I with List II.

| | List I | | List II |
|---|---|---|---|
| I. | Physical development | 1. | Developing qualities like cooperation , courtesy , sportsmanship etc. |
| II. | Emotional Development | 2. | Related to mental development of an individual. |
| III. | Social development | 3. | Ability to deal with jealousy , hate , anger, etc. appropriately. |
| IV. | Psychological development | 4. | Proper growth of the body. |

Options

(a) I-3, II-1, III-4, IV-2 (b) I-4, II-3, III-1, IV-2
(c) I-4, II-2, III-1, IV-3 (d) I-2, II-3, III-4, IV-1

**3.** Match the following List I with List II.

| | List I | | List II |
|---|---|---|---|
| I. | Sports coach | 1. | Organises sports events and manages teams. |
| II. | Physical education teacher | 2. | Trains individuals in physical fitness and exercise. |
| III. | Sports manager | 3. | Teaches physical education in schools and colleges. |
| IV. | Fitness trainer | 4. | Provides guidance on nutrition and fitness programs. |

**Options**

(a) I-3, II-1, III-4, IV-2
(b) I-4, II-3, III-1, IV-2
(c) I-2, II-3, III-1, IV-4
(d) I-2, II-4, III-3, IV-1

**4.** Match the following List I with List II.

| | List I | | List II |
|---|---|---|---|
| I. | Sports journalism | 1. | Ability to do some research and writing talent are the requirements to take up book writing as a career. |
| II. | Sports broadcasting | 2. | Provides live commentary and reports for radio, TV, or online sports events. |
| III. | Writing | 3. | Writes articles, columns, and reports about sporting events, teams and athletes. |
| IV. | Sports photography | 4. | Specialised in taking photographs for sports magazines, websites, or media outlets. |

**Options**

(a) I-4, II-1, III-3, IV-2 (b) I-3, II-2, III-4, IV-1
(c) I-2, II-4, III-3, IV-1 (d) I-3, II-2, III-1, IV-4

**5.** Match the following List I with List II.

| | List I | | List II |
|---|---|---|---|
| I. | Khelo India | 1. | Launched in 2019 to encourage fitness among citizens. |
| II. | Fit India movement | 2. | Launched in 2017-18 to promote sports at the grassroots level. |
| III. | State level Khelo India centre | 3. | A nationwide event encouraging people to run for fitness. |
| IV. | Fit India Freedom Run | 4. | Supporting better utilisation of sports infrastructure in states. |

**Options**

(a) I-3, II-4, III-2, IV-1
(b) I-2, II-1, III-4, IV-3
(c) I-4, II-3, III-1, IV-2
(d) I-1, II-2, III-4, IV-3

6. Match the following List I with List II.

| | List I (Events) | List II (Year) |
|---|---|---|
| I. | First ancient Olympic games | 1. 394 AD |
| II. | Ban on ancient Olympic games | 2. 776 BC |
| III. | Introduction of chariot racing in ancient Olympics | 3. 680 BC |
| IV. | Inclusion of boxing in ancient Olympics | 4. 688 BC |

**Options**
(a) I-3, II-1, III-4, IV-2 (b) I-2, II-1, III-3, IV-4
(c) I-2, II-4, III-1, IV-3 (d) I-4, II-3, III-2, IV-1

7. Match the following List I with List II.

| | List I | List II |
|---|---|---|
| I. | First modern Olympics | 1. 1896 |
| II. | First Olympic flag introduced | 2. 1913 |
| III. | First Olympic flame | 3. 1894 |
| IV. | First Olympic motto | 4. 1928 |

**Options**
(a) I-3, II-2, III-1, IV-4 (b) I-1, II-2, III-4, IV-3
(c) I-2, II-1, III-4, IV-3 (d) I-4, II-3, III-1, IV-2

8. Match the following List I with List II.

| | List I (Olympic Element) | List II (Year) |
|---|---|---|
| I. | Olympic mascot | 1. 1894 |
| II. | Olympic oath | 2. 1960 |
| III. | Olympic anthem in English | 3. 1920 |
| IV. | Formation of International Olympic Committee (IOC) | 4. 1972 |

**Options**
(a) I-4, II-3, III-2, IV-1 (b) I-1, II-4, III-3, IV-2
(c) I-4, II-2, III-3, IV-1 (d) I-2, II-4, III-3, IV-1

9. Match the following List I with List II.

| | List I (Olympic Value) | List II (Description) |
|---|---|---|
| I. | Excellence | 1. Building a better world through sport by promoting friendship and mutual understanding. |
| II. | Friendship | 2. Striving to achieve personal bests and pushing limits. |
| III. | Respect | 3. Respecting the rules, fair play, and the rights of others. |
| IV. | Inspiration | 4. Encouraging athletes and others to perform with integrity and commitment. |

**Options**
(a) I-2, II-1, III-3, IV-4 (b) I-4, II-3, III-2, IV-1
(c) I-2, II-4, III-1, IV-3 (d) I-1, II-3, III-4, IV-2

10. Match the following List I with List II.

| | List I (Source) | List II (Definition) |
|---|---|---|
| I. | Maharishi Ved Vyas | 1. Yoga is attaining the pose. |
| II. | Patanjali | 2. Suppression of modifications of the mind is Yoga. |
| III. | Agam | 3. Yoga is skill in action. |
| IV. | Bhagwad Gita | 4. The knowledge of Shiva and Shakti is Yoga. |

Options
(a) I-1, II-2, III-3, IV-4 (b) I-2, II-3, III-1, IV-4
(c) I-3, II-4, III-2, IV-1 (d) I-1, II-2, III-4, IV-3

11. Match the following List I with List II.

| | List I (Health Condition) | List II (Yoga Asanas) |
|---|---|---|
| I. | Poor functioning of thyroid gland | 1. Supta Matsyendrasana |
| II. | PCOS in women (excess male hormone production) | 2. Shishuasana |
| III. | Arthritis | 3. Dhanurasana |
| IV. | Lower back pain | 4. Halasana |

**Options**
(a) I-3, II-1, III-4, IV-2 (b) I-4, II-3, III-1, IV-2
(c) I-4, II-3, III-2, IV-1 (d) I-2, II-4, III-1, IV-3

12. Match the following List I with List II.

| | List I (Stage of Yoga) | List II (Description) |
|---|---|---|
| I. | Pratyahara | 1. Union with God. |
| II. | Dharana | 2. Complete constancy of mind. |
| III. | Dhyana | 3. Control our mind and senses. |
| IV. | Samadhi | 4. Concentration of the mind. |

**Options**
(a) I-3, II-4, III-2, IV-1 (b) I-2, II-3, III-4, IV-1
(c) I-3, II-4, III-1, IV-2 (d) I-2, II-4, III-3, IV-1

13. Match the following List I with List II.

| | List I (Pranayama Component) | List II (Meaning) |
|---|---|---|
| I. | Puraka | 1. Inhalation |
| II. | Kumbhaka | 2. Exhalation |
| III. | Rechaka | 3. Retention |
| IV. | Pranayama | 4. Breath Control |

**Options**
(a) I-1, II-2, III-3, IV-4 (b) I-2, II-3, III-1, IV-4
(c) I-3, II-1, III-2, IV-4 (d) I-1, II-3, III-2, IV-4

**14.** Match the following List I with List II.

| | List I (Pranayama Component) | | List II (Meaning) |
|---|---|---|---|
| I. | Counsellor | 1. | Helps children express themselves using speech, sounds, and gestures. |
| II. | Occupational therapist | 2. | Assists in developing fine and gross motor skills like eating and dressing. |
| III. | Physiotherapist | 3. | Helps children with movement disorders, balance, and posture. |
| IV. | Speech Therapist | 4. | Guides students in stress management, anger management, and emotional well-being. |

**Options**
(a) I-1, II-2, III-3, IV-4 (b) I-4, II-2, III-3, IV-1
(c) I-3, II-1, III-2, IV-4 (d) I-2, II-4, III-1, IV-3

**15.** Match the following List I with List II.

| | List I (Author) | | List II (Defintion) |
|---|---|---|---|
| I. | Hoskins | 1. | "It is the ability of a person to do daily routine work without fatigue, participate in playful activities, and meet any emergency." |
| II. | Kroles | 2. | "Physical fitness is the capacity to meet the present and potential physical challenges of life with success." |
| III. | Webster's Collegiate | 3. | "Physical fitness is the human body's ability to move with desired speed, balance, agility, and strength through proper exercise and nutrition." |
| IV. | David R. Lamb | 4. | "Physical fitness is the successful adaptation to the stresses of one's lifestyle." |

**Options**
(a) I-3, II-4, III-1, IV-2 (b) I-4, II-1, III-2, IV-3
(c) I-2, II-3, III-4, IV-1 (d) I-1, II-2, III-4, IV-3

**16.** Match the following List I with List II.

| | List I (Type of Wellness) | | List II (Description) |
|---|---|---|---|
| I. | Physical wellness | 1. | Control stress and anxiety |
| II. | Emotional wellness | 2. | Meditation and family values |
| III. | Social wellness | 3. | Communicate and interact |
| IV. | Spiritual wellness | 4. | Exercise and activities |

**Options**
(a) I-3, II-1, III-4, IV-2 (b) I-4, II-1, III-3, IV-2
(c) I-4, II-3, III-2, IV-1 (d) I-4, II-3, III-2, IV-1

**17.** Match the following List I with List II.

| | List I (Fitness Component) | | List II (Related Games/Activities) |
|---|---|---|---|
| I. | Cardiovascular endurance | 1. | Marathon running |
| II. | Muscular strength | 2. | Cycling |
| III. | Muscular Endurance | 3. | Weightlifting |
| IV. | Flexibility | 4. | Gymnastics |

**Options**
(a) I-1, II-2, III-3, IV-4 (b) I-2, II-3, III-1, IV-4
(c) I-1, II-3, III-2, IV-4 (d) I-1, II-3, III-4, IV-2

**18.** Match the following List I with List II.

| | List I (PRICE Component) | List II (Meaning) |
|---|---|---|
| I. | Protection | 1. Reduce movement |
| II. | Rest | 2. Prevent further injury |
| III. | Ice | 3. Reduce pain and swelling |
| IV. | Elevation | 4. Upper limb swelling |

**Options**
(a) I-2, II-4, III-1, IV-3 (b) I-3, II-1, III-4, IV-2
(c) I-2, II-1, III-3, IV-4 (d) I-4, II-3, III-2, IV-1

**19.** Match the following List I with List II.

| | List I (BMI/WHR Term) | | List II (Description) |
|---|---|---|---|
| I. | Overweight BMI category | 1. | BMI value between 18.5 – 24.9 |
| II. | Underweight BMI category | 2. | BMI value less than 18.5 |
| III. | Normal BMI category | 3. | BMI value between 25.0 – 29.9 |
| IV. | Obese-I BMI category | 4. | BMI value between 30.0-34.9 |

**Options**
(a) I-2, II-1, III-4, IV-3 (b) I-2, II-3, III-4, IV-1
(c) I-3, II-1, III-2, IV-4 (d) I-3, II-2, III-1, IV-4

**20.** Match the following List I with List II.

| | List I (Test/ Component) | | List II (Description) |
|---|---|---|---|
| I. | Kraus Weber test | 1. | Measures strength and flexibility of key muscle groups. |
| II. | Harvard step test | 2. | Measures cardiovascular fitness through recovery rate. |
| III. | Cardiovascular fitness test | 3. | Ability of the heart and lungs to supply oxygen to muscles for energy. |
| IV. | Muscular strength test | 4. | Measures muscular strength and flexibility of key muscle groups. |

**Options**
(a) I-4, II-2, III-3, IV-1 (b) I-3, II-2, III-4, IV-1
(c) I-2, II-4, III-1, IV-3 (d) I-1, II-3, III-4, IV-2

**21.** Match the following List I with List II.

| | List I (Bone) | | List II (Number of Bones) |
|---|---|---|---|
| I. | Skull | 1. | 26 |
| II. | Sternum | 2. | 24 |
| III. | Ribs | 3. | 1 |
| IV. | Vertebral column | 4. | 8 |

**Options**
(a) I-4, II-1, III-3, IV-2 (b) I-4, II-3, III-2, IV-1
(c) I-3, II-2, III-1, IV-4 (d) I-2, II-1, III-4, IV-3

**22.** Match the following List I with List II.

| | List I (Bones) | | List II (Examples) |
|---|---|---|---|
| I. | Long bones | 1. | Carpals, tarsals of anklets |
| II. | Short bones | 2. | Femur, tibia, fibula |
| III. | Flat bones | 3. | Vertebrae, some skull bones |
| IV. | Irregular bones | 4. | Skull, pelvis, Sternum, scapulae |

**Options**
(a) I-4, II-1, III-3, IV-2 (b) I-1, II-3, III-2, IV-4
(c) I-3, II-2, III-1, IV-4 (d) I-2, II-1, III-4, IV-3

**23.** Match the following List I with List II.

| | List I (Types of Joints) | | List II (Characteristics/Examples) |
|---|---|---|---|
| I. | Synarthrosis joints | 1. | Contains compressible fibro cartilage pad and allows limited movement. |
| II. | Amphiarthrosis joints | 2. | Contain hyaline cartilage and surrounded by fibrous articular capsules. |
| III. | Synovial joints | 3. | Contains cartilage between bones. |
| IV. | Symphysis joint | 4. | Found in the skull and face, held by fibrous tissue or ligaments. |

**Options**
(a) I-3, II-1, III-4, IV-2 (b) I-1, II-2, III-3, IV-4
(c) I-4, II-3, III-2, IV-1 (d) I-2, II-3, III-1, IV-4

**24.** Match the following List I with List II.

| | List I (Types of joints) | | List II (Characteristics/Examples) |
|---|---|---|---|
| I. | Gliding joint | 1. | Wrist and ankle joints, move on a single plane. |
| II. | Hinge joint | 2. | Elbow and knee joints, movement in one direction. |
| III. | Ball and socket joint | 3. | Hip and shoulder joints, movement on any axis. |
| IV. | Saddle joint | 4. | Thumb joint, allows crossing over the palm |

**Options**
(a) I-1, II-2, III-3, IV-4 (b) I-4, II-2, III-3, IV-1
(c) I-3, II-1, III-2, IV-4 (d) I-2, II-4, III-3, IV-1

**25.** Match the following List I with List II.

| | List I (Properties of Muscles) | | List II (Description) |
|---|---|---|---|
| I. | Contractility | 1. | Ability to respond to an electrical stimulus and react accordingly. |
| II. | Excitability | 2. | Ability to shortening of the muscle tissue when stimulated. |
| III. | Extensibility | 3. | Ability of the muscle to stretch beyond its resting length when relaxed. |
| IV. | Elasticity | 4. | Ability of the muscle to return to its normal length after being stretched or contracted. |

**Options**
(a) I-2, II-1, III-3, IV-4 (b) I-3, II-2, III-4, IV-1
(c) I-4, II-3, III-2, IV-1 (d) I-1, II-2, III-4, IV-3

**26.** Match the following List I with List II.

| | List I (Functions of Muscles) | | List II (Description/ Examples) |
|---|---|---|---|
| I. | Allows movement | 1. | Keeps the body stable and balanced without collapsing. |
| II. | Maintains posture | 2. | Facilitates voluntary action through coordinated efforts between tissues. |
| III. | Smooth functioning of the organs | 3. | Shields vital organs and bones from potential harm. |
| IV. | Protection of organs and bones | 4. | Supports processes like respiration and digestion. |

**Options**
(a) I-1, II-4, III-2, IV-3 (b) I-4, II-1, III-3, IV-2
(c) I-2, II-3, III-1, IV-4 (d) I-2, II-1, III-4, IV-3.

**27.** Match the following Lis I will Lis II.

| | List I (Parts of Respiratory System) | | List II (Description) |
|---|---|---|---|
| I. | Pharynx | 1. | Vocal sac and produces sound as air passes through it. |
| II. | Larynx | 2. | It is a cylindrical tube made of hyaline cartilage rings. |
| III. | Trachea | 3. | It is a funnel of muscle that opens through the larynx region into the trachea. |
| IV. | Bronchi | 4. | It carry the air into lobes of the lungs. |

**Options**
(a) I-3, II-1, III-2, IV-4 (b) I-4, II-1, III-3, IV-2
(c) I-3, II-2, III-1, IV-4 (d) I-4, II-3, III-2, IV-1

**28.** Match the following List I with List II.

| | **List I** (Parts of Respiratory System) | | **List II** (Description) |
|---|---|---|---|
| I. | Alveoli | 1. | Pair of spongy organs divided into lobes, site of air exchange. |
| II. | Lungs | 2. | Hollow cavities where oxygen and carbon dioxide are exchanged. |
| III. | Diaphragm | 3. | Large muscle below the lungs that aids in respiration by changing thoracic cavity volume. |
| IV. | Mouth | 4. | Secondary exterior opening for respiration, commonly used alongside the nose. |

**Options**
(a) I-1, II-2, III-3, IV-4 (b) I-2, II-3, III-4, IV-1
(c) I-1, II-2, III-4, IV-3 (d) I-2, II-1, III-3, IV-4

**29.** Match the following List I with List II.

| | **List I** (Functions of the Respiratory System) | | **List II** (Description/ Processes) |
|---|---|---|---|
| I. | Oxygenation of the blood | 1. | Release from the body through exhalation. |
| II. | Excretion of carbon Dioxide | 2. | Vibration in the larynx during inhalation. |
| III. | Production of sound | 3. | Enters the lungs and is distributed to the body organs. |
| IV. | Sense of smell | 4. | Olfactory fibres in nasal cavities detect chemicals in inhaled air. |

**Options**
(a) I-1, II-2, III-3, IV-4 (b) I-4, II-2, III-3, IV-1
(c) I-2, II-4, III-1, IV-3 (d) I-3, II-1, III-2, IV-4

**30.** Match the following List I with List II.

| | **List I** (Heart Chambers) | | **List II** (Function/ Description) |
|---|---|---|---|
| I. | Right atrium | 1. | Receives oxygenated blood from the lungs and passes it to the left ventricle. |
| II. | Right ventricle | 2. | Pumps oxygenated blood to the body and creates blood pressure. |
| III. | Left atrium | 3. | Receives blood with carbon dioxide from the veins and passes it to the right ventricle. |
| IV. | Left ventricle | 4. | Pumps deoxygenated blood to the lungs for oxygenation. |

**Options**
(a) I-3, II-2, III-1, IV-4 (b) I-2, II-3, III-4, IV-1
(c) I-4, II-3, III-1, IV-2 (d) I-3, II-4, III-1, IV-2

**31.** Match the following List I with List II.

| | **List I** (Heart Valves) | | **List II** (Function/ Description) |
|---|---|---|---|
| I. | Right atrioventricular valve | 1. | Allows blood flow from right ventricle to lungs only. |
| II. | Left atrioventricular valve | 2. | Allows blood flow from left auricle to left ventricle only. |
| III. | Pulmonary valve | 3. | Allows blood flow from right auricle to right ventricle only. |
| IV. | Aortic valve | 4. | Allows blood flow from left ventricle to body only. |

**Options**
(a) I-1, II-2, III-4, IV-3 (b) I-3, II-1, III-4, IV-2
(c) I-3, II-2, III-1, IV-4 (d) I-3, II-2, III-4, IV-1

**32.** Match the following List I with List II.

| | **List I** (Functions) | | **List II** (Processes) |
|---|---|---|---|
| I. | Transportation | 1. | WBCs clean up cellular debris and fight pathogens that have entered the body. |
| II. | Protection | 2. | Delivers essential nutrients and oxygen into the cells of the body |
| III. | Regulation | 3. | To maintain homeostatic control of several internal conditions. |
| IV. | Nutrition | 4. | Transfer of essential vitamins, minerals, amino acids as well as glucose to all parts of the body. |

**Options**
(a) I-2, II-1, III-3, IV-4 (b) I-1, II-3, III-4, IV-2
(c) I-4, II-2, III-1, IV-3 (d) I-2, II-4, III-3, IV-1

**33.** Match the following List I with List II.

| | **List I** (Concepts) | | **List II** (Explanations) |
|---|---|---|---|
| I. | Preventing injuries | 1. | Recovery from illness. |
| II. | Developing motor skills | 2. | Guides athletes in sport techniques. |
| III. | Rehabilitation | 3. | Reduces injury risks. |
| IV. | Preparing coaches | 4. | Helps in designing of equipment. |

**Options**
(a) I-3, II-2, III-4, IV-1 (b) I-4, II-3, III-1, IV-2
(c) I-3, II-4, III-1, IV-2 (d) I-4, II-2, III-3, IV-1

**34.** Match the following List I with List II.

| | List I (Terms) | | List II (Descriptions) |
|---|---|---|---|
| I. | Skill fix | 1. | Affects gear design |
| II. | Gear adjustment | 2. | Builds muscle endurance |
| III. | Injury reduction | 3. | Alters movement patterns |
| IV. | Body performance | 4. | Prevents harm |

Options

(a) I-1, II-3, III-4, IV-2 (b) I-2, II-1, III-4, IV-3
(c) I-4, II-2, III-3, IV-1 (d) I-3, II-2, III-1, IV-4

**35.** Match the following List I with List II.

| | List I (Principles of Biomechanics) | | List II (Application) |
|---|---|---|---|
| I. | Newton's first law of motion | 1. | A body at rest will remain at rest unless an external force is applied |
| II. | Newton's second law of motion | 2. | The acceleration of a body is proportional to the force applied. |
| III. | Newton's third law of motion | 3. | The rider bends forward to avoid falling when the horse suddenly stops. |
| IV. | Newton's law in swimming | 4. | The swimmer pushes their hand downward and backward to propel forward. |

**Options**

(a) I-2, II-4, III-1, IV-3 (b) I-3, II-2, III-1, IV-4
(c) I-1, II-2, III-3, IV-4 (d) I-4, II-3, III-2, IV-1

**36.** Match the following List I with List II.

| | List I (Movement Types) | | List II (Example) |
|---|---|---|---|
| I. | Flexion | 1. | Moving the arm downward after a badminton shot. |
| II. | Extension | 2. | Bending of the arm to decrease the angle between joints. |
| III. | Abduction | 3. | Performing a golf swing with the lead arm moving inward. |
| IV. | Adduction | 4. | Moving legs sideways to form a right angle with the body. |

**Options**

(a) I-1, II-2, III-3, IV-4
(b) I-3, II-4, III-1, IV-2
(c) I-2, II-1, III-4, IV-3
(d) I-1, II-2, III-4, IV-3

**37.** Match the following List I with List II.

| | List I (Movement Type) | | List II (Example) |
|---|---|---|---|
| I. | Circumduction | 1. | Rotation of the shoulder during a tennis serve. |
| II. | External rotation | 2. | Moving the forearm inward and shifting of weight. |
| III. | Internal rotation | 3. | Run up during javelin throw to generate momentum. |
| IV. | Supination of forearm | 4. | Evident during execution of the cricket ball. |

**Options**

(a) I-4, II-1, III-3, IV-2 (b) I-3, II-1, III-4, IV-2
(c) I-4, II-2, III-3, IV-1 (d) I-2, II-1, III-3, IV-4

**38.** Match the following List I with List II.

| | List I (Psychologist/ Source) | | List II (Definition) |
|---|---|---|---|
| I. | WB Pillsbury and JB Watson | 1. | Psychology deals with the activities of the individual in relation to the environment. |
| II. | Woodworth | 2. | Psychology is the scientific study of human mind and its functions, especially those affecting behaviour in a given context. |
| III. | Oxford Dictionary | 3. | Psychology is the science of human behaviour. |
| IV. | Crow and Crow | 4. | Psychology is the study of human behaviour and human relationships. |

**Options**

(a) I-4, II-1, III-3, IV-2 (b) I-3, II-4, III-1, IV-2
(c) I-3, II-1, III-2, IV-4 (d) I-2, II-3, III-4, IV-1

**39.** Match the following List I with List II.

| | List I (Psychologist/ Source) | | List II (Definition) |
|---|---|---|---|
| I. | RN Singer | 1. | Sports psychology is an applied psychology, more concerned with personalities, emotional or motivational aspects of sports and physical activities. |
| II. | Clark and Clark | 2. | Sports psychology is the branch of psychology that deals with the physical fitness of an individual through participation in games and sports. |

| | | | |
|---|---|---|---|
| III. | John Lauther | 3. | Sports psychology is an area that applies psychological facts and principles to learning performance and associated human behaviour in sports. |
| IV. | KM Burns | 4. | Sports psychology encompasses scholarly, educational, and practical activities associated with understanding and influencing behaviours in athletics. |

**Options**
(a) I-4, II-1, III-3, IV-2 (b) I-3, II-1, III-4, IV-2
(c) I-4, II-3, III-1, IV-2 (d) I-4, II-3, III-2, IV-1

**40.** Match the following List I with List II.

| | List I | | List II |
|---|---|---|---|
| I. | Physical growth in infancy | 1. | Development of muscle and nerves happens at a rapid rate. |
| II. | Muscular and nervous system development | 2. | Growth in height and weight is considerable during this stage. |
| III. | Motor skills development | 3. | Growth in activities that is spontaneous and developed by imitation or trial and error. |
| IV. | Physical activities growth | 4. | Development of skills such as walking, running and jumping. |

**Options**
(a) I-3, II-2, III-4, IV-1 (b) I-1, II-3, III-4, IV-2
(c) I-4, II-3, III-1, IV-2 (d) I-2, II-1, III-4, IV-3

**41.** Match the following List I with List II.

| | List I (Development during infancy) | | List II (Description) |
|---|---|---|---|
| I. | Brain development | 1. | The child's sentiments are not controlled and self-love becomes prominent. |
| II. | Language development | 2. | The child starts understanding words and develops a simple vocabulary. |
| III. | Development of curiosity | 3. | The child questioning increases on frequent topics. |
| IV. | Emotional and social development | 4. | The child's thinking abilities increase significantly. |

**Options**
(a) I-3, II-2, III-4, IV-1
(b) I-4, II-2, III-3, IV-1
(c) I-1, II-3, III-4, IV-2
(d) I-4, II-2, III-1, IV-3

**42.** Match the following List I with List II.

| | List I (Stage) | | List II (Characteristics) |
|---|---|---|---|
| I. | Early childhood (2-6 years) | 1. | Body proportions of the child changes and the baby look disappears. |
| II. | Physical characteristics in early childhood | 2. | Memory power increases, vocabulary grows, and social skills such as manners are learned. |
| III. | Cognitive Characteristics in Late Childhood | 3. | Problem-solving, critical thinking, and decision-making skills improve. |
| IV. | Late Childhood (6-12 years) | 4. | This stage is characterised by acquiring new skills, forming habits, and increased physical coordination. |

**Options**
(a) I-2, II-1, III-3, IV-4
(b) I-2, II-4, III-1, IV-3
(c) I-3, II-1, III-4, IV-2
(d) I-4, II-3, III-2, IV-1

**43.** Match the following List I with List II.

| | List I (Stage) | | List II (Description) |
|---|---|---|---|
| I. | Early childhood cognitive characteristics (2-6 years) | 1. | Development of muscular system and nervous system. |
| II. | Physical characteristics in early childhood | 2. | Memory power increases, vocabulary grows, and social habits to manners are learned. |
| III. | Cognitive characteristics in late childhood | 3. | It enhances problem-solving, critical thinking, and decision-making skills. |
| IV. | Late childhood (6-12 years) | 4. | It is also known as gang age. |

**Options**
(a) I-2, II-1, III-3, IV-4
(b) I-2, II-4, III-1, IV-3
(c) I-3, II-1, III-4, IV-2
(d) I-4, II-3, III-2, IV-1

**44.** Match the following List I with List II.

| | List I | | List II |
|---|---|---|---|
| I. | Adolescence phase | 1. | Development of abstract thinking and reasoning abilities. |
| II. | Adolescent cognitive development | 2. | Rapid growth, puberty, and hormonal changes. |
| III. | Adolescent emotional growth | 3. | Transition between childhood and adulthood with identity formation. |
| IV. | Adolescent physical changes | 4. | Increased emotional intensity, mood swings, and search for independence. |

**Options**
(a) I-3, II-1, III-4, IV-2 (b) I-2, II-1, III-4, IV-3
(c) I-2, II-3, III-4, IV-1 (d) I-3, II-2, III-4, IV-1

**45.** Match the following List I with List II.

| | List I | | List II |
|---|---|---|---|
| I. | Physical preparation | 1. | Analyse opponents and refine strategies. |
| II. | Technical preparation | 2. | Enhance fitness, strength, flexibility and coordination. |
| III. | Tactical preparation | 3. | Master sport-specific movements. |
| IV. | Psychological preparation | 4. | Build discipline, confidence, willpower, and perseverance. |

**Options**
(a) I-2, II-3, III-1, IV-4
(b) I-3, II-2, III-4, IV-1
(c) I-4, II-1, III-2, IV-3
(d) I-2, II-1, III-4, IV-3

**46.** Match the following List I with List II.

| | List I | | List II |
|---|---|---|---|
| I. | Principle of continuity | 1. | Proper mix of activities, diet and habits for optimal performance. |
| II. | Principle of balanced training | 2. | Regular and consistent training with rest intervals. |
| III. | Principle of individual differences | 3. | Adjusting training based on individual needs. |
| IV. | Principle of overload | 4. | Gradual increase in workload for progress. |

**Options**
(a) I-3, II-1, III-4, IV-2 (b) I-2, II-1, III-3, IV-4
(c) I-2, II-3, III-1, IV-4 (d) I-4, II-2, III-1, IV-3

**47.** Match the following List I with List II.

| | List I (Sports Principles) | | List II (Explanation) |
|---|---|---|---|
| I. | Principle of transfer | 1. | Normal training improves overall body function while specific preparation targets performance of sportsman directly. |
| II. | Principle of variation | 2. | Increases variety to avoid boredom and helps to maintain motivation. |
| III. | Principle of progression | 3. | Training load must gradually increase without causing injury, and adequate recovery. |
| IV. | Principle of general and specific preparation | 4. | Learning and performing one activity affects the performance of related skills and activities. |

**Options**
(a) I-4, II-2, III-3, IV-1
(b)I-2, II-4, III-1, IV-3
(c) I-3, II-4, III-1, IV-2
(d)I-4, II-3, III-1, IV-2

**48.** Match the following List I with List II.

| | List I (Types of Warming-up) | | List II (Description) |
|---|---|---|---|
| I. | Psychological warming-up | 1. | Uses external sources like massage, sunbath, and steam bath. |
| II. | Physiological warming-up | 2. | Prepares the athlete mentally for competition |
| III. | Active warming-up | 3. | Involves exercises like jogging, stretching and striding. |
| IV. | Passive warming-up | 4. | Prepares the body physically for performance |

**Options**
(a) I-1, II-2, III-4, IV-3 (b) I-2, II-4, III-3, IV-1
(c) I-1, II-2, III-3, IV-4 (d) I-4, II-3, III-2, IV-1